Plant Exploration for
LONGWOOD GARDENS

PLANT EXPLORATION FOR

Longwood Gardens

TOMASZ ANIŚKO

Foreword by Christopher Brickell

TIMBER PRESS

Frontispiece: An opening in a hornbeam hedge provides a glimpse of a misty flower garden at Longwood. Photo by Tomasz Aniśko.

Published in 2006 by

Timber Press, Inc.

The Haseltine Building

133 S.W. Second Avenue, Suite 450

Portland, Oregon 97204-3527, U.S.A.

www.timberpress.com

For contact information regarding editorial, sales, and distribution in the United Kingdom,
see www.timberpress.com/uk.

ISBN-13: 978-0-88192-738-2
ISBN-10: 0-88192-738-4

Printed through Colorcraft Ltd., Hong Kong

Library of Congress Cataloging-in-Publication Data

Aniśko, Tomasz, 1963-
  Plant exploration for Longwood Gardens / Tomasz Aniśko ; foreword by
Christopher Brickell.
      p. cm.
  Includes bibliographical references and index.
  ISBN-13: 978-0-88192-738-2
  ISBN-10: 0-88192-738-4
  1. Plant collection--History. 2. Phytogeography--History. 3.
Botanical specimens--Collection and preservation--History. 4. Longwood
Gardens (Kennett Square, Pa.)--History. I. Title.
  QK15.A55 2006
  580'.75--dc22   2005022139

A catalog record for this book is also available from the British Library.

In memory of

DR. RUSSELL J. SEIBERT,

the first director of

Longwood Gardens

Contents

Foreword

CHRISTOPHER BRICKELL

*Former director of the Royal Horticultural Society's Garden at Wisley
and retired director general of the RHS*

Longwood Gardens has long been valued by gardeners and botanists as one of the greatest gardens in the world, famed particularly for the magnificent displays of ornamental plants both in the very fine conservatories and outdoors in the historic park and arboretum. The art and aesthetics of horticulture are very evident wherever one goes at Longwood, as are the skills of the gardeners in growing the superb collections.

Less well known, however, is the very important role that Longwood has played in the introduction of plants from many areas of the world, starting during the second half of the twentieth century and continuing until the present day.

This quest for plants—plant exploration or plant hunting—has, over many centuries, intrigued and in some instances captivated botanists, gardeners and other travellers who possess an almost primaeval urge to search for and bring back plants to their own countries for both study and cultivation.

Much has been written about the exploits and dedication of such luminaries as Robert Fortune, David Douglas, Ernest H. Wilson, Reginald Farrer, Frank Kingdon Ward and many other plant hunters of the nineteenth and twentieth centuries, and there is little, if any, doubt that the scientific, economic and aesthetic value of their introductions has been immense. But until the publication of this very comprehensive survey of plant exploration, little has been written about the fifty important expeditions with which Longwood Gardens has been involved.

In 1956, Dr. Russell J. Seibert, the first director of Longwood Gardens, initiated a plant introduction programme, as he realised, soon after his appointment in 1955, that, while the collections were already very

diverse, it would be essential for the future of Longwood as a world-class public display garden to introduce "new blood" in the form of plant introductions from many other parts of the world so that the already fine collections of plants both under glass and outdoors could be greatly expanded and enhanced.

This introduction programme was followed in 1960 by a complementary programme of scientific research using a new range of experimental greenhouses to carry out trials and breeding programmes with newly introduced plants. A considerable number of the introductions proved new to cultivation, while some were new to science. Other collections of plants were reintroduced, and, although already known in gardens and commerce, these have provided a wider gene pool from which new cultivars have been selected; and yet others, like the now ubiquitous New Guinea *Impatiens,* have resulted from breeding programmes carried out at Longwood and elsewhere.

The other very considerable benefits resulting from the Longwood plant exploration and introduction scheme have been to enhance the already strong educational work of Longwood in association with the University of Delaware, as well as to enable selections from the new plant introductions to be made available through the nursery industry for the wider benefit of gardeners, particularly in the United States and Canada but also more widely in other parts of the world.

Additionally, authentic, well-documented living plant material from the wild, as well as the herbarium specimens brought back by these expeditions, have been very valuable for systematists in their taxonomic work.

While the plant introduction scheme was originally carried out in association with the New Crops Research

Branch of the U.S. Department of Agriculture (the USDA-Longwood plant exploration program), a very wide range of other institutions in the United States has also been involved during the fifty years this important and very successful project has been established. Such detailed organisation also demands the active assistance and cooperation of organisations and individuals in the countries visited, in itself a remarkable achievement bearing in mind the inevitable problems of finance, language, access, and legal and political problems that have been overcome.

As will be seen from the contents page, during the fifty years since this plant exploration scheme for Longwood Gardens was first activated, the fifty expeditions so far undertaken have taken place on six continents and in some fifty countries in search of plants to introduce both for their ornamental value and for research purposes.

For my part, these tales of plant exploration bring back nostalgic memories of my own past (and, I trust, future) forays to some of the wild and mountainous regions of the world and the excitement of searching for and finding plants in their natural habitats.

Others, I feel sure, will find this a very stimulating, readable and enjoyable account of the search for plants that admirably carries on the tradition of the many plant hunters of the past two centuries who so greatly enriched our gardens and contributed so much to our scientific understanding of the plant world.

It is very fitting that this account of the history of plant exploration at Longwood Gardens will not only celebrate the fiftieth anniversary of the first expedition of the plant introduction programme but will also mark the centennial of Longwood Gardens itself.

Preface

FREDERICK E. ROBERTS, *Director of Longwood Gardens*

Plant Exploration for Longwood Gardens describes a tradition of plant introduction as part of Longwood history for more than two centuries. In 1798 Samuel and Joshua Peirce, great grandsons of George Peirce, the first European owner of Longwood property, started an arboretum later to be known as Peirce's Park. By 1830 they had one of the finest collections of woody plants of any park or arboretum in the United States. Many plants in the arboretum were transplanted from the wooded areas of Pennsylvania; some were collected by the brothers as far north as the Catskill Mountains of New York and as far south as Maryland's cypress swamps; still others came from the famed explorers of that time such as John and William Bartram, Humphry and Moses Marshall, and André Michaux.

The Peirces also planted numerous species introduced from foreign lands, including Chinese ginkgo and European horse-chestnut. The early-nineteenth-century herbarium collection of William Darlington held at West Chester University in Chester County, Pennsylvania, gives an excellent survey of plants growing at Peirce's Park. The collection includes a large number of herbarium specimens, along with a herbarium catalogue that Darlington completed in 1843. Several of the Peirce specimens in the Darlington collection are of special significance, including the *Franklinia alatamaha,* commonly known as Franklin tree, collected in Peirce's Park on 7 August 1828, a direct descendant of the trees John Bartram discovered near the Altamaha River in Georgia.

By 1906, Peirce's Park had been under family ownership for several generations. Destruction of the park seemed inevitable when then-owner Lydia V. Bevan signed an agreement with a Lancaster lumber company granting permission for trees on the property to be cut and used for lumber. In an effort to save the old trees from destruction, Pierre S. du Pont, future chairman of the DuPont chemical company, bought the property in 1906. The heritage of the Peirce family and their development of the park is now integral to the history and tradition of Longwood Gardens. As Pierre S. du Pont developed Longwood Gardens as a private estate, he made a great effort to collect plants that he personally liked and thought would contribute to the quality of his garden. His trips to California inspired him to plant a grove featuring many of the magnificent West Coast conifers, none grander than giant sequoias. Du Pont frequently toured Europe's finest gardens, where he discovered French and Belgian camellias, which were imported to adorn newly built conservatories.

After Pierre S. du Pont's death in 1954, Longwood took on a new role as a public display garden, its mission to promote the art and enjoyment of horticulture while providing opportunities for research and learning. To answer the needs of a public institution with a vision of becoming the world's premier display garden, Longwood needed a greater variety of ornamental plants than were available in the United States at that time. Beginning in 1956 and over the next half century, a series of more than fifty expeditions were launched with a goal of finding and introducing new ornamental plants, an effort unprecedented in the history of horticulture in America.

Plants to a gardener are like oils to a painter. New plants offer new creative possibilities and aesthetic experiences. The great plant-collecting expeditions documented in this book exemplify how the introduction of new plants provides inspiration for the gardening community and thus allows the art of horticulture to continue to flourish. Many plants found on collecting expeditions were successfully introduced to American nursery growers and consequently found their way to millions of American gardens. In some instances, plants collected and introduced into cultivation have now been preserved, while their original native stands rapidly disappear. This aspect of plant conservation is critically important to the future. From the perspective of the past half century, dedication to plant exploration has contributed substantially to the great success Longwood has enjoyed in being recognized as a world-class garden.

Acknowledgments

TOMASZ ANIŚKO

I gratefully acknowledge the assistance of the many people without whom this book could not have been created. First and foremost, I am especially grateful to the plant explorers whose stories are told on these pages. Many of them contributed photographs and commentaries, which are reproduced and quoted throughout the book. Some allowed me access to their field notes, diaries, and personal letters. Still others offered their encouragement and constructive criticism in the course of preparing the manuscript.

I thank those who helped me to uncover publications, documents, and photographs related to the explorers and expeditions presented in this book, particularly Robin Everly and Kevin Tunison of the U.S. National Arboretum, Susan Fraser and Stephen Sinon of the LuEsther T. Mertz Library of the New York Botanical Garden, Susan Fugate and Sara Lee of the U.S. National Agricultural Library, Pauline Hubner and Joanna Wright of the Royal Geographical Society, Michael Nash of Hagley Museum and Library, Sandy Reber of Longwood Gardens Archives, Holly Reed of the U.S. National Archives and Records Administration, Alan Stoner and Karen Williams of the USDA Agricultural Research Service, Enola Teeter of Longwood Gardens Library, Judith Warnement of Harvard University Botany Libraries, and Emily Wood of Harvard University Herbaria.

I thank Longwood Gardens' volunteers, Richard Bitner, David Child, Marylou Sklar, and Frances Stapleton, and its interns, Amy Hall, Fowzia Karimi, and Sarah Lovinger, for their help in researching the archives and for proofreading the manuscript.

Note on Plant Nomenclature

Because of the historical character of this book, the scientific names of plants have been retained as used at the time of the expeditions despite taxonomical changes that might have affected them since. Therefore, for example, *Datura* of the 1950s is retained for plants classified today as *Brugmansia*.

Numbers given in parentheses after the scientific names are accession numbers assigned to plants grown at Longwood Gardens. The first two digits of the accession number refer to the year in which a plant was received. The subsequent digits are for the numerical order in which plants were received during that year. Thus *Dendrobium chrysotoxum* (5751) was the fifty-first plant received in 1957, while *Buxus sempervirens* (02647) was the 647th plant received in 2002.

HIMALAYA AND
ADJACENT REGIONS

THE LAST OF ITS KIND

"One can count oneself lucky to have lived in a golden age of horticultural exploration," wrote Frank Kingdon Ward (1956b) upon his return from Burma, now Myanmar, in 1956. "Hardy plant hunting in South-East Asia, as one knew it in the first half of the twentieth century, is on a fade-out basis." The rapidly changing political situation in the aftermath of World War II seemed to herald the end of the golden era of plant collecting. Kingdon Ward viewed his expedition as "among the last of its kind."

No one could be in a better position to voice such an opinion than Kingdon Ward, a veteran of forty-five years of plant exploration in Southeast Asia, with twenty-two expeditions behind him. As Sir George Taylor, director of the Royal Botanic Gardens, Kew, put it in an introduction to an annotated bibliography of Kingdon Ward, "No one travelled more widely in the area, wrote more perceptively about it, collected more discriminately and marshalled his observations so effectively. His record of publications on the region is unsurpassed, his reputation as one of the most eminent of horticultural collectors secure, and his geographical discoveries and stimulating topographical interpretations of the very highest order" (Schweinfurth and Schweinfurth-Marby 1975).

Uncharted mountain

In September of 1955, contemplating his twenty-third expedition, Kingdon Ward wrote to Dr. Russell J. Seibert, who had been appointed as the first director of Longwood Gardens just a few months earlier. He presented an outlook on an expedition to Mount Victoria (Natma Taung), 3053 m, in Burma's Chin Hills: "Practically nothing is known of the flora of Mount Victoria. . . . There are known to be several species of rhododendron, and I should expect to find a number of good trees, shrubs and herbaceous plants, both new species, or if botanically known, not in cultivation." He argued that although Mount Victoria had been frequently visited since its discovery in the late nineteenth century, very few of these visitors were botanists. "Thus we were woefully ignorant of the flora," he wrote later (1958). "There is, in fact, no literature on the botany of Mount Victoria—merely scattered references to and descriptions of isolated plants collected there at various times."

Kingdon Ward was not deterred by scarcity of published information on Mount Victoria or by the prospect of spending nearly a year on a mountain that was "remote from the main lines of communication," "little known to the people of Burma," and lacking "even the glamour that goes with a frontier outpost" (1958). Fortunately, neither were his supporters deterred. He managed to draw enough financial backing from organizations such as the British Museum, the Royal Horticultural Society, and Longwood Gardens to embark on an expedition accompanied by his wife, Jean Kingdon Ward, and Ingrid Alsterlund, assistant at the Gothenburg Botanic Garden.

The party left London on 5 January 1956, arriving in Rangoon, now Yangon, Burma's capital, in early Febru-

Myanmar occupies more than 670,000 km² in Southeast Asia between latitudes 10º north and 28º north. Most of the territory is hilly and mountainous, with the mountain ranges running north to south. The northern mountains, which include the highest peak of Myanmar, Hkakabo Razi, 5967 m, are the source of the great rivers Irrawaddy, Salween, Mekong, and Yangtze. The lower western mountain ranges, of which Chin Hills are part, have peaks 2000 to 3000 m in elevation and extend southward as far as the southern tip of the Arakan Peninsula. The eastern part of the country is occupied by the Shan Plateau, with an average altitude of 1000 m. Between the western ranges and the Shan Plateau is the central basin. The climate of Myanmar is primarily determined by the monsoon winds, although elevation and distance from the sea also affect the temperature and rainfall. The cool dry season lasts from October to February. It is followed by a hot dry season from March to mid-May, and a rainy season from May to October. While the coastal region and the mountains receive 5000 mm of rain, in the northern part of the central basin the rainfall is only 500 to 1000 mm. Nearly twelve thousand species of plants grow in Myanmar. The country is covered with forests of various types. Evergreen oaks and pines dominate above the frost line at 1000 m, with forests of rhododendrons above 2000 m. Evergreen tropical forests are found in areas with more than 2000 mm of rain. Monsoon forests, which are deciduous during the hot season, grow in regions receiving 1000 to 2000 mm of rain. Forest gradually gives way to scrubland in regions where the rainfall is less than 1000 mm.

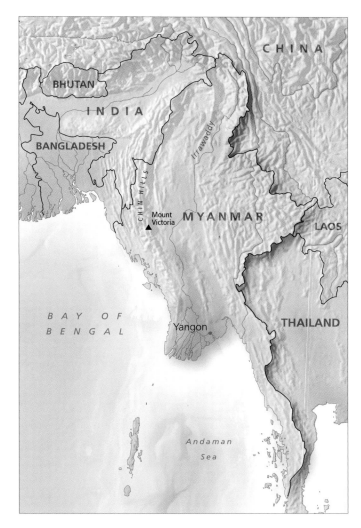

ary. In Rangoon it took them three weeks to comply with all the regulations before they could fly to Kyauktu on 28 February. Three days later they reached Mindat at the foot of Mount Victoria. There they established a base.

"Mindat stands on a pine-clad ridge running east–west, at an altitude of 4800 feet [1450 m]," wrote Kingdon Ward (1956b). "On either side is a deep valley, that to the south separating us from Mount Victoria, whose summit is just out of sight. At this altitude the variety of trees is not great, and the vegetation owes much to the attentions of man, cutting and burning for cultivation. Except in ravines, practically all forest is secondary, with three-needled pines (*P. insularis*), *Anneslea fragrans,* castanopsis and oak dominant. In gullies, however, one finds such trees as eugenia, stereospermum, sapindus, *Sideroxylon hookeri, Eriobotrya bengalensis* and *Melia azedarach*—plants which give a truer picture of the climax forest."

Arriving in the middle of the winter–spring drought, Kingdon Ward found Mindat looking "as though it had never rained since the beginning of time, and never would. The haze, compounded of dust coming up from the plains, and ashes dropping from the sky, reduced visibility to small dimensions. Sometimes the sun shone red as a hot plate; only a strong wind—there was plenty of that in March—could clear the air. However, we were told to wait: we would see all the rain we wanted when the time came" (Kingdon Ward 1956b).

A furnace of rhododendron blossom
Kingdon Ward hoped to start for Mount Victoria before 20 March, but it was only a week later that the first

Local children met by Kingdon Ward's party at the river below Mindat on the way to Mount Victoria. Photo by Frank Kingdon Ward.

Jean Kingdon Ward was put in charge of preparing and drying herbarium specimens. Photo by Frank Kingdon Ward.

driblet of porters from the Chin Hills turned up. "Our party needed thirty-one," he remembered, "and the best we could do was to send off fourteen in advance, with rice, stores, tents, and so forth, keeping back only the irreduceable minimum of everyday requirements. We were promised more porters the following day; but they never came, and we soon learnt to discount our chickens until they were hatched" (Kingdon Ward 1956c).

It was not until 30 March that another nine porters appeared. This was hardly enough, but Kingdon Ward decided to depart anyway. First the party had to cross the deep valley separating the Mindat ridge from Mount Victoria, which meant a descent of some 700 m, followed by a climb of 1000 m to Esakan.

On 2 April a full complement of porters arrived in Esakan, and Kingdon Ward resumed his march to

Ranchi, high up on the eastern ridge of Mount Victoria. While ascending along the ridge, which was covered by dry meadows of tall grass with scattered pines, alders, and oaks, Jean Kingdon Ward, "with a whoop of joy, noticed a beautiful white-flowered rhododendron in full bloom, and returned triumphantly with an armful" (Kingdon Ward 1956d). Its distinct sweet smell and yellow caste mark at the base of the corolla indicated that it was *R. cuffeanum* (57385), a little known epiphytic species named in honor of Lady Wheeler Cuffe, who introduced it into cultivation. At an elevation of about 2100 m, many trees were thickly clustered with orchids, among them species of *Dendrobium, Bulbophyllum, Vanda,* and *Coelogyne.* Even higher, above 2400 m, arisaemas and primulas became a common sight in the undergrowth. After a long march the party reached Ranchi at about

Kingdon Ward, left, assisted by Alsterlund and a Burmese officer, organizes the day's collections. Photo by Frank Kingdon Ward.

Kingdon Ward found these stunted oaks, *Quercus semecarpifolia,* growing at 2700 m on Mount Victoria. Photo by Frank Kingdon Ward.

2700 m and found an ample clearing in the forest with plenty of room to accommodate their tents.

The following day Kingdon Ward went on a reconnaissance along the east ridge. The crest of the ridge was covered with scrub and scattered trees. The north slope sheltered evergreen and semievergreen forest. In contrast, the southern slope displayed large areas of short grass painted mauve with thousands of plants of *Primula denticulata* (57379), while forest occupied only the gullies and hollows. In the scrub covering the ridge, Kingdon Ward found an attractive *Cotoneaster* (57347), a prostrate shrub hugging large rocks and displaying large brilliant scarlet fruits. He noticed that, "as for the trees which dared the tempest on the ridge—and they themselves showed by their streamlined limbs that it blows with gale force—they numbered three only: *Pinus insularis, Quercus semecarpifolia,* and *Rhododendron arboreum*— veteran warriors all. The pines best showed the direction and persistence of the wind; their gnarled limbs pointed like accusing fingers. The oaks never grew up into the wind, but were kept stunted. *Rhododendron arboreum* [57387] too, hunched itself up into a complete bundle, bristling with short twisted branches. But the shape of the last mattered not a jot, for every tree wore a halo of fiery carmine-cerise, which glowed with a luminous quality rarely seen in any flower. Indeed, I cannot recall ever to come across a more magnificent sight than *R. arboreum* on the summit ridge of Mount Victoria—centuries old

trees many of them were, bearing hundreds of trusses" (Kingdon Ward 1956d).

Three days later the party made a second excursion up the mountain that did not get much further than the first one. Then, on 9 April, they went straight to the summit. While ascending along the ridge, Kingdon Ward noted *Piptanthus nepalensis* (57374), with large, crisp yellow, pealike flowers, a rugged little *Symplocos* (57397) with "every twig thickly encrusted with flowers of old gold," and the ubiquitous *Prunus cerasoides* (57382), "such a gorgeous sight throughout the highlands of Burma" (Kingdon Ward 1956e). He recalled the last moments before reaching the summit: "The path, always easy to follow, diverged from the embossed ridge, now

Kingdon Ward collecting seeds on Mount Victoria in mid-April. Photo by Frank Kingdon Ward.

into the forest on the north face, now back to dry (or burnt) grass on the south face; then returned to the crest, interrupted by gaunt pines and a furnace of rhododendron blossom. There came a last sharp ascent, and almost without knowing it, we stood on the summit of Mount Victoria, 10,200 feet [3100 m] above sea level."

From the top of Mount Victoria, they had an uninterrupted view to the south and west, which was "insipid to the last degree," as Kingdon Ward described it (1956f). "We could see, indeed, a number of ranges, forest-clad, with long level ridges and rounded summits. But we looked in vain for the rugged peaks and fantastic rock pyramids, the bold escarpments and shattered screes of North Burma. They do not exist here; all we saw was hills, and more hills, smooth in outline, moderate in slope, and gentle in aspect, with deep but obviously harmless valleys between. The flowing lines of the forest

roof near at hand melted away into those of the hills, without a single jarring note; imperceptibly the near green drifted into the far blue, and a veil of haze levelled off the passive scene."

Although the summit appeared to be covered with nothing more than stunted rhododendron bushes and turf, "it was clear that a wealth of alpine and sub-alpine species jostled each other here, sufficient to transform the mountain in the rainy season," as Kingdon Ward noted (1956e). "It was with no little surprise that I collected appreciable quantities of rhododendron, iris, gentian, and even primula seeds so late in the season as mid-April—clear proof of the long drought. In more normal monsoon mountain climates, winter storms, early rains, or melting snow quickly scour out the capsules of these, and most other alpine plants." He spent the next several days exploring the forest around Ranchi, finding a fair variety of trees. On 16 April the party started back for Esakan and continued the next day to the base in Mindat.

Racing against a monsoon

As April passed into May, increasingly frequent thunderstorms heralded an early monsoon, which marked the beginning of the dead season for seed collecting. Kingdon Ward remained in Mindat for the next fortnight, exploring the surrounding forests. He was eager to make another trip before the rains broke and decided to explore a nearby mountain more than 2400 m high, situated some 16 km west of Mindat. On 20 May the party set out. They drove the first 11 km, to the end of the cart road, in a ramshackle truck. From there they followed on foot an old bridle path along the crest of the Mindat ridge. As the path grew steeper, the trees became laden with moss, ferns, and orchids.

Upon reaching a suitable place at an altitude of 2100 m, the party set up camp. That night the monsoon broke, and the next morning the campsite was engulfed in clouds. Kingdon Ward, despite feeling unwell, decided to stay there for a week and continue collecting. "The temperate forest at 7500 feet [2300 m] included many fine trees," he remembered, "especially oaks, chestnuts, hornbeam (*Carpinus viminea*), schima, engelhardtia, eriobotrya, elaeocarpus (in flower), and a second species of maple. Arisaemas were prominent as undergrowth and along the paths, with ferns, ophiopogon, alpinia and other zingibers" (Kingdon Ward 1956g).

After a week the party ran out of food supplies, so on 28 May, Kingdon Ward decided to return to Mindat, despite the fact that only a quarter of the porters that were needed to carry the loads had shown up in the camp. He, his wife, and two others started down only with essential loads, including a heavy basket of orchids, leaving the sodden tents standing, and some of the party in charge. "It rained in torrents the whole 10 miles [16 km]," wrote Kingdon Ward (1956g), "and we reached Mindat tired and half drowned, our plant paper, beds, bedding, clothing, diaries—everything, soaked. . . . The last four miles [6.5 km] along the cart road was like wading along an orange-ocre river. Except for a tall ground orchid with a foot of closely packed inflorescence, and a yellow-spiked chloranthus, we collected nothing en route. Indeed, in that blinding rain we could hardly see anything."

Orchid frenzy

By the middle of June the first powerful rush of the monsoon had exhausted itself, and the weather settled down to rainy spells with bright intervals. "By this time it seemed pretty certain that we were not going to find a large number of new first-class cool temperate plants," reminisced Kingdon Ward (1957a). "Even the discovery of two species of iris in Mindat could not make the flora as a whole a north temperate one. . . . We decided to turn our attention for the time being mainly to orchids. Because of the scattered or rare occurrence of some species, the far distance of others, it seemed advisable to bring most of them back to base as we found them, and plant them in likely places within easy reach; and this we had done from the beginning, so that by June we had quite a collection in Mindat."

The growing collection faced many threats, ranging from woodcutters insisting on lopping the very limbs on which the epiphytic orchids were planted, to village goats and ponies eating or trampling the terrestrial species. Nevertheless, Kingdon Ward was "much surprised to find what an obstinate hold many species have on life, so long as they are not actually diseased" (1957a). This was very apparent with one *Gastrochilus distichus* (5755), which was brought down from the misty ridge of Mount Victoria to be planted on trees 1200 m below. "It shrank visibly, like a leaky balloon, but valiantly continued to put out rootlets. Although gradually reduced to half its

Kingdon Ward inspects his day's catch of orchids. Photo by Frank Kingdon Ward.

original volume, it refused to give up the struggle, and continued to live."

The summit revisited

On 16 June, Kingdon Ward departed for his second visit to Mount Victoria. On the afternoon of that day, his party reached Esakan, and the next day they climbed to the Ranchi camp. Over the next several days Kingdon Ward explored the grassy slopes of the ridge leading to the summit. There he found a meadow mottled with *Roscoea purpurea* (57389): "At first glance it looks astonishingly like an orchid. It was not that, however, which drew my attention so much as an albino form. . . . Whether it is any improvement on the rich purple flower is a matter of opinion; at least it is different. I recalled that many years ago, in western China, I had come across an albino incarvillea, and passed it by. Never shall I forget

Kingdon Ward with *Dendrobium chrysotoxum* (5751) that he collected on Mount Victoria. Photo by Frank Kingdon Ward.

find the big gentian," he wrote, "fearing we might have just missed it in flower. But even at the beginning of November, by which time the rains had abated, I could see no sign of it. . . . It was on November 5 that, along the summit ridge of Mount Victoria, we at last found the first shy gentian-flowers. What a moment that was! So far as appearances went, the flowers were everything I had prayed for—large and trumpet-shaped, a little smaller, perhaps, than those of *G. sino-ornata,* in shape more like those of *G. szechenyii,* to which the plant was obviously related. But it was the wonderful colour which riveted our gaze. Slowly we took it in, from the wide band of pure Cambridge blue round the top, fading towards the base, to where the corolla is speckled with blue, green, and violet lights. The overall effect is that of a shining China-blue goblet" (Kingdon Ward 1960).

the astonished chagrin of an enthusiastic rock gardener when I made this awful confession" (Kingdon Ward 1957b).

When Kingdon Ward returned to this slope three days later, he found that the purple flowers of *Roscoea* were replaced with thousands of blue dwarf irises (57362) as thick as the *Roscoea* had been earlier. The fact that no iris flowers had been noticed only three days before, he attributed to "the evanescence of their fragile blooms, and to some distaste for the weather, which held them back; for there was none on the following day either" (Kingdon Ward 1957b). Remarkably, "with a glimpse of blue sky. . . a thousand dwarf irises briefly greeted the sunshine."

Later in Mindat, as Kingdon Ward prepared the first shipment of seeds and plants for Longwood, he wrote to Seibert: "You may be sure that all we send you will be of decorative value. It is only Botanical Gardens that want to be bothered nowadays with plants of purely botanical interest, without horticultural merit" (1956a).

Farewell to the mountain

In the middle of October, Kingdon Ward returned to Mount Victoria for the last time. Among the most memorable events of that excursion was an encounter with an undetermined species of *Gentiana* (57352). "I was agog to

In early December, Mr. and Mrs. Kingdon Ward left Burma for Sri Lanka, where they stayed for a couple of months before returning to London. In the meantime, a shipment of orchids arrived at Longwood Gardens after a considerable delay in transit. The orchids were dried out and in rather poor shape, but Longwood orchid growers managed to revive them. Soon Dr. Walter H. Hodge, the garden's head of education and research, was able to report back to Kingdon Ward: "You will be pleased to learn that without exception all orchids sent by you are now in good condition. There were only about four in poor condition, but we were able to save back bulbs of these. Even these are now throwing out new growth, the last one to break being *Arundina bambusifolia* [5756]. Certain of these orchids have already come into flower and one or two of them have been so good that they have been put on display. Especially noteworthy is a species of *Dendrobium* [5748] and *Thunia alba* [5757]. Several others will soon be in flower. From this you can realize that although some of the plants were rather low when they arrived, we have been able to nurse them all back into good health" (Hodge 1957b). One of these orchids, *Dendrobium chrysotoxum* (5751), can to this day be viewed in Longwood's conservatories where it dazzles visitors with brilliant orange flowers.

This trip to Burma's Chin Hills was to be Kingdon Ward's last expedition, for he died the following year. In his introduction to Kingdon Ward's *Pilgrimage for Plants,* published posthumously in 1960, William Stearn wrote of the author, "Scarcely a week before his sudden unexpected death he was discussing with me the possibilities of a plant-collecting expedition into the Caucasus or northern Persia." The relentless explorer, "the last of its kind," he never ceased dreaming of new adventures.

ON THE TRAIL OF THE HIMALAYAN ELMS

When researchers working in the Netherlands in the 1950s discovered that a clone of Himalayan elm, *Ulmus wallichiana,* received from the Arnold Arboretum of Harvard University in 1929 showed a certain level of resistance to Dutch elm disease (DED), they realized that in a wild population, trees with even greater resistance might be found. The tree received from the Arnold Arboretum was grown from seeds collected in 1919 in Thamba in the western Himalaya, overlooking the hot plains of Punjab, India, and proved not to be sufficiently cold-hardy in the Netherlands.

Hans M. Heybroek, plant pathologist and tree breeder at De Dorschkamp Forest Research Station in Wageningen, Netherlands, studied the tree. "We realized that this clone was no more than a chance seedling from a mild climate," he explains. "Therefore, in a wider collection, clones with a higher resistance to DED might be found, and trees from the inner valleys of the Himalayas, with their severe winters, should also be more cold hardy."

Seibert met with Heybroek at Floriade, a horticultural exhibition, in 1960: "I had the opportunity of meeting H. M. Heybroek during my recent stay in Rotterdam early in June concerning his project of collecting elms and other trees and shrubs in the Himalayas." Conversation with Heybroek convinced Seibert of the need to explore the Himalayan elms, and he agreed to support the expedition.

Dendrobium chrysotoxum (5751) that was collected by Kingdon Ward on Mount Victoria in 1956 can still be viewed in Longwood's conservatories. Photo by Rondel G. Peirson.

"Preparations were started," explains Heybroek. "Because of the tense political situation at that time, I decided to travel to India only, and avoid Pakistan and Nepal. One important decision I had to make was whether I should travel in late spring to collect elm seeds, or in early fall to collect scions. The first option required exact timing, because ripe seeds remain on elms for a period of only a week, and one can easily arrive too late or too early. Scions, on the other hand, can be collected over a period of months. Weighing these options, I decided to start the expedition in September, which is a better travelling season in the Himalayas anyway."

Old *chenar* trees, *Platanus orientalis,* line the canal in the Mogul gardens near Srinagar. Photo by Hans M. Heybroek.

Heybroek's companions from the Botanical Survey of India on one of the plant-hunting forays out of Srinagar. Photo by Hans M. Heybroek.

Beas was one the valleys east of Kashmir that Heybroek explored in search of *Ulmus wallichiana.* Photo by Hans M. Heybroek.

Revered elms

Heybroek arrived in New Delhi on 18 August 1960. On the ground in New Delhi, he secured help from both the Botanical Survey of India and the Forest Research Institute. The expedition began on 27 August with a journey northwest from New Delhi to Srinagar in the Valley of Kashmir.

"With its large Wular Lake at 1700 m, surrounded by mountains of 3000 m, the valley was breathtakingly beautiful," remembers Heybroek. "Before heading to the mountains, we visited the famous Mogul gardens near Srinagar. But there grew no elms in the Mogul gardens, just the great *chenar, Platanus orientalis.* These trees, favored by the Moguls, were introduced from their homeland Persia. Later they became an omnipresent motif in Kashmir art and also supplanted the native cherry bark elm, *Ulmus villosa,* as a revered tree for the

public areas. The elm, however, still retained the aura of sanctity. In some places in Kashmir and in the valley further east, it was the central village tree. Elms growing in the fields often had platforms built around their base, considered a good place for praying. This species proved later to be quite cold hardy in the Netherlands, and although it is not resistant to DED, it seems to be little bothered by it."

The main goal of the expedition was, however, the collection of *Ulmus wallichiana.* To find this tree, Heybroek and his team had to ascend the side valleys around Srinagar. "The forests at the higher elevations looked strangely familiar to me," he recalls. "The trees were of the same genera I knew from Europe—maples, cherries, oaks, birches, alders, poplars, pines, firs, spruces, and larches—just different species. Yew and ivy were no more than different subspecies. When looking down at the valleys covered by a coniferous forest, I had a feeling of being somewhere in the Alps, at least until I saw groups of monkeys crossing the stream."

Elm is for the cow

Heybroek remembers that his first encounter with *Ulmus wallichiana* was a bit puzzling. "Instead of a fine, majestic tree with a well proportioned crown, I saw a crooked stump devoid of branches. 'What is going on?' I asked myself. The answer came the next morning, when I met a shepherd, trekking with his flock of sheep and goats from the high pastures to the lower valleys. He told us that he supplemented his sheep's diet with elm leaves. When asked for a few twigs fit for grafting, he took off his

Ulmus wallichiana is lopped in late summer; its leafy twigs are then stored in a tree's crotch for winter. Photo by Hans M. Heybroek.

Between terraced fields, villagers grow many useful trees, including elms. Photo by Hans M. Heybroek.

shoes, put a small ax in his belt, and swiftly climbed into the top of an old elm standing in the forest, and chopped off at random several branches for us. Climbing was apparently a skill one needed to be a shepherd in Kashmir! As I was able to observe, this practice of mutilating forest trees for fodder eventually led to their decline. In contrast, trees growing along the fields and around villages were subject to a careful and sustainable practice of lopping branches for fodder. Farmers kept a well balanced framework of the main branches and lopping was carried out at a more or less regular rotation of two to four years. Elm leaf hay appeared to be an essential winter fodder as grass hay was very scarce. Villagers even planted new trees for this purpose. A farmer, who had planted a peach, an apricot, and an elm next to his house, explained: 'The fruits are for the man, the elm is

for the cow.' In the areas where *Ulmus wallichiana* occurred, it was the species favored for fodder, because of its high nutritional value, although certain other species were sometimes lopped too."

An elm that has been lopped will grow long, non-flowering shoots for many years. "As all elms I was finding on this expedition were lopped in some way," Heybroek explains, "I realized how fortunate my decision to go to the Himalayas in the fall rather than in the spring had been. Had I gone there in the spring there would be no seeds on these trees at all! Collecting scions is not without its own challenges. Scions can easily dry out, and when kept moist but warm, they deplete stored carbohydrates so that grafting fails later. Plant explorers before me had to carry metal tins to store the scions in. I had a new solution that revolutionized plant collecting—polyethyl-

Searching for elms, Heybroek explored several valleys in the western Himalaya, including the valley of the river Sutlej. Photo by Hans M. Heybroek.

ene bags. This material allows for gas exchange, but keeps the moisture in."

Sleeping on dynamite

On 22 September, Heybroek and his companions traveled southeast from the Valley of Kashmir to the Kulu Valley, where he collected near the towns of Kothi and Manali. A week later he relocated south to the next valley of the river Sutlej. On 17 October, Heybroek continued his journey southeast to the region of Kumaun, which borders Nepal on the east. There he spent nearly four weeks exploring mountains and valleys around Dehra Dun, Ranikhet, Almora, and Naini Tal.

"We traveled by car, by bus, in an open jeep, on horseback, and finally on foot, with two porters," Heybroek recalls. "Lodging was varied. Often it was a simple tent with two parts—one for cooking and eating, and the other for sleeping—set up on a surface paved with flat stones on which we would put our bedrolls. In a more fancy shelter, in which I had a small room with a cot, I naively asked about the restroom. The owner stared, amazed at me, then said with a broad gesture: 'The forest is all around, Sir.' One time we had to spend the night at a camp set up for construction workers widening a road high in the mountains. My guide found me a fine clean

tent where I could sleep on a large flat crate. After a quiet night, I discovered that the crate contained dynamite for the roadwork. But the finest lodging was in the forest resthouses. These were built for the forest managers travelling through the vast forest at convenient walking distances and always at beautiful locations. When the local attendant had an advance warning of our coming, the house provided luxuries such as a warm bath, an easy chair on the veranda, a few hours of electricity, a table to work on herbarium material, a good meal, and a quiet night on a cot."

Upon returning from Kumaun to New Delhi on 20 November, Heybroek arranged a short trip to Darjeeling, east of Nepal. "There, vegetation is drastically different from the western Himalayas," he says, "but there is one elm, *Ulmus lanceifolia,* an evergreen, primitive species of the tropical rainforest. This elm too was heavily lopped, while no other surrounding trees were. Apparently, this species also was a preferred source of fodder, like the elms in the west." Heybroek made there his last collections and on 2 December departed for the Netherlands. His collections of seeds were forwarded to the USDA Plant Industry Station in Beltsville, Maryland. Grafted elms followed some time later.

"The expedition brought back over sixty collections of elms, including several *Ulmus wallichiana* that proved to be hardy and reasonably resistant to DED," says Heybroek, summing up the expedition's accomplishments. "These were later used in crosses to develop DED-resistant hybrids. In addition, herbarium collections permitted recognition of three subspecies within *Ulmus wallichiana.* An elm, which I found growing in the mountains at lower elevation than *Ulmus wallichiana,* was determined to be a new species altogether. It was named *Ulmus chumlia.*"

"The expedition opened my eyes to the importance of leaf hay and of the lopping of deciduous trees for fodder. In some parts of Europe this was practiced until recently. In earlier centuries it was the mainstay of husbandry in many areas and in prehistoric times it may have played a decisive role in agriculture. Elm was always the preferred species as it had the highest nutritive value of all trees.

"Seeds of about sixty other species of trees, shrubs, and herbs were also collected, but their impact was small. Surprisingly, my collections of dandelion, *Taraxacum,* allowed for a discovery of several new species. As a result, there are now dandelions growing somewhere in the Himalayas that have been named in my honor *Taraxacum heybroekii;* a fact that people keep teasing me about."

Following the expedition, Heybroek used the elms he collected in the Himalaya in crosses to develop DED-resistant hybrids, as part of the broad Dutch elm breeding program. Over a period of sixty years, more than 200,000 seedlings were screened for resistance using artificial inoculations with the pathogen. The latest products of the program, the elm varieties 'Columella' and 'Nanguen', are fully resistant to the disease. Photo by Hans M. Heybroek.

ROADLESS KINGDOM

In his position as Longwood's director, Seibert recognized the importance of plant exploration, testing, and introduction. "New models of decorative plants are as much of value to man's welfare and economy as any other agricultural and horticultural plants," wrote Seibert (1970a). On this premise, in 1956 he approached the USDA with an offer of a cooperative agreement for the purpose of "encouraging the advancement of ornamental horticulture in the United States through the discovery and introduction of new or little known plants of the world which will have potential value to the future of ornamental horticulture and therefore to the rapidly increasing numbers of home gardeners and plant hobbyists" (Seibert 1956a).

The proposal was enthusiastically received by Dr. Carl O. Erlanson, head of the USDA Section of Plant

On his expedition to the western Himalaya, Heybroek discovered a new species of elm, *Ulmus chumlia,* in this forest in the Kalakhan area near Nainital. Photo by Hans M. Heybroek.

Introduction, and gained support from the trustees of Longwood Foundation. "It was felt that this basic work could in time benefit every homeowner, every commercial and professional gardener, horticulturist, florist, and plantsman," wrote Seibert (1970a). "It could brighten the

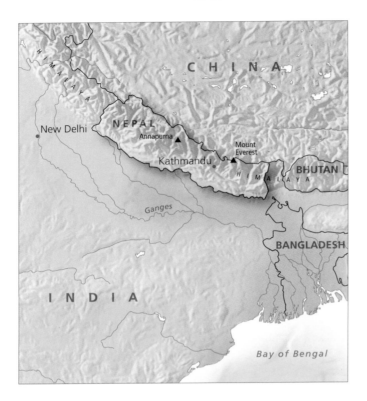

Among the most rugged countries in the world, Nepal occupies more than 145,000 km². About three-quarters of the country is covered by the Himalaya, which runs parallel to it for some 800 km. Only along the southern border with India is there any extensive area of flat land. Although Nepal is located in the subtropical latitude, its climate becomes progressively colder with the increase in elevation. At about 4800 m the temperature stays below freezing year-round. Rainfall ranges from about 1800 mm in the east to 750 mm in the west, most of it falling during the summer monsoon, but it may be as much as 2500 mm on the southern slopes of the Himalaya. Nepal has a rich flora comprising about seven thousand species of vascular plants. While eastern and central Nepal is considered an extension of the Sino-Japanese floristic region, western Nepal has strong affinities with the floras of the western Himalaya and even the Mediterranean. Southern parts of Nepal and river valleys of the midland hills, with an altitude below 1000 m, support tropical vegetation. In the subtropical zone, between 1000 and 2000 m, lauraceous and fagaceous forests dominate in the eastern and central part of the country, but in western Nepal these are largely replaced by pine forests. Above 2000 m, temperate flora thrives. While in eastern and central Nepal evergreen oaks, rhododendrons, and laurels are characteristic, further west, coniferous forests of cedars, cypresses, firs, and spruces become prominent. In the higher elevations a belt of hemlocks and rhododendrons separates the temperate broad-leaved forest from the subalpine flora, which develops above 3000 m. The subalpine zone supports fir forests at the lower elevation, while birches and rhododendrons predominate near the timberline at about 4000 m. The alpine scrub vegetation above 4000 m consists mostly of rhododendrons, junipers, barberries, and dwarf willows. Beyond the alpine scrub are rich meadows of herbs, grasses, and sedges.

outlook of the more than fifty million garden and horticultural hobbyists in the United States of America and it might even touch all but a few of the rest of the Americans who pause and reflect when they see a beautiful flower."

From its inception, the cooperative program had ambitious and far-reaching goals. "In most cases," wrote Seibert (1970a), "collectors, either by nature of their individual preferences, or because of the financial sponsors' stipulations are restrictive in the type of collections which are made. This program, however, having as its objectives new or potentially new as well as improved forms of existing ornamentals, cuts completely across the range of plants from abelias to zygopetalums; from desert to wetlands, from subarctic to torrid tropical; from seacoast to alpine. It seeks to cumulate into a United Nations of ornamental plants. It even provides for a continuing

exchange of ornamental plant materials between this country and the countries of exploration."

In 1962, when contemplating areas to be targeted under the USDA-Longwood plant exploration program, Seibert wrote to Dr. Howard L. Hyland of the USDA Agricultural Research Service, "I do feel that exploration for ornamental plant materials in Nepal would be highly desirable for American ornamental horticulture and I would hope it would be possible for this to be arranged."

The Himalayan kingdom of Nepal, tucked between India and Tibet, remained isolated from the rest of the world until 1947. At that time, the British and the Japanese made the first botanical surveys there. Travelers to Nepal coined the phrase "roadless kingdom" to reflect the scarcity of roads and abundance of footpaths and flimsy rope bridges throughout most of the country. Despite its

De Vos, center, with the expedition's cargo upon their arrival to Pokhara from Kathmandu. Photo by John L. Creech.

The expedition's first camp was set up on the way from Pokhara to Dana. Photo by John L. Creech.

remoteness, Nepal was particularly interesting as a destination for horticultural exploration because of its broad range of temperate-zone plants. Although latitudinally located in the subtropics, most of the country is in the high Himalaya and supports rich temperate flora with close affinity to that of China and Japan.

Dr. John L. Creech was asked to lead the expedition to Nepal, and Dr. Francis de Vos, assistant director of the U.S. National Arboretum in Washington, agreed to join the team. As the most opportune time for the collection of seeds of a wide range of woody and other species in that part of the world is in the period following the summer rains, Creech and de Vos decided to arrive in Nepal around the middle of September 1962.

The plan for the expedition was to make studies of the west-central part of Nepal, including the foothills of the Annapurna range, Kali Gandaki and Mardi Khola rivers, and in the hill country near Kathmandu. "Our party had grown," recorded de Vos (1963), "and included a young police trainee who was to serve as our liaison officer with the Nepalese government and two Sherpas, the high-altitude porters that had made it possible for others to climb such peaks as Everest and Annapurna. Our decision to hire the fifteen porters we needed in Pokhara, 90 miles [145 km] to the west, rather than in Kathmandu where they were cheaper, was based on a simple truth about roadless Nepal that must be faced by anyone who intends to explore the region outside the Kathmandu Valley. Whenever time is important, fly if possible. The flying time to Pokhara is forty minutes, but porters carrying 70 pound [32 kg] packs take ten days."

In the shadow of Annapurna

Thus Creech and de Vos flew from Kathmandu to Pokhara, Nepal's second largest city, situated at the foot of Annapurna, 8078 m, and used as the starting point for all expeditions to western Nepal. "The short flight brought us to the beautiful Pokhara valley where we landed on a grass airstrip and discharged our more than a half ton of cargo," remembers Creech. "A buffalo cart guided by two elderly ladies transported our baggage to the United States Operations Mission house. This would be our base to which we would return after each trek."

In Pokhara, Creech and de Vos hired a team of porters and on 11 October headed northwest to the town of Dana. "During this trek we established our protocol," recalls Creech. "De Vos and I, together with the police trainee and one of the Sherpas, would strike out at a faster pace in order to make side trips for collecting. The porters, having to break camp and marching at a slower pace, would follow. About 3 p.m. we would reach the selected camp site and the porters would arrive an hour later, set up camp, prepare the evening meal, and by 6 p.m. it would be dark and the evening was spent doing notes by gas lamp. We slept in our tent while the porters would gather under a large plastic cover for the night."

Dana was 60 km northwest of Pokhara and about the same distance from the Tibetan border. "The first part of our journey was along the Ghabung Khola at an elevation of 3300 to 5000 feet [1000–1500 m]," reported de Vos (1963). "Since Nepal is at the same latitude as central and northern Florida, the climate at this elevation was subtropical. The native vegetation along the way except for

The first part of the trek from Pokhara to Dana led along the river Ghabung Khola. Photo by John L. Creech.

"We had to negotiate several landslides of brilliant mica, crossed many streams by fording or narrow bridges. The water was so swift that fording above the knees was impossible. In this region, most slopes to the east, south and west were rather barren. The cattle which grazed there in summer were by then down at lower elevations. We used their abandoned sites for our camps because water, which was scarce, could be found there. All water we drank first had to be filtered because of the silica in it, which would tear out our stomachs, and then purified with iodine tablets."

the broad, spreading fig known botanically as *Ficus benjamina,* was of little interest. More than once, we were to rest ourselves and remove our packs at the porter stands so thoughtfully built beneath the shade of this magnificent tree. Citrus, bananas, and poinsettias were common, but most intriguing were the frangipani trees, native to Mexico and the West Indies. This tree, with its fragrant, white to pink flowers, is a favorite in Buddhist worship, and we saw it frequently on the grounds of Buddhist temples."

On the second day out, gradually, the hours of climbing up increased over those spent going down. "With the increase in elevation, we came into the temperate forest region at 7500 feet [2300 m]," noted de Vos (1963). "Giant rhododendron trees up to 60 feet [18 m] high and 3 feet [90 cm] in diameter were not uncommon. What a sight they must be in the spring when covered with trusses of bright, red flowers. In a shady, moist glen a blue *Primula* was in flower and the air was heavy with the fragrance of an autumn-blooming *Elaeagnus.* We were delighted with the change in the flora and collected seeds of a number of species including a low, red-berried evergreen *Cotoneaster* growing attractively over the rocks."

"The trail to Dana crossed many passes up to 2700 m but was easy to follow and direct," remembers Creech.

Five days after leaving Pokhara, the team arrived at Dana and within sight of the area in which they planned to establish their first base camp. "We camped that night on the grounds of a Hindu temple, feeling a little guilty, for our supplies included freeze-dehydrated steaks," wrote de Vos (1963). "After two days' delay in recruiting new porters, we left Dana at 4300 feet [1300 m] for the ridge above, so deceptively close but an agonizing two days' hike away. Despite the fact that we were carrying only about 25 pounds [11 kg], we could not keep up with our barefooted porters who were carrying 60 to 70 pound [27 to 32 kg] loads."

After two days of hard climbing, the expedition found a suitable camping site at about 2760 m where coniferous and broad-leaved forests mingled. "Each day for the next week we explored a different area between 7500 and 12,000 feet [2300–3650 m]," noted de Vos (1963). "In the simple language of our youngest Sherpa, our hike for the day was either 'up-going' or 'down-going.' On the ridges above us we collected seeds of the silver fir [*Abies spectabilis* 635], maples with long pendulous clusters of bright, red fruits, viburnums, barberries, roses, clematis, rhododendrons, iris, cotoneasters, mountain-ash, and a cherry. On the 12,000 foot [3650 m]

The expedition's team in their camp set up above Dana. Standing second from right is de Vos. Photo by John L. Creech.

Himalayan silver fir, *Abies spectabilis* (635), that Creech and de Vos collected on a ridge above their camp in Dana is found throughout the Himalaya at 2500 to 4000 m. Photo by Yoko Arakawa.

ridge low-growing willows, dwarf rhododendrons and grasses were the dominant vegetation. From this point we had our first good look at the solid white dome of Dhaulagiri [8172 m]. Since the British had collected extensively in the alpine meadows above us, we turned our attention to the broad-leaved evergreen forest below our base camp. We were amply rewarded as we found a red-fruited evergreen holly, more maples, and our first plants of *Magnolia campbellii*. Our joy turned to disappointment as we criss-crossed the slopes between 7500 and 9000 feet [2300–2750 m] looking in vain for fruiting specimens of this elusive magnolia, which is treasured in cultivation but goes unnoticed in the wild. We finally gave up, with the hope that in the area to the south we would find fruiting plants."

From Dana, the explorers headed south to Beni. "We had to hire nine extra porters for this short trip but we sold a bag of rice to the locals to make up for it," remembers Creech. "Porters and all purchases had to be made with coins, as paper money was not accepted, and porters expected to be paid daily. So we had a large metal trunk with money and porters would line up to be paid each afternoon. To satisfy auditors back in Washington, a signed receipt was required for each payment. Since the porters could not read or write, they simply put their thumb print on the form which must have caused the auditors fits. Furthermore, each porter expected a ration of local cigarettes and a mug of local spirits daily, and this did not appear on the receipt."

As the team followed the turbulent, slate-gray Kali Gandaki River, the terrain became more rugged and the trails more terrifying. Creech recorded how they traveled on a "path gouged out of the walls above this violent river, capped off by a crossing of a one-plank bridge with cables on either side for support—one miss and it is the Indian Ocean" (1962a). De Vos called this bridge "a real thriller" and noted how "a missing board at mid-stream added interest to the crossing" (1963).

On 25 October the team reached Beni, 65 km west of Pokhara. "When we left Dana and headed south to Beni, we soon found that even hills of 9000 feet [2750 m] were scarcely temperate," wrote Creech (1962b). "A few rhodies and *Pieris* at the very top and occasional hemlocks but not nearly so rewarding as at Dana which is certainly influenced by the cold coming down from Dhaulagiri and Annapurna."

In Beni the explorers had the first chance to send letters to the United States. "Collecting has been good,"

A pointed peak of Machhapuchhare, 7000 m, rises above Pokhara. Photo by Walter H. Hodge.

Crossing a suspension bridge over the Kali Gandaki. Photo by John L. Creech.

Kancha, a Sherpa accompanying Creech and de Vos, holds *Trichosanthes palmata* (6366), a cucurbit vine producing bright red fruits collected on the slopes of Machhapuchhare. Photo by John L. Creech.

Creech (1962a) wrote to Erlanson, "over 100 seed lots so far ranging from 3000 to 12,000 feet [900–3650 m]. At this writing we are sitting on a sandy field along the Kali Gandaki river. It is a grey, torrentuous stream, full of mica. Starting place is Tibet and it ends up in the Indian Ocean. Around us are scattered plants of *Pyracantha* and low-growing *Ziziphus* which is covered with fruits. We have to compete with our porters for fruit samples."

Fishtail mountain

"On the theory that we would find better temperate forests closer to the snow fields and where the cloud cover gathered each day on the slopes of the fishtail mountain called Machhapuchhare, we headed back to Pokhara to replenish our supplies," noted de Vos (1963). Machha-

puchhare, 7000 m, is an isolated spur of the Annapurna range, towering over Pokhara. Arriving in Pokhara on 1 November, the team rested for a day. "This one day break gives us a change of pace, an opportunity to deposit our collections here at Pokhara and lighten our loads," wrote Creech (1962b). "The weather has been entirely to our favor. One day of rain—yesterday, after we were in a house for the first time in over three weeks. Very convenient."

"As we ascended the slopes of Machhapuchhare," wrote de Vos (1963), "the forest became more luxuriant and the thrill of expectancy heightened with each turn of the trail. We did not have to wait long for at 6500 feet [2000 m] we found the most spectacular plant of our whole trip, a red-fruited cucurbit vine with fruits the size of large lemons [*Trichosanthes palmata* 6366]. What a

Creech, in red cap, and his team clean seeds of *Magnolia campbellii* (6343) collected at about 2250 m on the slopes of Machhapuchhare. Photo by John L. Creech.

Fruits of *Magnolia campbellii* (6343) found by Creech and de Vos on Machhapuchhare. Photo by John L. Creech.

show this plant would make when trained on a garden trellis!

"The following day was equally exciting, for we found our first plants of *Magnolia campbellii* but again we were to be disappointed as several fruits were without seeds. The same was true for the next specimen we found. Were we too late? We had our answer before the day was over for near the fringe of a clearing at 7500 feet [2300 m] a 60 foot [18 m] double-trunked specimen [6343] still held a number of partially open fruits on its upper most branches. Could we get the fruits down without shattering the cone-like fruits and losing the seeds in the dense vegetation on the forest floor? The final drama in the quest for seeds of this species gave us some anxious moments as we watched one of our porters saw off a fruiting branch while balanced precariously on another. Our relief was great when both porter and fruiting branch came down slowly and intact. The next day we found several more trees and many fruits with seeds, all on the ground. After two days more of successful collecting, we left Machhapuchhare with a warm feeling of accomplishment but chilled to the bone from exposure to the damp cold that prevailed on its cloud-shrouded slopes."

Hill country

On their return to Kathmandu, Creech and de Vos quickly reorganized and made plans for their next field trip. "We knew that above 8000 feet [2450 m] the nights would soon have temperatures below 20°F [-7°C] and that seeds would be getting hard to find," explained de Vos (1963). "First, we spent a very profitable three days with Dr. G. A.

C. Herklots, a British botanist, who, in cooperation with our AID [Agency for International Development] Mission to Nepal, is establishing a botanical garden for the Nepalese government. This remarkable man with boundless enthusiasm had in three years roughed out the beginnings of a botanical garden that will be an asset to the country and a delight to foreign botanists and horticulturists that are sure to visit this mountain kingdom in increasing numbers. Our visit culminated in his leading us a merry chase up a nearby mountain is search of orchids and seeds of delphinium, euonymus, evergreen oaks, and holly. Although he was more than twenty years our senior, he set the pace and we were the most anxious to stop for lunch and a rest. The physical agony of the day was dispelled by the good feeling of accomplishment, for our packs were full when we reached his home for tea and refreshments so tastefully prepared by Mrs. Herklots. Before leaving, he added some choice orchids and seeds of the autumn-blooming cherry, *Prunus cerasoides* [6352], that we had seen and admired on the hillsides around the botanical garden, as well as seeds of other species we had missed. Happily, we were able to reciprocate with some of *Magnolia campbellii* that we had worked so hard to collect."

On 16 November, Creech and de Vos planned to join Herklots on a trip south of Kathmandu to the Mahabharat range. "For this, fortunately, there is an actual road," wrote Creech (1962c) to Erlanson, "so we will travel by Landrover. The Nepalese have a drug garden in the mountains and we will combine collecting with a visit to that establishment." Traveling along the Rajpath, the sinuous and only road to India from the Kathmandu

A selection of *Cotoneaster microphyllus* (6322) collected by Creech and de Vos in the mountains above Dana was introduced in 1971 as 'Emerald Spray'. Photo by John L. Creech.

Valley, the explorers reached Dhaman in the Mahabharat range. "For five days we collected in the hills surrounding Dhaman at altitudes ranging from 7500 to 8600 feet [2300–2600 m]," recorded de Vos (1963). "Although the vegetation had been severely mutilated for fuel and fodder we made some interesting collections. *Pleione praecox* [621525–6], a terrestrial orchid spread in lavender carpets beneath the tree rhododendrons, pieris, and gaultheria shrubs." Before leaving this area, they added an unusual bittersweet, *Celastrus stylosus* (6319), and a large-fruited *Euonymus theaefolius* (6329).

Creech and de Vos hoped to go north of Kathmandu again on foot, but as the colder weather rapidly set in and snow accumulated in the mountains, they had to abandon this plan and prepare for departure. In addition, the echoes of the border fights between India and China reached the explorers. "To us it seems so remote and not of any cause for alarm," commented Creech (1962c). "The passes up there will soon close in and all will be quiet. We were concerned for a while because Indian Airlines stopped flying to Nepal and it is a long walk out of here. But the planes are back on schedule and all is again routine."

Creech and de Vos departed Nepal on 23 November. "All in all we considered it rather a successful venture, having made some 250 collections of lots of seeds and plants," wrote Creech (1962d) to Seibert after the trip. "I know that a number of these have never been in cultivation in the United States and probably not even in European gardens. Many of these sound like they will be good contributions to American horticulture."

One introduction from the expedition, *Prunus cerasoides,* for which both explorers had high hopes, did not live up to their expectations. "We thought this was going to be a real find for the southern United States," said Creech in 1974. "A cherry which flowered in November and December ought to be one that would be great in Florida and along the coast, but it has never really made it for this purpose." Another plant, however, *Cotoneaster microphyllus* (6322), one of the species collected above Dana at about 3000 m, did achieve widespread popularity. In the trials it proved to be an exceptionally attractive form, resistant to fire blight, and well suited as a landscape shrub in many parts of the United States. In 1971 this cotoneaster was released to the public under the name 'Emerald Spray'. It quickly gained recognition and remains widely grown.

RACING AGAINST THE MONSOON

In 1964 planning began for an expedition to Sikkim, a little kingdom in the Himalaya, hidden from the world between Nepal on the west and Bhutan on the east, never before explored by American collectors. A protectorate of India at that time, Sikkim later abolished monarchy and became a state of India in 1975. The expedition was intended as a sequel to the collecting undertaken in Nepal in 1962 but encompassed the more humid regions of the Himalaya. De Vos, who traveled to Nepal in 1962, and Dr. Edward G. Corbett, horticulturist at the USDA Plant Introduction Station in Glenn Dale, Maryland, led the expedition.

Situated in the eastern wing of the Himalaya, the hills of Sikkim and Darjeeling constitute the Sikkim Himalaya, a landlocked upland country forming a drainage basin for the river Tista. While the tops of the mountains are covered by snow, a lush tropical rain forest flourishes at lower elevations. Home to more than five thousand plant species, the Sikkim Himalaya has long been recognized as a center of a diverse number of ornamental genera of plants, *Rhododendron* among them. The goal set for this expedition was to collect any promising ornamental species encountered, with an emphasis on rhododendrons.

The expedition was planned for the spring of 1965 in order to overlap with the peak of rhododendron bloom. This enabled Corbett and de Vos to observe the range of natural hybridization among some thirty species growing wild in that region, and to make selections of outstanding types in the field. As Corbett remembers, the precise planning of the expedition played a critical role: "The exploration time was limited by the fact that the objective was primarily to see certain genera, *Rhododendron* in particular, in flower, and the flowering occurs just before the onset of the monsoon rains. With the beginning of the monsoon season the presence of large numbers of land leeches makes further exploration in the jungles impractical if not impossible." As the explorers expected to find only a very few seeds at that time of the year, they prepared for securing vegetative material, primarily cuttings, using plastic bags.

Sikkim on the horizon

On 4 April, Corbett and de Vos departed on their journey to the mysterious kingdom in the Himalaya, not being exactly sure what to expect there or which areas they would be able to visit. Three days later they arrived in New Delhi. There they were met by Dr. Som Pracash Mital from the Plant Introduction Office of the Indian Agricultural Research Institute, a botanist who would accompany them on this expedition.

Corbett and de Vos wanted to head for the Singalila Ridge separating Sikkim from Nepal and stay on the Sikkim side as they were moving northward along the border. "The Singalila Ridge extends from a point near Darjeeling north to the confluence of the borders of India, Nepal, and Sikkim, and then along the Sikkim-Nepal border," explains Corbett. "The ridge is at about 3000 to 4000 m and this is an area which had been explored in the middle of the nineteenth century and found to be rich in a variety of genera with horticultural interest." Circumstances, however, forced the explorers to change their plans.

Before the expedition began, access to the areas north and east of Gangtok, the capital of Sikkim, bordering on Tibet, was closed for security reasons, as border disputes between China and India intensified. The expedition was advised to instead visit western Sikkim and the neighboring regions of eastern Nepal. Upon arrival in India, however, even these plans had to change due to the last-minute cancellation of permission to collect in Sikkim and Nepal.

De Vos tried to enlist help from Her Highness, the Queen of Sikkim. On his behalf, Elizabeth Corning,

president of the Garden Club of America, wrote to Her Highness Hope Cooke, an American who in 1963 married the crown prince of Sikkim and two years later assumed the throne. Corning requested from Her Highness assistance in acquiring travel permits for the American explorers.

The party left New Delhi on 16 April on a flight first to Calcutta, then to Bagdogra, some 90 km southeast of Darjeeling, where they were met by Donald McKenzie from the nearby Bagracote Tea Estate. After being hosted in Bagracote by McKenzie for one night, de Vos, Corbett, and Mital left early on the morning of 18 April for a three-hour jeep ride to Darjeeling, elevation 2134 m.

As Corbett remembers, the difficulties in securing proper permissions for collecting seemed to never end: "One unanticipated factor on the trip was the bureaucratic red tape. We spent six days in New Delhi meeting people and getting final clearances which we had assumed had already been given. It seemed to take an inordinate amount of time to get those final permissions, and then we spent six more days in Darjeeling making final arrangements before we set off on the trail. Since we were working against the time limit of the onset of the monsoons it was a bit vexatious to lose that time."

"There is little hope for an excursion into Sikkim at this time," wrote de Vos (1965a) from Darjeeling. "This part of India is virtually one large armed camp, and soldiers are in evidence everywhere. Unless Her Highness intervenes, there is little chance that we will be allowed to cross the border. My contact, Mr. Donald McKenzie of Bagracote Tea Estate, was not very helpful. We had an interesting interlude at his place during which he managed to drink us under the table and then coax us out for nine holes of golf. Even under the best of conditions, I am a lousy golfer, but this game was a farce. There is no question that Mr. McKenzie knows the right people around here, but he didn't stay sober enough in the two days with him to help us much."

First collections

As the diplomatic efforts by Madame President and Her Highness did not result in granting permission to travel in Sikkim, Corbett and de Vos had to limit their activities to the southern part of the Singalila Ridge located in the Darjeeling district of India. In Darjeeling the party, consisting of Corbett, de Vos, and Mital, was joined by Baktiman Rai, a plant collector from the local Lloyds Botanic Garden.

Magnolia campbellii growing on Tiger Hill near Darjeeling. Photo by Edward G. Corbett.

Camp set up by Corbett and de Vos's team on the top of Tonglu. Photo by Edward G. Corbett.

On 22 April, de Vos (1965a) was finally able to report back: "After three frustrating weeks, we made our first plant collections today." It was done on Tiger Hill, 2580 m, about 11 km southeast of Darjeeling. With the horizon dominated by the tallest of the Himalayan peaks, Tiger Hill appeared to de Vos to be "a mere bump on the landscape around here." Nevertheless, on this "mere bump" they discovered a very diverse population of enormous—18 to 24 m tall—*Magnolia campbellii* with flowers ranging in color from red to nearly white. The scions collected from these trees were shipped to the United States by air the next day.

"Once in Darjeeling we learned that there is a road along the Singalila ridge which is accessible by four-wheel-drive vehicle from Darjeeling to Phalut, 3600 m, with guest houses, formerly called inspection bungalows, at Tonglu, Sandakphu and Phalut," remembers Corbett. "The party agreed to take the route from Darjeeling to Manibhanjang, 2134 m, by bus and on foot from there to Phalut along the ridge line, then returning by a lower route, 1800 to 2100 m, and passing through the towns of Rimbik, Palmajua, Ramam, and Batasi."

Through rhododendron country

On 23 April the party finally left Darjeeling for a trek, first to Tonglu, on the Singalila Ridge, some 60 km away, via Manibhanjang. The group included "our eight porters, the Indian botanist, Mital, and his helper, plus Ed and myself," recorded de Vos (1965b). "The rickety old Chevy bus got us there [Manibhanjang] all right but not without a few thrills. At Manibhanjang, we had the usual haggling over whose load was the heaviest but finally after an hour, got going. . . . The climb from Manibhanjang 6600 ft. [2000 m] to Tonglu 10,075 ft. [3020 m] reminded me of the climb from Dana to our first base camp. We made it but just barely. I am glad we rented the bungalow for the first night for we were in no condition to set up camp."

Reaching Tonglu, the explorers found that the conditions at 3000 m differed drastically from those in Darjeeling. "The weather at Tonglu was perfectly atrocious for the first two days," recorded de Vos (1965b). "The skies were clear until 8 a.m. then the clouds came rolling in on gale winds of about 45° [7°C]. Everyone from this area said this was most unusual and so it was, for the next two days have been magnificent."

Having the benefit of clear skies, on 26 April the party made a 24 km round trip exploring the slopes of Tonglu, down to 2300 m and then back up by a murderous hike to 3000 m. On the way they collected several rhododendrons. "We had expected that there would be white-flowered forms of many of the rhododendrons, particularly *R. arboreum* and *R. barbatum*," remembers Corbett. "This is precisely what we found and on one day we came upon an extensive hillside of *R. arboreum* with the color range we had hoped to find from the blood red type to white."

De Vos (1965b) reported on other botanical riches of these mountains: "The fruit of *Mahonia nepalensis* is plentiful here and we will collect seeds in about three weeks. *Daphne cannabina* is abundant between 2400 m and 3000 m, and varies from nearly white to deep

Color variation in flowers of *Rhododendron arboreum* found by Corbett and de Vos on Tonglu. Photo by Edward G. Corbett.

Corbett and de Vos found *Daphne cannabina* on the slopes of Tonglu between 2400 m and 3000 m. Photo by Francis de Vos.

purple—wish there was a way to get more vegetative propagations back. Arisaemas are very abundant here in about six species. On the east slope of Tonglu, Corbett and de Vos collected an epiphytic orchid, *Coelogyne corymbosa* (65661), which was spotted growing on an evergreen oak at 2550 m. A few hundred meters higher on the same slope they found *Pieris formosa* (68425), an evergreen shrub with profuse white flowers and reddish new growth. The party continued collecting on Tonglu for several days, often wandering onto the Nepalese side of the mountain.

Kanchenjunga, 8585 m, the third highest mountain in the world, as viewed by the expedition from Tonglu. Photo by Edward G. Corbett.

The place of the winds

On 1 May the expedition left Tonglu and continued the trek toward Sandakphu. The trail led them first to Gairibas, 2620 m, then to Kali Pokahari, 2950 m, where they stopped for a light lunch. Past Kali Pokahari a steep climb brought the party to the top of Sandakphu, 3580 m, by late afternoon. While ascending Sandakphu, they found at about 3000 m another orchid, this time *Coelogyne cristata* (65662), and more rhododendrons, including *Rhododendron falconeri* (691193) and *R. grande* (691194).

The Singalila trek took the expedition through sparsely populated areas. Corbett recalls their infrequent encounters with the inhabitants of the country: "The villages in the mountains are rather isolated. There is a road

The expedition's porters on a trail from Sandakphu to Phalut. Photo by Edward G. Corbett.

Corbett crosses a bamboo bridge. Photo by Edward G. Corbett.

of sorts but almost everything comes in by pack animal or porters using A-frame backpacks. Judging from the reactions of the people, especially the children, we were the first westerners who had been there in some time."

The party spent several days on Sandakphu. Being up early to take advantage of clear mornings, Corbett and de Vos hiked down from the top of the mountain, often through nearly impenetrable thickets of roses, brambles, and bamboo, then climbed back to return to the base before the clouds closed in. Their findings included, among others, *Abies spectabilis* (7112), *Acer pectinatum* (68565), *Roscoea alpina* (66256), and a wide array of rhododendrons. "It has been a real treat to see the rhododendrons in flower," wrote de Vos (1965c). "I am sure that we have seen the full range of color in *R. arboreum*—from nearly white to red and enough atypical plants to add fuel to controversy over hybridization in the wild."

In the evenings Corbett, de Vos, Mital, Rai, and their helpers gathered around a fireplace in a smoky room of a shabby bungalow, sipping tea and sherry, and writing up the day's collections, while rain, lighting, thunder, and howling winds blasted outside. "After a week of collecting in Sandakphu—the place of the winds—we are moving on to Phalut and hopefully to better weather," wrote de Vos (1965c).

Through orchid country

The party left Sandakphu on the early morning of 9 May and reached Phalut, 3600 m, the northernmost mountain on their trek, in the afternoon. The next day they hiked north along the Singalila Ridge a few kilometers into Sikkim and back without seeing a soul.

Two days later they began to work their way back south to Manibhanjang, mostly along the 2400 m contour of the Singalila Ridge. First the party hiked east from Phalut and descended to a village, Samanden, situated in a valley filled with cultivated fields. Near Samanden they collected several epiphytic orchids, including *Cymbidium grandiflorum* (65663) and *C. longifolium* (65667). On 14 May the expedition departed Samanden and headed first for Shirikhola, 2115 m, then after crossing a river on a suspension bridge, reached Rimbik, 2286 m. The following day the party explored the hills surrounding Rimbik, where they found more orchids, including *Eria graminifolia* (65669) and an unknown *Bulbophyllum* (65668).

On 16 May, de Vos, Corbett, and their team reached a forest station in Palmajua. Along the trails from Rimbik to Palmajua they collected more orchids. As the station was completely deserted, the party pitched tents in front of one of the bungalows. Corbett remembers that day: "By the time we reached Palmajua the monsoon had set in in earnest and attempts to collect or observe much of anything were no longer possible." Heavy rain came in that night and the tents were put to the ultimate test. To complicate matters even further, Mital received news that he must return to Delhi earlier than previously planned, so the party decided to cut short their stay in Palmajua and depart for their next stop, Batasi, the following morning. Along the trail leading to Batasi, they contin-

De Vos with *Rhododendron aucklandii* on Phalut. Photo by Edward G. Corbett.

Children gathered around Rai and de Vos in Rimbik. Photo by Edward G. Corbett.

ued collecting orchids, including *Dendrobium* sp. (65675) and *Liparis* sp. (65674). Upon reaching Manibhanjang a couple of days later, the expedition closed the circle. In Manibhanjang they boarded a bus that took them back to Darjeeling.

The party arrived in Darjeeling on 20 May. "We have just returned to Darjeeling after trekking about 200 miles [320 km] through the Singalila Range," wrote de Vos (1965d) to Creech. "Aside from our failure to do anything with rhododendron cuttings, I feel that our trip has been well worthwhile. Over a third of our present 180 collections are either plants or seeds. The rest are flowering herbarium specimens."

By that time it was apparent to de Vos that the expedition's collecting activities might be compromised. "The spring flowering season is over and the pre-monsoon rains have begun," he reported (1965d). "During the past week we had rain every afternoon or evening, and with 1 to 2 inches [25–50 mm] of rain a day the leeches have come out of hibernation. Our whole party of seventeen had one or more leeches during our trek to Manibhanjang this morning."

Corbett and de Vos spent the next several days in Darjeeling organizing collections and hoping for a change in weather. They took advantage of plant collections maintained in the Lloyds Botanic Garden and with the help of Rai procured seeds of sixty additional species native to the Darjeeling region. Corbett and de Vos also made some purchases in a seed house of G. Ghose and Sons in Darjeeling, which turned out to be fairly well stocked with

The expedition's porters in Palmajua. Photo by Edward G. Corbett.

seeds of local plants. Unfortunately, the monsoon was settling over Darjeeling and the Singalila Ridge for good. The explorers decided to prepare for departure. On 26 May the expedition left Darjeeling to return to the United States by way of Bagdogra, Calcutta, and Delhi.

"Although we were disappointed that we did not get permission to enter Nepal or Sikkim we were quite pleased with the collections that we made," said de Vos (1965e). "Among the material brought back were 59 collections of living plants comprised of cuttings, seedlings, and rootstock, and seed of 136 species. We also made about 500 herbarium specimens."

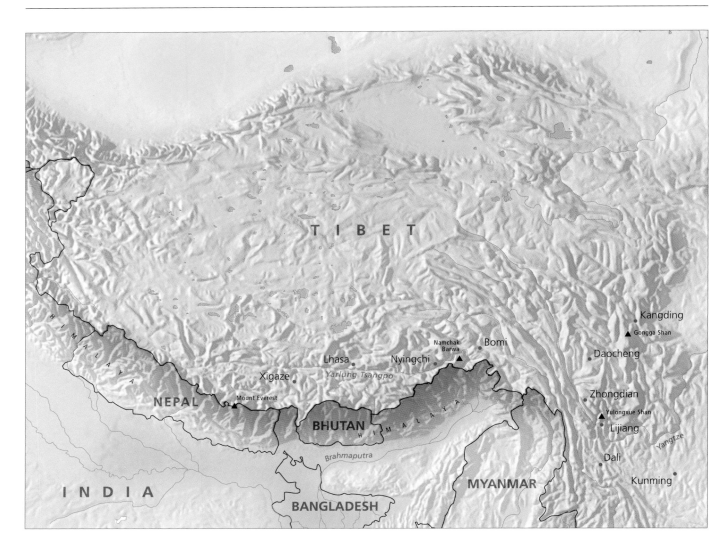

The Tibetan plateau occupies 2.3 million km² in central Asia, about half of which lies in the Tibetan Autonomous Region of China, with the rest divided between four Chinese provinces—Qinghai, Gansu, Sichuan, and Yunnan. Although most of Tibet's territory is relatively level, its topography extends from the Himalayan peaks, 8000 m in altitude, to the low-lying, deep southeastern river gorges with elevations below 1200 m. The Himalaya, the world's highest range, comprises 110 peaks more than 7300 m high and extends for nearly 2500 km from Nanga Parbat, 8126 m, in the west to Namchak Barwa, 7756 m, in the east. While in the western part of the plateau high plains predominate, mountain ranges and river gorges are the dominant feature of the eastern part. Most of Tibet is subject to a severe, dry, continental climate. While the arctic air has unhindered access to Tibet from the north, the warm, humid air masses from the south can barely penetrate the Himalaya. As a result the annual precipitation on the northern slopes of the Himalaya can be as low as 150 mm, whereas on the south side it varies from 1500 to 3000 mm. The gorges of southeastern Tibet are more accessible to the air masses from the south, which bring a higher annual precipitation, about 500 mm. The vegetation of Tibet reflects the diversity of its climates, and the number of vascular plants exceeds six thousand. Forests are limited to southern Tibet, with the southeast being the most densely forested. Deserts occupy the northern part, while grasslands are found in the northeast. The flora of the mountains is differentiated according to the elevation. Tropical vegetation can be found below 1200 m, subtropical vegetation between 1200 and 2200 m, and temperate vegetation from 2200 to 3500 m. Above that, alpine vegetation develops.

ON THE FRINGES OF TIBET

Longwood exploration of the Himalayan region in the 1950s and 1960s was limited to the areas south of the main crest of the Himalaya. Tibet, like the rest of China, was not accessible to Western explorers during that period. It was not until China removed some of the restrictions on travel to Tibet in the 1990s that it became possible to send plant-collecting expeditions to that part of the world.

In 2000 I joined the team organized by Dr. Zsolt Debreczy and Dr. István Rácz, principal investigators of the International Dendrological Research Institute in Wellesley, Massachusetts, to travel to eastern Tibet, a region administered by Sichuan and Yunnan provinces. In the early 1970s, Debreczy and Rácz had begun the paramount task of preparing the *Dendrological Atlas;* in the decades that followed, both traveled to nearly every corner of the temperate climate zone to study and document trees and shrubs. The focus of the 2000 expedition to eastern Tibet was conifers, the subject of the first four volumes of the atlas. Debreczy, Rácz, and I were joined by Ethan W. Johnson of the Holden Arboretum in Kirtland, Ohio, and a group of volunteers, including Mary Campbell, Patricia A. Fox, Erhard Lorenz, Craig D. Sickel, and Isabell Voss. Our guides during the trip were Yang Yong and Kang Yun, researchers from the Beijing Herbarium of the Chinese Academy of Sciences.

Tali Range

Our team assembled in Beijing and departed on 23 September for Kunming in Yunnan. The next day we headed to Xi Shan, also known as Western Hills, overlooking Kunming and Lake Dian. An abundance of *Cercis yunnanensis,* growing out of sheer rock cliffs overlooking the lake, made us realize what a spectacular site this must be in the spring, when these trees are in bloom. Rich, mixed forest covered the mountain with *Cupressus duclouxiana, Keteleeria evelyniana,* and *Pinus yunnanensis,* the most prominent coniferous trees in the area. One deciduous *Ilex macrocarpa* (001375), growing along the road, caught our attention with its profusion of cherrylike, shiny black fruits.

On 25 September we paid a visit to the Black Dragon Pool Park located in the suburbs of Kunming, which offers fine examples of Taoist and Buddhist temples. The main reason for our visit was a massive specimen of *Cupressus funebris,* commonly called mourning cypress,

Cupressus funebris, alleged to be seven hundred years old, grows on the grounds of a temple in the Black Dragon Pool Park in Kunming. Photo by Tomasz Aniśko.

estimated to be some seven hundred years old. Other arboreal delights included aged *Chionanthus retusus, Cryptomeria japonica,* and *Lagerstroemia indica,* and a sky-high grove of *Glyptostrobus pensilis,* the Chinese relative of the American swamp cypress, *Taxodium distichum.*

The next morning we left Kunming and traveled northwest to the town of Dali, where we intended to explore Diancang Shan, also known as the Tali Range. This range, its highest peaks reaching 4122 m, stretches some 50 km from north to south, overlooking Dali and Lake Er. To expedite our ascent from the town on the lake shore—elevation 1980 m—to the high peaks, we resorted to a cable lift, which took us halfway to the top of the mountain and saved a good several hours of hiking. Our collecting began at about 3300 m. The most important find of the day were cones of *Abies delavayi,* a species of

Diancang Shan, previously known as the Tali Range, rises above Dali. Photo by Tomasz Aniśko.

A caravan of Tibetan horses is prepared to take our group to Yunshan Ping on the slopes of Yulongxue Shan near Lijiang. Photo by Tomasz Aniśko.

Collecting plants on the slopes of Diancang Shan near Dali are, left to right, Sickel, Campbell, Debreczy, Rácz, Fox, Kang, and Yang. Photo by Tomasz Aniśko.

fir inhabiting the uppermost ridges of Diancang Shan, but our collections also included *Arisaema yunnanense* (001376), *Rodgersia sambucifolia* (001387), and *Sorbus rufopilosa* (001388).

Nakhi kingdom

From Dali we continued north to the city of Lijiang, the historical capital of the ancient Nakhi kingdom. The city is backed by the majestic Yulongxue Shan, or Jade Dragon Snow Mountain, 5596 m, standing on the edge of Tibet. The mountain is home to half of Yunnan's thirteen thousand plant species, including four hundred species of trees.

After checking into a hotel, our group decided to do a quick reconnaissance on the mountain. We drove

toward Yunshan Ping, an alpine meadow on the east side of the Yulongxue Shan, which would be our destination the next day. To our delight, at a turn in the road we spotted a specimen of *Abies salouenensis* decorated prolifically with cones. While Debreczy and Rácz climbed the tree to collect the cones, the rest of the group surveyed the vegetation around the site. *Viburnum, Buddleja,* and *Rhododendron* abounded, as did herbaceous plants, peonies, and primroses.

The next day we returned with the intent to reach Yunshan Ping, surrounded on three sides by a virgin forest with thousand-year-old *Abies forrestii* (001396) and *Picea likiangensis.* A small caravan of Tibetan horses was hired to carry us to the meadow, from where a further ascent would begin. The unimposing stature of these horses revealed nothing about their incredible strength and ability to maneuver along narrow and steep mountain paths. The forest above the meadow had clearly been used for grazing by the very same horses, as the understory vegetation was severely impacted. Only upon reaching the alpine zone, where loose dolomitic rock covering the ground kept horses away, did we see a greater diversity of plants. Here firs and spruces were replaced by *Betula calcicola, Juniperus squamata,* and *J. pingii.* Many dwarf shrubs, including a curious *Buxus rugulosa* var. *prostrata* (001613), hugged the ground.

Hutiao Gorge, or Leaping Tiger Gorge, said to be the deepest gorge in the world, was our destination for 30 September. Extending 15 km, from Yulongxue Shan in the south to Habaxue Shan in the north, it is traversed by

The author dwarfed by the massive trunks of *Abies forrestii* (001396) growing in Yunshan Ping on the slopes of Yulongxue Shan near Lijiang. Photo by Tomasz Aniśko.

Standing on the eastern rim of Hutiao Gorge at its northern end where the Yangtze river emerges after dropping some 300 m in a series of eighteen rapids. Photo by Tomasz Aniśko.

Ascending to the plateau

The next day we headed north from Lijiang to Zhongdian following the course of the Zhongdian River, one of the tributaries of the Yangtze. Zhongdian is the seat of Dechen Tibetan Autonomous Prefecture, which occupies the northwestern corner of Yunnan. As the road we were traveling on steadily climbed to higher altitudes, rapid changes in the landscape, vegetation, and architecture, as well as the sudden appearance of horsemen and herds of yaks, announced our entry into historical Tibet. Enticed by the rich, lush vegetation along the river, we decided to return there later and to dedicate a whole day to collecting in this valley.

The valley along the Zhondian River fulfilled our every expectation. Despite constant rain and bloodthirsty leeches, which were curiously attracted to our faces, plant collecting was very fruitful. Particularly attractive at that time of year, and richly adorned with colorful fruits, were *Schisandra chinensis* (001585), *Sorbus prattii* (001587), and *Viburnum kansuense* (001586). However, of all the plants collected, none caused as much excitement as a spurge, *Euphorbia nematocypha* (001400), decorated with fire-red leaves. To our dismay, hardly any fruit was present on these plants. After searching through dozens of plants for half an hour, we found only five precious seeds.

On 5 October we continued north to Daocheng in Sichuan. The dirt road between Zhongdian and Daocheng leads through rugged terrain that under normal conditions can be traversed only by four-wheel-drive vehicles and is frequently impassable due to land-

the mighty Yangtze River and bounded by two peaks towering 3900 m above it. While rushing through the gorge, the Yangtze drops about 300 m in a series of eighteen rapids. Our goal was to explore the north end of the gorge, which is more difficult to reach than the south end and therefore less visited. The dirt road we were traveling on ended abruptly at the gorge only to reveal an unearthly landscape shaped by unimaginable forces of nature. Standing on the rim of the gorge, we were overpowered by the scale of the awesome geological formation around us. The seemingly uninhabited land before us was Tibet. The only sign of human presence was a small shack manned by two people selling soft drinks, potato chips, and instant noodles.

The valley of the Zhongdian River, which flows south from Tibet to Yunnan, was a rich plant hunting area. Photo by Tomasz Aniśko.

Blazing red foliage of spurge, *Euphorbia nematocypha* (001400), growing in the Zhongdian River valley. Photo by Tomasz Aniśko.

slides. It took us a whole day in Zhongdian to find several drivers brave enough to undertake such an arduous trip. A convoy of four vehicles was assembled to accommodate our team with an ever-increasing load of plants and herbarium specimens. Not being sure of the road conditions ahead of us, we left Zhongdian at the first light of dawn. Our Tibetan drivers warned us that in good weather it took more than ten hours to reach Daocheng. Little did they realize the group they had agreed to transport over these mountains would not resist the temptation to stop at every picture-worthy tree along the road. To assure our movement at a reasonable pace, the Tibetan drivers learned quickly to call us back to the vehicles using the one English phrase they knew—"Let's go!"— shouted with a commanding tone. In the afternoon our

advances were further delayed by several mechanical failures, which afflicted our vehicles one by one, and eventually by a flat tire. It was shortly before midnight when we saw the lights of Daocheng.

Before departing from Daocheng the following morning, we replaced our convoy of jeeps, which had served us so well, with a small bus. To reach Yajiang, our next destination, we had to cross a large section of the Tibetan plateau, rising some 4000 m above sea level. As we ascended to higher altitudes, the coniferous forest was gradually replaced by grassland and finally by alpine desert with scarce cushion herbs and dwarf rhododendrons hiding between crumbled rocks. Several species of *Gentiana* with brilliant blue flowers, rivaling the azure sky above, frequented these high altitudes. High moun-

Our small convoy of jeeps at one of the many stops along the road from Zhongdian to Daocheng. Photo by Tomasz Aniśko.

Pinus densata was among the conifers seen en route from Zhongdian to Daocheng. Photo by Tomasz Aniśko.

Habitat of *Abies squamata* near Daocheng. Photo by Tomasz Aniśko.

tain pastures stretching over rolling hills dominated the landscape.

Mountain of natural wonders

On 7 October, on the way from Yajiang to Kangding, we were frequently able to admire the snowcapped peaks of Gongga Shan proudly guarding the entrance to Tibet. Widespread along our route were *Abies squamata, Larix potaninii,* and *Picea likiangensis* var. *rubescens*. A dwarf *Cotoneaster adpressa* (001595) was very attractive in its autumnal attire, exceptionally richly decorated with large, red, shiny fruits. After crossing Zheduo Pass at 4150 m, in order to reach Kangding located in a deep river gorge, we had to descend rather rapidly some 1500 m. This required the driver to stop frequently to allow the

Groves of poplars in an otherwise treeless landscape near Daocheng announce to travelers that they are approaching a settlement. Photo by Tomasz Aniśko.

Hailougou, a glaciated valley located on the eastern slope of Gongga Shan near Kangding. Photo by Tomasz Aniśko.

vehicle's brakes to cool—not an unwelcome event on this long and strenuous ride.

Kangding, the seat of the Ganzi Tibetan Autonomous Prefecture, is a major trading post on the route from Beijing to Lhasa and has been historically regarded as the gateway to Tibet. It is also among the most important towns in the history of botanical exploration. Plant collectors such as Ernest H. Wilson, Antwerp E. Pratt, Jean André Soulie, Grigori N. Potanin, and Joseph F. Rock chose Kangding as a base from which to explore eastern Tibet.

Gongga Shan, or Minya Konka, 7556 m, is the highest mountain in China outside the Himalaya. The mountain abounds in natural wonders, including glaciers, hot springs, and most importantly a virgin forest with nearly twenty-four hundred species of seed plants. The only road on the mountain led us to Hailougou, a glaciated valley located on the eastern slope of Gongga Shan. The sixteen-hundred-year-old glacier is 15 km long and 80 to 200 m high. Our hike began at an altitude of about 3000 m and took us through a magnificent forest of centuries-old *Abies faberi, Larix potaninii,* and *Picea brachytyla,* with understory vegetation dominated by

rhododendrons, viburnums, and mountain-ashes. Debreczy and Rácz claimed this was the most beautiful coniferous forest they had ever seen in their travels around the world. We were able to reach the timberline, but darkness quickly set over the mountain, preventing us from exploring it further.

On 9 October, after spending the night on Gongga Shan, the team decided to split into several groups taking different trails to cover more ground before we had to return to Kangding. Johnson and I headed down toward the glacial tongue terminating at a cave at the altitude of 2850 m. We were especially amazed to observe so many floristic parallels between this forest on the edge of Tibet and the forest of the Appalachian Mountains in North America. Similarities went beyond cohabitation of hemlocks and spruces with rhododendrons, viburnums, maples, and magnolias, to include herbaceous plants such as *Clintonia, Polygonatum, Smilacina,* and *Trillium.* Needless to say, we felt very much at home. The arrival of autumn was apparent, but the spectacle of fall leaf color was rather muted compared to what we were used to in eastern North America, and limited to mainly maples and mountain-ashes. What this forest lacked in leaf color, however, was very generously compensated for by an abundance of colorful berries.

Upon returning to Kangding, we cleaned and organized the seventy collections made on this trip. The next morning we started on an all-day drive to Chengdu, the capital of Sichuan, from where we flew back to Beijing on 11 October. In Beijing I met with Gao Jiying, a researcher at the Subtropical Forestry Research Institute in Fuyang, Zhejiang. Gao had been collaborating with Longwood Gardens, Descanso Gardens in La Cañada, California, and Dr. Clifford R. Parks of the University of

North Carolina at Chapel Hill on a joint project aimed at collecting all species of camellias known to occur in China. Having been informed about our expedition returning from Tibet, Gao offered to meet with me and share forty camellias from his collection. The most treasured of these was *Camellia azalea* (001113), a species only discovered in 1984 and never before introduced into cultivation. Most importantly, this is the only camellia known to bloom throughout the year.

TIBET'S GORGES AND MOUNTAIN PASSES

The 2000 expedition permitted only limited collecting along the eastern fringes of Tibet, but it opened our eyes to the immense floristic riches of that region. The southeastern part of Tibet, which receives the highest rainfall, is the location of the largest concentration of plant life. This makes that region an exceptionally attractive place for plant explorers looking for prospective garden-worthy plants.

Southeastern Tibet is recognized for its large number of *Rhododendron* species. Even though these shrubs were not the sole focus of the trip planned for 2002, rhododendron experts Ronald R. Rabideau, nursery manager of Rare Find Nursery in Jackson, New Jersey, and Scott Vergara, license manager of the Conard-Pyle Company in West Grove, Pennsylvania, joined me on this expedition. The trip was organized in collaboration with the Institute of Botany in Beijing. Yudan Tang, curator of the institute's garden, coordinated the trip, while Wang Ta of Lhasa guided us through Tibet.

Fresh snow in the mountains
Our group assembled in Beijing on 6 October and the same day we flew to Lhasa, the capital of Tibet, situated at about 3600 m. On 8 October, after a day of rest and acclimatization to high altitude, we headed northeast to Lake Pasum. Driving along the Lhasa River, we gradually gained elevation from 3600 m to about 5000 m at Milha Pass. Before reaching the pass we stopped in several locations and collected a number of perennials, including *Thalictrum diffusiflorum* (02961), and a couple of shrubs, including *Wikstroemia scytophylla* (02962). At higher elevations snow was already on the ground, but herds of yaks still grazed in areas that remained green.

Camellia azalea (001113), discovered in southern China in 1984, blooms throughout the year. Photo by Tomasz Aniśko.

From Milha Pass we descended to Lake Pasum at about 3500 m. It was late at night when we arrived at the village of Tsomjuk on the lake's shore, and what appeared to be a campsite with rudimentary cabins. Chilled to the bone, we woke the next morning to a beautiful view of the mountains on the other side of the lake catching the rising sun on their snow-dusted peaks. This made us appreciate how brief the growing season is here, and how quickly winter can set in at such high elevations. Everything around us quickly thawed, as did we. Revitalized with a couple of cups of hot tea, we were ready to explore the shores of the lake. Most of the time we followed the road being constructed along the south side of the lake, leading to a military base. The road took us as far as the village of Je, beyond which we were not permitted to

Scarlet berries of *Triosteum himalayanum* (02968) found growing on the shores of Lake Pasum. Photo by Tomasz Aniśko.

Namchak Barwa revealed its glory when the expedition reached Serkhyem La traveling from Nyingchi to Bomi. Photo by Tomasz Aniśko.

Nyingchi occupies the valley at the confluence of Nyang Chu and Yarlung Tsangpo. Photo by Tomasz Aniśko.

wander. Before night we returned to our campsite carrying a day's worth of collections, including seeds of *Larix griffithiana* (02974), *Podophyllum hexandrum* (02967), and *Triosteum himalayanum* (02968).

On the morning of 10 October we drove south from Lake Pasum to Nyingchi, a busy city and administrative center on the banks of Nyang Chu, not far from its confluence with Yarlung Tsangpo, the main river of southern Tibet. Traveling to Nyingchi, we descended to about 3000 m. Our goal the following day was to reach Serkhyem La, a mountain pass northeast of the city, through which one of the few roads connecting Tibet with China was being built. Construction, taking place simultaneously on the entire stretch of the road between Nyingchi and Serkhyem La, slowed down our progress

considerably, and at times stopped us altogether. We soon realized we would not be able to reach the pass and return to Nyingchi before dark. After a long and grueling drive, we ascended to about 3800 m, at which point we decided to turn around. Fresh snow was already on the ground at that altitude, thus reducing our prospects of finding plants. Stopping at several sites, we made a number of collections. Among them were *Ceratostigma griffithii* (02977), *Primula florindae* (02979), *Rabdosia pseudo-irrorata* (02978), and several rhododendrons.

On 12 October, in order to reach our next destination, the town of Bomi on Parlung Tsangpo, a tributary of Yarlung Tsangpo, we had to cross Serkhyem La at high noon. To avoid the worst traffic jams on the construction sites along the road leading up to Serkhyem La, we departed Nyingchi at dawn. To assure our timely arrival in Bomi, we resisted any temptation to stop before reaching Serkhyem La at about 4300 m. Upon reaching the pass, a magnificent view opened before us. The sacred mountain of Namchak Barwa, 7756 m, stood high on the horizon, dwarfing the surrounding peaks of a mere 4000 m that were clad in dark forests. The mountain appeared as if crudely chiseled out of a solid block of ice. In its whiteness it seemed more akin to the passing clouds, sliced by its knife-sharp ridges, than to the earth below.

The prospect of spending several more hours on the road to reach Bomi prevented us from taking more time to contemplate the beauty of this site; after collecting seeds of a few plants, we began our descent to the valley of Rong Chu some 1800 m below. Rong Chu flows north

The valley of Parlung Tsangpo, a tributary of Yarlung Tsangpo, near Bomi. Photo by Tomasz Aniśko.

Fruits of *Malus rockii* (02988) growing in the valley of Parlung Tsangpo. Photo by Tomasz Aniśko.

and discharges its water to the river Tongkyuk, which in turn is a tributary of Parlung Tsangpo. Stopping along the way, we collected *Rodgersia aesculifolia* (02982), *Salvia przewalskii* (02985), and *Viburnum mullaha* var. *glabrescens* (02984).

Yak-butter tea time

For the next two days we made excursions out of Bomi to explore areas to the west and east of the town. Unfortunately, the local authority denied us permission to cross to the other side of Parlung Tsangpo, where we intended to explore the mountain passes south of the town. The proximity of the border with India makes this area militarily sensitive. On 13 October we drove west from the town on the same road we had traveled the day before. There we explored several sites along the river as well as the lower slopes of the surrounding hills. Among the plants collected were *Deutzia compacta* var. *multiradiata* (02987), *Malus rockii* (02988), and *Senecio echaetus* (02990).

The day ended with a spontaneous visit to a monastery that we spotted nestled on a small island in the middle of Parlung Tsangpo, connected to the outside world by a shaky suspension bridge. Driven by curiosity and a desire to find out what plants were cultivated by the monks, we crossed the bridge and wandered into the monastery. Not entirely certain what kind of reception we could expect inside, we proceeded cautiously, but to our delight, the first monk we met invited us into his living quarters for a cup of steaming yak-butter tea. Our conversation over tea quickly turned into the subject of

A fall-flowering vine, *Senecio echaetus* (02990), growing on shaded slopes along Parlung Tsangpo. Photo by Tomasz Aniśko.

plants, and we were greatly impressed by the breadth of knowledge the monks had about the wild plants growing in the monastery's environs.

On 15 October we left Bomi with the intention of driving east to the town of Yiong on Yiong Tsangpo, a tributary of Parlung Tsangpo. The valley of Yiong Tsangpo provided a convincing testimony to how geologically young this landscape was. The river mercilessly undercut the entire sides of the mountains. The valley was littered with immense boulders as if it were some playground for unimaginable giants. Driving on a road barely scraped out of this river of stone, we wondered how often the boulders came down. Our journey came to an end when we learned that a landslide ahead of us had destroyed the road completely. We were thus forced to

The expedition's vehicles are dwarfed by giant boulders scattered along Yiong Tsangpo. Photo by Tomasz Aniśko.

return to the town of Tangme at the confluence of Yiong Tsangpo and Parlung Tsangpo. The area around Tangme, at 2000 m, was the lowest elevation point of the entire trip. At this relatively low altitude, the warm and humid air moving from the south through the Tsangpo Gorge supported lush subtropical vegetation. One of the more striking plants at that time of year was *Hedychium sino-aureum* (02993), decorated by bright red fruits and seeds backed by gingerlike foliage.

Crawling up Tra La

On 16 October we retraced our steps from Tangme to the valley of Rong Chu. The road squeezed through the gorges of Parlung Tsangpo and Tongkyuk, and climbed some 1000 m in elevation, before the broad valley opened before us. Several stops along the route allowed us to botanize in the gorges, which resulted in collections of *Gaultheria trichoclada* (021002), *Hydrangea robusta* (021006), and *Rhododendron nuttallii* (021007), among others. Before night we arrived at Lunang, a quintessential frontier town that must be a welcome sight to the

truck drivers traveling on the treacherous road between Bomi and Nyingchi. Exhausted from long hours of tense driving, we gratefully accepted accommodations in what might be, under the circumstances, generously called a motel.

Waking up the next morning to the subfreezing temperatures inside our cabins and a light cover of snow on the ground, we set off on a hike to Tra La, a 4000 m mountain pass above Lunang separating the valley of Rong Chu to the west from that of Yarlung Tsangpo to the east. This required a murderous climb of seven hundred vertical meters from the floor of the valley. To add to the challenge, while there were no recognizable paths of any kind, the steep slopes we climbed were covered with thick moss, which made them extremely slippery. Crawling on our hands and knees most of the time and grasping every possible sturdy branch, we finally reached the pass several hours later. We accomplished the descent back to the valley mostly by sliding down on the thick, plush moss, dodging the low branches and dense thickets. For all this effort we were well rewarded with

A typical farmstead in the valley of Rong Chu near Lunang. Photo by Tomasz Aniśko.

interesting collections, which included *Abies georgei* var. *smithii* (021039), *Podophyllum hexandrum* (021008, 021013), and undetermined species of *Aconitum* (021012, 021014), *Iris* (021009), and *Meconopsis* (021011, 021015), as well as several rhododendrons.

On the edge of the world

On 18 October we traveled from Lunang over Serkhyem La back to Nyingchi, and the next day we drove to the small village of Yeku on the south side of Tsangpo at the foot of the Himalaya. On the way we stopped at the site of a ruined monastery, where we found a large colony of *Paeonia delavayi* var. *lutea* (021038). We suspected the plants had been cultivated by the monks and persisted after the destruction of the monastery.

Situated near the end of the road paralleling Yarlung Tsangpo, Yeku had the aura of a place on the edge of the world. Beyond it lay the roadless hidden country where the mighty Yarlung Tsangpo is forced between 7000 m peaks into a series of narrow gorges. After dropping more than 2000 m through the gorges, it emerges on the Indian side of the Himalaya as the river Brahmaputra. Yeku was not much more than a trading post for the porters buying goods and carrying them over the mountain passes to Pemakö, a region isolated from the rest of the world by high mountains and by the territorial dispute between China and India.

One of these passes, Doshong La, was our destination on 20 October. A winding road brought us to a boggy area near the timberline at about 3700 m, from where a 500 m climb to Doshong La began. This site had

Bright red fruits of *Podophyllum hexandrum* (021008, 021013) found on the slopes leading up to Tra La east of Lunang. Photo by Tomasz Aniśko.

Vergara, left, and Rabideau are surrounded by *Paeonia delavayi* var. *lutea* (021038) reaching 2 to 2.5 m in height. Photo by Tomasz Aniśko.

A bungalow in Yeku which served as a starting point for our excursions to Doshong La and Namu La. Photo by Tomasz Aniśko.

Rabideau, left, and the author atop Doshong La. Photo by Tomasz Aniśko.

The small bog at 3700 m marked the end of the road and the beginning of the footpath leading to Doshong La. Photo by Tomasz Aniśko.

Yarlung Tsangpo as seen from the path leading to Namu La, north of Doshong La, before the river enters the narrow gorge between Namchak Barwa, 7756 m, and Gyala Peri, 7151 m. Photo by Tomasz Aniśko.

Glossy leaves of *Bergenia purpurascens* (021018) showed their scarlet fall color along the path leading to Doshong La. Photo by Tomasz Aniśko.

Desert habitat of *Oxytropis* sp. (021037) along Yarlung Tsangpo near Xigaze. Photo by Tomasz Aniśko.

been known as rich plant-hunting ground since Kingdon Ward collected there in 1924. For us the time spent on Doshang La turned out to be the single most fruitful day of the entire expedition. Among our collections were many perennials, such as *Bergenia purpurascens* (021018) and *Triosteum himalayanum* (021025), and shrubs, such as *Cotoneaster hebephyllus* (021022), *Gaultheria tetramera* (021019), and *Lonicera tomentella* (021023). At length, the day's collections were complemented by numerous rhododendrons.

Yeku marked the turning point for the expedition. On 22 October we left the village to begin a three-day drive west along Yarlong Tsangpo to Xigaze, Tibet's second largest city, some 280 km west of Lhasa. As we traveled west the climate became drier, the lush forests of

Namchak Barwa giving way to sparse xerophytic vegetation and then deserts. But to our surprise, even among the shifting sand dunes along Yarlung Tsangpo, we found interesting plants adapted to this extreme environment, such as species of *Oxytropis* (021037).

On 25 October we returned to Lhasa, spent a day cleaning and preparing seeds, plants, and bulbs for a phytosanitary inspection, and on 27 October flew back to Beijing. While waiting in Beijing for the phytosanitary documents to be processed, we met again with Longwood collaborator Gao, who shared with us sixty-two camellias from his collection. These were added to our own 224 collections and carried back to the United States a few days later.

JAPAN

FORESTED ARCHIPELAGO

The first expedition organized under the collaborative agreement between Longwood Gardens and the USDA was undertaken in 1956. It targeted southern Japan and, as Dr. Walter H. Hodge, Longwood's head of education and research, explained, "was concentrated in the remote forest regions of the southern part of the archipelago on the Islands of Kyūshū, Shikoku, and lower Honshū . . . whose warm temperate climate is similar to parts of the southeastern and gulf coasts of the United States as well as the milder coastal belt of the Pacific Northwest" (1959d).

Dr. John L. Creech, horticulturist with the USDA Agricultural Research Service, who had collected ornamental plants in Japan a year earlier, was selected as the explorer. Western plant collectors explored Japan in the late nineteenth and early twentieth centuries, concentrating their efforts on plants suitable for northern climates. "Most collectors, however," said Creech (1957), "have neglected the regions of warm temperate Japan, perhaps partly because the Japanese themselves are not entirely familiar with these places. We would anticipate that the plants native to areas with warm-temperate and even subtropical conditions might have distinct limitations in the United States. Yet, an agro-climatic study will show that in terms of yearly variations in climate southern Japan is remarkably like parts of southern United States."

Creech attributed the great potential for finding new plants in Japan to the fact that Japan is among the most heavily forested countries. "High rainfall during the growing season, accompanied by adequate temperatures, have caused these forests to be luxuriant in woody plants," he wrote (1957). "Because the Japanese have practiced careful silviculture for many centuries, great forests are under imperial control and certain parts of them are allowed to remain in a natural state of development."

Late bloomer of Yatsugatake

Creech arrived in Tokyo on 30 September. He was greeted by Dr. Hideo Takeda, botanist with the Military Geology Section of the U.S. Army. "This outstanding Japanese botanist acted as interpreter, guide, and photographer during the entire period covered by this expedition," noted Creech (1957). A week later the two men headed to the Yatsugatake Mountains, situated west of Tokyo, in central Honshū.

"We traveled from Tokyo by rail to a small town called Chino, not far from Suwa Lake, where a mountain innkeeper had arranged to meet us with a jeep," recorded Creech (1957). "The mountain roads are pitifully poor at this time of the year. It required about four hours to grind our way up to Shibuyo Onsen (inn) which is situated at 4950 feet [1500 m] altitude. Since we had collected here during the summer of 1955, we were familiar with much of the terrain and the vegetation. Our main interest was to collect late-flowering forms of *Rhododendron japonicum* [60623]. This azalea inhabits open fields, especially the more boggy plateaus. It normally flowers in early

May. Both yellow and orange forms grow wild on this mountain. We had observed several orange-flowered plants in bloom on July 20, 1955, but owing to the time of year it was impossible to secure living collections. Therefore, our local collector had visited this meadow during the summer of 1956 and had placed large stakes in the late-blooming clumps. When we arrived in October, the majority of *R. japonicum* had already defoliated, but those which were late-flowering held their green leaves even at this late date."

Creech began his exploration of Japan in the Yatsugatake Mountains in central Honshū. Photo by John L. Creech.

The Yatsugatake region contained a number of familiar woody plants, many of which were in cultivation in the United States, but there were also species that had not yet succeeded in cultivation. "Of these, *Ilex geniculata,* a deciduous holly with red fruits on long stalks was the most noteworthy," wrote Creech (1957). "The edges of the fields and wooded slopes contained such species as: *Hydrangea paniculata; Clethra barbinervis* that grew stiffly upright to about 10 feet [3 m] and terminated in nodding clusters of fruits; *Ligustrum ciliatum,* a spreading privet that usually remained less than 4 feet [1.2 m] high; and *Sorbus rufoferruginea,* readily discerned by the brilliance of the red autumnal foliage. Isolated colonies of *Chamaecyparis obtusa* [592109] occurred in open places."

Two capes of Shikoku

On 14 October, Creech and Takeda left Tokyo for southern Shikoku, the smallest of the four principal islands of Japan, located south of Honshū and east of Kyūshū. "Southern Shikoku is characterized by two prominent land features—the capes of Muroto and Ashizuri," noted Creech (1957). "The climate of this part of Japan simulates central Georgia across to Mississippi, inclusive of the gulf area. The terrain is extensively mountainous. The land may drop to the ocean in steep cliffs that support only herbaceous plants or the descent may be more gradual where broad-leaved evergreen forests grew down to the narrow, rocky beaches."

The starting place for any travels to southern Shikoku is the city of Kōchi, lying inland from Tosa Bay. Creech's first exploration in this area was to Cape Muroto, east of Kōchi. "We reached it by traveling on a winding dirt road along a coastline where the black sand beaches were lined with huge trees of *Pinus thunbergii,* the Japanese black pine," wrote Creech (1957). "Standing on the beach road at Muroto, one can see a great broad-leaved forest that ascends steeply, presenting a mosaic of greens. . . . Along the beach, *Quercus wrightii* [572446], with gnarled wind-form, grew among huge rocks. Other salt-spray tolerant plants found just behind the beach were *Rhaphiolepis umbellata, Pittosporum tobira, Ficus erecta,* and *Eurya emarginata* [58174]. The narrow, level beach was covered by small stones. Here, *Rosa wichuraiana* [82749]; *Dianthus japonicus,* with bright pink flowers; *Lactuca keiskeana* [572070], yellow-flowered and with succulent leaves; *Lathyrus maritimus;* and a prostrate legume, *Indigofera pseudotinctoria,* a rugged plant with a deep extensive root system that strongly defied the

CHINA

RUSSIA

HOKKAIDŌ

Sapporo
▲ Izari-dake

Hidaka

NORTH
KOREA

Cape Erimo

Matsumae

▲ Hakkōda-san

SEA OF JAPAN

SOUTH
KOREA

Gayō-san ▲ Kamaishi

Shizugawa
Ayukawa

Ōtakine
▲ Tomioka

JAPAN

Abukuma

Tsukuba-san ▲

Chino   Kashima

Tokyo
▲ Fuji   Chiba

Nagoya

Ōsaka

Hiroshima   Ise

Kotohira   KII
               PENINSULA
                              Shingū
SHIKOKU
Fukuoka   Shirahama
Hirado   Kurume   Kōchi   Ōshima
          Kusu   Cape Muroto

Kumamoto   Cape Ashizuri

KYŪSHŪ

Kirishima
Kagoshima   PACIFIC OCEAN

ŌSUMI
PENINSULA

                Tanegashima
Yakushima

HONSHŪ

Japan (left) comprises four main islands, Honshū, Shikoku, Kyūshū, and Hokkaidō, and many smaller islands, with a total area of more than 370,000 km². It extends nearly 1400 km from south to north, between latitudes 30° north and 45° north. Mountains cover about 65 percent of Japan's land area. Many peaks reach 2000 to 3000 m in altitude, the highest being Fuji, 3776 m, on southern Honshū. Japan's climate is influenced by the country's latitudinal extent, the surrounding oceans, and the neighboring Asian landmass. In winter, cold air from eastern Siberia flows over the Sea of Japan and brings monsoons, which cause rain and snow in the west part of Japan and dry weather in the east. The summer monsoons, in contrast, caused by winds from the east and south, bring warmer temperatures and rain. In addition, the southern islands are affected by the warm Japan Current flowing from the southwest, while in the north the cold Kurile Current has a pronounced cooling effect. Precipitation ranges from 900 mm on Hokkaidō to 4000 mm in central Honshū, most of it falling in early summer. Japan supports a very diverse flora in proportion to its size. More than four thousand species of plants are native to Japan, and about a quarter are endemic to these islands. The southern areas of Japan are dominated by evergreen, broad-leaved, woody plants. Lush vegetation of that region contains many plants with affinities to floras of southern Korea and China, highlands of the Himalaya, Myanmar, and Indochina. Japan's temperate regions support mixed forests of deciduous and coniferous trees, with a close relationship to floras of central China, high mountains of the Himalaya, and Malaysia. The boreal region of Japan is characterized by coniferous forests, with many species having a wide circumboreal distribution.

Lush forests of southern Shikoku are filled with many species of woody plants. Photo by Walter H. Hodge.

removal of the shrub, spread rampantly. The forest was rich in cryptogamic flora. Several interesting ferns, such as the tiny *Pteris cretica* var. *albo-lineata, Rumohra aristata,* and *Osmunda bromeliifolia* [592154], flourished. *Psilotum nudum* [591624] occasionally could be found among rotted tree stumps."

Creech's next destination, Cape Ashizuri, is situated at the southern end of Shikoku, southwest of Kōchi. The cape is rather isolated and heavily forested except for a narrow road that traverses mountain passes. "Along the valleys, *Camellia sasanqua* [602333] was found in bloom," noted Creech (1957). "The trees were 18 to 25 feet [5.4–7.5 m] tall, evidently escapes for I saw only one locality where this species was probably natural. We journeyed to Nakamura village and traveled through magnificent reforested areas of *Cryptomeria* to the small port of Shimizu. From here, we traveled to the very tip of the cape, making our headquarters at the forestry bureau official's residence."

Cape Ashizuri ends in a precipitous sea cliff. "The abrupt rocky sea walls encouraged no woody plants but extensive colonies of *Hemerocallis aurantiaca* var. *littorea* abound," noted Creech (1957). "It was a most rewarding sight to approach the sea-cliff through groves of gnarled *Camellia japonica* and to step out onto a terrace of *Zoysia japonica* to find this beautiful daylily in bloom by the thousands. *Peucedanum japonicum* [571619] with large columbine-like leaves and heads of white flowers was scattered among them. From the sea-cliff, we returned to the dense undergrowth, heavily populated by gray, distorted, multi-stemmed clumps of camellia."

From Cape Ashizuri, Creech and his party returned to Kōchi and went on to Kotohira City in northern Shikoku. "In the enormous Shinto shrine area, many large trees of *Camellia sasanqua* have been culti-vated for centuries," reported Creech (1957). "Because these were quite ancient plants and large-flowered, we secured cut-tings of each type despite the fact that they were unnamed [572038–41, 602334–6]." Two days later Creech returned by steamer across the Inland Sea to Okayama and jour-neyed by rail back to Tokyo.

Shrine forests of southern Honshū

On 24 October, Creech started yet another excur-sion, this time to Kii

The rugged coastline of southern Shikoku between Kōchi and Cape Ashizuri. Photo by John L. Creech.

Peninsula, the southernmost part of Honshū. "Kii Penin-sula, lacking alluvial plains, is isolated by rugged moun-tains and is one of the least populated areas of southern Japan," wrote Creech (1957). "Transportation is mostly by coastal shipping or over poor, dirt roads that wind tediously through the mountains. Knowledge of the plants is mostly local but it is said to be unusually rich in various types of evergreen woody plants of a warm tem-perate and subtropical nature."

After exploring briefly the tiny island of Kashima, near Tanabe, Creech continued across the bay to Shira-hama, a former pearl culturing center: "It was here that *Ardisia villosa* [572062] was first encountered and grew as a restricted ground-covering plant in shady places. The area was rather disturbed and only a few wild plants of interest were noted. . . . Therefore, we left the locality and traveled by 3rd class train down to the lowest point of the Kii Peninsula, stopping at Kushimoto. From there we took passage to a small island called Ōshima. This is a typical fishing community where little agriculture is prac-ticed. Occasionally we found small orchards of a citrus, *Fortunella margarita*. The natives surrounded their homes with tall hedges formed from *Distylium racemosum* [572073], an evergreen tree native to the island" (Creech 1957).

Colonies of *Hemerocallis aurantiaca* var. *littorea* cover precipitous sea cliffs of Cape Ashizuri. Photo by John L. Creech.

The exploration continued on Nachi-san near Shingū, on the eastern shore of Kii Peninsula. "At Nachi, there is a densely forested tract that is a part of the famous Kumano Gongen Shrine," recorded Creech (1957). "Several small streams flow through the region that merge into a waterfall about 400 feet [120 m] high. We pursued a trail above this fall through a planted forest of *Cryp-tomeria japonica* and into an uncut jungle of vines and dense shrubs. . . . After traveling up through the forest for several hours, we reached the top of the pass where hemlocks and false cypress towered. There were the usual orchid epiphytes, but it was impossible to reach them as the trees grew off at an angle from the edge of the cliff. Even the local forester, who normally would climb any tree, declined to attempt the collection. Frequently, we collected orchids where cryptomerias had recently been cut and still lay on the ground."

Descending from the pass, the group plunged into a damp, gloomy woods along the stream and came upon a second but smaller waterfall. "Here, the filmy ferns, *Hymenophyllum,* grew in the stream-eroded, dripping walls," remarked Creech (1957). "At drier localities we observed several ericads, such as *Rhododendron serpyllifolium* [602323], the azalea with the smallest leaves being less than one-fourth inch [6 mm] long. . . . A cold rain dampened the whole aspect during the return journey. Later at the city of Shingū we paused to inspect a floating sphagnum bog and found it to be a composite of cool-temperate and warm-temperate plants. *Ilex sugerokii, I. serrata* [581699], *Photinia villosa* [572441], and *Daphniphyllum humile* were all characteristic of northern Japan. During some era, warm-temperate plants such as *Vaccinium bracteatum, Ardisia villosa, Pittosporum tobira,* and *Myrica rubra* had invaded the bog to thrive in this soggy environment."

From Shingū the group traveled by jeep and bus along the coast over Yanokawa Pass to Owase. Then they continued north to Ise. "Our final stop on Kii Peninsula was the forest of the Grand Shrine of Ise, particularly in the Jingu shrine," wrote Creech (1957). "This is the finest example of Shintō shrine architecture. The temples are constructed entirely of Hinoki cypress [*Chamaecyparis obtusa*], polished to a brilliant orange. To provide the timber to continue the erection of new structures, a large forest of Hinoki cypress is maintained. A part of the forest is permitted to develop naturally and collecting is rarely sanctioned. Fortunately, the chief forester was a student of our guide, Dr. Takeda, and we gained entrance."

The rich forest surrounding the Jingu shrine yielded many collections. One plant that made a strong impression on Creech was a species of *Damnacanthus*: "We had seen *Damnacanthus indicus* several times earlier. This is a remarkable small plant, with its foliage and branches in fanlike arrangements. But a different species occurred here. This was *D. macrophyllus* [571612], a larger shrub,

This *Psilotum nudum* (591662) from Taihaku Nursery in Goso near Osaka was among more than twenty rare varieties of *Psilotum* that Creech obtained in Japan. Photo by Tomasz Aniśko.

with leaves about 1 to 2 inches [25–50 mm] long, purple colored when young. It is spined and has red berries" (Creech 1957).

During his stay in Ise, Creech visited a grower of curious varieties of *Psilotum nudum* (581237–8, 581240–5, 591625–6). "This rare cryptogam was in vogue for centuries," he noted (1957). "As many as two hundred varieties had been developed with cristate and distorted stems. This leafless plant makes an interesting pot subject and is easy to cultivate. Gradually, interest in this plant has diminished; today, scarcely thirty types are cultivated. Several kinds were purchased and brought back to the United States for observation because they are not known in our culture and will shortly cease to exist in Japan."

Imperial flower

After returning to Tokyo on 30 October, Creech dedicated the next two weeks to visiting chrysanthemum nurseries and shows. "This weekend, I leave for a round of visits to mum growers and the big shows which have just started to open today," Creech (1956a) wrote to Hodge. "It is quite true that the Japanese grow bizarre types of mums, the like of which will certainly make a show in the United States if they are grown in a manner similar to that used here."

Creech's trip coincided with the flowering and exhibition of chrysanthemums, which enabled him to make a rather complete collection of the modern Japanese varieties. "Since the chrysanthemum is the flower of the imperial family of Japan, considerable importance is attached to its culture, development, and display," he

A giant plant of *Chrysanthemum* ×*morifolium* trained to produce four hundred blooms and exhibited in Yasukuni Shrine in Tokyo. Photo by Walter H. Hodge.

Hirakata Park in Hirakata City has one of the most visited chrysanthemum shows in Japan. Photo by John L. Creech.

The fall flower show in Kyōto Botanic Garden, like many others held around Japan, celebrates the traditional art of growing chrysanthemums. Photo by Walter H. Hodge.

A startling array of unique chrysanthemum selections is exhibited every year in Yasukuni Shrine in Tokyo. Photo by Walter H. Hodge.

explained (1957). "For display purposes each show employs its own staff of cultural experts and breeders. Often the varieties raised for a particular exhibit are not released for general distribution and this results in types peculiar to that show. Thus, to see all of the kinds of chrysanthemums, ultimately every show should be observed."

Upon his return to Tokyo on 10 November, Creech reported, "It was, by and large an interesting trip as I visited the several large growers of chrysanthemums and also the major mum shows. They are going to send me small suckers of all of the leading types of chrysanthemums grown in Japan and it was as I had hoped. There are many types of mums grown here which we have not ever attempted in the United States, especially in the category of large-flowered and show types. . . . Now after these are established in Glenn Dale, there will be the problem of growing them for show purposes but I am sure the Longwood people will do a good job with a bit of coaching on Japanese techniques. As a result, there could be at Longwood, a chrysanthemum display the like of which has never been seen in the United States" (Creech 1956b).

A plant collector's paradise

Creech's last trip was to take him to Kyūshū, the southernmost of the main islands of Japan, and to Yakushima and Tanegashima, small islands about 100 km south of the Kyūshū port of Kagoshima. "These islands have been a constant collecting ground for Japanese botanists," remarked Creech (1957). "Yakushima, in particular, has been noted for the extent of its woody flora and E. H. Wilson considered it a plant collector's paradise."

The departure was set for 16 November. "It will be a long and interesting trip but rather difficult to accomplish," wrote Creech (1956b) to Dr. Howard L. Hyland of the USDA Agricultural Research Service in Beltsville, Maryland. "The weather is getting quite cold in certain areas and with no heat in the Japanese hotels, you can imagine that it is difficult to crawl out of a warmed bed when you can see your breath in the room. I think the worst problem is that of getting wet while in the field and having no way to dry out. So far, that has occurred on every trip and usually my clothes dry out while I am still wearing them."

Before heading to Yakushima, Creech and his team stopped at the agricultural experiment station at Kurume in northern Kyūshū to outline the course of the exploration. Two members of the Kurume station staff, Sadeo Abe and Teruo Tamoura, joined the team, acting as guides and collecting plants that were of interest to them.

Yakushima is a small island about 22 km across. It is surmounted by the highest peak of the Kyūshū area, Miyanoura-dake, 1935 m. "A coastal savanna occurs along the river estuaries," noted Creech (1957). "Near the mouth of the Kurio, a true mangrove formation of *Kandelia candel* has developed. The broadleaved evergreen forests occur up to about 1800 feet [550 m] altitude. Above this is a vast stand of conifers, mainly cryptomeria and fir, with some deciduous trees, up to 5500 feet [1700 m]. Above the forested zone, a subalpine climate prevails; here, the plants are mostly dwarfed."

Creech's team in Yakushima. Abe, Takeda, and Creech, left to right, are in the back row. Photo by John L. Creech.

Forestry is the major agricultural pursuit of Yakushima, and cryptomeria wood from this island is especially prized for its beautiful grain. "The population of Yakushima is scattered around the perimeter of the island in a series of small villages, of which Ambō is the largest, and Miyanoura is next," explained Creech (1957). "Both ports are shipping centers for cryptomeria logs. A single mountain village occurs about 2500 feet [750 m] altitude at Kosugidani and it can only be reached by a narrow-gauge lumber railroad."

A steamer from Kagoshima brought the group to Miyanoura, on the northern shore of Yakushima, where Creech established a base camp in a small inn. They traveled first east from Miyanoura along the coast as far as the Nagata Light. Upon reaching Isso River, "we followed its twisting course back up into the hills, often crossing from bank to bank by leaping over gigantic granite boulders that were lodged in the streambed," wrote Creech (1957). "Often the trees and shrubs grew in midstream where the rocks had accumulated debris and soil. It was in such a locality that we found *Ilex liukiuensis* [572052]. This evergreen holly was prolific in its fruiting habit and the berries were bright red. It has never been in cultivation. . . . Returning along the sea road, we found *Smilax china* scrambling on the sunny banks. This vine is almost thornless and has large red berries. *Kadsura japonica* [581701], *Morinda umbellata* [58188], and *Alpinia kumatake* [572426] were abundant on the roadsides. *Elaeagnus crispa* [58173] was widespread in abandoned fields and along the roadsides. The berries sometimes were quite large and edible."

Creech followed the course of Isso River in order to explore the interior of Yakushima. Photo by John L. Creech.

Neofinetia falcata (580120) was among the orchids Creech collected on his hike along the Isso River. Photo by Rondel G. Peirson.

Creech collected *Damnacanthus indicus* (58171) in the upper reaches of Miyanoura River in Mannō National Forest on Yakushima. Photo by Gottlieb A. Hampfler.

Creech's next trip surveyed the Miyanoura River, which drops gently from the hills and has a broad alluvial plain. "The outstanding shrubs along the trail were *Callicarpa japonica* var. *luxurians* [572430] and *C. tosaensis* [572431]," noted Creech (1957). "These grew to 15 feet [4.5 m], overarched by ponderous clusters of purple fruit. I have never observed *Callicarpa* fruiting so abundantly in cultivation. . . . As we reached higher elevations, the vertical, eroded stream walls were pocketed with small plants of *Rhododendron indicum* and in midstream the plants developed into dense, low thickets. Surprisingly, many of the plants were in full bloom although it was November. . . . Stepping back a few paces into the damp forest, we found the small but always delightful *Damnacanthus indicus* [58171] covered with red berries."

Having explored the broad-leaved evergreen forests of northern Yakushima, Creech moved his base camp to the forestry office at Ambō, on the eastern shore of the island. From Ambō the team headed for Miyanoura-dake. "We ascended Miyanoura-dake by a small lumber train to as far as the camp called Kosugidani, about 2500 feet [750 m] altitude," Creech reported (1957). "The trail to the upper meadows of Miyanoura-dake led through the large forests of cryptomeria and firs. Along the way, large clumps of *Rhododendron metternichii* grew everywhere. Sometimes, large branches of the conifers, sweeping off at a low angle, would accumulate forest duff and the rhododendrons would spring up on the branches almost in an epiphytic manner."

This small lumber train carried Creech and his party up Miyanoura-dake, Yakushima. Photo by John L. Creech.

Lagerstroemia fauriei (572438) that Creech collected on Yakushima was later used by Donald Egolf at the U.S. National Arboretum to develop a series of hybrids resistant to powdery mildew. Two superior selections from Creech's collection were introduced as 'Fantasy' and 'Townhouse', pictured here, by the North Carolina State University Arboretum. Photo by Tomasz Aniśko.

Trochodendron aralioides (59506), growing in Longwood's Hillside Garden, was collected by Creech on his hike on Miyanoura-dake, above Kosugidani, Yakushima, at an altitude of about 1300 m. Photo by Tomasz Aniśko.

Creech related his experiences on the mountain in a letter to Hyland: "We went up to a sphagnum bog at 1600 m, collecting along the way, returning to the terminal of the railroad at 7 p.m. and rode a cart, free wheeling down the track to 700 m, at night guided by a flashlight! Next time we went on the car, the brakes failed to work and we all had to jump off to stop the cart. But the collections are well worth the excitement" (1956c).

The next excursion from Ambō took Creech and his team around the south coast to the town of Kurio. "This region had been heavily felled for logs and was in a state of semi-devastation," remarked Creech (1957). "In these hills, we found *Lagerstroemia fauriei* [572438]. This deciduous tree with brown and green flaky bark grows to 30 feet [9 m]. The flowers are white. Only a few trees of this endemic species were noted; it was evident that it would soon be extinct in the wild."

Back in Miyanoura, Creech wrote to Hyland: "Collecting has reached expedition size. When we returned from Ambō today it required two jeeps to carry the baggage, including plants, herbarium specimens, food, clothing, and collecting equipment. . . . It is a great expedition! Wilson was so right, Yakushima is a plant collector's paradise" (1956c).

On 1 December the group embarked on a steamer for the short journey to Tanegashima, only some 20 km

Chrysanthemums collected by Creech in Japan were displayed for the first time in Longwood's Azalea House in fall of 1957. Photo by Gottlieb A. Hampfler.

Back at Longwood, Creech inspects the chrysanthemums he collected in Japan in 1956. Photo by Gottlieb A. Hampfler.

east of Yakushima. Tanegashima is a narrow island approximately 60 km long and 13 km wide. It is devoid of high mountains and largely given over to agricultural crops. Creech and his team headed first to Tachimoto Forest in the southern part of the island. "Although mostly planted to cryptomeria, a number of evergreen oaks have survived, *Lithocarpus edulis* [591592] being common," commented Creech (1957). In Furuta National Forest, the group's next stop in the northern part of the island, evergreen oaks were also plentiful. "These were generally accompanied by the usual epiphytic orchids, climbing ferns, and cycads," wrote Creech. "Of the orchids, *Phajus maculatus* [58102] was the most striking. We came upon it while climbing up a shaded hillside. This terrestrial species first appeared to have small spots of sunlight flickering across the leaves but in reality this mirage was a multitude of large yellow variegations. The pattern was consistent among wild specimens and of a genetic nature."

Winter storms, dashing the surf high above the breakwater, prevented Creech's leaving Tanegashima until 7 December, and on that date he returned to Kagoshima aboard a steamer. A few days later the group traveled from Kagoshima back to Kurume. "Our arrival in Kurume was accompanied by cold weather and a light snowfall making living in poorly heated Japanese quarters rather gloomy," remembered Creech (1957). "It also heralded the end of our collecting trip. On December 10 we returned to Tokyo with our collections of seeds, plants, and herbarium specimens."

On 20 December, Creech concluded his expedition and returned to the United States. From this exploration, 668 plants were introduced, half being from the wild. Among them were 219 cultivars of chrysanthemums. An exhibit of these chrysanthemums was shown for the first time at Longwood Gardens during the fall of 1957. Soon Creech's chrysanthemums were distributed to major growers in the United States. One was later renamed 'Tokyo' by Yoder Brothers in Berberton, Ohio, and when released to the trade in 1962 turned out to be a great commercial success.

JAPAN'S WILD SIDE

Results of the 1956 expedition to southern Japan convinced Dr. Russell J. Seibert, Longwood's director, and his collaborators in the USDA of the richness of that island's flora that still awaited discovery and introduction into cultivation. While the 1956 trip concentrated on collecting plants new to American horticulture, planning for the next expedition emphasized the need to introduce plants that would contribute traits of improved hardiness and appearance to already important groups of garden plants.

Because of his previous experience collecting plants in Japan, Creech was asked to lead this expedition. He explained the task ahead of him: "Objectives were to investigate the geographical distribution of selected woody and herbaceous plants of Japan and to collect propagating material from important variations of species valuable as ornamentals in American horticulture. . . . During the exploration of Japan in the fall and winter of 1956, I was content to bring to the United States species that would add variety to southern gardens without considering hardiness relative to origin. Additional study of the Japanese literature showed that many species are found in Japan far north of places where collections were made earlier" (Creech 1966b).

Azaleas' most favored island

The expedition began in April to coincide with the beginning of the azalea flowering season in southern Kyūshū. "Japan is the center of distribution of azaleas in the Orient," explained Creech (1966b), "and Kyūshū is the most favored locality for azaleas in Japan. Combination of a highly acid porous volcanic soil and a mild maritime climate with moderate, evenly distributed rainfall provides an ideal environment for the development of extensive colonies of azaleas."

Although Kyūshū was undoubtedly the right locale for collecting azaleas, especially those believed to be the prototypes of Kurume azaleas, timing was equally important. "One of the really good points in planning this trip," wrote Creech (1961c), "was to arrive here during the early azalea season, for without the opportunity to see the plants in bloom, a number of good things would have escaped my eye. For out of bloom the plants all are pretty much alike."

Creech arrived in Kyūshū on 22 April 1961 and began the four-week exploration of the island in the southern city of Kagoshima. "Three mountains," he noted, "provide the most plausible clues as to the origin of the Kurume azaleas, foremost of the cultivars that have evolved from the species found in Kyūshū. These mountains are Sakurajima [1118 m], a unique, active volcano overlooking the city of Kagoshima; Takakuma [1236 m], a mountain chain adjacent to Sakurajima; and Kirishima [1700 m], a group of high volcanic cones famous for hot springs. These mountains are all within a 30-mile [50 km] radius of Kagoshima" (Creech 1966b).

Two days later Creech was on a ferry crossing the 4 km stretch of water separating Kagoshima from the active volcano. "Sakurajima, an isolated, symmetrical volcanic cone, juts out into Kagoshima Bay, overshadowing Kagoshima City," he noted (1966b). "The slopes of this active volcano are so covered with fresh lava rocks from

On Sakurajima, Creech found a puzzling array of wild azaleas varying in color from light pink to strong reddish purple. Photo by John L. Creech.

constant eruptions that the upper portions do not support a forest cover. Yet, among huge lava boulders, azaleas thrive in profusion and present a variable array of colors from light pink to strong, reddish purple. I spent the entire day of April 24 wandering the paths that wind around the slopes of Sakurajima trying to draw some conclusions."

The following morning, Creech and his Japanese colleagues departed by jeep for Takakuma, the ash-covered mountain chain paralleling the coast of Ōsumi Peninsula and consisting of a series of peaks that gradually ascend to the highest point on the peninsula called Onogara. The route led through gorges inhabited by broad-leaved evergreens, and in one of these, called Sarugajo, the party spent the better part of the day collecting plants. "The finest of the flowering trees in these dense forests is *Symplocos prunifolia* [621488]," noted Creech (1966b). "The tree grows to a height of 50 feet [15 m] and the flowers are white, fragrant, and borne in dense terminal racemes."

By evening Creech and his group reached the cottage of the Kagoshima University Forestry Station in the Takakuma mountains. "The azaleas are the conspicuous feature of the open meadows of Takakuma," Creech recorded (1966b). "From sea level to about 500 m, *Rhododendron kaempferi* [621466] abounds on rock outcroppings and on ledges along trails. The flowers are typically brick red and the leaves large and scattered along the branches. At about 500 m, a new azalea appeared. This is *R. sataense* Nakai [621460, 621473]. These plants are dense and moundlike, with flowers that range from

Calanthe discolor f. *sieboldii* (61750), distinguished by its clear yellow flowers, was collected by Creech in the Takakuma mountains on Ōsumi Peninsula. Photo by Walter H. Hodge.

Cypripedium japonicum (61751), found by Creech in the Takakuma mountains, inhabits moist woods in southern Japan. Photo by Walter H. Hodge.

Creech found *Rhododendron sataense* (621460, 621473) growing in open meadows in Takakuma mountains on Ōsumi Peninsula. Photo by John L. Creech.

pink to purple with broadly overlapping petals and shiny leaves that are flat to convex."

Camellia japonica also grew abundantly on Takakuma, and Creech wanted to determine to what elevations this tree was limited. "We set off early on April 26," he wrote, "and ascended during a drenching rain through magnificent forests of *Cryptomeria* interspersed with the usual broadleaf evergreens. The trail led around the outer ledges of the mountain where andromeda, hollies, and rhododendrons grew in quantity. . . . We penetrated the forest again and as we approached 1000 m, the broadleaf evergreens began to be noticeably reduced in number and stunted in habit. The last specimens of *Camellia japonica* [64203], at approximately 1050 m, were ungainly, sparsely branched trees reaching a height of up to 3 m. It surpassed any other broadleaf evergreen in number. The ground beneath the trees was littered with fallen blossoms, and occasional flowers continued to drop onto the bare, muddy soil" (Creech 1966b).

As there were no small camellia seedlings to be seen anywhere, Creech concluded that either the fruits were washed down the mountainside or fertile seeds were rarely produced. "It is difficult to imagine what the winter conditions must be like in these mountains but certainly the weather is bitterly cold," he commented (1961a). "Survival of camellias at this elevation is probably due to the slowness with which the weather modifies in the spring, and the resulting lateness of bloom. The fact that the trees are sheltered by conifers affords a considerable degree of protection from winds. Then, too, precipitation is sufficiently high in winter that there is no desiccation of the plants, for the forests are shrouded with dripping fogs most of the winter."

Back in Kagoshima, Creech prepared for the next excursion and on 28 April, accompanied by his Japanese guides, departed for Kirishima. "The Kirishima mountains are the highest volcanic cones in southern Kyūshū," he noted (1966b). "On the evergreen-clad lower slopes and in the grassy meadows at higher elevations occurs a complex of azaleas that have figured largely in the literature on the development of the famous Kurume azaleas. In 1955, I had climbed to the rim of the volcanic cone Karakuni-dake (1700 m) to observe the colonies of *Rhododendron kiusianum,* a small-leaved, purple-flowered azalea. When this azalea hybridizes with *R. kaempferi* from lower elevations, a bewildering array of seedlings with pink, scarlet, crimson, and purple flowers results."

Azaleas of Hirado

Having completed the exploration of the mountains around Kagoshima, Creech relocated to the northern part of Kyūshū. His first destination there was Hirado Island which is home to the famous Hirado azaleas. "This island, which is now relegated to the occupation of fishing and subsistence farming, is steeped in Japanese history and romance," said Creech (1966b). "Being isolated and scenic, Hirado became a favorite spot for the feudal samurai of older Japan and their palaces dotted the gentle slopes. It might also be said that many of these noblemen delved into the smuggling trade with the Chinese pirates and thus enhanced their fortunes. But the gentlemen did have elaborate gardens and these were

An array of Hirado azaleas collected by Creech on Hirado Island of the northwest coast of Kyūshū. Photo by John L. Creech.

planted largely to azaleas. . . . The azaleas of Hirado are a distinct group characterized by unusually large flowers, some measuring up to 13 cm across and this character can easily by traced to *R. scabrum.* The color range is from pink through red to purple, which suggests the infusion of *R. mucronatum* and *R. phoeniceum.* . . . The Hirado azaleas are located in individual private gardens so one has to visit many places to see them all. Some of these gardens date back more than 300 years during which time selections were continually made from the spontaneous populations that sprang up among the original azalea plantings. Today, approximately 230 varieties of Hirado azaleas are recognized."

Creech managed to acquire thirty varieties (611456–69, 611512–4, 62133–8, 621254–5) that were representative of the range of variation in the Hirado race. "I have brought together the best types, some as plants, others as cuttings," he wrote to Hodge. "These will go to Glenn Dale on 8 May and if we have any luck should definitely establish this race in America. I want a set to go to Longwood just as soon as safely established at Glenn Dale. You would be surprised at the difficulty there is to delicately pry loose material from these gardens because the plants are zealously guarded" (Creech 1961b).

During his last few days in Kyūshū, Creech concentrated on the mountains in the central part of the island. On a small peak at Seidagawa, 520 m, isolated in the hot central plain, he found *Rhododendron japonicum* growing profusely: "Above the town of Kusu in a pine-chestnut region, *R. japonicum* [621257–8] grows in hot sunny meadows, quite different from the cool bog habitats ordi-

Creech collecting *Rhododendron japonicum* in the meadows above Kusu, Kyūshū. Photo by John L. Creech.

The prostrate, compact, small-leaved selection of *Euonymus fortunei* var. *radicans* (621437) collected by Creech on Tsukuba-san in Ibaraki Prefecture proved later to be exceptionally hardy and was introduced in the United States as a cultivar, 'Longwood'. Photo by Tomasz Aniśko.

narily frequented by this azalea. Furthermore, here can be found the broadest range of color variation occurring in the species. The colony includes the yellow form, *aureum*. Despite earlier observations by Wilson to the effect that the yellow form is rather rare, it accounts for about a third of the colony I visited at Seidagawa" (Creech 1966b).

On 16 May, Creech departed Kyūshū and traveled back to Tokyo. After four weeks of field work, he welcomed the prospect of spending a few days in the city. "As you well know," he wrote to Hodge, "collecting straight for a month without letup is pretty tiring and I will be glad to get back to Tokyo for some food other than fish but the excitement of finding so many interesting plants in this part of Japan keeps me going" (Creech 1961b).

Region of transition

The second part of the expedition encompassed a survey of the Pacific coast of central Honshū, from Kashima north to Tomioka. This is a region of transition from the predominantly broad-leaved evergreen vegetation of southern Japan to the mixed and deciduous forests of northern Japan.

"Our first collecting area was in the Takahagi Forestry District near Ibaraki City," reported Creech (1966b). "The most interesting localities were the beach areas. These were planted to forests of the black pine (*Pinus thunbergii*) for sand-dune control. The shore juniper, *Juniperus conferta* [611560], has invaded the

pinewoods. In the shelter of the pines, the shore juniper grows to 18 inches [46 cm], but on the open sands it spreads prostrate and carpets miles of beach front. . . . At many points the cliffs abruptly erode into the ocean and provide the picturesque scenery so typical of Japan. An orange-yellow daylily in full flower dominates the open areas. This is *Hemerocallis longituba* [64923], the earliest of the species to flower. Collections of these May-flowering plants have now provided breeders with the full range of flowering sequence."

Further north, Creech made a stop at Ōtakine, west of Tomioka, which at 1193 m is the highest peak in the Abukuma range: "We traveled part way by jeep along a logging road and on foot to the severely cutover meadows at the top. On this mountain, the winter snow accumulates to 7 m and the temperature falls to -15° to -20°C . . . . A large tree of *Camellia japonica* [64209], single flowered, grew along the roadside here. Cuttings were taken from this tree since it was the only specimen I had seen at so high an elevation in this region (605 m)" (Creech 1966b).

Having traveled the length of the Abukuma range, from seacoast to the highest peaks, Creech headed next to Tsukuba-san, 876 m, an isolated mountain sitting in the Kanto Plain. Among the plants he collected on Tsukuba-san was *Euonymus fortunei* var. *radicans* [621437], "an especially diminutive type from a cliff face," later introduced to the trade under the name 'Longwood'. Then he traveled by boat across Kasumiga Lake to the Kashima

Shrine. "At Kashima, the only collections of interest were *Damnacanthus indicus* [621434] and *Fatsia japonica*," Creech recorded (1966b). "The area resembles southern Japan with plants requiring a warm, temperate climate, including epiphytic orchids and evergreen ferns. This is also the last of the truly evergreen forests along the outer coast of Honshū."

Northernmost camellia outposts

Back in Tokyo, Creech shipped his collections to the United States and prepared for the trip that would take him to the Pacific coast of northern Honshū. This time he was accompanied by S. Kurata of the University of Tokyo. "Along the coast of this region," explained Creech (1966b), "I hoped to visit the most northern habitat of *Camellia japonica* and to determine the manner in which this and other broadleaf evergreens completed their distribution in northern Japan." He noted that the habitat of *C. japonica* along the Pacific coast of Honshū is remarkably different from that observed in Kyūshū. "Here, the camellia is in strictly sea coast environment, and as might be expected, the plants associated with the camellia differ, too, from those found in Kyūshū" (Creech 1961a).

Creech began his collecting in the forests around the port of Ayukawa. "Here I located the most extensive colonies of *Ardisia japonica* [621423] I have seen in Japan," he noted (1966b). "This evergreen ground cover grows in the same dense fashion as the familiar *Pachysandra* but it has red fruit and lustrous green leaves. It spreads by underground stolons." Near Ayukawa, Creech also collected *Camellia japonica* (64211), which was approaching the northern limit of this species' distribution: "In this area *Camellia japonica* grows on the faces of the sea cliffs, along with deciduous oaks and black pines. It is a scrubby tree showing much winter damage but is said to bloom from December to March."

Creech and Kurata's next stop further north along the coast were two islands near Shizugawa: Tsubaki-jima and Areshima. "Tsubaki-jima [or 'Camellia Island'], so named because it is a dense jungle of camellias, is a small, round island, black on the horizon, because of the thick evergreens, especially *Machilus thunbergii* [621450]," wrote Creech (1966b). "This handsome relative to the camphor-tree has not been introduced previously although it exceeds both the camphor-tree and the evergreen oaks in

hardiness. In the spring the young growth flushes brilliant orange, not unlike that of *Pieris japonica*."

Areshima is an island similar to Tsubaki-jima but closer to shore. On Areshima, Creech noted that "*Camellia japonica* [64213] develops a distorted habit on rock faces. On the beach fronts, it clings to the rocks within a foot [30 cm] of the tidal limit, attesting to its salt tolerance. Within the forest it reaches 12 inches [30 cm] in diameter and attains 12 feet [3.6 m] in height" (1966b).

On 15 June, Creech and Kurata continued driving northward from Shizugawa toward Gayō-san, 1341 m. "Barley is the main crop in this region and camellias are frequently planted in the vicinity of the grainfields," recorded Creech (1966b). "At a small town, Rikuzen-Takeda, the seeds of *Camellia japonica* [64215] are pressed for oil that is used for cooking and as a hairdressing." At the top of Gayō-san they found azaleas in flower: "*Rhododendron kaempferi* [65429] was just at the end of its flowering period. The flowers are small, dark red with a heavy blotch. *R. japonicum* was also in flower with rather uniform orange-red blooms. These azaleas were now found in deciduous forests, mostly birch and maple."

Driving from Gayō-san to the village of Kamaishi on the coast, Creech and Kurata stopped at Cape Funakoshi. "Funakoshi is the northernmost locality for truly wild stands of *Camellia japonica* [64216]," wrote Creech (1966b). "Here in the protection of large *Cryptomeria* trees in a swale behind the seacoast, some thirty or forty straggly trees are grouped together." Surprisingly, these camellias showed no evidence of poor growth that might be accredited to winter injury. More camellias grew along the roads leading to and from Funakoshi, and some of these trees were even several kilometers in from the coast: "The colonies were often growing at the edges of persimmon and apple orchards, and frequently I passed through ripened barley fields to reach camellias. Although the time of year was late June, I found sufficient numbers of partially decomposed flowers lying under the trees to confirm the statements of the local inhabitants that the camellias bloomed in May" (Creech 1961a).

The northernmost place on the Pacific coast of Honshū where Creech found *Camellia japonica* (64219) being cultivated was the tiny fishing village of Raga. "The trees are in shrine gardens and around one or two dwellings," he wrote (1966b). "An elderly farmer assured me that these were native plants and flowered in May. He generously permitted me to collect cuttings and pre-

Camellia japonica growing along the road near Raga in Honshū. Photo by John L. Creech.

Creech found *Lysichiton camtschatcense* (611030) growing abundantly in sphagnum bogs on Mount Hakkoda, Honshū. Photo by Walter H. Hodge.

Creech considered the northernmost population of *Rhododendron japonicum* (621464) growing on Mount Hakkōda in northern Honshū to be "the finest form of the species." Photo by Walter H. Hodge.

sented a bag of seeds. These were, as usual, part of the oilseed harvest."

From Iwate Prefecture, Creech traveled to Aomori Prefecture in northern Honshū, where his first destination was Hakkōda-san, 1585 m. "Mount Hakkōda is capped with perpetual snow and replete with moorlands colonized by ericaceous and other subalpine plants," noted Creech (1966b). "We climbed from one bog to the next, collecting seeds and cuttings of hollies. *Ilex sugerokii* [68583] is the most vigorous holly species on Mount Hakkōda. It is a shrubby species rarely exceeding 8 feet [2.4 m]. . . . *I. crenata* var. *radicans* [65117] grows in and around the bog pools while *I. rugosa* completely prostrate can be found considerably higher on rocky ledges and

hidden under dense clumps of *Pinus pumila.*" The most spectacular plant on the mountain was, however, *Rhododendron japonicum* (621464): "This is the northern limit of natural distribution and a remarkable contrast to the colonies found blooming in Kyūshū in early May. It was in full bloom on June 24. The plants were scattered throughout the bogs, often at the very edges of the pools. It is a meadow plant here as elsewhere in Japan. At its northern limit, *R. japonicum* is a vigorous plant with large glaucous leaves. The flowers are uniform in color throughout the stands. It is a glowing orange red and trusses of ten to twelve flowers are compactly borne. By far, this is the finest form of the species I have ever observed in Japan."

Place for daylilies

Hokkaidō, the northernmost of Japan's main islands, was the final chapter of Creech's expedition. On 8 July, starting from Sapporo, Creech traveled south to Lake Shikotsu. Except for one large peak, Izari-dake, 1318 m, the terrain around the lake is high moorland inhabited by scrub trees and ericaceous plants, including three azaleas: *Rhododendron kaempferi* (66474), *R. tschonoskii,* and *R. albrechtii.* From Lake Shikotsu, Creech journeyed down the coast of Hokkaidō along the Hidaka Mountains to Cape Erimo.

"Driving along this road, carved casually out of massive looming cliffs, is an easily recalled experience," he wrote (1966b). "Along the narrow seafront, the beaches were often ribbonned with extensive gatherings of giant kelps. These had been brought from deep water and were being dried for food. *Rosa rugosa* grew in numerous colonies behind the beach. It is one of the best dune-holding plants of this region. Inland from the narrow beach, loose shale affords little room for woody shrubs. Herbaceous species of plants predominated. Without doubt, Hokkaidō is the place to search for daylilies. More extensive colonies are found here than anywhere else in the Japanese Empire. Facing the ocean as it does the Hidaka Mountain Range is a rich floristic locality. This range was so dense with fog that nearby climbers could be heard but could not be seen."

From Cape Erimo, Creech returned to Sapporo and proceeded to Matsumae, an ancient city located at the southernmost tip of Hokkaidō. "Along the coastal road near Esashi I spent a morning in a fine meadow filled with daylilies, *Hemerocallis middendorfii* [64926–7], and collected plants to express some of the variations of this robust orange-yellow daylily," he recorded (1966b). "The flowers varied from those with narrow straplike segments to others with broad ovate overlapping segments and flowers 15 cm across. Others had multiple buds with many flowers open at one time."

Matsumae was the only place in Hokkaidō where Creech found cultivated large plants of *Camellia japonica* (64220–2). "I am sure the feudal lords arriving in this harsh land longed for the warm, sophisticated culture of Kyōto and transplanted as much of that as possible, including plants. What significance can be attached to these plants is conjecture, but at least a number of garden camellias flourish and may be the hardier remnants of the

Creech found various forms of *Hemerocallis middendorfii* (64926–7) growing along the southern seacoast of Hokkaidō, and *H. middendorfii* var. *esculenta,* shown here, along the Pacific coast of northern Honshū. Photo by Walter H. Hodge.

varieties transported to this place. All are late flowering here—April to June—and include singles and doubles in both white and pink. It is the northernmost center of camellia culture in Japan" (Creech 1966b).

From Hokkaidō, Creech returned to Tokyo on 21 July and two days later departed for the United States. "In retrospect, this was my most rewarding journey to Japan, replete with new locations for important ornamental plants," wrote Creech (1966b). "This exploration did not yield much in the way of introducing new species for this was not the intent. Rather, this effort to improve significant garden plants has provided the broadest base of breeding stocks of documented origin yet available to those concerned with Japanese plants."

A total of 347 collections of plants, cuttings, and seeds were shipped during the course of the trip. In addition, arrangements were made for the collection of seed from important localities when the seed matured. "I believe that I have brought to America the greatest collection of breeding stocks of important Japanese plants than any-one previous," wrote Creech (1961d) to Hodge. "This is with all due respect to my own earlier trips and other collectors. We now have all the wild camellia, holly, azalea, and similar materials to do some really fine breeding and developmental work with these plants."

TREASURE HOUSE

Almost a quarter century passed since Creech's 1961 trip before Longwood Gardens had another opportunity to introduce plants from Japan. Unlike Creech's expeditions in 1956 and 1961, the trip, planned jointly with the U.S. National Arboretum for 1985, was to be dedicated primarily to cultivated plants. It was thought that during a short five-week trip, more could be accomplished by selecting new introductions from plants already in cultivation in Japan, rather than by collecting in the wild. The team consisted of two explorers: Rick Darke, Longwood's curator of plants, and Sylvester G. March, chief horticulturist at the National Arboretum and a veteran of plant exploration in Japan.

"Japan is an invariable treasure house for garden plants," wrote March (1985). "The focus of the trip was on visiting arboreta, botanic gardens, prefectural research stations, nursery specialists, and private collections in the Tokyo area and south to Hakone, Nagoya, Tsu, Kyoto, Ōsaka, Hiroshima, Iwakuni, and Kumamato." With their goals thus set, Darke and March departed for Japan in mid-October.

Magical blend of Jindai
Upon their arrival in Tokyo, Darke and March spent the first several days visiting sites in the city and its vicinity. On 16 October they toured Aritaki Arboretum, a private establishment in Koshigaya with a reputation for being a source for elite plants. The arboretum's curator, Tadahiko Aritaki, had traveled and collected plants throughout Asia. Darke and March were especially interested in the plants Aritaki had introduced from Taiwan.

The next day Darke and March were taken to Kawaguchi, in the northern suburbs of Tokyo, to visit several nurseries. First they stopped at the nursery owned by the Nihonkaki Corporation, where they purchased a number of plants, including several species of *Tricyrtis,* such as *T. macranthopsis* (85881), *T. ohsumiensis* (85884), and *T. perfoliata* (85885). Then, in Kabayashi Maple Nursery, Darke and March selected a number of unusual cultivars of *Acer buergerianum, A. shirasawanum,* and *A. sieboldianum.* A rare red-flowered form of *Rhododendron mucronulatum* (85865) and a white-flowered form of *Allium thunbergii* (85810) were found in the Kairo-en Nursery. Finally, a visit to Suzuki Sanyasō Nursery resulted in two dwarf varieties of goldenrod, *Solidago virga-aurea* var. *minutissima* (85873) and *S. virga-aurea* var. *praeflorens* (85874).

On 20 October the explorers went to the Jindai Botanical Garden in Tokyo. March considered it a good example of how Japan's botanical gardens "excel in having the magical blend of attractions to draw a broad audience to learn and enjoy at their gardens—people of all ages sketching and painting; families spread out on broad expanses of grass taking in the beauty of the surroundings; and throngs of people viewing outdoor chrysanthemum exhibitions; all making the gardens a vibrant part of the fabric of daily life" (March 1985). The daylong browsing through Jindai's plant collections resulted in only one acquisition, that of *Aster tataricus* (85813). "At Jindai Botanical Garden I noticed a plant of *Aster tataricus* that was evidently lower-growing than the typical forms in cultivation in the United States," remembers Darke. "Since the typical *Aster tataricus* is too tall and aggressively spreading for the average sized garden, this compact form offered a promising alternative. It was named 'Jindai' to honor its origin and, when introduced commercially in the United States, quickly gained popularity."

Camellias of the samurai
On 26 October, Darke and March began their journey southwest of Tokyo. A couple of days later the explorers arrived in Nagoya, the capital of Aichi Prefecture, situated at the head of Ise Bay. Here they paid a visit to the Fukukaen Nursery and Bulb Company to learn about their breeding of new cut flower and pot plant crops. Then they toured the Nagoya Fruit Garden, a municipal garden completed only a year earlier, which is devoted to

Aster tataricus 'Jindai' (85813), introduced by Darke and March from the Jindai Botanical Garden in Tokyo, is a lower-growing form of this vigorous perennial native to east Asia. Photo by Tomasz Aniśko.

Hirose, left, and Karasawa with *Miconia magnifica* (85855) obtained from Hiroshima Botanical Garden by Darke and March. Photo by Rick Darke.

a broad range of fruit-bearing plants. According to March it was "without a doubt, the most impressive garden visited" (1985).

By 7 November, the explorers reached Ōsaka on the northeastern shore of Ōsaka Bay, where they stopped at the Yoshida Bonsai Center and the Yamashoji Kokujuen Nursery. From the extensive offerings of these two nurseries, several unique plants were selected, among them *Ardisia crispa* (85811), a white-flowered form of *Cercis chinensis* (85826), and *Stachyurus praecox* var. *matsuzakii* (85875).

From Ōsaka the explorers headed west to Hiroshima, a prefectural capital situated at the west end of Japan's Inland Sea. Their destination was Hiroshima Botanical

Garden, a relatively young municipal garden established in 1976, featuring extensive collections of orchids, begonias, fuchsias, water lilies, and others plants from around the world. They toured the garden accompanied by Kohji Karasawa, director, and Yoshimichi Hirose, expert on variegated plants. One plant that impressed Darke and March was *Miconia magnifica* (85855), a small tree from Central America. With its enormous leaves colored green above and purple-blue below, it is considered among the most striking foliage plants.

By 11 November the team arrived on the island of Kyūshū, heading for the city of Kurume in Fukuoka Prefecture, where the federal Vegetable and Ornamental Crops Research Station is located. Darke and March were

A weeping form of *Ilex serrata* (85848), acquired from Shimabichi Nursery in Kawaguchi by Darke and March, was introduced in the United States as a cultivar, 'Longwood Firefall'. Photo by Rick Darke.

Yokoi, left, and Darke with *Ilex crenata* 'Sky Pencil' (85847), growing in Longwood's nursery eleven years after it was introduced from Yokoi's garden. Photo by Rick Darke.

especially interested in seeing the results of the ever-green azalea breeding carried out at the station. While there, they picked up one recently introduced red-flow-ered cultivar, 'Benifusha' (8624), notable for its exceptional hardiness.

From Kurume the explorers traveled to Kumamoto, the home of Higo camellias, which date back to the times of the samurai. The origin of Higo camellias is shrouded in mystery, but their flowers are unique and distinct because of their very large and iridescent petals and large number of showy, brightly colored stamens. Among the many Higo camellias acquired by Darke and March in Kumamoto were the pink 'Osaraku' (85820), red 'Kobai' (85818), and white 'Fuji' (85816).

Feeling overwhelmed

Back in Tokyo, Darke and March dedicated their last couple of days in Japan to visiting more nurseries. They spent a good part of 17 November selecting unusual plants from Shimabichi Nursery in Kawaguchi. To their delight, it turned out to be the most productive day of the whole trip. From Shimabichi's exceptionally diverse and interesting offering, they picked forty-seven plants, including a number of rare selections of *Enkianthus campanulatus* (85830–4) and dwarf forms of *Styrax japonica* (85876), *Clethra barbinervis* (85827), and *Magnolia stellata* (85852). A weeping form of *Ilex serrata* (85848) acquired from Shimabichi was later introduced in the United States as 'Longwood Firefall'.

While in Kawaguchi, Darke and March also paid a visit to the garden of Dr. Masao Yokoi, professor at the Laboratory of Floriculture and Ornamental Horticulture at Chiba University, and according to March, one of the best-known plant specialists in Japan at that time. "Dr. Yokoi's garden at Kawaguchi City can only be described as a paradise for those interested in variegated plants," wrote March (1985). "Every square meter of the garden and greenhouse is jam packed with variegated plants. Because there is no space to walk, he waters the green-house by standing in the doorway and aiming the hose." Yokoi graciously shared with the explorers some of the plants from his outstanding collection, including two that later gained widespread popularity in the United

Miscanthus sinensis 'Cabaret' (91599) obtained by Darke and March from Yokoi was displayed in Longwood's Idea Garden. Photo by Tomasz Aniśko.

States: a columnar form of *Ilex crenata* (85847) named 'Sky Pencil' and a variegated *Miscanthus sinensis* (91599) named 'Cabaret'.

The trip concluded on 23 November. In addition to the 292 plants they collected in Japan, Darke and March returned home with an immense respect and admiration for the country's gardening tradition and fascination with ornamental plants. "No matter how frequently I travel there in search of garden plants," said March (1985), "I cannot come away without feeling overwhelmed by the intensity and wealth of horticulture."

Yokoi, left, and Darke in Yokoi's garden in Kawaguchi. Photo by Rick Darke.

SOUTH KOREA

REDISCOVERING KOREAN FLORA

The scars of the Korean War were still fresh when Dr. Edward G. Corbett, research horticulturist of the New Crops Research Branch of the USDA Agricultural Research Service in Glenn Dale, Maryland, and Dr. Richard W. Lighty, geneticist at Longwood Gardens, undertook an ambitious expedition to South Korea in 1966. Horticultural exploration of the peninsula had barely begun at that time. Aside from sporadic port calls by Russian ships in the nineteenth century, a visit by the English nurseryman John Gould Veitch in 1860, and brief exploration in the early twentieth century by Ernest H. Wilson and John G. Jack of the Arnold Arboretum of Harvard University, the wealth of the flora was unknown in the West.

"Nevertheless," recalls Lighty, "it was well known that the flora of Korea, like that of adjacent China, Manchuria, and Japan, is closely related to that of the eastern United States and that collections there would have value similar to those from earlier trips to Japan. Furthermore, Korea is climatically similar to that region with summer precipitation, heat, and humidity that match that of our east coast from Maine to Florida. Winters also match ours in terms of temperature extremes. Other reasons for projecting this exploration were the inaccessibility of the even richer flora of China, our lack of knowledge of botanic gardens and arboretums that could be relied upon to collect under contract, and

the presence of an outstanding field botanist, Dr. Lee Tchang Bok, professor of Seoul National University. He had a personal familiarity with the flora of the entire country beyond that of other Korean botanists."

The trip was planned to encompass much of the growing season, culminating in autumn as seed ripened. The length of time, almost four months, allowed repeat visits to areas of high interest, assuring that desirable plants were secured.

Climbing a volcano

"When we arrived in Seoul on 7 July, it was raining hard as though to affirm the heralded summer precipitation," remembers Lighty. The explorers spent the first few days taking care of organizational details. "These included obtaining permission to use facilities of the Eighth United States Army base at Yongsan, in the heart of Seoul; making arrangements to access the regions where the animosity between North and South Korea continued to make travel dangerous; and establishing procedures for cashing checks, holding our mail, and seeing to it that, on return to Seoul after each foray, our plants were quickly placed in the next diplomatic pouch to leave for the United States."

Although an itinerary had been drawn up prior to the trip, it had to be altered as circumstances dictated. "Transportation difficulties, flooding, and new and more accurate information on the distribution of target species all affected, in a practical way, when and where we went,"

The Korean peninsula extends southward from eastern Siberia and Manchuria to within about 110 km of Japan at its southern end. Approximately 960 km long and up to 320 km wide, the peninsula covers more than 220,000 km^2. Mountains and hills occupy nearly 70 percent of Korea's territory. The highest peak, Mount Paektu, 2744 m, is located on the border between North Korea and China. The main areas of lowlands are in the western and southern parts of the peninsula. The climate of Korea is influenced by polar, tropical, and continental air masses moving in from surrounding areas. During winter, northerly winds bring dry and cold weather from Siberia. In contrast, summer monsoons bring abundant moisture and warm air from the south. In the northern parts of the peninsula, winter temperatures can drop to below -37ºC, while summer temperatures in the south can reach as high as 35ºC. The rainfall ranges from 500 mm in the northwestern highlands to 1800 mm in the southeastern coastal areas. About three thousand species of vascular plants are native to Korea, and of those about 14 percent are endemic. The flora of the southern regions is more diverse than that of the north. Rich, coniferous forests predominate in the inland regions, while evergreen, broad-leaved forests are widespread on the warmer islands. Many trees in northern Korea are closely related to those found on other regions of the Northern Hemisphere. Others, less common elsewhere in the temperate regions, were able to survive the glaciation in the mountain refuges on the peninsula. A number of species found in the coastal regions of southern Korea are related to the genera distributed throughout the Southern Hemisphere.

recalls Lighty. "In general we covered all of the places we had anticipated visiting."

Corbett and Lighty's first trip was to Cheju, an island off the southern tip of the peninsula. "It is dominated by the beautiful volcanic peak, Mount Halla, which is similar in form to Mount Fuji of Japan," remembers Lighty. "At 1950 m in height, it is South Korea's highest peak and, at higher altitudes, can have cold and snowy winters. At sea level, Cheju Island is subtropical, and the deep and fertile soils have an ancient history of agriculture. Many elements of the Japanese flora are represented here along with Korean-Manchurian species typical of the peninsula. Among the plants collected here were *Aruncus aethusifolius* (69190), *Hemerocallis coreana* (67344), *Lindera erythrocarpa* (69216), and a number of rhododendrons."

These first collections did not come without paying a price. As Lighty recalls, he "suffered a sunstroke while at the top of Mount Halla following a grueling climb." In a letter sent to Dr. Russell J. Seibert (1966a) he confessed, "In two days I had two cans of warm beer and four slices of spam. When we got down, the MD said I had sunstroke. If so I think it was in combination with something else." Later he admitted, "I had made the mistake of carrying my 30 kg pack up the mountain. Fatigue and ultraviolet exposure at an altitude of 1950 m left me with an inability to keep water or food down."

Most of the collecting on Cheju was done on Mount Halla, since the expedition's primary focus was on temperate plants. "Each evening we would go over the day's collections, wash soil from the roots of plants, and repackage living material, wrapped in slightly damp paper and placed in sealed plastic bags," explains Lighty. "These would be carefully packed to withstand the rigors of the remaining time in the field and, along with copies of the field notes, sent to Washington on our return to Seoul. We returned from Cheju Island on 18 July and sent our collections off through the American Embassy, provisioned for the trip to Ullung Island, and rested."

Close to heaven

"Ullung Island was a destination I had looked forward to since reading Ernest H. Wilson's account of his brief visit there," recalls Lighty. "The island was still without wheeled vehicles and had only limited locally generated electricity in Todong, the largest village on the 90 km² island. The one refrigerator was used alternatively to make ice cream or cool beer, never both at the same time. Ullung Island is in the middle of the Sea of Japan, and therefore quite hot and humid; one might say sweltering when the wind was not blowing."

Lighty leads the group on their first day of hiking on Mount Halla on Cheju Island. Photo by Richard W. Lighty.

The party left Seoul on 24 July and, after a five-hour train ride and nearly as long a ride in a crowded bus over flooded roads, reached Pohang harbor in the evening. In Pohang they boarded the small freighter for a ten-hour ride to Ullung. "Now I know what inaccessible means!" wrote Lighty (1966b) to Seibert. "Then too—all the spaces in their transportation system are made for men 5 feet 5 inches [1.7 m] tall—I have not fit yet."

Lighty recalls this boat ride: "Still suffering from the effects of the sun, and having difficulty fitting into the dresser drawer–sized bunks, I spent the night on the canvas cover over the hold, and fell asleep watching the mast play across a brilliant, star-filled sky. I awoke at first light and watched as the rising sun brought the steep lava cliffs of Ullung Island into bright relief. My first thoughts were that this must have been how it appeared to Wilson! There followed a remarkable feat of seamanship as the captain dropped anchor, and backed the ship into the tight little harbor; then dispatched two other lines to secure the stern to the cliffs on our left and the breakwater on our right. After that, we were lightered in to the beach where we disembarked. Ullung Island is a resort of sorts, but it was quickly clear that few if any Westerners had been there within the memory of children under fifteen years of age. We were followed everywhere and closely watched at all times, from windows, roofs, and doorways, by battalions of children. Only by drawing the curtains were we able to get a little privacy."

Ullung is "famous to botanists as the home of a number of endemics—but to the world at large, it is the origin of squid. . . . Each night all the eligible males went to sea and caught squid like fury" (Lighty 1966b). On several occasions Lighty observed these daily routines: "The boats return at first light, and the women and children take over the job of gutting and cleaning the catch. The squid are hung on bamboo racks to dry in the wind for

Steep lava cliffs of Ullung Island as they appeared to Corbett and Lighty. Photo by R. William Thomas.

several days before being bundled for storage and shipment, mainly to Japan. All of the tiny villages of Ullung-do are set in small coves at the base of sheer cliffs; and all are characterized by vast numbers of drying-racks, looking like laundry drying-yards for hundreds of people." However picturesque the drying squid might have appeared, Lighty was unequivocal in his appreciation of them: "I hope I never see another."

The island also posed other challenges. "I had been coming down with dysentery since we returned from Cheju Island," explains Lighty, "and it now started to have its full effect in terms of enervation. A visit to a Catholic hospital, a shot in the buttocks with a horse syringe, and several doses of powders would keep it at bay, but I had lost 10 kg, and most of my energy. In addition to the heat and exhaustion, we now found that the island had, literally, no level land." In a letter to Seibert, Lighty wrote, "The most rugged terrain I've ever seen. Up and down are the only two directions of that island of volcanic origin" (1966b). Lighty recalls an old saying from Ullung: "When the farmers go out to plant, they take seed and an equal number of tacks to hold the seeds on the hillside."

It was these sheer walls that the explorers had to climb to do the collecting. They soon found a way to

Squid-drying racks in Todong on Ullung Island. Photo by Richard W. Lighty.

avoid the overland difficulty: "On several occasions we engaged an off-duty squid boat to take us part way around the island to one or the other of the tiny villages, many of which did not have docks or breakwaters," recalls Lighty. "We would disembark and begin climbing immediately. It would have been a trying experience for healthy, vigorous people, and that we were not. Despite this, we took full advantage of the flora of this remarkable island. It is the only place on earth, with the possible exception of a small area around Vladivostok, Russia, where *Lilium hansonii* (681258) is found. This was the most important of a number of lilies I hoped to collect, as it was represented in the West by only a single clone which, like most lilies, was self-incompatible. Yet it was one parent of the important hybrid lily group, the Martagon Hybrids."

While not battling the sheer cliffs guarding the mysterious interior of Ullung against intruders, Corbett and Lighty occasionally experienced the gentler nature of the island. "Returning to Todong from one foray," remembers Lighty, "we joined a group of high school-aged girls and boys participating in a work camp on the island. We boarded as the sun was setting, and as we skimmed over the crystal-clear water, we could see deep down 15 m to house-sized boulders rounded by the action of the sea. We were sitting on rice-straw blankets covering a huge load of braided garlic while a brilliant half-moon rose above us, and we all joined in singing the usual camp songs that seem to be known the world around. As we basked in the moment, the high cliffs with pounding surf on one side, and the squid boat lights winking on the other, Ullung Island seemed a place closer to heaven than to the hell it had seemed at high noon. This is the Ullung Island that I remember."

The tranquility of this place seems to have had a soothing effect on Lighty: "By this time I was down to 70 kg, the least I had weighed since I was twelve, but the sunstroke was gone, and the dysentery on the wane, so my vigor and ambition were returning. On 30 July, we had to leave. The freighter was back in harbor, its lights blazing and its amplifiers blasting the town with Korean, American, and other flavors of music. The captain had been to America as a young man, and liked all things American—including us. He looked the other way as I went back to my canvas bed under the brilliant night sky."

Demilitarized mountain

"Back in Seoul on 2 August we checked on arrangements, made previously, to go to Mount Sorak, 1708 m, area," recalls Lighty. "This mountain is the southern-most expression of the Diamond Mountains. It is above the 38th parallel, but outside the demilitarized zone between North and South Korea, and was the scene of intense fighting on several occasions during the Korean War. We were told by an American advisor to the Korean National Police that the area was closed to tourists and that his

office could do little to help. He suggested we go to the military."

Meanwhile, to use the time effectively the explorers went to Mount Kwanak, outside of Seoul, which, as Lighty explains, "had also been a battlefield on several occasions and a refugee camp following the Korean War. What vegetation had not been blasted off by bombs and artillery had been eaten or burned for fuel by the starving refugees. There was no soil, only pulverized rock, but by 1966 it had begun to recover, and a young scrub of adventive species had begun to grow."

Returning to Seoul, Corbett and Lighty found that it was possible for them to explore the Mount Sorak region. Although the exact conditions under which they would be allowed to work were still unclear, they departed on 8 August. One venue for collecting was the resort village of Osaek. The party spent three nights there in a motel offering Korean-style accommodations, which, noted Lighty, "require a different set of bones than God gave me" (1966c). The resort of Osaek grew around naturally carbonated springs, whose healthful waters are collected by visitors and taken back to Seoul and elsewhere.

Cool spring water in Osaek, healthful or not, was much welcomed by the explorers. "My major problem in Korea is liquid—cold liquid," wrote Lighty (1966c) in a letter sent to Longwood. "One can buy beer (quite good lager), or cola, or something they call cider but which never saw an apple, but to get these properly cooled takes much management. We use wells and springs where there is no ice (includes most of rural Korea) and then we drink it warm if all else fails. I am worse off than Ed here because much of the natural water of Korea has a high humus content and actually makes me retch. He can drink most any water after putting iodine pills in it. I haven't had any water since we left Seoul."

On 12 August, Lighty reported back to Longwood regarding the difficulties they faced while collecting on Mount Sorak: "Each day we climbed in a different direction but we were always stopped less than halfway up the mountain by ROK [Republic of Korea] Army. The infiltrators are becoming quite a problem—every night several are spotted and/or killed. . . . Today we were going to try climbing from this side of the mountain but discovered on awakening that three infiltrators had been spotted here last night and the ROK Army is all out after them. We did, however, get a lieutenant and two soldiers to accompany us up one part of the mountain" (Lighty

The military escorted Corbett and Lighty on the climb up Mount Sorak. Photo by Richard W. Lighty.

Coniogramme fraxinea var. *intermedia* (66747) collected by Corbett and Lighty on Mount Sorak. Photo by Richard W. Lighty.

Aceriphyllum rossii (70758) growing along a stream on Mount Sorak. Photo by Richard W. Lighty.

The team near Mount Odae, including, left to right, Park, Corbett, Cho, Lee Moon Ho, Lee Tchang Bok, and Lighty. Photo by Edward G. Corbett.

1966c). Despite these difficulties the party made several forays from Osaek. In September they revisited this area to collect the seeds that were not ripe on the first visit. Among the plants collected on Mount Sorak were *Aceriphyllum rossii* (70758), *Coniogramme fraxinea* var. *intermedia* (66747), *Forsythia ovata* (681242), *Rhododendron brachycarpum* (68743), and *Syringa amurensis* (681256).

Another fertile collecting area in that region was a relatively mature forest surrounding a Buddhist temple on Mount Odae, 1563 m, some 160 km east of Seoul. Here Corbett and Lighty collected *Athyrium coreanum* (66596), *Spiraea salicifolia* (681254), and *Thalictrum uchiyamai* (68609), among other plants. According to Corbett, the presence of Buddhist monasteries with extensive land holdings was one particular advantage of collecting in Korea: "The Buddhist philosophy includes a

strong interest in preserving the natural environment, and this meant that those areas were rich floristically." Lighty adds that "throughout our travels we found that such temple forests had been protected for centuries by the monks, and had generally been spared destruction in the war."

Led by the monks
On 17 August the party returned to Seoul. To reach the capital they had to drive over what Lighty noted were "some of the dustiest and bumpiest roads I have experienced (and we have traveled some bad ones). . . . The number of washouts from the terrible flooding they have had is astounding" (1966d). He attributed the flooding to the widespread deforestation: "The only really good collecting areas in Korea lie on the high mountains and

Lycoris koreana (68598) collected at Paegyang-sa near Kwangju. Photo by Richard W. Lighty.

in the temple forests. Outside of these . . . they cut all the trees right down to one-inch [25 mm] saplings—the regrowth is cut off as it appears. Then they sickle off all the weeds and grasses to feed their animals. The rule seems to be, 'if in doubt—cut it off before your neighbor does.' Most of the hillsides (those not terraced for rice) look, as a result, like they are plowed each year. Soil erosion is rampant and the flooding we've just had is the result" (Lighty 1966e).

In Seoul, Corbett and Lighty packed and dispatched their collections before getting ready to fly to Kwangju. Their destination was the nearby temple preserve at Paegyang-sa, the southernmost of the collecting sites on the peninsula. The specific goal for this excursion was to collect *Lycoris koreana* (68598), an orange-flowered species never cultivated in the West. "One monastery we visited there had the only known wild population of

Lycoris koreana," remembers Corbett, "and Dr. Lee was able to persuade the monks to allow us to collect some bulbs. A couple of monks agreed to lead us to the plants, and we started out up a steep rocky slope which was traversed only with great difficulty. Near the summit we were shown a cave with a mineral spring reputed to have healing qualities. We had to sample the water and then we again set out by a circuitous route to find *Lycoris*. Finally, after about five hours of walking we came to the stand of *Lycoris koreana* within several hundred meters of the entrance to the monastery, our starting point."

Caught in a typhoon

"On return to Seoul," remembers Lighty, "we dispatched our collections and went on to Suwŏn, where the Agricultural College of Seoul National University was located. We had the comparative luxury of staying at the University's guest house, a Victorian building dating to the Japanese occupation" (1966e). The guesthouse offered a welcome respite from the accommodations generally available in small and remote villages. Corbett and Lighty rejoiced: "Our two-day stay at Suwŏn has considerably improved our digestive tracts—we had a western-style cook and housekeeper who really knew how to cook like home! She even had refrigerated boiled water for us."

Corbett and Lighty then turned their attention to Mount Chiri, 1915 m. "It was fairly far south, so we took a train to Kurye, then hired a truck to reach the largest temple in Korea, located at the base of Mount Chiri," explains Lighty. "The climb was not steep, but it took five hours to reach our campsite, a summer resort for Presbyterian missionaries that had been built here in the early 1900s, but had been destroyed during the Japanese occupation. The remains of sixteen stone lodges, tennis courts, swimming pools, and other amenities suggested that life was not always hard for missionaries in the field." The surrounding forests of maple, birch, hornbeam, and oak were cut through by cold, rapidly flowing brooks cascading over granite boulders. Crystal-clear pools punctuated the woods and invited the tired explorers to enjoy "swimming—that is to say bathing—for the first time in four days" (Lighty 1966f).

After the second day, plant collecting was somewhat curtailed by heavy, cold rains and fog related to a typhoon that had come off the East China Sea. The downpour was more than the party was prepared for. "Our tents were worse than useless—since we had had some degree of confidence in them," recalls Lighty. "They leaked like sieves and, at the height of the storm, one took off and was damaged. Fortunately there was a peasant's hut close at hand where we could take refuge—and we did!" (Lighty 1966f). In spite of the weather, the team managed to make most of the collections they had come for. Among the notable plants collected on Mount Chiri were *Alangium platanifolium* (70759), *Davallia mariesii* (66618), and *Rhododendron tschonoskii* (69226).

Following the excursion to Mount Chiri, Lighty wrote to Seibert: "We have almost completed the first phase of our trip—the exploration and study of new areas. After a brief stay at Suwŏn with several short trips to close-by areas, we will begin to re-cover the areas we have already seen, this time collecting seed. Seed is spotty this year—in some areas a given species has produced none while in other areas the same species has produced abundantly" (1966f).

Surrounded by reminders of war

On 22 September the party returned to Mount Sorak to see it in its full fall glory. "At its peak, the color rivals that of New England, and many of the same genera contribute to the show there," reminisces Lighty. "*Acer pseudosieboldianum* and *Carpinus laxiflora* were among the most colorful species at this early stage. We were seeking seed of the dwarf form of *Pinus pumila,* a plant which in South Korea is found only in the alpine zone of Mount Sorak. We saw extensive mats of this pine, but there was no seed to be found. Collecting was made difficult by the steady cold rain which accompanied us for most of the climb and turned to sleet as we reached the top."

The most memorable climb took place on 24 and 25 September. Lighty described it in a letter to Seibert: "That evening, just before we reached the temple below the peak, a cold rain hit us. We afterward found out that this was the start of another typhoon. Why must we always meet typhoons while at the top of mountains? We were fairly well soaked by the time we got inside the government-built lodge. Fortunately the foresters had arrived early and built roaring fires, and the floors were radiantly hot. We dried out and worked over our collections while rice was cooking—then after dark had descended we ate supper . . . . Next morning we awoke to heavy fog and high winds—bitter cold. We ate breakfast and put on all the clothes we had and forced ourselves out into it. Fortunately the last several kilometers were steep and we kept warm by

Corbett soaked after a rainstorm. Photo by Edward G. Corbett.

exertion, for not five minutes after we set out, the rain came with renewed fury. We were quickly wet through to the skin! We made several collections as we wended our way upward. Finally we were above the tree line, and there the wind, rain, and sleet—almost hail—hit us with terrific force. All we could think about was moving on—getting out of it. We lost our way twice and had to return 2 km— very frustrating when you're in the middle of a storm! All around us were the remains of the Korean war—cartridge cases, ammo boxes, bullets, and cartridges and even a few human bones. They say there were many more for the first few years after the war. All of Korea had this same sort of thing. Finally after eight hours we arrived at the village of Osaek—a village where we had stayed before. . . . It was good to be back—and not only to get warm once again. We both caught colds—mine mild—Ed's worse. Lucky that is all we got" (Lighty 1966g).

The prostrate form of *Caryopteris incana* (69860) found by Corbett and Lighty along the beach on Cheju Island was later introduced in the United States as a cultivar, 'Blue Billows'. Photo by Richard W. Lighty.

Magnolia sieboldii (68599) collected by Corbett and Lighty along a rocky streambed on Mount Sokni, some 130 km southeast of Seoul, flowers at Longwood Gardens nearly forty years later. Photo by Tomasz Aniśko.

Being discriminating

After returning to Seoul on 28 September, the party once again flew to Cheju. "This time we were fit and healthy, and the climb that had consumed three agonizing days in July was accomplished in one long day," remembers Lighty. "This time we also worked at sea level. In an ancient plantation of *Torreya nucifera* (68612), traditionally employed as a vermifuge, we found *Calanthe discolor* (66570) which, on return, proved hardy with protection at Longwood. Along the beach we found a most interesting form of *Caryopteris incana* (69860), with prostrate stems arching at the ends to hold the typical blue flower clusters 15 cm above the ground."

The expedition's final Korean collecting was done in the vicinity of Suwŏn, again at Mount Kwanak and at a temple nearby. Shortly before their departure, Lighty wrote to Seibert: "The end is drawing near—and we feel it has been a most fruitful trip. Our collection numbers are in the 460s and will probably end up a little lower than 500. Both Ed and I started out with the idea of being discriminating—and we hope we have not lost this quality. The flora here is rich, and the possibility of hardiness in most of the material has somewhat increased its potential scope of use. Of course we realize that only a minute fraction of the total has any chance of becoming widely used as outstanding ornamentals" (Lighty 1966h).

IN PURSUIT OF COLD-HARDY CAMELLIAS

"Most if not all of the *Camellia japonica* varieties traditionally grown in the United States are originally of Japanese origin," wrote Barry R. Yinger (1989), curator of Asian plant collections at the U.S. National Arboretum. "They were first widely grown in the deep South where cold hardiness was not considered a serious problem, but in recent years, with dramatically colder winters in parts of the South too, it has become clear that Japanese camellias are, in general, less hardy than they should be to be a reliable part of the landscape. We know now that if we want to have significantly hardier camellias we must look beyond Japan. Fortunately, the wild type of *Camellia japonica*, from which all the cultivated forms were developed through selection and breeding, has a very broad range extending beyond Japan through the coastal regions and islands of Korea deep into China. . . . I found (as many had before me) that the Korean climate, even near the coast, is harsher than Japan's climate. Korea is on the edge of the Asian land mass with its continental climate. . . . The prevailing winter winds are strong, frequent, cold, and dry. In general, Korean winters are harder on both plants and people."

Based on this premise, in 1983 Yinger had circulated a proposal for collecting and studying plants in South Korea. Longwood Gardens, along with several other institutions, expressed interest in joining that effort, and in July of the following year the first expedition, focused on Korea's northwestern islands and coastal areas, was launched.

Apps, March, and Yinger's expedition began on Taechong Island near the coast of North Korea. Photo by Paul W. Meyer.

Remnants of wild populations of *Camellia japonica* on Taechong Island. Photo by Paul W. Meyer.

In addition to Yinger, the team of plant collectors included Dr. Darrel A. Apps, head of Longwood's education division, and Sylvester G. March, chief horticulturist at the U.S. National Arboretum. Young June Chang, a student at the Seoul National University, served as the expedition's interpreter and guide.

Flowery minefields

The explorers planned to travel to several islands in the Yellow Sea off the northwest coast of South Korea and to the sites on the Taean Peninsula. The expedition began on 29 July with the exploration of three islands, Taechong, Paengyong, and Sochong, which are situated just below latitude 38° north and which are within sight of the North Korean territory. This is the northern limit of the distribution of *Camellia japonica* and several other broad-leaved evergreens.

"Getting to the islands was no small feat," remembered Apps. "Arrangements were made through the United States Embassy with the Korean Navy and Korean Intelligence Agency to have our collecting team transported by boat. The trip from Inchon to Paengyong is nearly twelve hours by commercial carrier. By Korean Navy fast boats it takes six hours. Since military maneuvers were the navy's main mission we were, so to speak, excess baggage. To our surprise we were usually transferred from boat to boat about every two hours (two transfers per trip). When jumping from deck to deck in four to eight foot [1.2 to 2.4 m] waves one starts thinking about his mortality!" (Apps and Batdorf 1988).

Taechong, Paengyong, and Sochong, being near the coast of North Korea, are of strategic military importance to South Korea. "Because of their location the various military branches maintain round-the-clock surveillance," noted Apps. "Korean Marines are dug in around the coast of each island. Mine fields are laid between encampments to maintain an impenetrable security. Essentially we were guests of the military and did our plant collecting under the watchful eye of armed guards. It is not too surprising that the best undisturbed plant communities were in the mine field. We also can report that these plants are still there!" (Apps and Batdorf 1988).

After a few days on Taechong, the team had made thirty-eight collections of *Camellia japonica* and forty of other plants, including *Cimicifuga heracleifolia* (85348), *Cymbidium goeringii* (85351), and *Polygonatum odoratum* var. *pluriflorum* (85368). Three days of collecting on Paengyong, the largest of the three islands, added another thirty-one collections, among them *Sanguisorba officinalis* (85370, *Scilla scilloides* (85372), and *Sedum oryzifolium* (85377). Then, on 10 August, the group headed to the island of Sochong.

"Our main plant target on this island was *Camellia japonica*," recalled Apps. "Sochong boasts a natural stand of a score or more of trees that are 20 feet [6 m] tall and ten inches [25 cm] or more in diameter. The trees are located on a wind-swept hill that rises a couple of hundred feet over a quaint bay. On our collecting day it was nearly 95 degrees Fahrenheit [35°C] with winds blowing 30 miles [48 km] an hour. Those of us with

Camellia japonica grows on Sochong Island on exposed, windswept hillsides overlooking the Yellow Sea. Photo by Paul W. Meyer.

Fruits of *Camellia japonica* (84882) collected on Sochong Island. Photo by Paul W. Meyer.

glasses had to continually wipe off the caking salt spray" (Apps and Batdorf 1988).

The explorers were struck by the dramatic difference between the common perception of where camellias ought to be growing in the wild, and the reality of the site. "Based on my experience with camellias in gardens, I expected them to be woodland shrubs growing in the shade of forest trees," wrote Yinger (1989b). "This face-to-face contact with wild camellias made it clear that camellias thrive at seaside and possess remarkable salt tolerance, which suggests strong resistance to urban pollution as well. They are also clearly much more tolerant of sun and wind than I had expected. In fact, the extra exposure seemed to produce exceptional flowering and strong compact growth. These camellias clearly preferred very well-drained soil and were thriving among rocks."

Yinger estimated the camellias on Sochong to be about 150 years old: "Hard living had not made these plants any less beautiful. Their smooth gray trunks were solidly muscular, topped with dense crowns of rich, glossy dark green leaves. Their overall aspect was of rude good health under great stress, a description which could be applied to many of the human inhabitants of the island too. . . . The dark brown seeds, the size of a rather large bean, covered the ground as thick as a gravel walk in some places. Despite this enormous crop of seeds, there were no seedlings or young plants at all. The goats and cattle which had stripped the leaves from the trees as high as they could reach had made short work of any young plants, and it

was obvious that when these trees were gone, there would be none to replace them" (Yinger 1989b).

This lack of seedling regeneration concerned the explorers. "We were saddened when we realized that the prognosis for this native stand of *Camellia* was bleak," wrote Apps. "Unfortunately, the rapid industrialization of Korea seems to preoccupy all of its citizenry—preserving native habitats is a long way from being a political agenda item" (Apps and Batdorf 1988).

After collecting cuttings from twenty different camellias, the group headed for a rocky cliff where they saw large colonies of flowering daylilies, *Hemerocallis*. "It turned out that this was one of the few times that we were left alone by our military assistants and it was also a time when we nearly got into serious trouble," remembered Apps. "Near the top of the bank was a stunning clump of an almost yellow daylily; most of the others were a soft orange-apricot self. . . . After a struggle with falling rocks and a very thorny *Rosa rugosa* patch the yellow daylily was at hand. Suddenly from among the large rocks near the ocean floor we heard shouts of native women. Our interpreter Young June Chang yelled, 'Stop!' It was more than a little disconcerting to learn that the edge of a mine field had, or was about to be entered! The yellow daylily was carefully extracted from the rocky soil and the return trip made ever so carefully in an attempt at backtracking. Those hostile thorny roses seemed more friendly this time as bare hands held on to prevent a slip or a rock slide down the cliff" (Apps and Batdorf 1988).

Offshore of North Korea

On 15 August the explorers started off for their next destination, Taeyonpyong and Soyonpyong, two islands in the Yellow Sea, east of the Paengyong island group. "Again there was much adventure associated with our naval transport system," recorded Apps. "Toothy grins were everywhere as the young naval men watched us load plant presses, dryers, pruning poles, and other paraphernalia into their boat. They seemed to enjoy a little diversion from their normal routine. We had left Inchon at 10 a.m. and arrived at a floating military docking station at 3 p.m. in the Yellow Sea near Taeyonpyong. Then we transferred to a smaller craft that took us to the island. We were met by an Intelligence officer who escorted us to military quarters. He informed us that we were one and one-half kilometers from North Korea and that nearly one-half of the villagers on these islands were sympathetic to the North Korean political ideology. As we walked along the edges of the island we could see North Korean fishing boats—a reminder that the land mass extended farther north and that there were probably some interesting plants there too, but, not available to us just yet!" (Apps and Batdorf 1988).

The following morning the group headed to Soyonpyong for a day excursion. On the island they made twenty collections, including several undetermined daylilies, *Hemerocallis* (861088): "Along with the daylilies on this island were handsome clumps of *Pennisetum alopecuroides*. Both dark and blond-headed forms were often growing side by side. Nearby were patches of a campanulate flower *Adenophora*. These three plants together, *Hemerocallis, Pennisetum,* and *Adenophora,* would make a striking perennial border combination" (Apps and Batdorf 1988).

The next day the team of explorers stayed on Taeyonpyong. In the course of daylong botanizing on the island, they were able to add seventeen new collections: "On Taeyonpyong we made several significant other plant finds. A large shrub *Lindera glauca* variety *salicifolia* [88374] had been reported to exist but was thought to be a sterile form. One day we found many plants and some that were fruiting. Seeds were collected on a second trip later that fall. Near our original landing site, on a steep bank, we found one plant of a most unusual form of *Scilla scilloides* [871222]. Its flower stalk was branched and had a rich ruby-red color. On the ends of each

In fall the foliage of *Lindera glauca* var. *salicifolia* (88374) turns blazing orange and contrasts with shiny black fruits.
Photo by Tomasz Aniśko.

branch were multiple white cauliflower-like miniature flowers" (Apps and Batdorf 1988).

Collecting for preservation

The last leg of the trip took the explorers south to Taean Peninsula on the west coast of South Korea, and to several nearby offshore islands, including Anmyon and Taebaengi. Two days of scouting on these islands resulted in more than thirty collections, including *Clematis patens* (85349), *Convallaria keiskei* (85350), *Peucedanum japonicum* (84756), and several camellias. After a five-week journey through some of the most remote locations in northwestern South Korea, Apps, March, and Yinger returned to the United States carrying 235 plants, cuttings, bulbs, and rhizomes.

March shows fruits of *Cornus kousa* (86469) collected in October when he returned to Korea with Bristol, Meyer, and Yinger. Photo by Paul W. Meyer.

This *Camellia japonica* (84881), raised from seeds collected on Sochong Island in the Yellow Sea, proved to be the most cold-hardy of Korean camellias trialed at Longwood Gardens. Photo by Tomasz Aniśko.

Visits to the offshore islands made the explorers acutely aware of the extent of the habitat destruction threatening the existence of many plants there. "There is no mystery in what is happening to the plants—there is simply the condition of more people, more land cultivation, and more domestic animals to destroy native plant communities," wrote Apps. "For the most part we can have little influence on site preservation in other countries. About the only opportunity we have is collecting . . . . It occurred to us that American gardens might become repositories for Korean germplasm—a bit like providing a sanctuary for a deposed political figure who may or may not return" (Apps and Batdorf 1988).

A month later March and Yinger returned to Korea in order to collect seeds from many of the plants seen

earlier. They were joined by Peter W. Bristol, director of horticulture at the Holden Arboretum in Kirtland, Ohio, and Paul W. Meyer, director of horticulture at the Morris Arboretum in Philadelphia. The four-week trip added another 250 plants for introduction to the United States.

Plants collected in South Korea were distributed among the participating institutions, and a long process of evaluations began. Two years later Apps wrote to Dr. H. Marc Cathey, director of the U.S. National Arboretum: "Our trip two years ago has given us several good perennials. We have selected three *Chrysanthemum* sp. for potential fall display, we have picked out a good form of *Gypsophila oldhamiana* [84894–5], we are real excited about *Astilbe chinensis* var. *davidii* [85339], and I personally have fallen for eight-foot-tall [2.4 m tall] *Echinops setifer* [855]. Besides these perennials there are several more plants that have promise as ornamentals—we are hoping to name a form of *Serissa foetida* [8540]" (Apps 1986).

The greatest impact the 1984 Korean expeditions had on American horticulture was, however, through the introduction of cold-hardy *Camellia japonica* germplasm. Trials at Longwood Gardens, Morris Arboretum, and elsewhere showed that these plants can withstand harsh Pennsylvania winters and flower reliably every spring. One superior plant raised from seed collected on Sochong (84882) was selected and named 'Korean Fire' by Yinger. In 2003 this cultivar was awarded the Gold Medal by the Pennsylvania Horticultural Society. Through the efforts of plant collectors and plant breeders, the Korean camellias, which evolved on the small windswept islands along the North Korean coast, may extend the range in which camellias can be grown and thus introduce many gardeners living in the northern climes to these exquisite flowers.

SEVEN MOUNTAINS

The 1984 trips to Korea explored the flora of the west coast and of the islands of the Yellow Sea. Subsequently, in 1986, plans were made to continue the search for superior landscape plants in the eastern part of the Korean Peninsula. Cathey wrote to Frederick E. Roberts, Longwood's director: "We are seeking to discover new and elite woody plants which can be brought to the United States in cooperation with botanists and horticulturists in Korea. It is one of a series of trips we are taking to Korea to locate plants which can be used in our breeding programs at the arboretum" (Cathey 1986).

It was three years later that such an expedition was launched. The principal target areas for collecting were chosen in the mountainous province of Kangwŏn in the northeastern part of South Korea, including the island of Ullung, which lies about 150 km off the east coast of Kangwŏn Province. Seven major mountains were selected as the collecting sites. Because of the severe climate of Kangwŏn, collecting in that region offered opportunities for introduction of trees, shrubs, and perennials with superior cold hardiness and stress tolerance. The goals for the expedition emphasized collecting species with significant landscape potential, documenting the native flora of

Members of the 1989 fall expedition to Korea, including, left to right, Thomas, March, Kim, and Bristol. Photo by Paul W. Meyer.

Kangwŏn Province and Ullung, and assisting in the conservation of rare and endangered Korean native plants.

The seed-collecting expedition planned for the fall of 1989 was preceded by a reconnaissance trip in the spring of the same year to identify sites where desired plants could be found. March and Meyer led both trips. In the spring they were accompanied by Dr. Richard G. Hawke of the Chicago Botanic Garden and Dr. James E. Henrich of the Missouri Botanical Garden, whereas in the fall they were joined by Bristol and R. William Thomas, Longwood's education division manager. Daegon Kim of Yeungham University served as the guide for the fall expedition.

Mount Odae and Mount Kariwang
The team assembled in Seoul on 17 September. Three days later they departed for Mount Odae, which had been explored by Corbett and Lighty twenty-three years earlier. On the morning of 21 September, the group climbed to the top of the mountain. The dominant vegetation on this ridge, which was all dwarfed and stunted, included *Abies nephrolepis* (90755), *Quercus mongolica*, and *Taxus cuspidata*. "On the sheltered slope below the peak were ancient, 20 m tall trees of *Taxus*," recalls Thomas. "Through the mist and clouds of that day, the trees could easily have been mistaken for large specimens of *Cedrus*." Meyer describes some of the more widespread species on Mount Odae: "*Viburnum sargentii* was a common shrub across the exposed mountain top but was seldom seen at the lower elevations. *Acer tschonoskii* var. *rubripes* frequented these higher elevations and it was col-

Bristol leads the group to the top of Mount Odae through the forest of maples, oaks, and firs. Photo by Paul W. Meyer.

March, left, and Meyer with an ancient specimen of *Taxus cuspidata* growing on Mount Odae. Photo by R. William Thomas.

oring up with brilliant orange-red color, whereas *Acer tegmentosum* with clear yellow fall color was found further down the ridge." The group's collections on Mount Odae were not limited to trees and shrubs; there were many herbaceous plants as well, such as *Cimicifuga simplex* (90769) with its slender racemes of white flowers, *Hepatica maxima* (91543) with its beautiful, large, shiny leaves, and *Hypericum ascyron* (90774) with its golden yellow star-shaped flowers up to 8 cm wide.

From Mount Odae the expedition continued on 23 September to Mount Kariwang, 1560 m, located about 40 km to the south. Two days of botanizing on this mountain turned out to be exceedingly fruitful. At the foot of Mount Kariwang, about 500 m in elevation, they collected, among others, *Carpinus cordata* (90767), *Iris sanguinea* (90775), and *Rodgersia podophylla* (91551).

Higher up, at about 800 m, the explorers found *Acer pseudosieboldianum* (90756), *Actinidia polygama* (90762), and *Kalopanax pictus* (90776). Finally, at 1100 m, they encountered *Acer ukurunduense* (90761), *Alangium platanifolium* var. *macrophyllum* (91534–5), and *Smilacina japonica* (90786).

Mount Chiak and Mount Taebaek

On 25 September the group traveled to the town of Wŏnju, some 100 km southeast of Seoul, where they planned to explore the nearby Mount Chiak, 1288 m. The following morning the team hiked to the summit. "It was probably the hardest climb of the trip, up very loose rocky inclines," recalls Meyer. "The peak was covered with *Acer pseudosieboldianum*, *Quercus mongolica*, *Rhododendron schlippenbachii*, and *R. mucronulatum*. All the trees on the highest part of the mountain were dwarfed. On the ridge, a little down from the peak, we collected *Carpinus laxiflora* (90768). Its leaves were turning yellow and orange at the time of our visit. This species seemed to be confined to the higher, dryer areas, between 750 and 1200 m, and did not occur in the valleys. Just below the summit we found *Betula ermanii* (90766), notable for its grayish white, exfoliating bark."

The next day it rained heavily and the explorers dedicated the whole day to processing their seeds and herbarium collections. On 28 September the weather improved enough for the team to spend the morning exploring the forest at the lower elevation on Mount Chiak, after which they headed back to Seoul.

Pinus densiflora, P. koraiensis, and *Abies nephrolepis* inhabit rocky ridges on Mount Chiak. Photo by R. William Thomas.

Slopes of Mount Taebaek were rich in maple species, including *Acer tegmentosum* (90757), *A. triflorum* (90759), and *A. tschonoskii* var. *rubripes* (90760). Photo by Paul W. Meyer.

In Seoul the group spent a couple of days cleaning seeds and processing herbarium specimens before traveling to their next destination, Mount Taebaek, 1561 m. This mountain is situated some 100 km southeast of Mount Chiak in the Taebaek mountain range, South Korea's major mountain range paralleling the east coast of the peninsula. Two days on the mountain allowed the explorers to survey its vegetation from the valleys to the summit. On the slopes many maples, including *Acer tegmentosum* (90757), *A. triflorum* (90759), and *A. tschonoskii* var. *rubripes* (90760), were putting on spectacular fall colors. In an open woodland at about 1300 m, the group came upon a colony of *Thuja koraiensis* (91545), notable for its dark green leaves with conspicuous silver-white bands underneath. Despite extensive searching on the sprawling plants, no seeds were found,

and so stem cuttings were collected instead. In contrast, *Pinus densiflora* (90781) growing at the same elevation provided an ample crop of seeds.

Mount Sobaek

On 4 October the team traveled southwest from Mount Taebaek to the town of Tanyang, some 70 km away. They intended to explore Mount Sobaek, 1421 m, the southernmost peak of the expedition. On the way the group stopped at several locations identified during the spring reconnaissance trip as good plant-hunting sites. "Earlier in the spring we had identified sites of *Syringa velutina* and *Syringa reticulata* var. *mandschurica*," remembers Meyer. "We were able to relocate these but seed was sparse. In the course of looking for the lilacs at a site 2 km south of Tongjom railroad station, we spotted a number

Meyer reaching out for the seed capsules of *Stewartia koreana* (90790) growing in the valley of Huibangsa on the lower slopes of Mount Sobaek. Photo by Paul W. Meyer.

Valleys on the eastern slopes of Mount Sorak were home to many trees of *Acer triflorum*, one of the expedition's target species. Photo by Paul W. Meyer.

bers Meyer. "It grows commonly over the steep limestone slopes near Tanyang. We found many plants, most of which were under 1 m tall (91536–8). The hills they grew on were relatively devoid of other woody vegetation. Scattered here and there were *Juniperus rigida, Quercus dentata,* and naturalized *Robinia pseudoacacia.*"

Mount Sorak

The expedition's next destination was Mount Sorak, located in the northeastern corner of the country. "On 11 October we collected in relatively low elevations along a trail

of small plants of summer-blooming *Rhododendron micranthum* (90783). Large colonies were growing in thin soil atop rocky escarpment and near vertical rock faces in very exposed situations, in virtually full sun. This led me to believe that they would be heat and drought tolerant and hardy much farther to the north of Philadelphia."

The next morning the group headed for Mount Sobaek. "The main collection we wanted to make there was *Stewartia koreana,*" explains Meyer. "The trees were plentiful in the valley of Huibangsa on the lower elevations of Mount Sobaek. We were finding many capsules but unfortunately most had only sterile seeds and only a few well developed seeds were recovered (90790). The trees we saw were growing in a protected valley, in the moist area along a stream as well as in pockets of seemingly fertile, organic soil along the base of rocky ledges. They were just beginning to show tints of red and yellow fall color." Thomas adds, "The sight of these tall trees with stunningly attractive bark was one the explorers would never forget."

On 6 October, after a morning of drying herbarium specimens and processing seeds, the team explored an area northwest of Tanyang. "We hiked for several kilometers in search of *Buxus microphylla* var. *koreana,*" remem-

leading from the village Sorak to the main peak of Mount Sorak," recalls Meyer. "The principal target species in this area was *Acer triflorum*. It was plentiful in the lower valleys on the eastern slopes of Mount Sorak but we did not find any seed at all. We were more successful in collecting seeds of *Sapium japonicum* (90784). We were surprised to find *Sapium* there to be tree-like, unlike those seen elsewhere, which were shrubby. A tree-form *Sapium* would potentially be more useful in the American gardens. Some trees were still green with no signs of fall color; others had taken on shades of brilliant red and orange. This species grows primarily in the lower parts of the valley although it is high enough to be above the flood plain of the streams."

During the next two days, collecting efforts were somewhat impaired by rain, but on 14 October the explorers woke to a beautiful blue sky. "We took the trail that started above the village of Osaek, at about 1000 m, and led to the summit of Mount Sorak," recalls Meyer. "As we ascended the mountain, we could look out and see clouds which had settled into the nearby valleys. Occasionally, the sea of clouds was pierced by neighboring mountains giving the effect of islands. Once we got into higher elevations the deciduous plants had already

While ascending to the top of Mount Sorak, the explorers traversed a forest of *Quercus mongolica*. Photo by Paul W. Meyer.

Bristol collects seeds of *Rhododendron brachycarpum* from plants growing just below the summit of Mount Songin on Ullung Island. Photo by Paul W. Meyer.

dropped their foliage. The most prominent tree along the trail was *Quercus mongolica,* but *Abies nephrolepis* and *Pinus koraiensis* were also common. On a ridge at about 1400 m we found also *Thuja koraiensis* (91548) and *Betula costata* (90765). The latter one was exceedingly variable and possibly some of the plants had resulted from hybridization with another species."

Mount Songin

The expedition's last excursion took them on 18 October to the island of Ullung, visited by Corbett and Lighty in 1966. The team took a ferry from Pohang to the port town of Todong on the east side of the island. The following morning they began hunting for plants in the hills above Todong. Their exploration of a ridge about 100 m above sea level resulted in a number of collections, including *Aphananthe aspera* (90763), *Campanula takesimana* (91539), and *Neolitsea sericea* (90780).

The next day the explorers crossed the island going through a forest of *Pinus parviflora* (91544) and *Tsuga sieboldii.* "Though we collected some seedlings of both species we were disappointed that no seeds were found," recalls Meyer. "Both trees were loaded with cones but they had already shed all their seeds. The pine and hemlock grew together and the ecological association was reminiscent of the white pine and hemlock forest of Pennsylvania."

On 20 October the expedition's destination was Mount Songin. At 984 m, it was the highest peak on the island, though the lowest of the seven mountains explored on this expedition. "In the morning we were able to catch a truck ride up to the foot of the mountain,"

remembers Meyer. "This saved us a couple of hours and allowed more time for collecting. The forest canopy consisted there of *Acer okamotoanum, Fagus multinervis* (91533), *Sorbus commixta,* and *Styrax obassia.* Most of the trees were multiple-stemmed and we speculated that they had been coppiced many years ago. From the ground layer we collected *Smilacina dahurica,* which had bright red fruits in terminal spikes, and *Disporum viridescens* (91541) with steel blue fruits. We reached the top of Mount Songin by mid-afternoon and found there large colonies of *Rhododendron brachycarpum* heavy with seed. Interestingly, none of the trees growing on the peak had any viable seeds. Rhododendrons were confined to the area just below the summit on the northern slopes. Some of them were completely exposed to full sun and wind."

Two days later the group returned by ferry to Pohang and continued their journey back to Seoul. On 28 October the expedition came to an end, and the explorers departed for the United States carrying with them 230 collections representing some of the best plants the seven mountains had to offer for contemporary gardens.

"We were totally enchanted with the Korean peninsula," reminisces Thomas. "The memories of warm, friendly, smiling people, rich Korean culture, and beautiful mountainsides clothed in brilliant reds, oranges, and yellows, would not be forgotten." Meyer, recognizing that this expedition only barely began to uncover the botanical treasures of this part of Korea, adds that "because of its floristic diversity and harsh continental climate, this region continues to offer much untapped potential for plant exploration."

CHINA

TAIWAN "OFF-LIMITS"

When contemplating a destination for the eleventh joint USDA-Longwood plant-collecting expedition, Dr. John L. Creech, chief of the USDA New Crops Research Branch, suggested Taiwan. "This island with its rich subtropical and temperate floras was considered by Ernest H. Wilson as especially important," he wrote to Dr. Russell J. Seibert, Longwood's director. "To my knowledge, no one has collected there since his time [1918]. Yet some of our most important azaleas including those used in the Glenn Dale hybrids and our forcing types come from Formosa [Taiwan]. Most of these collections do not exist any longer, yet we certainly need them to combine with the northern types I brought back from Japan. In all, there are forty species of *Rhododendron* on Formosa, eleven nominal *Camellia* species, plus a tremendous array of broadleaved evergreen trees and shrubs" (Creech 1966a).

Seibert agreed and saw one other reason for exploring Taiwan: "This area skirts the China mainland from where it has not been possible for this country [the United States] to obtain ornamental plant materials for many years. Many of the species from this island are co-specific or similar to those on the adjoining mainland. Taiwan is currently relatively easy to penetrate since the high mountains have radar installations accessible by road. Accessibility, however, is limited to official personnel mutually cleared by the United States and Taiwan govern-

ments. It is therefore important that this area be explored for potential ornamental plants at this time" (R. J. Seibert 1967d).

Retracing Wilson's steps

Preparations for the expedition to Taiwan began in early 1967. Creech planned to retrace Wilson's steps, both as to time and place. In addition, he wanted to visit areas not explored previously from a botanical aspect, but which recently became easily accessible thanks to a newly opened highway cutting across Taiwan from east to west.

"Taiwan bristles with mountains that run from north to south separating the island into a flat, fertile plain on the western side and a rugged, scarcely populated eastern region," explained Creech (1967c). "This particular exploration was restricted to the temperate zone vegetation which begins at 1800 m and ends with alpine elements on top of Mount Morrison, or Yushan, at 3997 m. This is the highest peak of all eastern Asia. Included in the array of genera to be found in these mountains are rhododendrons, camellias, hollies, and conifers which will be useful as breeding materials or for direct introduction into the nursery trade."

Creech arrived in Taipei on 8 November 1967. He was met there by the staff of the Botany Department of the National Taiwan University. Two botanists from the university, Dr. Hsu Chienchang and Dr. Huang Tsengchieng, and a professional plant collector, Kao Muhtsuen, accompanied Creech during his travels in Taiwan.

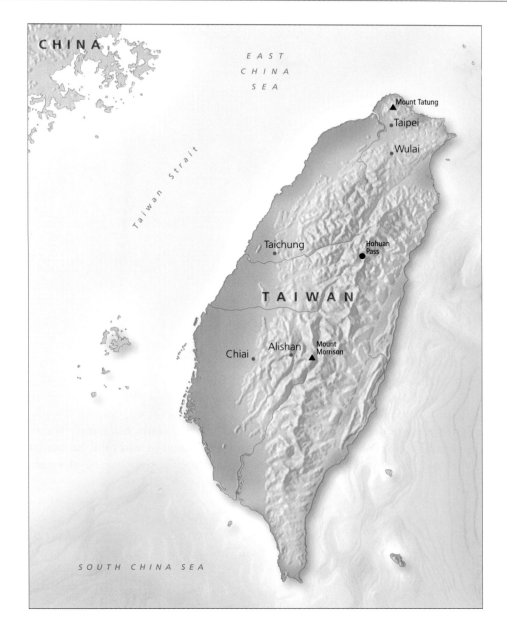

Taiwan, an island off the southeast coast of China, is about 450 km long, 140 km wide at its maximum breadth, and has an area exceeding 35,000 km². The mountain ranges, which dominate Taiwan's landscape, run north to south for nearly the whole length of the island. There are forty-eight peaks more than 3000 m in elevation, with Mount Morrison being the highest at 3997 m. Taiwan lies astride the Tropic of Cancer, and its climate is moderated by the warm Japan Current, resulting in long warm summers and mild winters. The amount of precipitation varies from 1200 mm on the west coast to more than 6500 mm on the mountain slopes facing the southeastern sea, most of it coming in the summer. The mild climate and abundant rainfall result in luxuriant vegetation. There are nearly four thousand species of flowering plants and ferns, about 40 percent of which are endemic. Tropical and subtropical plants, including many bamboos and palms, grow below 500 m. The most luxuriant, warm-temperate, mixed forests of conifers and broad-leaved trees are found below 1800 m. The cool-temperate, coniferous forest with many broad-leaved evergreen species in the understory occupies areas between 1800 and 2500 m. Above 2500 m, pure stands of conifers become prominent. Above the timberline at 3500 m, the vegetation transitions from a dense scrub of mostly junipers, rhododendrons, and barberries to the alpine tundra found on the highest peaks at about 3800 m.

North of Taipei on Mount Tatung, Creech collected *Rhododendron oldhamii,* an azalea species that blooms year-round. It was later used in the development of fall-flowering hybrid azaleas. Photo by John L. Creech.

Creech's party traveled from Alishan to Tungpu by a small logging train. Photo by John L. Creech.

Four days later Creech and his team went on the first excursion to Tatung, a 1080 m high volcanic peak just north Taipei. "It was a good exercise," remembers Creech, "because in the sulfur outcroppings on the mountain we encountered many azaleas and ericaceous plants, including *Rhododendron oldhamii* and *Lyonia ovalifolia* (69219)."

Atop eastern Asia

Creech's major collecting was to take place on Mount Morrison. On 15 November he started from Chiai by a small diesel train to Alishan, a logging village and mountain resort at the base of Mount Morrison. "The trip took about four hours over a frightfully narrow track," remembers Creech. "There are over seventy bridges and more than forty tunnels as black as pitch and just large enough for the train. Up to 1200 m, the vegetation was subtropical. Shortly conifers appeared, *Cunninghamia lanceolata* and *Cryptomeria japonica,* and with them came fog. But around 2000 m we broke into sunshine and the peaks were bathed to a golden brown. The sky was streaked with gold and the fog settled below like a soft blanket."

Typhoon Gilda held Creech's party in Alishan for a couple of days, but eventually they were able to take a logging train up Mount Morrison. "Few visitors traveled beyond Alishan, and I soon learned why," wrote Creech (1987). "The logging train, a series of flatcars and a small caboose, departed Alishan early on November 18. My next stop was Tungpu, a logging terminal about two hours away. I chose to ride one of the flatcars rather than

the caboose, which was staffed with people, baggage, chickens, hunks of pork and every logging equipment to the point where something of every category stuck out the windows. Arriving at Tungpu, at an elevation of around 2600 m, I soon realized that there was no Hilton here—just a series of unpainted huts with no electricity or outside communications. The accommodations were primitive and the food suspicious. But the locals were exceedingly friendly and concerned for my welfare. Unfortunately, typhoon Gilda arrived with me. . . . The rain and wind dissipated shortly, and I was able to spend the day collecting among some magnificent colonies of *Pieris taiwanensis* [70598–9]. The color of the young growth was so intense that it painted the hillsides bright orange." Alishan is part of a plateau-like range with peaks varying from 1000 to 2800 m, situated to the west of Mount Morrison. While exploring the slopes of Alishan, Creech collected, at about 2300 m, *Chamaecyparis obtusa* var. *formosana* (691179) and two rhododendrons, *Rhododendron morii* (70580) and *R. kawakamii* (70579).

Creech, accompanied by two Taiwanese collectors and two porter-guides, left Tungpu early on 19 November: "Like all trails at high elevations, our footpath led through forested areas to the outer rock ledge, where it became extremely dangerous. In several places, the route crossed narrow ledges—with the sheer mountainside above and drops of several hundred feet below. And there were no handholds" (Creech 1987).

"At one point I was sufficiently scared by the trail that I wanted to turn back," admitted Creech (1967a), "but

Creech collected seeds of *Tsuga chinensis* var. *formosana* near Tungpu at 2600 m, where it was the dominant coniferous tree. Photo by John L. Creech.

Creech's party on a trail from Tungpu to the summit of Mount Morrison. Photo by John L. Creech.

Kao Muhtsuen, a member of Creech's team, collects seeds of *Juniperus squamata* below the summit of Mount Morrison. Photo by John L. Creech.

my guide helped me along some 20 feet [6 m] of a 1-foot [30 cm] ledge at 11,000 feet [3350 m] with the pole pruner. When I got on the other side I was shaking because I knew I had to retrace that point. And these guys do it all the time!"

For his effort Creech was rewarded with superb collecting and excellent seed crop along the trail: "A handsome prostrate evergreen species, *Cotoneaster morrisonensis* [681238] lay in broad sheets over the face of the rocks. We saw *Rhododendron oldhamii,* usually with large, bright red flowers above densely hairy stems, and once a shrubby *Euonymus* [*E. pallidifolius* 681240] with such pink fruits and bright red arils that it looked like a flowering quince at a distance. The handsome *Lilium philippinense* [69215] was everywhere along the trail, both in flower and with seed capsules" (Creech 1987).

By late afternoon Creech's team reached a small hut below the summit at a place called Taipingshan. "The imperfect weather had cleared earlier in the day, so we had a clear view of the massif above us," remembered Creech (1987). "It was a mixture of the greens of rhododendrons and junipers with bright red barberry foliage in a broad band, while above us was a pale mass of loose shale. I spent the rest of the day collecting from individual rhododendrons while Kao and a porter picked juniper berries and barberry fruits. The rhododendron, *R. pseudochrysanthum* [71247–53], occurs only above 3000 m and is almost prostrate near the mountain's peak, with shiny ovate leaves that are heavily matted beneath. The plants grow in large colonies in open, rocky, windswept situations and are said to be a grand sight when they bloom in April and May."

Mixed forest of *Tsuga chinensis* var. *formosana* and *Juniperus squamata* below the summit of Mount Morrison. Photo by John L. Creech.

A view west towards China from the top of Mount Morrison. Photo by John L. Creech.

Creech at the summit of Mount Morrison. Photo by John L. Creech.

The next morning the group rose early and were on their way to the top by 7:30 a.m. "As we ascended we continued our collecting until we passed the stands of juniper and barberry," wrote Creech (1987). "Now the path provided only narrow footing, causing us to wander back and forth just for purchase. We reached a place called the 'wind-hole,' a gully that fell for over a thousand feet [300 m]. 'Danger' said a red sign in Chinese—for strong winds have been known to sweep climbers to their death at this point. We passed across the gully several times and finally scrambled up to the top of Mount Morrison. There we stood surveying the distant valleys and looking toward the mainland of China. . . . Although it was early afternoon, and the sun was bright and warm, long cloud fingers were beginning to stretch up from the valleys below. We knew it was time to descend. The

downward trip was more sliding and faster than going up. Soon we were at the hut, where steaming bowls of rice flavored with sugar and dried daylily flowers were passed around. The next morning, November 21, we retraced our path downward, much more aware of the dangerous footing. We reached the logging road in about six hours. Exhilarated by the successes of the climb, we spent the night in Tungpu. We returned to Alishan on the morning of the 22nd by logging train. This time we rode in the caboose, which was now hooked onto a chain of flatcars each bearing three gigantic logs that appeared rather loosely tied."

After this exhausting ascent to Mount Morrison, Creech confessed in a letter to Seibert, "At first I intended to collect at the lower elevations, 6000–8000 feet [1850–2450 m], but by the time I had gotten there, I had risked my neck enough on the trails that I finally climbed to the summit, 3997 m, and collected a fine lot of material, some much desired rhododendrons and a large quantity of seed of *Juniperus squamata,* from the summit of the mountain. I believe I am the first American collector to ascend Mount Morrison since Ernest Wilson in 1918. After making the climb myself, I marvel at what he did under certainly lesser conditions. But I am sure the trail is no different for if it were worse, he probably would not have made it" (Creech 1967b).

Back in Taipei, Creech undertook short day-trips to the mountains south of Taipei, where mostly subtropical species may be found. "On 28 November, we had a short trip to the village of Wulai," he recalls. "This is a hilly area through which the Hokusei River winds. The road ends at Wulai and from there we used local transportation. This consisted of 75 cm single rail track and a flat car pushed by a driver who kneeled as one might do in a child's wagon. The passengers sat on small boxes and away we went, first at foot speed, later at a moderate clip, according to the grade. We stopped from time to time to collect but were always on the lookout for cars coming in the opposite direction. In such instances, we jumped off, and the driver merely flips the cart off the track to a 'lay-by' as the other car passes." Collecting near Wulai at an elevation of about 300 to 400 m, Creech found pink-flowered *Lagerstroemia subcostata* (69213), *Lasianthus chinensis* (691183), and *Rhododendron kanehiraei* (70578).

Creech, center, and his party at a stop along the East-West Highway. Photo by John L. Creech.

Kao reaches out for the fruit-laden branches of a holly growing near Hohuan Pass. Photo by John L. Creech.

Following the East-West Highway

The second part of Creech's trip was by jeep over a newly opened East-West Highway. This road, completed only two years earlier, opened up rugged territory previously untapped by plant collectors. On 1 December, Creech and his party left Taipei to undertake a collecting trip to Hohuan Pass, 3178 m, along the East-West Highway.

"Unfortunately, the direct route to Lishan near Hohuan Pass had been washed out and we had to follow a secondary road," recalls Creech. "It was a one way track and as we ascended, the fog closed in and by 6 p.m. it was so thick that the driver was afraid to go on so we stopped at a small forestry station for the night. The next morning, the weather had cleared and found us on the road again where we passed through some fine evergreen forests around 1700 to 2300 m. The road was simply cut into the steep slope and there was no way to go up or down but along the roadside there were ample opportunities to collect and we paused to walk to take advantage of this."

After a night at another forestry station, they woke to find snow on the ground, with more falling. "We drove over the pass and stopped in the shelter of a ledge from where we climbed on foot," remembers Creech. "But the wind was so fierce we could only make a few collections of rhododendrons and junipers and drive down to lower elevations."

From Hohuan Pass, Creech's team drove to Lishan, a popular mountain resort. While driving through lush forests covering mountain slopes above 2000 m, Creech made several stops. Azaleas, rhododendrons, camellias, evergreen oaks, and conifers flourished along the route, and Creech collected a number of plants, including

Creech collects seedlings of *Taiwania cryptomerioides* (69231) at the National Forestry Bureau's Experimental Forest at Chito near Taichung. Photo by John L. Creech.

Camellia nokoensis (71327), *Gordonia axillaris* (69198), and *Hydrangea integrifolia* (70591), a rare evergreen vine climbing on oaks.

"By early afternoon we were hungry and returned to the forestry station at Hohuan Pass," recalls Creech. "Again the fog moved in and it snowed with a bitter wind. We searched the rocky ravines near the station for rhododendrons despite ice forming on the plants. After a fine day of collecting we returned to the station and an evening by the fireside was especially pleasant even though the thermometer seemed stuck at 10°C."

The following morning the team started back to Taichung by a new road. "It was interesting to see the alpine bamboo—solid brown, except where conifers stood gnarled and twisted covered with moss and lichens," notes Creech. "In shale ravines and meadows,

the rhododendrons stood out bright green. On rocky walls, *Cotoneaster morrisonensis* hung like strands of red beads and junipers almost dripped off the ledges, their branches were so pendulous. It was a harsh landscape and no place for agriculture." The route took Creech's team to Sun Moon Lake, where they visited a small forestry station. At the station they acquired a number of woody plants, including *Castanopsis carlesii* (69193) and *Keteleeria davidiana* (69212). Near the lake Creech collected broad-leaved evergreen shrubs such as *Daphniphyllum pentandrum* var. *oldhamii* (70761), *Rhododendron lasiostylum* (73554), and *Tutcheria shinkoensis* (71336).

Unhappy collector

Creech returned from his Hohuan trip on 6 December and spent the following two days working in the herbarium of the National Taiwan University. Then, on 9 and 10 December, he visited the National Forestry Bureau's Experimental Forest at Chito near Taichung. "Here, the rare *Taiwania cryptomerioides* [69231] is still grown in a natural state," wrote Creech (1967c). "A nursery planting will replenish this conifer and here I obtained both seed and seedlings to introduce into the United States." This handsome evergreen with drooping branches is related to cypress, *Cupressus,* and is becoming rare as a wild tree in Taiwan.

A few days later the course of this expedition was abruptly altered. On 15 December, Creech was standing on a plaza at National Taiwan University about to enter a taxi. "Suddenly, I heard a terrific roar," he recalled. "I was thrown up in the air and landed in total dismay with the same roaring in my face. A student on a motorcycle had been speeding across the plaza and had somehow lost control. As he passed me from the rear he caught my leg with the motorcycle's footrest. I staggered to my feet, dazed but still conscious enough to know that I did not want to go to any hospital but an American one. So I collapsed into the taxi and shouted, 'American Embassy!'" (Creech 1987).

Creech was taken to an emergency room of an American military hospital, where he was treated. "Fortunately, there were no broken bones," he wrote to Seibert, "but sufficient muscle damage to my right leg and tail that the Navy doctor decided I was finished as far as field work was concerned" (Creech 1968).

Thus Creech spent the next two days packing his collections and departed Taipei on 18 December: "So ended the Taiwan collecting, several weeks before my scheduled return. Fortunately there was no permanent damage—but it surely was an unhappy collector who struggled onto a plane for the long flight home" (Creech 1987).

Creech returned home with about 150 collections. "In general, collecting in Taiwan presents no difficulties provided one has official assistance," he concluded (1967c). "All mountain areas are 'off-limits' and require special passes for entry, both by locals and foreigners. . . . Native stands of plants are fast disappearing and as roads are developed, the forests are heavily cut and replaced by introduced species. There are, however, some regions such as at Mount Morrison which are so steep that they are still untouched."

STEPPING ONTO THE MAINLAND

Ever since the United States lifted the ban on travel to China in 1972 and the relations between the two countries began to normalize, horticulturists and botanists alike made plans for exploration of China's floristic resources. In 1974 the National Academy of Sciences sent the first Plant Studies Delegation to China. Creech, who was among the delegates, recalls: "One goal of the delegation was to discuss ways for exchange of germplasm and to undertake collection of important plants. The delegation brought seed samples including seed from the U.S. National Arboretum and Longwood Gardens, and received seed collections from the People's Republic of China in return."

Official delegation exchanges in the 1970s paved the way in 1980 for the first joint plant-collecting expedition to China sponsored by the Botanical Society of America and the Chinese Academy of Sciences. With new opportunities arising in China, a number of institutions with an interest in plant exploration and botanical exchanges formed in 1991 the North American–China Plant Exploration Consortium (NACPEC). Longwood Gardens joined this consortium the following year. NACPEC's main goal was to facilitate cooperation between the botanical gardens and arboreta in North America and similar institutions in China in the area of plant exploration. NACPEC member institutions included, in addition to Longwood Gardens, Arnold Arboretum of Harvard University in Jamaica Plain, Massachusetts; Holden Arboretum in Kirtland, Ohio; Morris Arboretum

Left to right, with their Chinese hosts, are Meyer, Thomas, Del Tredici, and Conrad, assembled in Nanjing, Jiangsu Province, on 6 September 1994. Photo by Paul W. Meyer.

of the University of Pennsylvania in Philadelphia; Morton Arboretum in Lisle, Illinois; the U.S. National Arboretum in Washington; the University of British Columbia Botanical Garden in Vancouver; and the USDA Woody Landscape Plants Germplasm Repository in Glenn Dale, Maryland.

Hubei's Taoist epicenter

In 1994, R. William Thomas, Longwood's education division manager, joined NACPEC's plant-collecting expedition to the Wudang Mountains in northern Hubei Province. Alongside Thomas, the team was made up of Kevin P. Conrad, curator of the herbarium at the U.S. National Arboretum, Paul W. Meyer, director of the Morris Arboretum, and Dr. Peter Del Tredici, director of living collections at the Arnold Arboretum.

The team assembled on 6 September in Nanjing, the capital of Jiangsu Province on the banks of the Yangtze. They were greeted by Professor He Shanan, director of the Nanjing Botanical Garden, who helped organize the expedition. Two botanists from the garden, Mao Cailiang and Hao Riming, were assigned to accompany the explorers to Wudang Mountains in Hubei Province, located some 700 km west of Nanjing.

Five days later the team reached the village of Guan Shan in the foothills of the Wudang Mountains. "We arrived at Guan Shan around midday and were immediately met by the local officials," recalls Meyer. "Our group was received very cordially and the officials promised to do everything they could to facilitate our visit. We

China (left), with an area of more than 9.5 million km², is the largest country in east Asia. Mountains—among them the world's highest, Mount Everest, 8848 m—make up about a third of China's territory. Highlands with elevations above 4500 m occupy an additional fifth of the land area. These two prominent features of China's topography, along with the proximity of Siberia to the north and the Pacific to the east, directly affect its climate and vegetation. The mean annual temperature decreases from about 20°C in the south to below 0°C in the north. The rainfall generally decreases from the southeast to the northwest. While the annual rainfall may exceed 2000 mm along the southeast coast, in desert areas of the northwest it is less than 10 mm. Most of the rain falls during the summer months. China can be divided into two major floristic regions: the dry northwestern areas belong to the Irano-Turanian region, the humid southeastern areas to the Eastern Asiatic region. In addition, the most southerly parts of the mainland and the islands of the South China Sea support tropical vegetation. With the exception of tundra, all types of the Northern Hemisphere's vegetation types can be found in China. The number of species of seed plants in China is estimated at about thirty thousand. Lack of extensive topographic barriers between tropical, temperate, and cold regions has led to a great variety and intermixture of tropical and temperate plants in China. The tropical forests of southern China bear close affinity to those of other regions of southeastern Asia, whereas the vegetation of northwestern China resembles that of Kazakhstan, Mongolia, and Russia.

were told we were the first Westerners to ever visit this village."

Stretching across 400 km, the Wudang Mountains boast seventy-two jagged peaks, of which Tianzhu Feng, at 1612 m, is the highest. These mountains were chosen as the target for the expedition because of their exceptionally diverse flora, considered among the richest in China, portions of which still remain in a relatively undisturbed state. The Wudang Mountains were an important Taoist center during the Ming Dynasty (1368–1644), dozens of temples, shrines, and pavilions erected on their slopes.

"Remnants of ancient forest in China are typically found only in the vicinity of Buddhist or Taoist temples," explains Del Tredici, "hence the relatively good condition of the forests of the Wudang Mountains. At lower elevations, below about 600 m, the forests have either been replaced by field crops or are being intensely managed for fuel wood production through coppicing. The relatively undisturbed forest still exists above 900 m on slopes punctuated by inaccessible peaks, steep cliff faces, and boulder-strewn valleys."

This is just one of many temples erected on the slopes of Tianzhu Feng, a reflection of this mountain's significance as a Taoist religious center. Photo by Paul W. Meyer.

On 12 September, the first day of collecting, the explorers woke up to blaring loudspeakers. "To our dismay, the speakers, located just outside our bedroom window, broadcasted political messages throughout the village," explains Meyer. "After a bountiful breakfast, we boarded a van and proceeded to the trailhead. It had rained the night before and the dirt roads that were cut into the mountainside were dangerously slippery. The driver soon informed us that he could not risk going any further and that we would have to walk to the trailhead. This added another 6 km to the day's journey. All the vegetation on the roadside was heavily disturbed. Only a few wild plants grew on the cliffs and small areas between the fields. As we ascended the mountain, we entered a secondary growth forest dominated by *Quercus variabilis*

(95480). A particularly interesting collection of that day was *Catalpa bungei*. It was growing in the middle of a steep, terraced hillside of soybeans and corn." Del Tredici considers this "the most beautiful of all *Catalpa* species."

Botanical pilgrimage

On 14 September the team relocated to Wudang Shan at the foot of Tianzhu Feng. After a day of working on herbarium specimens, they pushed toward the mountains despite steady rain. The paved road took them up Tianzhu Feng to about 900 m, from where they continued on the trail leading to Nanyan Palace, dating from the Tang Dynasty (618–907), and to a group of temples built directly into the cliff face. "As we looked down from the temples into the valley below, we could see nothing but the gray fog," remembers Meyer. "The swirling mist which blew into the temple through the window grates gave it a mystical atmosphere." For two days the explorers botanized on the coppiced slopes of Tianzhu Feng between 600 and 900 m, where they found many shrubs, including *Deutzia grandiflora* (98334), *Rhododendron mariesii* (98347), and *Wikstroemia pampaninii* (9626).

On 18 September they set out early in the morning for a hike up the slopes of Tianzhu Feng to about 1400 m. A steep stone path led to the summit, crowned by a Taoist temple. While the vegetation in the immediate vicinity of the stone path was impacted by thousands of pilgrims, a well-preserved forest was accessible through a network of less-traveled secondary trails.

"Once we left the main trail, we began to see for the first time the mature forest that we had come to Hubei for," recalls Meyer. "Soon we came upon *Euptelea pleiosperma* (95558), a small tree with smooth gray bark and a heavy load of winged fruits, and *Acer davidii* (95562), a striped-bark maple growing on a rocky ledge. Further up the ravine we found a colony of a low-growing *Hydrangea aspera* (98339). On the other side of the ravine, I spotted a tree that appeared to have white flowers. We worked our way across to the plant and discovered that we were seeing persistent bracts of *Emmenopterys henryi* (98335)."

The following day the team chose an easier paved path and a series of stone stairs used by the pilgrims that took them all the way to the summit of Tianzhu Feng. This is where the temple stood, topped with its golden roof. On the way down the explorers followed a less-trav-

eled, muddy, treacherous path on the north side of the mountain. This allowed them access to relatively undisturbed forest where they made many collections, including *Acanthopanax henryi* (961037), *Staphylea bumalda* (95559), and *Viburnum erosum* (96384).

Heavenly forest

On 20 September the explorers hiked on the east face of Tianzhu Feng. "The weather was alternately foggy and rainy creating a mysterious mood in the forest," remembers Del Tredici. "Shortly after leaving the main trail leading to the summit, we entered a forest dominated by large specimens *Pinus tabulaeformis* and *Quercus aliena*. Our local guide, Zeng, a collector of medicinal plants, pointed out two specimens of *Stewartia sinensis* with beautiful, smooth cinnamon-red bark, a wonder to behold and touch. Growing nearby were several *Cornus kousa* and a small specimen of *Acer griseum*. The Americans in the group could hardly contain their excitement, as though they had died and gone to horticultural heaven. The only thing missing, sadly, was seed on any of the plants, probably due to the previous summer's drought. The understory of this exquisite forest consisted of the beautiful evergreen holly, *Ilex pernyi*; the ubiquitous Chinese spicebush, *Lindera glauca*; and *Lyonia ovalifolia* var. *elliptica* (98343). The forest floor was carpeted with a bewildering array of ferns and herbaceous perennials, including species of *Aconitum*, *Cimicifuga*, and *Ligularia*, all in flower. Jack-in-the-pulpits, *Arisaema*, were everywhere, their stalks heavy with seed, along with species of *Epimedium* and *Rodgersia aesculifolia* (95490)."

About noontime, the group found a small cave at the base of a cliff, where they took shelter from the cold rain and warmed up by the fire. In the afternoon, collecting continued. Growing on a cliff face was an ancient specimen of *Zelkova sinica* consisting of five massive trunks covered with bright orange, exfoliating bark that stood out of the thick mist.

"A little way beyond the *Zelkova*, we found *Hamamelis mollis* (95560), loaded with unopened seed capsules," recalls Del Tredici. "We were particularly pleased to collect this winter-blooming species, which had recently been gaining popularity. After seeing so many plants without seed, it was a treat to find one in fruit, and we greedily collected every seed capsule we could find."

In the lower-elevation areas of the Wudang mountains, the forests have been replaced by field crops or are intensely coppiced for fuel wood. Photo by Paul W. Meyer.

Del Tredici crosses a creek on the west side of the town of Yan Chi He. Photo by Paul W. Meyer.

Meyer, Mao, Del Tredici, and Hao, left to right, head to the mountains around the town of Yan Chi He. Photo by R. William Thomas.

Small but very sweet nuts of *Castanea henryi* (95485) collected from a moist ravine north of the town of Yan Chi He. Photo by Paul W. Meyer.

Good fortune

The following day the group came down from the mountain to Wudang Shan, spent a day organizing their collections, and on 23 September headed off southeast toward the town of Yan Chi He. During the next three days they explored the mountains around the town. In the hills west of Yan Chi He, at an elevation of 750 m, they collected *Callicarpa japonica* (98332), *Philadelphus pekinensis* (97360), and several rhododendrons. In a moist ravine north of the town they found *Kolkwitzia amabilis* (98341), while a hike along a creek on the west side of Yan Chi He resulted in collections of *Camellia oleifera* (96856) and *Pistacia chinensis* (95568), both oil-bearing plants, and *Castanea henryi* (95485), said to have small but very sweet nuts.

From Yan Chi He, the expedition traveled to the town of Lang He. For the next two days the team collected on the hillsides surrounding the nearby village of Bai Yang Ping. "Although the hillsides closest to the village had been recently coppiced, we still found a number of interesting species," remembers Meyer. "Among the species collected the first day were *Fortunearia sinensis* (95576), *Hovenia acerba* (96569), and *Mallotus apelta* (98344). The second day we entered a deep gorge with mature trees. The further we went up the gorge, the larger the trees we saw. The path we followed worked its way up the narrow gorge, often crossing over moss covered and slippery rocks. At times the path disappeared altogether and we waded up the stream. The superb and exotic scenery compensated for the treacher-

Thanks to its orange exfoliating bark, *Zelkova sinica* stood out in the thick mist of the forest on the slopes of Tianzhu Feng. Photo by Paul W. Meyer.

This 20 m tall *Emmenopterys henryi* (96568) was found in an isolated valley on the northwestern side of Tianzhu Feng. Zeng climbed it barefoot to collect seeds. Photo by Paul W. Meyer.

ous hiking. *Pterostyrax psilophylla* (96570), growing among the rocks on the stream edge, was the most exciting find of the day. We had only spotted one tree of this species on the whole trip and fortunately it had fertile seeds. Also growing along the stream edge was *Pterocarya hupehensis* (95564). We tried to collect seed of this tree before but found nothing but sterile seeds. This time we were lucky to find a small number of viable seeds."

Return to the holy mountain

On 30 September the expedition departed Lang He to return to Tianzhu Feng. "We felt that the last few days of the trip could be best spent in rich areas that we had seen previously, but had relatively little time to collect," explains Meyer. Arriving at Wudang Shan in midmorn-

ing, they set off to the area where they had seen *Acer griseum* a few days earlier.

"At about 900 m on a steep northwest-facing slope, we found two large specimens of *Acer griseum* (95570), covered with seed," remembers Del Tredici. "Throughout this area of mature forest, we saw numerous saplings and seedlings of this species growing in dense shade on very steep, well-drained terrain. *Acer griseum* appeared to be clearly able to persist under conditions of deep shade, periodic drought, and intense root competition. When a gap in the forest canopy develops, this maple is perfectly positioned to expand into the newly available space. Our excitement at finding *Acer griseum* was exceeded only when we noticed two other trees with bright orange bark farther up the slope. More *Stewartia sinensis,* we thought at first, but on closer examination we discovered them to be specimens of *Zelkova sinica.* Its orange bark exfoliating in discrete plates like pieces of a jigsaw puzzle, was every bit as spectacular as that of *Acer griseum.*"

The next day the group headed up another isolated valley facing northwest on Tianzhu Feng. "Climbing a steep, moist ravine, almost immediately we were in the midst of numerous herbaceous plants, many in full flower," says Del Tredici. "Further up the slope, at about 1200 m in elevation, we came upon a particularly exciting find—a giant specimen of *Emmenopterys henryi* (96568), some 20 m tall. Its persistent bracts subtending flower clusters were taking on a rose-to-tan color as the small fruits ripened. Our local guide, Zeng, showed no hesitation about climbing the tree barefoot in order to collect some seed. For the Americans, it was a thrill to find this species considered by some, one of the most strikingly beautiful trees of the Chinese forests."

Upon completing their work on Tianzhu Feng, the explorers headed back to Lang He, and on 4 October the team began their week-long trip back to the United States. The expedition returned home with 192 lots of seed, cuttings, and small plants. Del Tredici characterizes their collections: "We have succeeded in bringing in new germplasm of species already in cultivation in North America but represented by only one or two prior collections that may or may not include the hardiest ecotype available. We also made a contribution to the *ex situ* conservation of several rare Chinese plants, such as *Emmenopterys henryi,* that were threatened by extinction due to widespread habitat destruction. And, finally, we introduced into cultivation several species that had never been grown in the United States. We were all struck by how little natural vegetation remained in Hubei. Even in remote mountain areas, agriculture has encroached on all but the steepest mountainsides. It is only in the most remote mountain valleys that the remnants of the diverse flora of Hubei can be found. It was clear that the natural flora is on the edge of being eradicated. Collections from this trip will contribute to the preservation of the biodiversity of the Wudang Mountains."

TAPPING THE QINLING MOUNTAINS

The next expedition to China, organized under the auspices of NACPEC, took place in 1996. Conrad and Rick

J. Lewandowski, curator and director of horticulture at the Morris Arboretum, jointly led the team, which included Dr. James R. Ault, representing Longwood Gardens, and Kunso Kim, curator of the Norfolk Botanical Garden in Norfolk, Virginia. The Qinling Mountains of Shaanxi and Gansu provinces were chosen as the area to be explored. "Our objectives were to collect, protect, and preserve plant materials from an area previously ignored by plant collectors," wrote Kim (1997). "Attracted by the rich and diverse Chinese flora, botanists around the world . . . explored many parts of the country, but curiously, the plant communities of the Qinling Mountains in Shaanxi Province in central China remained untapped."

The rich floristic diversity of these mountains offered much that these plant explorers wanted to tap. "The Qinling Mountain Range stretches from northeast of Beijing to southwestern China, ending west of Xian City in Shaanxi Province," explained Kim (1997). "This mountain range has precipitous slopes, deep gorges, and rugged peaks. Breathtaking mountains stretch as far as the eye can see, and the sharply rising peaks appear to be a series of saw teeth on the flat plain of the horizon. The Qinling Mountain Range runs from east to west and acts as a geographic barrier blocking the dry, wintry wind blowing from the north and capturing the heavy precipitation from the summer monsoons carried from the south. The southern slopes of the Qinling Mountain Range have an average minimum temperature just above the freezing point. This provides a mild climate and supports mixtures of subtropical and temperate plant communities. More than 1500 species are native to the Qinling Mountains."

Unfortunately, the diversity of plants in the Qinling Mountains has been threatened, as in other parts of China, by extensive deforestation: "The overexploitation of natural resources has inevitably resulted in the extinction of many beautiful plants. With a sense of urgency due to this habitat destruction, NACPEC organized the plant exploration in Shaanxi and Gansu provinces to save and bring back garden-worthy and endangered plants" (Kim 1997).

With their compass set on the Qinling Mountains, the team assembled in Xian, the capital of Shaanxi Province, on 2 September. They were met by Professor Cui Tiecheng, deputy director of the Xian Botanical Garden, who would guide the expedition through Shaanxi and Gansu.

Bright red seeds of *Paris polyphylla* (9724) collected in the Liping Forest Station in Qinling Mountains. Photo by James R. Ault.

Hydrangea aspera ssp. *strigosa* (961593) was collected at 1700 m in the Liping Forest Station in Qinling Mountains. Photo by Rick J. Lewandowski.

A stream led the explorers up a ravine deep into the Foping Nature Reserve in Qinling Mountains. Photo by Rick J. Lewandowski.

Floating in the mist

The expedition started with a trip to the town of Foping, some 150 km southwest of Xian. "Our first collection site was Foping Nature Reserve," noted Kim (1997). "After leaving Xian City, which was our home base, and driving in the two land cruisers for five hours through the countryside of endless flat corn fields, everyone was excited at the sight of the mountain peaks appearing to float in the mist. As we approached the mountains, a dramatic view was revealed—sheer, steep cliffs and rock faces jutting out above the road."

During the first three days of exploring the Foping Nature Reserve, the group collected a wealth of plants. Among the plants collected were trees such as *Acer stachyophyllum* (98261–2), *Magnolia sprengeri* (98258),

and *Tsuga chinensis* (9754); shrubs such as *Deutzia vilmorinae* (961584–5), *Euptelea pleiosperma* (961586), and *Viburnum erosum* (9761); and garden-worthy perennials such as *Actaea asiatica* (961615), *Cimicifuga foetida* (961612), and *Tricyrtis latifolia* (9752).

"On 9 September," noted Kim (1997), "we left Foping Reserve in order to move to Yue Ba Station; while still within the reserve it is located eighty miles [130 km] from the previous station. We drove an unpaved and bumpy road, the conditions being especially bad after heavy rains for more than a week." Collections around the Yue Ba Station during the following couple of days were especially fruitful and resulted in the acquisition of seeds of many tree and shrub species, including, among others, *Idesia polycarpa* var. *vestita* (98274), *Magnolia biondii* (98259), and *Sinowilsonia henryi* (9742).

Atop Ning Shan are, left to right, Conrad, Ault, Kim, and Lewandowski. Photo by Rick J. Lewandowski.

Kim, Conrad, and Lewandowski, left to right, collect seeds of *Abies fargesii* (961565) on Ning Shan in Qinling Mountains. Photo by Rick J. Lewandowski.

Conrad, left, and Kim with seeds of *Paeonia mairei* (9721) collected on Ning Shan in Qinling Mountains. Photo by Rick J. Lewandowski.

On 14 September the group traveled south to Liping, a small town near the border between Shaanxi and Sichuan. The next three days were spent collecting around the Liping Forest Station. Among the plants collected were several new perennials, including *Lilium brownii* var. *colchesteri* (976), *Paris polyphylla* (9724), and *Tricyrtis macropoda* (9753); shrubs, including *Camellia oleifera* (961576), *Euptelea pleiosperma* (961587), and *Hydrangea aspera* ssp. *strigosa* (961593); and trees, including *Betula utilis* (98264), *Crataegus wilsonii* (98272), and *Pinus henryi* (9729).

Blue-carpeted mountain

A couple of days later the group crossed the main range of the Qinling Mountains again and found themselves on its south side. Their destination was Ning Shan County and the mountain of the same name, 2840 m high.

"This mountain exemplifies the diverse flora occurring in different plant communities," noted Kim (1997). "We started climbing at 1400 feet [420 m] elevation at Ning Shan and hiked up to 9000 feet [2750 m]. Vegetation changes as we ascended were fascinating. Broad-leaved evergreens, including *Machilus, Phoebe, Ilex, Holboellia, Sinofranchetia,* and *Cephalotaxus,* dominate the low elevation. An array of interesting perennials, such as *Rodgersia, Paeonia,* and *Ligularia,* occur as ground covers. As we went higher, the vegetation gradually changed to mixed forest and included maples, oaks, mountain-ashes, roses, and lilacs. The high atmospheric moisture and rich organic soil present throughout the mountains create a favorable growing habitat. At over 6000 feet [1850 m], rhododendrons, firs, and *Cimicifuga* make their home. The surface of the ground was so thickly covered with moss that it felt as if we were stepping on sponge carpet. . . . Above 8000 feet [2450 m] the rhododendron forest abruptly ended and a barren peak appeared and as we reached the fog-laden peak, a field of blue greeted us. In between the windswept *Potentilla, Rhododendron, Berberis, Salix,* and *Juniperus,* a large field of blue-flowered gentians in full bloom formed a carpet that covered the whole peak."

This rich area kept the explorers busy for four days. The low-elevation forest afforded such finds as *Cephalotaxus fortunei* (961580), *Lindera neesiana* (977), *Phoebe faberi* (9726), and three species of *Ligularia*: *L. dolichobotrys* (961599), *L. nelumbifolia* (961601), and

Drupelike seeds of the Chinese plum-yew, *Cephalotaxus sinensis* (961581), the expedition found near Dang Chuan Forest Station. Photo by Tomasz Aniśko.

Widespread deforestation was observed by the explorers on the slopes of Ning Shan in Qinling Mountains. Photo by Rick J. Lewandowski.

L. veitchiana (961598, 961600). In the mixed forests higher up, the team collected *Acer davidii* (961566), *Sorbus koehneana* (98281, 98283), and *Syringa pubescens* ssp. *microphylla* (9749). Two species of *Cimicifuga, C. foetida* (961611) and *C. acerina* (961609), which were making their home among rhododendrons and firs, provided an ample supply of seed. The windswept *Potentilla* turned out to be *P. glabra* var. *veitchii* (9735), while the flower that painted the top of the mountain blue was *Gentiana apiata* (961589).

Dreaming of a hot tub

After a month of exploring southern Shaanxi, the group boarded an overnight train to travel from Xian to Tianshui, in eastern Gansu Province, on the north side of

Qinling Mountains. Their plan called for three days of collecting on Maiji Shan.

First they headed to Dang Chuan Forest Station. "There was a misty rain when we arrived at the station, but the rain became heavier as the day progressed," recalls Lewandowski. "Being in pouring rain for several hours, we were soaking wet and chilled by 5°C temperatures. The day, although we experienced the worst weather by far of the trip, was not without its rewards. We collected, among other plants, *Carpinus cordata* (961579), *Cephalotaxus sinensis* (961581), and an excellent collection of *Cimicifuga foetida* (961610)."

On 6 October the group visited a nearby Guang Ying Forest Station. "It appeared we were in for more rain and chilly weather, but we decided to go into the field anyway," says Lewandowski. "The drive to the station took two hours, but the beautiful scenery, and a bus window that shattered unexpectedly, broke the trip's monotony. After less than an hour in the field, heavy rains started. The air was frigid, a bone chilling cold that forced us to cut our collecting short. Nevertheless, we found several outstanding plants, including *Cornus kousa* var. *chinensis* (98269), *C. controversa* (98268), and *Quercus aliena* var. *acuteserrata* (961607)." On their last day in Gansu the explorers added to the collections *Sinofranchetia chinensis* (9741) and *Hydrangea aspera* (961591), which they found in the forests surrounding Maiji Shan Botanical Garden.

Back in Xian the group dedicated a couple of days to cleaning and organizing their collections, and on 13

October departed for the United States by way of Beijing. They returned home carrying 256 collections of some of the most garden-worthy plants of the Qinling Mountains.

"The excitement of finding our target plants and many unexpected species kept our enthusiasm high, but the long and strenuous hiking exhausted us," reminisced Kim (1997). "As we descended the mountain each day, often soaked in sweat or rain, our dream of submerging ourselves in a hot bathtub often turned out to be unfulfilled. Is plant exploration in such remote Chinese mountains worth the hardship? Yes, it definitely is. It is distressing to witness the rapid destruction of the pristine forest that is home to so many beautiful plants. Every day we passed piles of timber lying by the road waiting to be carried somewhere."

FRONTIER MOUNTAINS

The next opportunity for Longwood staff to join the NACPEC group on an expedition to China came in 1997, when plans were made to travel to the Changbai Mountains in the province of Jilin, stretching along China's frontier with North Korea. The Changbai range was chosen as the destination for the expedition because of the rich flora that evolved there in a climate with very cold winters. It was expected that many exceptionally hardy forms of species previously collected from more southern locations in China and Korea would be found in these mountains.

Jeffrey Lynch, section gardener in charge of Longwood's nursery, joined the team, which included Kris R. Bachtell, horticulturist at the Morton Arboretum, Meyer, Del Tredici, and Charles E. Tubesing, propagator at the Holden Arboretum. The group assembled first in Nanjing, where they were hosted again by He Shanan, who provided the organizational support for the expedition. He arranged for Sheng Ning, botanist at the Nanjing Botanical Garden, to accompany the NACPEC group on this expedition.

On 31 August the group flew from Nanjing to Shenyang, the capital of Liaoning Province, neighboring Jilin to the east. In Shenyang they were met by Dr. He Xingyuan, director of the Institute of Applied Ecology. The next morning the group visited the institute's arboretum. "It was raining hard," remembers Meyer, "but we did get a feel for the place. It was quite small and was structured along ecological themes, featuring native plants, rare and endangered plants, nitrogen-fixing plants, and various other plantings, grouped by genus."

On 2 September the expedition loaded into vehicles and left Shenyang for Tonghua in southern Jilin, at the foot of the Changbai Mountains. Upon arriving in Tonghua, the group met with Dr. Cao Wei, taxonomist from the Shenyang Institute of Applied Ecology, who would guide them through the mountains.

Close call

The next morning the explorers left Tonghua for the town of Changbai on the bank of the Yalu River, separating China from North Korea. "We made a slight detour because the main road to Changbai that followed the Yalu River was closed," recalls Meyer. "Then a second detour forced us off the road and into a river. Our van had to cross the river several times, but this road took us through a beautiful old growth forest filled with maples, birches, and poplars. It was just sensational! Unfortunately, we could not spend much time in this forest. There was lots of concern about how to get to the Changbai Mountains, given that the detours had thrown us completely off course. How far it was, or when we would get to our destination, were unknowns."

By 4 p.m. the explorers caught the first glimpse of the mountains in the distance. All along the road were signs of recent logging, and the group's van frequently passed carelessly loaded trucks with long log ends trailing behind and raising clouds of dust. "At one point we encountered a terrifying close call," remembers Lynch. "As a logging truck was approaching our van, the load of large logs evidently shifted and one of the logs swung free of the truck. Acting like a medieval joust, it rammed the front of the van, tearing off the entire driver's side door. Only by chance was no one in our group injured or killed." Meyer adds: "After all the joking about how dangerous China was, we were now fully enmeshed in a head-on collision. In the fading light we walked down to look at the logging truck and saw our van door wrapped around the butt end of a large, 12 m long log of *Tilia mandshurica,* one of the species we hoped to collect on this expedition."

About an hour later the police arrived to investigate the accident and by 8 p.m. the group was allowed to board another vehicle that arrived from a nearby forestry station and took them to the town of Changbai on the

Yalu River, upstream from Changbai, separates China from North Korea. Photo by Paul W. Meyer.

Yalu River. This town would serve as a base from which the expedition would launch day-trips to the southern slopes of the Changbai Mountains.

South side
"The Changbai Mountains are relatively untouched and unexplored," explains Lynch. "This mountain range features several climatic zones and is home to over 1300 plant species. The highest peak in the range, Baiyun, 2691 m, is a magnificent volcano atop a wide lava plateau. Within the volcano's crater is the huge Lake Tian."

While in Changbai the group was helped by Sun Longxing, director of the local forestry department. On 4 September their first collecting mission was underway. "The trip began on the south side of the mountains," says Lynch. "With an inventory of the plants that we wanted

to collect, the group ventured along the Yalu River, finding *Astilboides tabularis* (971671), and *Chosenia arbutifolia* (99246), a member of the willow family that has never been introduced to western cultivation. The plant we collected was the only one found in the area with viable seed."

The next morning the explorers headed north from Changbai. "Our first stop was along the highway where we collected *Sorbus, Acer,* and a charming little plant, *Lychnis fulgens* (971683) with sensational coral-red flowers, over 5 cm across," explains Meyer. "A little further on we turned off onto a logging road, where we collected *Cornus alba* (971688), *Rosa acicularis* (971691), and *Tripterygium regelii* (971687)."

"We then ventured up the mountain and, at 1000 m, encountered a mixed forest of broad-leaved and coniferous shrubs and trees," remembers Lynch. "The bulk of

Habitat of *Astilboides tabularis* (971671) along the Yalu River near Changbai. Photo by Paul W. Meyer.

Chosenia arbutifolia (99246) growing on the banks of the Yalu River. Photo by Paul W. Meyer.

Tubesing leads the group through a colony of *Oplopanax elatus* (971692) growing in a mixed forest north of Changbai. Photo by Paul W. Meyer.

the material collected on this trip was found in this zone because of its similarity to Pennsylvania's climate. Examples of plants found in this zone included *Abies holophylla, Acer mono, Fraxinus mandshurica, Pinus koraiensis, Quercus mongolica,* and *Tilia amurensis* (971681)."

On 6 September the group drove north out of town again, this time along a dirt road where active logging was underway. Meyer remembers that the "first stop to collect *Sorbus* also produced an abundance of *Paeonia obovata* (971693) growing everywhere in the disturbed understory, in moist soils and in partial shade. As a species, it seems to have benefited from logging. The seed heads were very filled with shiny, blue-black seeds sitting on a plush mass of scarlet arils. One couldn't possibly invent a more sensual combination."

A little further on along the road they noticed a colony of *Thuja koraiensis* (971695) covering an eroded

slope with plants up to 1 m tall. "On the upper slopes, the plants were much taller, up to 8 m, with cones on their topmost branches," explains Meyer. "Beneath *Thuja* was a mat of pure sphagnum moss and below that a bed of coarse shale. The plant was clearly clonal, and all the small plants were layered lateral branches, as indicated by a characteristic bow shaped base. After a little searching, with the rain pouring down, we found one specimen with a fair number of fresh cones on it, and got permission from Sun to cut down one specimen that was 5 m tall, with lots of fresh cones."

On 9 September, Sun led the group north from Changbai into the coniferous zone that extended from 1000 to 1700 m. "The plan was to hike to the top of a nearby mountain to see and collect seed of *Pinus pumila,*" recalls Meyer. "Unfortunately, Sun was unsure of the correct way to go and we promptly got lost, marching

Paeonia obovata (971693), collected in the vicinity of Changbai, enticed the explorers with its shiny blue-black seeds backed by scarlet arils. Photo by Tomasz Aniśko.

Lynch, left, and Meyer on a plant-collecting foray near the town of Changbai. Photo by Kris R. Bachtell.

Betula ermanii (971717) inhabiting southern slopes of Changbai Mountains. Photo by Paul W. Meyer.

around in a big circle in the pouring rain. Because of the problems with the weather and the directions, the decision was made not to climb the mountain, but instead to walk back down the road, collecting as we went. *Betula ermanii* (971717) and *Syringa wolfii* were common, along with *Abies nephrolepis* (971718)."

Northern slopes

The expedition continued their collecting around the town of Changbai until 13 September, when they said farewells to Sun and prepared for their trip to the northern side of the Changbai Mountains. "Ten days after our departure to the south side of the Changbai Mountains, we embarked on a fourteen-hour drive to the north slopes," remembers Lynch. "Despite the need for armed

guards and many border crossings where other armed guards searched the vehicle, our journey went on well."

In the afternoon the group reached a research station near the town of Erdao Baihe at the base of the northern slopes of Changbai Mountains, their home for the next several days, where they were met by Dr. Dai Limin, the head of the station. "The next morning we departed for the summit of Baiyun," recalls Lynch. "This was the last day that it would be accessible due to the fact that it had not rained in weeks and a wildfire warning was in effect. Upon reaching the top the scenery was breathtaking. The wind was howling over the beautifully sculpted pumice peaks, and the clouds left ominous shadows on the surrounding hills. The tundra floor was a deep red color from the cranberry bushes that had adapted themselves to the harsh climate. The last time the volcano was active was about four hundred years ago, and now amidst its enormous crater is Lake Tian."

"On the way down we walked through *Betula ermanii* forest," describes Meyer. "Admiring the twisted, windswept trunks of the birches, we reached the base of a 68 m tall waterfall that formed near the point where Lake Tian flowed out of its crater to form Songhua River. Our next stop on the way down was in the conifer belt, about 1200 m, where *Abies, Picea,* and *Larix* dominated. Then, at around 800 m, we stopped in the mixed conifer–deciduous forest belt. The forest floor was littered with moss-covered trunks and branches. There we collected seeds from large *Pinus koraiensis* (9811) trees. Scattered among them were *Pinus densiflora* var. *sylvestriformis.*"

Lake Tian occupies an enormous crater atop Baiyun, the tallest peak of Changbai Mountains. Photo by Paul W. Meyer.

The group spent 15 September collecting in a mixed forest at about 750 m. Under the canopy of giant pines, oaks, ashes, and poplars, they found *Acer triflorum* (98137) growing on the banks of a small streambed. "At a stop along the river we collected *Alnus hirsuta* (9815) and more *Acer triflorum* (9816)," remembers Meyer. "Then we went looking for *Acer mandshuricum* (98138), which was everywhere, but with very little seed. We finally collected seed from a tree growing under a giant *Populus koreana*."

On the rainy morning of 17 September the group drove northwest from Erdao Baihe with the goal of reaching a forest where *Taxus cuspidata* once grew. "The forest was excellent," recalls Meyer. "We immediately found *Carpinus cordata* (9828) mixed with giant *Abies holophylla*, *Betula costata*, *Pinus koraiensis*, *Quercus mongolica*, and *Tilia mandshurica*. In the understory were *Acer pseu-*

dosieboldianum, A. tegmentosum, and *Deutzia glabrata* (9829). The herb layer was also rich, with *Actaea asiatica* (9832) and *Caulophyllum robustum* (9833). *Taxus cuspidata* was formerly plentiful in the area, but in recent years, it had been heavily cut for use in medicine. Near the end of the day, after we had given up on finding any, we located a mature specimen and a few seedlings from which cuttings were collected."

This was the expedition's last day of collecting in the mountains. On 19 September the explorers woke at 5 a.m. for the drive back to Shenyang, arriving there fifteen hours later after a long detour and a flat tire. From Shenyang the group traveled back to Nanjing, where they spent a couple of days cleaning, inventorying, and allocating the 143 collections for each participating institution. On 24 September they departed for the United States.

"The most important contribution made by this expedition is a comprehensive collection of many trees—especially in genera *Acer, Abies, Picea,* and *Pinus*—from areas where winter temperatures can drop to -40°C," recalls Meyer, summing up the results of the expedition. "Changbai Mountains are the northern extreme for many species from Korea, which are cherished as garden plants and cultivated in the United States. Collections we made are going to be among the hardiest one can find."

Songhua River begins as a waterfall flowing out of the crater containing Lake Tian. Photo by Paul W. Meyer.

HEMLOCK HUNTING

An important aspect of plant exploration is the introduction of new species or varieties that may be resistant to, or tolerant of, certain diseases and pests that afflict plants in cultivation. One such group of plants that has been of great concern is the much beloved hemlocks of the eastern United States, *Tsuga canadensis* and *T. caroliniana,* which have been under severe attack from the Asian hemlock wooly adelgid, *Adelges tsugae,* since the 1950s. In addition to the extensive research undertaken to characterize the pest's biology and spread, starting from the 1990s, efforts have been made to introduce Asian hemlocks that may be resistant to the wooly adelgid. A study, conducted in 1991 by the Morris Arboretum, indicated that from among various *Tsuga* species cultivated in the United States only *T. chinensis,* native to China, was free of the pest. Based on these encouraging results, Morris Arboretum, jointly with the U.S. National Arboretum, spearheaded an effort to collect *Tsuga* germplasm throughout China and subject it to testing for resistance to the wooly adelgid.

In 1999 Longwood Gardens joined this project, when Jerry S. Stites, Longwood's horticulture department head, embarked on an expedition with Dr. Edward J. Garvey, botanist at the USDA Agricultural Research

Del Tredici, left, and Lynch, assisted by their Chinese colleagues, collect fruits of *Acer triflorum* (98137). Photo by Paul W. Meyer.

Service, and Shawn V. Belt, horticulturist at the U.S. National Arboretum, to travel to China's southwestern province of Sichuan.

Reaching for the cones
The team assembled in Beijing on 1 October and from there flew to Chengdu, the capital of Sichuan Province and the starting point for the expedition. In Chengdu the team met with Wang Qing of the Nanjing Botanical

Garden, who would be their guide. After a hard day of traveling north from Chengdu, the explorers arrived at the Wolong Panda Reserve, near Wenchuan.

The team's first collecting day came on 4 October when they headed up the trail that led to Wuyepeng panda observation station. "We crossed a raging white water river on a wooden footbridge and started a relentless climb up the mountain with beautiful views across the valley," remembers Stites. "Tiny cabbage patches and cornfields created an amazing

In the hills above Miyalou the expedition found a sizeable population of *Tsuga chinensis*. Photo by Edward J. Garvey.

patchwork quilt on the other side of the mountain. Hemlocks were found between 2500 and 3000 m altitude. We climbed for three hours before we reached the remote observation station where we had lunch. Another hour of climbing and we came upon a relatively flat area with several large hemlocks, *Tsuga dumosa*. All of the branches were too high to reach and most of the cones were from last year. We finally found a tree with cones about 8 m above the ground. After several attempts, we got the rope saw in place and cut the branch off. We collected immature green cones and some of the old cones hoping to get a few viable seeds. At 4 p.m., we headed back down the mountain. The trail down was wet, slick, and very steep adding to our fatigue with every rubber-legged step."

The next day the group made "pretty good collections" in the nearby Wen Xiang Gou Reserve. "A number of healthy hemlocks, *Tsuga chinensis*, were within sight but only several were accessible," recorded Stites in his field notes. The following day the group traveled west to Miyalou near Li Xian. "For every day of collecting we spent at least two long, grueling days driving to the next site," explains Stites. "Usually it required climbing a mountain pass on a windy gravel road to get to the next valley. Often one side of the road dropped hundreds of meters into a raging river and the other was a steep slope

prone to rock slides. We were delayed more than once while the road was being cleared by hand from rock slides. The roads were a maze of potholes and surprises. Our driver was skilled at dodging broken down trucks, yaks, and old women carrying loads that dwarfed their size. He relied on the car's horns more than the brakes to navigate his way through."

The day after arriving in Miyalou the team started off on an all-day hike up the mountains. After an extremely difficult climb, they reached an area at 2500 m where hemlocks, *Tsuga chinensis*, grew. As in previous sites, most cones were inaccessible, but they managed to cut lower cone-bearing limbs from several trees.

Over the Qionglai Mountains

On 8 October the expedition departed Miyalou for Danba, a town at the confluence of the Xiaojin and Dajin rivers, on the west side of the Qionglai Mountains. "On our way to Danba we crested a summit at 4100 m and saw the sun for the first time of the trip," describes Stites. "Blue sky, a few clouds, and snow-capped mountains made spectacular scenery. By 4 p.m., we had traveled only 210 km of our 300 km journey. Wang suggested we spend the night in Guishuan since the final 90 km could take five more hours. Guishuan is not open to foreigners

The snow-capped Gongga Shan appeared in its full glory as the expedition crossed Qionglai Mountains on their way to Danba. Photo by Jerry S. Stites.

Collecting *Tsuga chinensis* var. *oblongisquamata* (01289) along the Kuangyong River. Garvey, right, speaks with Songji, holding pole pruners, and Wang while Belt photographs the tree. Photo by Jerry S. Stites.

Belt with *Tsuga chinensis* var. *oblongisquamata* (01289) along the Kuangyong River. Photo by Edward J. Garvey.

Traveling from Miyalou to Guishuan, the group stopped for lunch in the little village of Tadong. Photo by Jerry S. Stites.

and it was apparent by the stares we received. Wherever we went we drew a crowd. After checking into our hotel, Belt, Garvey, and I took a walk to see the sights. Wandering around the market was quite an experience. We discovered a roof-top bar where we could be anonymous observers and enjoy a few beers."

After reaching Danba, the group made excursions over the next couple of days to sites several hours' drive away on rough roads. "On 10 October it was a bone-jarring, three-hour drive to the forest station in the Kuangyong Valley," remembers Stites. "With our local guide, Songji Longkai, we had four people and gear crammed into the back seat of our jeep. In the valley several families lived at the primitive forest station. We went to a small room with a bare light bulb hanging from the ceiling and crowded around an electric hot plate for

The group crosses a stream in Dongma Valley near Danba, where they collected *Tsuga chinensis* var. *oblongisquamata* (01290). Photo by Jerry S. Stites.

lunch. Lunch was all you can eat pig's ears, pig's feet, and other unidentified parts. After lunch we walked from the forest station along a dirt road and had an easy and fruitful day of collecting. Along Kuangyong River we found many trees of *Tsuga chinensis* var. *oblongisquamata* (01289), which provided an ample crop of seeds. This made the long drive back worthwhile."

Trekking south

On 12 October, on the way south from Danba to Kanding, the group stopped in Caqilongba Valley, where they found easily accessible trees of *Tsuga chinensis* (01288) growing along the river. Out of Kanding the expedition undertook a couple of excursions. In Yangchang Valley and Tonglin Valley, in moist woodlands along riverbanks, they made more collections of *T. chinensis* var. *oblongisquamata* (01287, 01366).

On 15 October the expedition continued south to Luding. The next morning they undertook a trip to Hailougou Glacier on the slopes of Gongga Shan, 7556 m. At about 2800 m another species of hemlock, *Tsuga dumosa*, inhabited moist woodland. Although no cones could be found within reach of a rope saw, a number of small seedlings were collected on that site. The group's next destination was the town of Mianning, some 200 km south of Luding. While hiking in the nearby Yuanbao Valley, the team found two populations of *T. dumosa* growing between 2600 and 2800 m.

In their pursuit of hemlocks, after a long day's drive, the expedition reached Dechang, a town situated on the banks of Anning River, on 19 October. "The following day we had a relatively short drive to the small village of Liuchong," remembers Stites. "Most of the male villagers crowded around us to see what we were up to. They were

The group traveled from Kanding to Gongga Shan by way of Luding, site of the heroic capture of the bridge over the Dadu River during the Long March of the Red Army in 1935. Standing on the bridge are, left to right, Stites, Belt, and Garvey. Photo by Edward J. Garvey.

enamored with our telescopic pruners. After the customary delays and confusion our local guide showed up and we started trekking up the mountain. Just above the village, at about 1700 m, stood a lonely *Tsuga chinensis* var. *oblongisquamata* (011652). We were told that all other hemlocks near the village had been harvested. Our only hope to find these trees was to climb higher. A couple of weeks of hiking in the mountains had not prepared us for today's trail. The trail was very steep and muddy making forward progress slow and difficult. Our local guide was getting impatient with his poky Americans. We continued up the trail with Wang bringing up the rear. The trail was getting steeper and we were clinging to trees and shrubs to keep from slipping backwards. Our ascent continued until we reached a rocky ridge at about 2500 m with a few small hemlocks, *Tsuga forrestii* or possibly *T. dumosa*. A thorough examination of the trees turned up no cones. Apparently the cone-bearing trees Wang had seen in this location earlier in the summer had been cut down."

Upon their return to Dechang, the team members decided to skip the last of the collecting sites planned for this trip. "The last site near the town of Miyi, some 100 km downstream from Dechang, was a two-day drive on roads worse than what we had been experiencing," explains Stites. "Wang confessed that he was unable to reach the site in the summer pre-investigation trip because the road was washed out. He did not know if the road was repaired and could not call ahead to find out."

Uncertain about the prospects of finding hemlocks in that location, the group decided to conclude the expedition and return to Chengdu. A couple days later, Belt, Garvey, and Stites returned to the United States, bringing with them seventeen collections of hemlocks. As Stites points out, "Whether wooly adelgid resistant forms will be found among them, only time will tell."

CHINA'S CAMELLIA LANDS

Since Longwood's conservatories first opened, camellias have been an essential part of the indoor display. "They furnish one of Longwood Gardens' outstanding displays," wrote Dr. Donald G. Huttleston, Longwood's taxonomist, about camellias in 1960. "The Longwood Gardens' camellia collection was begun in 1919 at a time when but one small conservatory had been completed. In the spring of that year thirty-four varieties of Japanese camellias were obtained from Belgium through John Scheepers, Inc., of New York. . . . In the spring of 1920, when the large conservatories were well under way, an additional thirty-seven varieties were obtained from France." In time more varieties were added, mostly from Europe, so that by 1960 the camellia collection had grown to 211 cultivars. By then there was an understandable desire to expand camellia display into the outdoor gardens. There was, however, one major obstacle to overcome: the available camellias were not hardy in this part of the United States. To remedy the situation, a daring project aimed at finding and testing cold-hardy camellias was started at Longwood in the 1960s—a project which has continued, with its ups and downs, through the present day.

If one has sufficient ambition and stamina to undertake such a seemingly impossible task as finding cold-hardy camellias, one has to go where the wealth of camellia diversity still hides: China. An opportunity to tap into China's wealth of camellias came for Longwood Gardens in 2000, when Dr. Clifford R. Parks, professor of the University of North Carolina at Chapel Hill, with forty years of experience researching camellias, assembled a team to travel to China's southern provinces of Yunnan, Sichuan, Guangxi, and Hunan. Lynch and I represented Longwood. The team also included Dr. Betty McConaughy of the University of Washington in Seattle; David Parks of the Camellia Forest Nursery in Chapel

Long, left, asks a villager if he has seen camellias on Lion Mountain near Wuding. Photo by Tomasz Aniśko.

Denuded mountains around Dukou, Sichuan, are home to *Camellia kangdianica*. Photo by Tomasz Aniśko.

Hill, North Carolina; Ronald R. Rabideau of Rare Find Nursery in Jackson, New Jersey; Katherine Rankin of the Smithsonian Institution in Washington; Tim Thibault of Descanso Gardens in La Cañada, California; Jennifer Trehane, a camellia expert from Dorset, England; and Dr. Xiao Tiaojiang and Dr. Barbara Thakor, both from the University of North Carolina at Chapel Hill.

The team assembled in Kunming, the capital of Yunnan, on 14 February. Our host for the entire trip was Long Chunli, researcher from Kunming Institute of Botany. The expedition was timed to coincide with the blooming of most of the camellia species in that part of China. Although it was not the season to find seeds on camellias, we were able to collect pollen from the flowers, which would later be used in cross-breeding camellias in the United States.

The following morning we headed north toward the border with Sichuan. What began as a modern, comfortable highway quickly became a bumpy gravel road. The stark scenery with its dry, denuded hills resembled the American Southwest, with the exception of ever-present terraced fields carved out of the mountainsides and greening up with winter wheat and leafy vegetables. Lion Mountain near Wuding, our first collecting site, is famous for its Buddhist temple. While botanizing there, we were often passed by pilgrims and newlyweds carrying incense sticks as offerings. Several populations of *Camellia pitardii* var. *yunnanica,* our first encounter with wild camellias, were found there growing amidst evergreen oaks.

After crossing into Sichuan the next day, we reached Dukou, an industrial city surrounded by mountain ranges where rich coal deposits abound. A narrow road led us up the mountains through several mining villages. Our bus had to make frequent stops and maneuver carefully in order to allow trucks loaded with coal to pass by. Effects of habitat destruction and industrial pollution made the whole scenery rather depressing. Despite almost complete deforestation in that area, we found a stand of *Camellia kangdianica,* considered by some to be a variant of *C. reticulata,* along the edge of a cultivated field. Camellias proved to be exceptionally resilient and capable of regenerating from the rootstock even after the forest that had provided shade and shelter was cut down. However, the future of these remnant colonies, subjected repeatedly to harvesting for firewood and grazing, is uncertain.

Through the lands of the Yi
On 16 February the trip continued north to Yanbian with a stop in a forest conservation park located in an area inhabited predominantly by the people of Yi nationality, one of the many minority groups living in Yunnan. The rural landscape, with picturesque villages nestled between the mountains, offered a much welcome relief after a day spent in Dukou. While Lynch and Thibault tried to find fruits of *Schima argentea,* a handsome evergreen tree from the tea family, the rest of the group assembled around a large camellia, awaiting its identification from Clifford Parks and Xiao. Their determination "unknown species" made us all aware of how complicated the taxonomy of this genus is.

In order to reach all the sites planned for the following day around the village of Guosheng, north of Yanbian,

Terraced hillsides near Yanbian, Sichuan, are greened up with winter wheat. Photo by Tomasz Aniśko.

Crossing a stream near Guosheng, are, left to right, David Parks, Clifford Parks, and Thibault. Photo by Tomasz Aniśko.

Yi women selling camellia flowers picked in the wild. Photo by Tomasz Aniśko.

Camellia brevigyna found near Guosheng. Photo by Tomasz Aniśko.

we had to hire two small pickup trucks, because the road we were to travel was too rough for our bus. In addition to finding several populations of *Camellia brevigyna, C. minor,* and a small plantation of *C. sinensis,* we came across a giant *Astilbe grandis* (00234) with huge leaves hanging over a small stream coming down a rocky cliff.

Our route changed direction on 19 February as we traveled east toward Huili when a casual road stop resulted in an unexpected discovery. To our great excitement, we found a colony of a camellia of uncertain identity that for the time being was declared to be *Camellia boreali-yunnanica.* Later that day, a visit to Yuza, the site of the original discovery of *C. huiliensis,* revealed that most of the plants from that population had been destroyed. Even during our visit there we could observe a group of presumably local women and children picking camellia flowers which were later sold from roadside

Camellia tenuivalvis (00269, 00274) growing near the summit of Longzhou Shan, north of Huili. Photo by Tomasz Aniśko.

stands. This situation exemplified the urgent need to collect seeds, pollen, and herbarium specimens before these camellias disappear from the wild.

Longzhou Shan, an impressive mountain north of Huili, awaited us the next morning. The peaks on the northern side were clad with an evergreen forest of *Lithocarpus* trees, while the southern side featured large colonies of *Camellia tenuivalvis* (00269, 00274). At 3200 m, this is likely the highest elevation where camellias can be found. The near-freezing temperature and patches of snow on the ground helped us to appreciate this fact. Other species of evergreen plants flowering with the camellias caught our attention. Especially delightful was *Illicium simonsii* (00276), a species of anise tree with very showy, creamy yellow, fragrant flowers backed by soft green, dense foliage.

Valley of the poisonous anise tree

To reach our next destination, Xichang, we took the road running along a valley cut through the mountains by the river Anning. Sugar cane plantations abounded on both sides of the river. From time to time bright red flowers of silk-cotton trees, *Bombax ceiba,* growing near the road created a great deal of excitement on our bus. Stamens of this tree are considered a culinary delicacy, and we sampled them; the silky fiber embedding the seed is also used for stuffing pillows.

"After two weeks in China, some of the novelty had worn off," remembers Thibault. "We had come to expect noodles for breakfast, a crammed bus ride, a couple of sites with camellias, a modest hotel room, cold shower, huge dinner, and an evening of recording data. Nevertheless, the first of our collecting sites around Xichang proved a unique experience. The day started with the usual noodles and bus ride. That day our bus had an escort of Chinese government officials accompanying us to the village of Guojimou. We were off to the land of the Yi, and a Chinese botanist had recently been attacked at this site. Our Chinese hosts did not want any trouble. Neither did we, but we also hoped for a good local guide. The local leader of the Yi seemed receptive to the requests of the Chinese officials. He did not object to us collecting plants in their lands and as a result we had a host of guides accompanying us that morning."

As far as road conditions permitted, the bus drove up the mountains east of Xichang, through the Mangcaogou Valley, or valley of the poisonous anise tree, which takes its name from *Illicium simonsii*. In order to reach the camellia site we had to continue on foot for another 3 km. "The first plants we saw blooming there were very appropriate for the valley named after them—*Illicium simonsii*," recalls Thibault. "Continuing on up the Mangcaogou Valley, from a distance we spotted one spectacular camellia tree covered with large white flowers. Upon closer inspection it was decided that it was a highly variable *Camellia boreali-yunnanica* (00277). The plants were around 5 m and very floriferous. The flowers themselves were large, approaching 12 cm judging by the palm of my hand, with a color varying among plants from almost white to almost purple, including two-tones."

As the morning went on, more and more of the Yi came out from the nearby village of Guojimou to have a look at us. "We were supposedly the first Westerners on this site," explains Thibault. "We had been invited to

Illicium simonsii growing in the Mangcaogou Valley, east of Xichang. Photo by Tomasz Aniśko.

Color variants of *Camellia boreali-yunnanica* (00277) in the Mangcaogou Valley, east of Xichang. Photo by Tomasz Aniśko

lunch in the village. A young couple was curious about us, enough to slaughter one of their pigs in our honor. They provided a quick introduction into Yi life. The house we were invited to was obviously a new construction, with freshly white washed mud walls holding a satellite dish on top of them. The satellite dish, television and electricity were apparently compliments of the Chinese government as a way to keep farmers updated on new techniques and world events. We watched a few minutes of the Chinese agriculture channel together before roast pork and chicken soup were served in wooden bowls set on the floor. Fear had turned to friendship."

Rock's village

On return to Yunnan Province we were greeted by an overcast sky and drizzle—not a frequent occurrence during the dry winter season. On 25 February, driving from Huaping in northern Yunnan to Wuping Reservoir, we saw numerous herds of black goats. This made us a little skeptical about how diverse the plant life might be at the site. From what we were able to observe, grazing goats consumed everything in their path with the exception of poisonous plants or plants armed with thorns. Animals grazing on plants and people cutting plants for firewood appear to be two major factors preventing natural reforestation in these mountains. Our efforts were rewarded, however, when we found flowering specimens of camellias, identified as a diploid form of *Camellia reticulata,* growing together with *Rhododendron spinuliferum,* an association frequently seen in the areas visited during this trip.

Continuing east from Huaping to Lijiang, the cultural center of the Nakhi minority, we made a stop in Nanhua Township at the site of a large colony of *Camellia saluenensis.* Growing among the camellias was a rare palm, *Trachycarpus nana,* not previously known to occur in the area.

The road from Huaping to Lijiang steadily climbed up the mountain ranges and became increasingly winding. Every turn revealed yet another spectacular view of deep valleys below, green fields of winter wheat contrasting with steep tan slopes. For several kilometers the road followed along the gorge of the Yangtze.

We decided to visit Yufengsi Temple, located on a mountainside some 10 km northwest of Lijiang. At the highest level of the temple, a special courtyard housed an enormous ancient *Camellia reticulata* tree, famed for

Camellia saluenensis was found growing among Chinese windmill palms, *Trachycarpus nana,* in Nanhua Township. Photo by Tomasz Aniśko.

Members of the expedition pose with women in traditional Nakhi costumes in front of the ancient *Camellia reticulata* tree in Yufengsi Temple. In the back row are, left to right, Lynch, Thakor, Clifford Parks, McConaughy, and Xiao; in the front row are Rabideau, the author, and David Parks. Photo by Tomasz Aniśko.

The house of Joseph F. Rock in Nguluko near Lijiang. Photo by Tomasz Aniśko.

A specimen of *Camellia reticulata,* claimed to be six hundred years old, grows on the grounds of Jing Le Yan, a Buddhist nunnery west of Kunming. Photo by Tomasz Aniśko.

opening twenty thousand flowers every spring. The tree was constantly surrounded by pilgrims and tourists, each cherishing it equally.

In contrast, our second destination that day, the home of Dr. Joseph F. Rock, was rarely visited. With some difficulty we found Nguluko, the small village where Rock, one of the greatest plant explorers of the twentieth century, had spent twenty-nine years of his life. His house was no different from others in the village. A wall surrounded it, a gateway opening onto a three-sided courtyard, with the residence ahead and the wood and animal shelters to the side. One of the shelters is now a small museum displaying photographs and a few personal items, including Rock's much worn coat. The residence is mostly empty, though Rock's bed and curious folding table remain.

Protected by monks and nuns

Our route changed direction again, and on 29 February we began traveling south to Kunming. On the way there we stopped at Zixi Shan, one of Buddhism's holy mountains, located near Chuxiong. It escaped deforestation in the past thanks to several temples situated there. Our guide for the day was Zhang Fangyu, who had dedicated many years of his life to the preservation of Zixi Shan and had coauthored a biological survey of the mountain, which listed twelve hundred species of flowering plants, including eight species of camellias. This mountain is also home to numerous ancient cultivars of *Camellia reticulata,* which differ from the wild plants in having larger, double flowers.

Before returning to Kunming on 3 March, we stopped at Jing Le Yan, a Buddhist nunnery, to see an old specimen of *Camellia reticulata.* While hiking up the hill we admired massive trees of *Calocedrus macrolepis* that looked to have been at least several hundred years old. Their trunks were decorated with colorful sticks of incense left by pilgrims, who, in our view, could not have chosen a more appropriate tree for such a ritual, this being the Asian counterpart to the American incense cedar, *C. decurrens.* Inside the nunnery we found a specimen of *Camellia reticulata* claimed to be six hundred years old, sheltered by high walls. Understandably, no collecting was permitted on this sacred ground.

Epimedium remedy

On 5 March we left Yunnan and flew to Guilin, the capital of Guangxi Province. The next morning we traveled by boat along the famous Li River to Yangshuo, a small town four hours away. The boat ride provided us an opportunity to admire the scenery so often depicted on Chinese paintings. Li River passes through an area where limestone hills exposed to erosion have acquired fantastic shapes. To add to the mystique of the landscape, the hills are bathed in mist and fog most of the year, as they were on the day of our visit.

"Leaving the boat in Yangshuo, we ran the gauntlet of hawkers, wandering through the old city streets," remembers Rabideau. "As we made our way further from the dock, we found ourselves in a large, busy, and colorful produce market. One section was devoted to traditional Chinese medicine. To us, these baskets and bowls of dried bark, sticks, fungi, and numerous other things, were interesting places to look for plants. It was at one of these vendors where Lynch pointed out to me a fresh leafy bundle he had recognized as *Epimedium,* a genus I had been looking for and had not yet found in the wild. Excitedly yet discreetly so as not to negotiate the price too high, I called over Xiao to bargain for me. They talked for a while, with the vendor exchanging odd glances at me occasionally. Next I was asked how much I wanted. 'The whole bunch,' I said. My response led to more discussion between Xiao and the vendor, and even more odd glances. I could tell my friend was driving a hard bargain. Xiao, a fervent believer in traditional Chinese medicine himself, began to throw curious looks my way as well. 'Why do you want it all?' he asked. 'Well, to grow, of course,' I replied. He looked as though he doubted my intentions. 'Do you know what it is for? No? Well, it is an aphrodisiac,' he laughed. Aphrodisiac or not I wanted to grow it, so I bought the whole bunch and my purchase went into a plastic bag. Some time later, while at another stall, I received a curious knowing smile from the female shopkeeper. I glanced down and noticed one of the *Epimedium* leaves was showing!"

Grown in Bojia

On 7 March we drove north to the neighboring province of Hunan. In the town of Dongan, where we were staying for the night, we met with Gao Jiyin of the Subtropical Forestry Research Institute in Fuyang, Zhejiang, who had been collaborating with Dr. Clifford R. Parks, Longwood Gardens, and Descanso Gardens on a joint project aimed at collecting all the species of camellias native to China. Gao was returning from one of his collecting ventures and shared with us a number of camellia seeds and cuttings he had found.

The next day we explored Shunhuang Shan Forest Park, situated near Damiaokou, not far from the border between Hunan and Guangxi. Hiking in constant rain, we were surprised to meet a group of women from a nearby town celebrating International Women's Day in the park. They were equally intrigued by our group, who had traveled halfway around the world to look for camellias in their park. With the help of a park ranger skilled in climbing, we were able to collect flowers of *Camellia tunganica.* The best spectacle, however, was produced by trees of *Litsea cubeba,* which even on that gloomy day glistened with creamy yellow flowers. In the afternoon we were taken to nearby Camellia Mountain. After a brisk and strenuous hike, we found a stand of *Camellia hunan-*

Limestone hills along Li River near Guilin, Guangxi, shrouded in fog and mist, evoke impressions of fantastic creatures. Photo by Tomasz Aniśko.

ica. But the most exciting find of the day was a small shrub bearing iridescent blue fruits of great beauty, identified as *Dichroa febrifuga* (00251).

The following morning began with a visit to the local Forestry Institute, where we were greeted by the director emeritus, Lou Zhongchun, who in the 1950s discovered a new species of coniferous tree, *Cathaya argyrophylla,* belonging to a previously unknown genus. Only about three thousand trees have been found in the wild since then. The Forestry Institute works on developing methods of propagation and utilization of these rare trees in reforestation. Lou accompanied us to nearby Lang Shan National Park, known for its dramatic scenery, with limestone mountains immersed in fog and rain most of the year. There we found *Camellia handelii,* a species smaller in stature, with diminutive leaves and flowers.

This month-long expedition culminated on 11 March with a trip to Bojia Township in Liuyang County, near Changsha, the capital of Hunan Province. Bojia is said to have the highest concentration of nursery production in China. In a township with an area of 90 km² and twenty-one thousand inhabitants, there are sixty-one hundred nurseries. In a meeting with the mayor we were told that twelve hundred kinds of plants were produced there, but as far as we were able to determine the overwhelming majority of these plants come from a very limited selection of several genera, including *Camellia, Ginkgo, Loropetalum, Magnolia, Osmanthus, Pinus,* and *Podocarpus.* All the nurseries we visited offered large specimens of trees transplanted from the wild, among them *Loropetalum,* which had scions of purple-leaved selections grafted onto them.

Trees of *Litsea cubeba* glisten with creamy yellow flowers in Shunhuang Shan Forest Park near Damiaokou. Photo by Tomasz Aniśko.

Lou with young trees of *Cathaya argyrophylla*, a species he discovered in the 1950s. Photo by Tomasz Aniśko.

We left Bojia with mixed feelings. Transplanting mature trees from the wild did not meet with our approval. On the other hand, the remarkably high success rate in moving such large trees, when no specialized equipment was available, astounded us. Who could tell what this spontaneous outburst of nursery entrepreneurship might lead to in the future? Maybe there would no longer be any need for Westerners to travel halfway around the globe to collect plants in China. Instead, mail-order catalogs of Bojia nurseries could offer anything one could ever wish to grow.

We departed Changsha on 12 March and returned to the United States with fifty collections of cuttings and seeds, including twenty-six camellias, in addition to twenty-six collections of camellia pollen.

AUSTRALASIA

DOWN UNDER

The first Longwood plant-collecting expedition to Australia was organized in 1958 under the auspices of the USDA-Longwood plant exploration program. Two explorers selected for this expedition were Dr. Walter H. Hodge, head of education and research at Longwood Gardens, and George H. Spalding, superintendent of the Los Angeles State and County Arboretum in Arcadia, California.

Explaining the rationale for the trip, Spalding remarked that "Australia, with a highly endemic flora, was selected as the locale of the expedition, because the flora of this continent 'down under' has long been appreciated as one of the richest in the world. . . . Obviously, it was impossible to visit all of the Australian States on the five-month trip. Only those areas where we could fulfill our objectives most profitably were visited. Principal areas selected for exploration included parts of Western Australia, South Australia, Victoria, Australian Capital Territory, and New South Wales" (Spalding 1962).

The rarest of the lot

Western Australia is the largest of the Australian states, about 2400 km long north to south and 1600 km wide east to west. "The northern one-third is a tropical summer rainfall area," wrote Spalding (1962), "gradually changing to a warm-temperate and temperate winter rainfall area in the southern part. The State can be divided, very broadly, into two physical regions—an inland tableland (Great Plateau) and a low-lying coastal strip (Coastal Plain)."

Hodge and Spalding arrived in Perth, Western Australia, on 3 September. The next day they headed north to Three Springs, some 320 km north of Perth, in the company of Neil Gayfer, an agriculturist with the Commonwealth Scientific and Industrial Research Organization (CSIRO). At Coorow, about 24 km from Three Springs, they left the main highway and turned west on the road to the coastal town of Green Head. At this point they found wild flowers in great profusion, but the trip ended abruptly after about 16 km when flooding made the road impassable. "On the return to Perth via Moora, Mogumber, Gingin, and Yanchep, we traversed large areas cleared of native vegetation to permit grazing of sheep," noted Spalding (1962). "In several places we were pleased to discover that an uncleared strip, varying from 50 to 100 feet [15–30 m] in width, is preserved on both sides of the road where native plants abound."

On 8 September, Hodge and Spalding headed north again, this time for a three-day trip in the company of Charles A. Gardner, state government botanist, "who is reputed to know the native plants of Western Australia better than anyone else," commented Hodge (1958b). "He is a self-trained Englishman who fell in love with the plants hereabouts and has spent his life studying them. He also is self-assertive and lets everyone know that he is without peer in this field." Hodge added: "We were

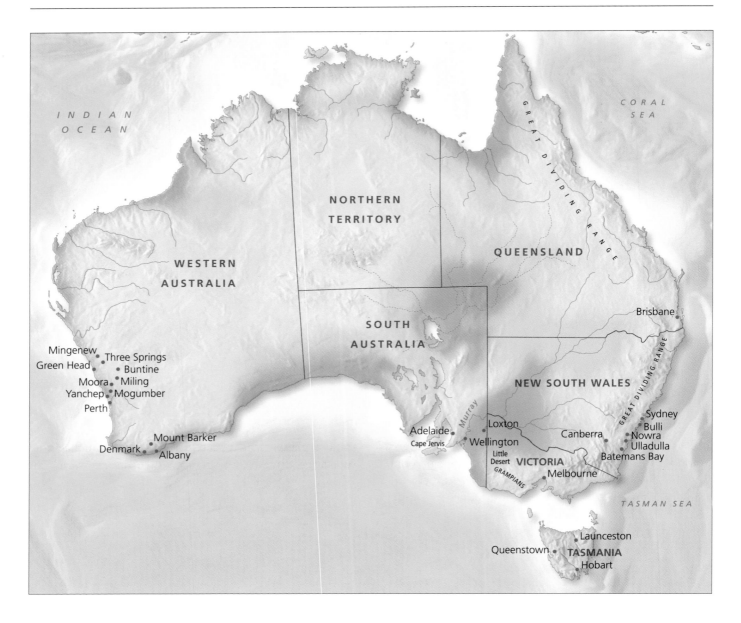

Australia, with an area of 7.7 million km², extends latitudinally from about 10° south to 44° south and shows considerable diversity in climates and soils. It is a relatively arid land except for mountainous areas, largely limited to the Great Dividing Range along the east coast, and the wet coastal areas of Queensland and the Northern Territory. Most of Australia is frost-free. Snow is a yearly feature only in parts of the Australian Alps in the southeast corner of New South Wales. The total number of vascular plants growing in Australia is estimated at about twenty thousand. Because of its long isolation, the flora of Australia has been free to develop without contact with other areas; therefore it is characterized by a very high proportion of endemic species. At the same time, it has common relationships with certain groups of plants in South Africa and South America, which date back to the time when these landmasses were part of the ancient continent Gondwanaland. Dry climates, poor soils, and frequent fires also contributed to the uniqueness of growth forms and flower types of Australian plants. While the remnants of tropical forests can be found only in the north, the forests of the east and southwest are dominated by *Eucalyptus*, and those of the southeast and Tasmania by *Nothofagus*. Southern heaths of Epacridaceae are common in the south and southwest. The semiarid interior of Australia is covered by savanna of scattered *Eucalyptus* and grasses, while in the central desert areas savanna is replaced by scrub of low-growing *Acacia*.

Blackboys, *Xanthorrhoea preissii,* growing on a hill near Bindoon. Photo by Walter H. Hodge.

Flowers of *Byblis gigantea* (59203), a giant sundew found near Mogumber by Hodge and Spalding. Photo by Walter H. Hodge.

happy to return to the same area we had been since now we could be with someone who literally knew all the plants he saw. It was an advantage for us for we now could put names on a number of the showy things that we had seen a few days before. Even better, we could learn whether there were better plants than even the ones we saw" (1958c).

At Bindoon near Mingenew, located 400 km north of Perth, "a large group of blackboys (*Xanthorrhoea preissii* Endl.) made an impressive sight on the slope of a hill," noted Spalding (1962). "This arborescent member of the Liliaceae stands 6 to 8 feet [1.8–2.4 m] high with simple or unbranched trunks, often blackened by frequent fires which sweep the region. The common name 'blackboys' for this species was coined by the early settlers in allusion to the appearance of this bizarre plant in late afternoon as the sun casts spearlike shadows through the grassy foliage in contrast with the thick black trunks."

Hodge and Spalding's next journey into the hinterland took them north from Perth to Coorow, Waddi Forest, Maya, Buntine, Wubin, Miling and back to Perth via the Great Northern Highway. Among the most exciting finds of that trip was spotted near Mogumber, about 80 km north of Perth. Hodge wrote of it in a letter to Longwood: "Today George and I had the good fortune to locate a colony of *Byblis gigantea* [59203], an insectivorous plant which looks like a giant, erect, linear-leaved sundew. This is one of the genera we would like to get established at Longwood so George is planning to forward about nine small plants on by air tomorrow via the USDA Inspection House to Longwood. We hope at least some of them will make it and can be established.

They grow in almost pure sand (wet) with good drainage. Their roots are long and fragile so handle with care" (1958d). Hodge thought *Byblis* was "a collector's item not only because of the interest generated by its carnivorous habit, but also for its very showy flowers" (1960a). These are borne on loose racemes, average about 3.5 cm in diameter, and show various shades of rose-purple. The flowers are backed by yellowish green leaves covered by minute glands which secrete a glistening mucilaginous substance attractive to small gnatlike insects, which are effectively "snared as on flypaper."

On 11 September, Hodge hired a car and drove to Albany on the south coast while Spalding stayed behind in Perth. The prime purpose of this trip, as Hodge explained (1958e), was in "seeing a district famous in Western Australia for its wildflowers as well as being the site of an especially interesting endemic genus, *Cephalotus follicularis,* the Albany pitcher plant." He "arrived in Mount Barker, about 30 miles [48 km] from Albany, around 6 p.m. so took time out to eat. In Australia one has to be sure and stop to eat between 6 and 7 else everything is shut down (even in the hotels) and you are out of luck. Mostly one depends upon the hotels to eat for there are few, if any, restaurants, especially in small towns and in Australia, outside of Perth, Adelaide, Melbourne, Canberra, Sydney and Brisbane, all other places are small."

The next day Hodge headed to Denmark, a hamlet about 50 km west of Albany, "looking all the way into all the swampy areas for *Cephalotus* which I had a pretty good idea of its looks though not its size. Finally stopped at a farm near Denmark and asked the farmer if he was familiar with this local pitcher plant. Luckily he was, so

Albany pitcher plants, *Cephalotus follicularis* (581780), collected by Hodge near Denmark. Photo by Walter H. Hodge.

Lothian, left, and Spalding cook lunch by the roadside near Cape Jervis. Photo by Walter H. Hodge.

pitcher which appears on the outer margins of the rosette in late winter and spring in ample time to be ready to trap prey in the main insect-hunting season of summertime" (Hodge 1962). Hodge took notice of the most exotic morphological features of this plant: "The diminutive pitchers (actually transformed leaf petioles) are elegant structures, well designed for holding water for trapping such terrestrial game as ants. Three girder-like structures aid not only to strengthen the one-to-two-inch-long [2.5 to 5 cm] vessel, but also serve as a sort of living 'barbed-wire fence,' directing insects upwards to the 'one-way-only' orifice of the trap. A formidable barricade of down-pointing teeth at the trap mouth plus the usual slick surface on the upper inner walls of the pitcher assure that entering prey will seldom escape" (Hodge 1962).

Their lovely natives

On 13 September, Hodge and Spalding relocated their headquarters to Adelaide, the capital of South Australia. The explorers were greeted there by Noel Lothian, director of the Adelaide Botanical Garden. "Upon our arrival in town Lothian incidentally had supplied us each with a typed day-by-day program for our Adelaide visit, plus maps of South Australia and the city of Adelaide, plus a typed account of the vegetation of the State—all of which was a very nice thing to have to get us oriented. It indicates the type of chap he is—on the ball!" wrote Hodge (1958f).

Collecting in South Australia covered about 800 km over some of the more interesting floristic areas east and southeast of Adelaide. The first trip south from Adelaide took Hodge and Spalding through Yankalilla to Cape

sent his young son and daughter to show me a location about 2 ½ miles [4 km] back on the road I had just come on" (Hodge 1958e). There they found the elusive *Cephalotus follicularis* (581780), "the rarest of the pitcher plant lot," as Hodge described it (1962).

"For a stranger to find plants in the wild is not always an easy matter," he wrote, "for although *Cephalotus* grows in peaty soil in moist open spots along streams and swamps, its earth-hugging rosettes are hidden beneath an overgrowth of grasses and sedges which usually dominate the scene. . . . Unlike our American pitcher plants, two types of leaves are produced. One is a normal, flat, somewhat fleshy, green foliage leaf, ovate or elliptical in shape and produced, in the fall, in the center of the rosette; these function as photosynthetic over-wintering leaves. The other leaf type is the curious little carnivorous

Jervis. They reached Cape Jervis about noon, "in time to cook out our lunch by the roadside in eucalypt bush," wrote Hodge (1958g). "Made ourselves a fire of eucalypt wood and grilled (with sticks) the standard fare of tender lamb chops (wonderful!) along with 'billy tea'—tea made in a pot over a campfire." From Cape Jervis they continued east to the shores of Lake Alexandrina. In Wellington, on the north end of the lake, the explorers crossed the Murray River over a cable ferry and reached Tailem Bend before nightfall.

The following day they headed northeast to Loxton. On the way they traversed parklike countryside, with shrubby species of *Eucalyptus,* called mallee, covering large tracts interspersed with other shrubby vegetation. "In the early days before roads, many people without adequate vantage points were lost in the almost unbroken cover of mallee in gently rolling countryside," explained Spalding (1962). "The slender mallee trunks are too limber to support the weight of a man for climbing."

From Loxton the explorers continued north to Berri, where they turned west to return to Adelaide. While in Adelaide, Hodge and Spalding visited several private gardens of "special interest to plantsmen." One of them was Alison Ashby's garden in Blackwood, an Adelaide suburb, known for its collection of myrtaceous plants, especially *Callistemon* and *Melaleuca,* described by Hodge as "really outstanding." Among the species procured from Ashby's collection were *Callistemon phoeniceus* (59551), with brilliant red inflorescences, and *Melaleuca pentagona* (59788), with profuse heads of pink flowers. Hodge and Spalding also stopped at the Sanctuary, a nursery in Ashton, recognized for its collections of Australian and South African plants. The owner of the Sanctuary, F. C. Payne, "has been at the job of growing natives for some thirty years, so knows a bit about them," noted Hodge (1958h), "and by so doing he is encouraging by demonstration and by the sale of plants—the planting of natives in Adelaide gardens. By and large few Australians would think of growing their lovely natives. . . . The great advantage of a nursery of this type is that it saves plant collectors a great deal of time in looking up the plants in the wild and they can be seen all in one spot."

Swanson's flower beds

On 21 September the explorers arrived in Melbourne, the capital of Victoria, located on the southeastern tip of the continent. "Many areas of the State are favored by a rela-

tively high rainfall and fertile soil," noted Spalding (1962). "Farming and grazing, although rewarding occupations, in many areas have brought about widespread destruction of vast tracts of native vegetation."

Hodge and Spalding spent the first several days in Melbourne scouting collections of plants at the Royal Botanic Gardens, the second oldest botanic gardens in Australia, founded in 1846, and described by Spalding as the "world's most beautiful." Around Melbourne they visited a number of nurseries, including Swanson's Native Plant Nursery in Frankston, specializing in South African and Australian species, grown primarily for cut flowers for the florist trade in Melbourne. "The plants he has now in bloom," wrote Hodge (1958i), "are gorgeous, and we were able to see many things that we had seen in the wild but not always in as good condition." Spalding added, "For color effect only the wildflower fields of Western Australia surpassed Mr. Swanson's cut-flower beds" (1962). Hodge thought it noteworthy that "the land on which this material is being grown is a light sandy soil much like the areas in which you find the things in nature. The soil is of little value for other agricultural use and so makes a wonderful sort of location for growing these plants."

The wealth of plants in Swanson's nursery inspired the explorers to modify their plans: "Upon seeing this place, George, who had planned to go on with me to Tasmania, decided to withdraw and stay on in the Melbourne area while I go on. This will enable him to absorb a little better some of the things we had been seeing around the Melbourne area" (Hodge 1958i).

Tasmania's eucalypts and acacias

On 27 September, Hodge flew from Melbourne to Hobart, Tasmania, where he was met by Dr. Don Martin of CSIRO. The next day Hodge and Martin joined several local botanists on an excursion to the Florentine Valley and Frenchman's Cap National Park. "We traveled northwest of Hobart up the valley of the Derwent River which is the main river, emptying into Hobart harbor. . . . Our destination was the so-called Florentine Valley which has some of the finest temperate rain forest in Tasmania. . . . In the trip up from Hobart to the Florentine we ran from a rather low rainfall to a rainfall which was upwards of 70 inches [1800 mm] a year which is rather considerable for this part of the world. The giant eucalyptus trees which were to be seen ran on an average of from

A forest of *Nothofagus cunninghamii* at Frenchman's Cap, 1444 m. Photo by Walter H. Hodge.

220 to 250 feet [65–75 m] high with an age of around 350 years" (Hodge 1958j).

After lunch the group drove north, turning off on a road running up from the river valley to the plateau country and leading to the national park. "The forests in the river valley where the rainfall begins to increase are largely mountain ash, *Eucalyptus regnans,* which reaches pretty maximum size in such areas, but as one moves upwards to the plateau country, the trees are replaced by other types of eucalyptus, particularly subalpine forms and including such species as *Eucalyptus urnigera, E. coccifera* [582168], and *E. gunnii* [582170], all three of which are among the hardiest of the Tasmanian eucalypts. As one got higher, the rain and wind began to increase and the weather was really rotten, blowing and cold and feeling like the 'Roaring Forties.' There was a great deal of beauty in the eucalyptus trunks at this higher elevation,

because in the wet the blotched grey or yellow or even reddish trunks showed up beautifully in the eery light" (Hodge 1958j). Among several of the most promising Tasmanian species of *Eucalyptus* that Martin collected later and sent to Longwood were *E. gigantea* (582169), *E. pauciflora* (582171), *E. perriniana* (582172), *E. simmondsii* (582173–4), and *E. tasmanica* (582177).

On the morning of 29 September, Hodge and Martin started on a trip through the plateau country of Tasmania. They began by heading northwest on a main highway to Queenstown, located about midway on the west coast of Tasmania, but it soon turned into a dirt road. "We traveled over the highland areas following the headwaters of the Derwent River as far as Derwent Bridge which is nothing much more than a wide spot in the road with a gasoline station and a hotel which is more a place for people to get lunch rather than to overnight.

Forest of stately trees of mountain ash, *Eucalyptus regnans.* Photo by Walter H. Hodge.

Acacia dealbata, one of the large tree acacias, still standing despite forest clearing in the Golden Valley in Tasmania. Photo by Walter H. Hodge.

Most of this highland area is covered either with a sclerophyll eucalypt forest or with moorlands, wherever it is too wet for eucalypts to grow. . . . In former years, when the native Tasmanians used to live here, these were regularly fired since they were the only source of herbage for game and consequently this is where the natives caught their wallabies or other animals" (Hodge 1958j).

Then Hodge and Martin proceeded to the western side of the Great Lake. "The lake itself lies at about 3000 feet [900 m]," explained Hodge (1958j), "and so to get out of its basin one has to go up to about 4000 feet [1200 m] on a pass and then down an escarpment which drops one immediately to the northern lowlands of Tasmania. At this pass there is a great deal of the native pencil-pines, *Athrotaxis,* which are typical high country trees, scrubby, often with unusual form caused by wind. . . . At the pass level we came across a small mountain tarn called Pine

Lake from these pencil-pines, so we stopped and spent a couple of hours here collecting and looking at the plants. It is from such a place that one might expect to find hardy materials. One of the things was an alpine podocarp, *Podocarpus alpinus,* which forms little mats growing among big masses of rocks. *Drimys* bushes are also common, growing to perhaps a maximum of 8 to 10 feet [2.4–3 m], but with very nice form, very much like *Drimys winteri* of South America."

From Pine Lake, Hodge and Martin started down the escarpment which brought them to the lowland area. "The valley into which we were descending was called Golden Valley because at this time of year in former years it was occupied almost solely by gorgeous display of *Acacia dealbata* which even now was just coming into good color," recorded Hodge (1958j). "These are beauti-

Flowers of *Doryanthes excelsa* (59990) encountered by Hodge and Spalding near Bulli Point. Photo by Walter H. Hodge.

ful acacias, the largest growing species that I have seen, growing probably to 50 or 60 feet [15–18 m] tall with trunks one or two feet [30–60 cm] in diameter presumably, and completely covered with yellow flowers at this season of the year. Apparently the people, in clearing the forests, spare this acacia and so even on the cleared areas which we ran into below, these trees would stand out on the beautiful green slopes which were devoted to fattening or feeding lambs and sheep as well as cattle." Hodge's trip to Tasmania came to a close when he and Martin reached Launceston, the island's second largest city. The following morning Hodge flew out of Launceston to Melbourne and then Canberra, where he was reunited with Spalding several days later.

North to Sydney
In Canberra, the capital of the Commonwealth, Hodge and Spalding consulted with Dr. William H. Hartley, principal plant introduction officer of CSIRO, who helped to plan and organize the expedition. Accompanied by Hartley and Nancy T. Burbidge, botanist in charge of the CSIRO herbarium, Hodge and Spalding drove to Sydney on 8 October. The party followed the coastal route via Braidwood to Batemans Bay, Ulladulla, Nowra, and Bulli.

"The coast range begins just east of Braidwood," noted Spalding (1962). "Here, on the western slopes, the forest is composed largely of *Eucalyptus maculata* Hook. In several localities the cycad, *Macrozamia spiralis* Miq. (Cycadaceae) forms a nearly solid understory. . . . At Nowra, we diverted the route slightly with a short trip

inland to the Cambewarra Mountains for a short inspection of the vegetation growing there. The terrain is very steep with a dense covering of evergreen shrubby vegetation covering part of the area. . . . We proceeded north, still along the coast, through the scenic Kangaroo Valley, an agricultural area, to Bulli Point. In the National Park north of Bulli Point, *Doryanthes excelsa* Correa (Amaryllidaceae) [59990] is a prominent plant of the bush. This striking member of the amaryllis family with broad straplike leaves about 4 feet [1.2 m] long, produces a globular head of red flowers about 1 foot [30 cm] in diameter at the summit of leafy stalks 8 to 10 feet [2.4–3 m] long; the flowers are each subtended by colored bracts."

Upon reaching Sydney, Hodge and Spalding paid a visit to the Royal Botanical Gardens, located on the foreshore of Port Jackson. From their base in Sydney they undertook excursions to several sites in the northern part of New South Wales. Just north of Sydney they explored the Ku-ring-gai Chase, an area set aside as a national park. "Here we saw the waratah, *Telopea speciosissima* [59718], Proteaceae, the state flower of New South Wales," recorded Spalding (1962). "This highly attractive protead is an evergreen multiple-stemmed shrub to 6 feet [1.8 m] high with large heads of bright red flowers. In the wild the waratah prefers the light shade of ravines, although in cultivation near Gosford we saw this plant thriving in light sandy soil in full sun."

Queensland's rain forest
In mid-October, Hodge and Spalding made a trip to Brisbane, located in the southeastern corner of Queensland. "The climate here is warm-temperate to subtropical with comparable vegetation to be seen in gardens and parks of the area," noted Spalding (1962). "On both visits to Brisbane, the botanic gardens were the principal center in our search for ornamentals."

One of the exceptionally showy plants obtained from the Brisbane Botanic Gardens was *Tecomanthe venusta* (59519), a vigorous woody vine native to New Guinea. "The main ornamental feature of the plant," wrote Hodge (1960b), "lies in the beautiful, pendant, trumpet-shaped flowers which appear in axillary, umbell-like clusters (up to 16 in a cluster on our specimen) on the old wood of the climbing stems." The tubular flowers, about 8 cm long, are a light magenta-rose on the outside of the tube, fading to a paler rose and creamy yellow on the inner surfaces of the spreading lobes and inside of the

Specimens of *Tecomanthe venusta* (59519) that were collected by Hodge and Spalding at the Brisbane Botanic Gardens were exhibited in Longwood conservatories for thirty years. Photo by Walter H. Hodge.

tube, which also sports numerous narrow red lines running down to its base.

Outside Brisbane, the explorers visited Mount Glorious in the Maiala National Park, located some 50 km northwest of the city, for a brief survey of the rain forest vegetation there. "As we got higher up and the amount of rainfall increased, we began seeing characteristic signs of wetness such as tree ferns and some of the palms, in particular species of *Archontophoenix* and *Livistona,* both growing together in more open eucalypt areas," remarked Hodge (1958k). "It was immediately evident that this was not a rain forest in the sense of a tropical American or tropical Malayan rain forest in that the rainfall very definitely was not as heavy."

On 17 October the explorers separated again. Hodge left Australia for Indonesia, from whence he continued on to Singapore. Spalding retraced their routes across Australia to return to the sites visited by both explorers since late August, this time to collect seeds.

Everything so green
Arriving the next morning in Jakarta, Hodge was picked up by Jan Schuurman of the Bogor Botanic Garden, the former Dutch Buitenzorg Botanical Garden. Together they drove to Bogor, about 80 km to the south. En route, Hodge immediately noted how "everything appeared so green after Australia, a light, bright green which hits you right in the face. Apparently, there is never any shortage of water, and crops can be grown continuously around the year" (Hodge 1958k).

Palm collection in Bogor Botanic Garden. Photo by Walter H. Hodge.

Driving to Bogor, Hodge and Schuurman left the coastal plains of Java and gradually ascended the highlands, with an elevation of about 360 m. Bogor Botanic Garden was situated in the center of the city. "From books of David Fairchild and the like," wrote Hodge (1958k), "I was prepared for the majesty of the plantings which are very mature, having been there in many cases for 100 or 150 or perhaps more years. Mature rainforest trees with great buttresses, wonderful lianas, and a medley of palms greeted the eyes as we drove up to the Treub Laboratory." In the garden they were met by Anwari Dilmy, keeper of the herbarium, and Soedjana-Kassan, curator of living plants.

The following morning Hodge, accompanied by Dilmy and Soedjana-Kassan, set off for Cibodas, a branch of the garden at Bogor, also established by the Dutch and situated about 300 m higher on the slope of

Mature specimens of sealing-wax palm, *Cyrtostachys lakka,* in Bogor Botanic Garden. Photo by Walter H. Hodge.

Dimorphic flowers of *Dimorphorchis lowii* (582051) acquired by Hodge from Singapore Botanic Gardens. Photo by Richard F. Keen.

and *Mucuna bennettii* and sealing-wax palms [*Cyrtostachys lakka*] and certain ferns and lycopodiums that I knew would be of interest," he wrote (1958k). "Probably the most interesting collections from our standpoint at the gardens are the fine collections of monocots, particularly gingers, Marantaceae, Araceae, and the like. There are a number of species in these groups that I do not think I have ever seen before and some of them would make very attractive ornamentals in tropical gardens though space would be required for many since they are large terrestrial things."

Plagued by monkeys

On 21 October, Hodge returned to Jakarta and from there flew to Singapore. The following morning he paid a visit to the Singapore Botanic Gardens and met with George Addison, acting director.

"In general," noted Hodge (1958k), "the garden looked well-cared for and attractive, but Addison tells me that the place chosen was unfortunate for such an organization since the soil is very poor and it is difficult to grow almost anything without continuous heavy fertilizing. On account of this, many things cannot be grown here and even many Malayan things will not do well. Because of this, the representation in the garden is rather poor. It is probably because of this that the development of the large orchid collection and the production of hybrids especially for growing in the Singapore area, has received a great deal of attention for, of course, these plants do not need to be put in soil and thus can be readily handled in pots. . . . There is a great deal of trouble in protecting the

Mount Gede-Pangrango. At Cibodas, in addition to the developed part of the garden, a large tract of native forest had been set aside as the Wild Garden. "Here one really can get a glimpse of what is true rain forest, not the sort seen in Queensland," commented Hodge (1958k). "None of the visitors to the garden go into this part any longer because rumor has it that it's infested with bandits. Apparently, there are bandits and what they are I do not know, whether they are just plain bandits or nationalists or anti-communists, or what have you. No one was willing to explain except to state that there was nothing to be concerned about because they [the garden staff] like this rumor since it keeps the public from destroying wild things."

Back in Bogor the next day, Hodge continued browsing through the garden's collections. "I looked up such things as the jade vine [*Strongylodon macrobotrys* 582061]

Nepenthes ×hookeriana, a natural hybrid between *N. rafflesiana* and *N. ampullaria*, found by Hodge in a secondary scrub woodland outside Singapore. Photo by Walter H. Hodge.

collections not only from man, since many of the plants are worth hundreds of dollars, but even more so from the monkeys which plague the gardens."

One of the noteworthy plants Hodge collected at the Singapore Botanic Gardens was *Hoya lacunosa* (582062), native to Indonesia. "In habit and foliage this woody climber is much prettier than the familiar wax-plant [*Hoya carnosa*]," wrote Hodge (1960c). The delicately fragrant flowers of this plant have greenish yellow petals whose inner surfaces sport a corona of velvety hairs. Among other botanical gems uncovered by Hodge in Singapore were *Acrotrema costatum* (582049), *Mussaenda philippica* 'Doña Aurora' (582054), and a number of orchids, including *Dimorphorchis lowii* (582051), *Oncidium* 'Golden Showers' (582055), and ×*Vandachnis* Premier grex (582058).

The next day Addison took Hodge to a secondary scrub woodland on the outskirts of the city to show him wild species of tropical pitcher plants of the genus *Nepenthes*. "One could tell from the height of the forest that the land was rather poor because most of the trees did not grow much more than 40 or 50 feet [12–15 m] tall and the underbrush was rather open. The soil was a red clay. As we walked into the scrub area we found quite a number of pitcher plants trailing along the ground or scrambling into the low bushes and sometimes even up the trees. The species involved were *Nepenthes gracilis* with a slender pitcher, *N. ampullaria* which has little short stubby pitchers many of which are arranged in concentric rings, it would seem, around the stems of whatever the plant is climbing upon, and the largest of all, *N.*

rafflesiana, which looks like the hybrid types which we have growing at Longwood. We were also lucky enough to see a natural hybrid, *N.* ×*hookeriana,* which is a hybrid between *rafflesiana* and *ampullaria*" (Hodge 1958k).

On 23 October, Hodge concluded his visit to Singapore and the entire two-month trip. After a brief stopover in Ceylon (Sri Lanka), he returned to Philadelphia a couple of days later. Spalding stayed in Australia for another three months and returned to the United States in February 1959, having collected nearly four hundred plants.

INDONESIA'S KEBUN RAYA

The brief stay at the Bogor Botanic Garden in October of 1958 inspired Hodge to return to the Kebun Raya, as this garden is now known in Indonesia, the following year. This time he was accompanied by his wife, Barbara (Bobbie), who served as "chief assistant, general package carrier, and enthusiastic enjoyer."

"Although plant exchanges effected by correspondence between botanic gardens can be fruitful," reasoned Hodge (1961a), "nothing can equal an on-the-spot visit by a plant hunter, particularly if he is looking for ornamental plants which must be tailored to specific needs. . . . With new conservatory space available for display of tropical ornamentals, Longwood Gardens . . . was interested in a sampling of unusual Indonesian plants. My visit to the Kebun Raya saved endless weeks or months of activity in the field."

Great garden

The Hodges arrived at Jakarta on 29 September. Following a few hours' drive south from the capital, they reached Bogor in early afternoon, met Dr. Kusnoto Setyodiwiryo, director of the garden, and checked into one of the guesthouses for visiting scientists.

"In the Indonesian language," wrote Hodge (1961a), "Kebun Raya denotes 'great garden.' To most Indonesians the phrase refers to but one spot, the beautiful Javanese garden at Bogor, known in Dutch colonial days as Buitenzorg. Today, after nearly 150 years of existence, the Kebun Raya at Bogor, still is the most famous of all tropical gardens. . . . During its long existence, thousands of different kinds of plants have been cultivated at Bogor. At the present time about 10,000 to 12,000 living species

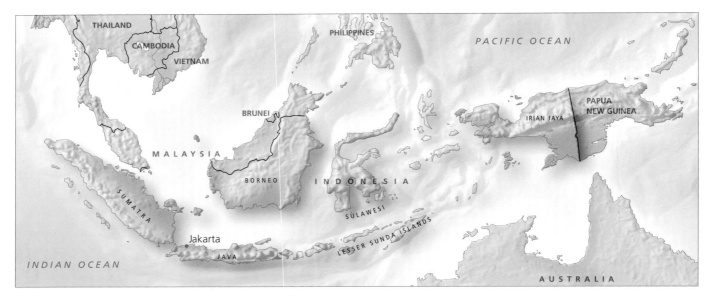

Indonesia, the largest country in Southeast Asia, composed of 13,667 islands in the Indian and Pacific oceans, extends from east to west for about 5400 km and covers more than 2 million km². The major islands feature rugged, volcanic mountains, which slope down to coastal plains with frequent alluvial swamps. Indonesia's position astride the equator assures that temperatures are high and fairly uniform throughout the year, and that they are moderated only at higher elevations. Most of Indonesia receives heavy rainfall, with the highest amounts from December to March. From central Java eastward, the dry season becomes more pronounced. The annual precipitation ranges from more than 2000 mm in Borneo,

Sumatra, and Java to 1000 mm in parts of the Lesser Sunda Islands. Most of Indonesia is covered by tropical rain forest. About thirty thousand species of flowering plants are native to Indonesia, including about five thousand orchids. The most prevalent type of vegetation is mixed lowland and hill tropical rain forest, characterized by the presence of a large number of buttressed trees, woody lianas, epiphytes, saprophytes, and parasites. Above 1500 m, mountainous evergreen rain forest composed of oaks and laurels dominates, while mangrove forests are widespread along the swampy shores.

are inventoried on the Kebun Raya's grounds, and others are found at branch gardens in Indonesia."

The day after the Hodges arrived, Walter Hodge, armed with lists of plants desired for Longwood, "roamed the garden and mapped out his plan of attack" (B. Hodge 1959a). He later explained his strategy: "From a published catalogue of plants available at the Kebun Raya as well as from notes taken during a prior visit, I already had upon my arrival at Bogor completed lists of plants that were to be collected. I was interested in conservatory plants that could be grown at Longwood Gardens or sister establishments, or species that could be planted outdoors in tropical or subtropical locations in the United States" (Hodge 1961a).

Work begins

The next five weeks were dedicated to scrupulous studies of the collections in the garden and choosing the most

desired species. In their daily routines the Hodges were helped by Soedjana-Kassan and Tati, his assistant.

"Our workday here starts at 7 a.m. like all over Indonesia where people work till 2 p.m. then have the balance of the day off, when it is hottest," Hodge reported to Longwood (1959c). "Weather here is not as hot and sticky as in Jakarta, an hour away, but it is still warm, running probably between 78° and 90°F [26°C–32°C]. Usually it rains in the late afternoon and this brings a little cooling weather for sleeping. Otherwise you can depend on fair weather every morning when work has to be done."

The first shipment of plants was sent out to the United States on 5 October. "We had a regular production line going," noted Bobbie Hodge (1959b). "Soedjana-Kassan and his men brought material from greenhouses and gardens for us, Walt selected and prepared, I wrote necessary slips, etc." Preparation of plant

Torch-ginger, *Etlingera elatior* (592335), was one of many ornamental gingers native to Indonesia and procured by Hodge at Bogor. Photo by Walter H. Hodge.

Hodge and Tati, curatorial assistant, who helped the Hodges with their work at the Kebun Raya. Photo by Walter H. Hodge.

Bobbie Hodge cleaned seeds collected at the Kebun Raya and prepared them for shipment. Photo by Walter H. Hodge.

shipments had to be synchronized with airline flight schedules in Java, and special arrangements had to be made for living plants to be carried in the plane's heated compartments. "The rapidity of modern air transport is assurance that certain plants, that can be shipped only as seeds (palms, for example), will reach their destination in living condition," explained Walter Hodge (1961a). "This is important, for seeds of some palms remain viable for scarcely more than a week or so after collection. The majority of plants could be sent as fresh cuttings. Wrapped in plastic bags, vegetative propagations are almost assured of safe arrival."

World's largest orchid

On 7 October the Hodges traveled, in the company of Soedjana-Kassan, to Cibodas, a satellite garden of the Kebun Raya. "Cibodas is located on the eastern slopes of the Gedeh mountains at an elevation of just over 1500 m," Hodge explains. "It was established to accommodate introductions requiring a cooler and rainier climate than at Bogor—such as *Cinchona,* source of quinine, which was first introduced into Java from Peru and Bolivia in the 1850s."

Hodge was familiar with the collection at Cibodas from his previous visit to Java. "Walt had hoped to stay two days there," wrote Bobbie Hodge (1959b), "but as there are supposed to be robbers which descend on the place at night, we were not allowed to stay." Despite these restrictions, Walter Hodge managed to collect a number of interesting plants at Cibodas, including *Medinilla verrucosa* (592307), an epiphyte with showy blue fruits;

Wild Vietnamese banana, *Musa coccinea* (592295), ornate with scarlet bracts, was acquired by Hodge at the Cibodas branch of the Kebun Raya. Photo by Walter H. Hodge.

Dipteris conjugata (592287), a large terrestrial fern collected by Hodge at the Cibodas branch of the Kebun Raya. Photo by Walter H. Hodge.

Musa coccinea (592295), a showy wild banana with upright scarlet inflorescences, native to Vietnam; *Rhododendron javanicum* (592299), an epiphytic species with orange flowers, found growing wild around Cibodas; and several attractive large ferns native to Java, among them *Dipteris conjugata* (592287), *Leucostegia hymenophylloides* (592284), and *Oleandra neriiformis* (592285).

Upon their return from Cibodas to Bogor, the Hodges prepared another consignment of seeds and living plants to be shipped to Longwood. Subsequently the shipments were made at about weekly intervals. In a letter sent to Seibert at Longwood, Hodge reported on the progress they were making: "Of special items for us I have gotten seed, seedlings, and small plants of *Cyrtostachys* [592225–6, 592296, 592319]; a good sized *Grammatophyllum* [*G. speciosum* 592274]; seeds and

seedlings of *Victoria amazonica* [592317] (do not know whether the latter will carry well as plants); several interesting epiphytic species of *Lycopodium* [592300–1, 592342]; and a very nice selection of large-leaved monocots" (1959b).

One extraordinary plant collected at Kebun Raya was *Grammatophyllum speciosum*, sugarcane orchid, considered to be the world's largest epiphytic orchid, growing on a number of the larger trees in the garden. "This is a spectacular thing with the mottled brown flowers and very large leafy stems which may be 10 feet [3 m] long," wrote Hodge (1958k).

Scraping the surface

By 20 October, Hodge had finished up his collecting activities in Bogor. "As originally planned I have been

Sugarcane orchid, *Grammatophyllum speciosum* (592274), the largest of the epiphytic orchids, with an inflorescence up to 3 m in length, and each plant with up to a hundred flowers, was collected by Hodge at Kebun Raya. Photo by Walter H. Hodge.

Impressive clumps of palms, *Oncosperma horridum,* grace an alley at the Bogor Botanic Garden. A single seedling acquired by Hodge was forwarded to Fairchild Tropical Garden in Miami. Photo by Walter H. Hodge.

focusing primary attention on the foliage plants," he wrote to Seibert, "particularly the showy monocots, and including some of the rarer palms that are in seed. A lot of the latter are best for the Fairchild Tropical Garden but there are several very nice small palms endemic to Indonesia and New Guinea that I have been able to get and which would be nice for us to try. . . . To date I have close to two hundred things collected and by tomorrow or the next day (my deadline for final collecting here) that total may increase perhaps twenty-five to fifty numbers. If we get out of this a dozen nice things we should be satisfied" (1959b).

After making the last shipment on 22 October, Hodge wrote to Longwood: "Something over two hundred species have been collected. There still remains a

gold mine of material here. I have only scraped the surface though much could not be used under glass and would be better for outdoor gardens in the subtropics or tropics of America" (1959c).

The Hodges' time in Indonesia came to an end on 26 October, when they said farewells to their hosts at Kebun Raya, and returned to the United States by way of Thailand and Japan. A total of 218 species were collected in Indonesia. A large number of these were shared with the Fairchild Tropical Garden. Palms, orchids, gingers, arums, ferns, and club-mosses were all prominently featured among the collections.

One of the more intriguing collections made by Hodge on this trip were seeds of an unknown *Amorphophallus* (592216) native to Sumatra. When germi-

A titan arum, *Amorphophallus titanum* (571638), received from Sumatra in 1957, flowered at Longwood in April 1961. Hodge photographs the tiny flowers inside the leaflike spathe of the inflorescence, while Elaine Hampfler, research assistant, and Richard W. Lighty, geneticist, observe. This was only the second time such an event took place in the Western Hemisphere, after the 1937 blooming of a titan arum at the New York Botanical Garden. Photo by Gottlieb A. Hampfler.

Flowers of a titan arum inflorescence, *Amorphophallus titanum* (571638), as seen on the spadix through a hole cut in the leaflike spathe. Contrary to its being sometimes proclaimed "the world's largest flower," the titan arum has thousands of tiny flowers tightly arranged on the spadix and forming an inflorescence. Unopened male flowers are seen above the much larger, jug-shaped female flowers. Photo by Walter H. Hodge.

nated at Longwood the species was identified as *A. forbesii*. It produced quite imposing inflorescences. These, however, paled in comparison to those produced by another Sumatran native, titan arum, *A. titanum* (571638), which had arrived at Longwood from that island two years earlier.

A BIG LUMP OF COUNTRY

The first opportunity to acquire plants from New Guinea for Longwood's collections came when a letter arrived from Dr. Leonard J. Brass one winter day in 1959. Brass, an Australian botanist, was a member of Archbold Expeditions of the American Museum of Natural History. "We are planning a Sixth Archbold Expedition," Brass wrote to Seibert, "and on the recommendation of Dr. Swallen of the U.S. National Herbarium and Dr. Harold E. Anthony of our Museum, I should like to offer to collect and send you seeds of ornamental herbaceous plants" (Brass 1959). As Seibert was away at that time, collecting plants in South America, Hodge replied enthusiastically to Brass's offer: "I believe it would be safe to say that, realizing the limitations of greenhouse culture, we are interested in anything (except large trees) which could be considered of outstanding ornamental value" (Hodge 1959a).

Although, in the end, Brass's 1959 collections for Longwood were limited almost exclusively to ferns—*Papuapteris linearis* (591781), *Leptopteris alpina* (59458), and several *Cyathea* species (591776–80) among them—he managed to convince Seibert of New Guinea's immense floristic resources. "One can achieve a lot in specialized, not bulky, collecting in a month or two," wrote Brass (1960), "but New Guinea is a big lump of country, and very diversified ecologically, and a longer period could well be spent in it for ornamental plants." Brass advised Seibert that an expedition to collect ornamental plants in New Guinea was "quite feasible in concept, and one which should prove very profitable for the gardens."

It was not, however, until ten years later, when Longwood and the USDA launched an expedition to New Guinea that these ideas would come to fruition. Two explorers, Harold F. Winters, research horticulturist, and Dr. Joseph J. Higgins, plant physiologist, both from the USDA New Crops Research Branch in Beltsville, Maryland, were selected to undertake this trip.

Rhododendron zoelleri and the other 156 species of New Guinea rhododendrons belong to section *Vireya,* named after French naturalist Julien Joseph Virey. Of nearly three hundred species of Vireya rhododendrons, all but seven are found in Malesia, comprising the Malay Peninsula and Malay Archipelago, of which New Guinea is a part. Vireya rhododendrons distinguish themselves by flowering repeatedly throughout the year, producing flowers in colors of a clarity and intensity not seen in other rhododendrons, and by their ability to grow epiphytically. Photo by Joseph J. Higgins.

Winters explained the rationale for selecting New Guinea: "It was chosen for exploration because it is one of the world's most primitive regions and has been less thoroughly explored for plants than most other parts of the world. It was largely bypassed during the colonial expansion period of European nations until late in the nineteenth century. Some of its highland tribes were not pacified until air transportation opened up the country during and after World War II. . . . Ornamental plant collection from this area was timely. The inland peoples of New Guinea support themselves entirely by agriculture. Civilizing influences of the Australian administration have stopped cannibalism and tribal wars, and instituted health programs. The resulting increase in population causes greater pressure on the land for food. Consequently, forested land is being cleared for gardens at a greater rate than previously; and the cleared areas are extending farther up the mountain sides. Even above the frost line the native vegetation is being destroyed by logging and wood cutting operations and by roving herds of pigs" (Winters 1970f).

The expedition's collecting was fairly broadly defined but rhododendrons were given high priority. "Of approximately 850 known species in this genus," explained Winters (1970f), "about 157 occur in New Guinea. All

The Island of New Guinea lies between the equator and latitude 11° south, directly north of Australia. Its flora bears affinities to that of Southeast Asia, the Greater Sunda Islands, and Australia. New Guinea ranks among the most diverse regions of the world, with twenty-one thousand plant species. The dominant physiographic feature of New Guinea is a rugged central mountain range stretching over the entire island. This consists of a complex series of ranges trending east to west, intervening upland plains, and frequent volcanic cones and domes. Parallel to the central ranges are the much narrower northern ranges, separated by the intermontane valley, which also runs the entire length of the island. Western New Guinea is part of the Indonesian province of Irian Jaya, while the eastern half of the island, together with the Bismarck Archipel-

ago, and North Solomon Islands, forms the state of Papua New Guinea. The main island, which occupies more than 808,000 km², is the second largest island in the world, after Greenland. Most of the land area is covered by forest. Rain forest develops in lowland areas below 1000 to 1400 m that receive annual rainfall in excess of 2500 mm. It is floristically very rich, with more than twelve hundred species of trees forming canopy and subcanopy. In regions receiving less rainfall, a dry evergreen forest develops, which is replaced by savanna in areas with a marked dry season. Above 1000 to 1400 m, montane rain forest predominates, interspersed by man-induced grasslands, largely in the valleys. Upward from the natural tree limit at 3000 to 3900 m is the subalpine vegetation of low shrubs, herbs, and grasses.

Winters, left, assisted by Michael Corabasson, collects samples of *Neocallitropsis araucarioides* in New Caledonia. Photo by Joseph J. Higgins.

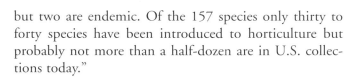

Millar, who assisted Winters and Higgins in their collecting in New Guinea, holds a flowering specimen of *Saurania*. Photo by Joseph J. Higgins.

Wau Valley viewed from a road leading to Edie Creek. Photo by Joseph J. Higgins.

but two are endemic. Of the 157 species only thirty to forty species have been introduced to horticulture but probably not more than a half-dozen are in U.S. collections today."

Ten cents an armload

Departing from Baltimore on 4 January 1970, Higgins and Winters stopped in Hawaii in order to consult with experts on the New Guinea flora. On 8 January the explorers continued their journey across the Pacific to Noumea in New Caledonia. The purpose of their visit in New Caledonia was to collect samples of two endemic conifers, *Neocallitropsis araucarioides* and *Austrotaxus spicata,* needed for a cancer screening program in the United States.

Leaving New Caledonia, Higgins and Winters paid a brief visit to the Queensland Herbarium in Brisbane, Australia, and a few day later landed in New Guinea, arriving at Lae, the second largest city, situated on the coast of Huon Gulf. At Lae they were most cordially received by John S. Womersley, chief of the Division of Botany in the Department of Forests, and by Andrée Millar, curator of Lae Botanic Garden. "This area of Lae resembles coastal Puerto Rico to a great extent, warm, humid," wrote Winters (1970a), describing his first impressions. "It is in the dry season so we have had only a little rain so far."

For their first field trip the explorers were taken by Millar to Wau, a town south of Lae, situated at the foot of Mount Amungwiwa, 3277 m. Operating out of Wau,

Flowers of *Rhododendron aurigeranum* (73567–8) collected on the grassy slope of Beenleigh Peak varied in color from pure yellow and orange to apricot. Photo by Joseph J. Higgins.

Various forms of *Impatiens hawkeri* found at Namie Creek showed intriguing variation in flower color. Photo by Joseph J. Higgins.

Rhododendron konori (73573) impressed the explorers with its huge flowers up to 15 cm wide. Higgins considered it among the most beautiful rhododendrons in New Guinea. Photo by Joseph J. Higgins.

they made several excursions to various sites, including Edie Creek, Meri Creek, and Bulolo River gorge.

"On our first excursion out of Wau, we collected our first rhododendron on the grassy slope of Beenleigh Peak, at about 1450 m," recalls Winters. "Some years previously the area had been cleared of forest. Rhododendron seeds, being winged and light in weight, are easily carried to such areas by the wind. Vireya rhododendrons are good colonizers, readily establishing themselves in such locations. We had a picnic collecting seeds and cuttings of *Rhododendron aurigeranum* (73567–8) in colors ranging from pure yellow and orange to apricot."

As Higgins remembers, when they stopped at Namie Creek, on the way from Wau to Edie Creek, at an eleva-tion of about 1200 m, "*Impatiens hawkeri* appeared, the first of many impatiens collected. We were attracted to its potential for horticultural value because of the large flowers, some 7 cm in diameter." They found various forms of this species growing along wet stream banks, the flowers ranging from pink (71202) and rose (71203–9) to pale salmon and white (71210–14).

"In search of other plants we climbed to 2100 m," notes Higgins, "where one of the most beautiful rhododendrons was encountered of the many we were ultimately to collect. This was *Rhododendron konori* (73573). Its white flowers were nearly 15 cm across and had unusually numbered seven petals flaring at the end of its tube." More rhododendrons were collected from old

Many children in Patep II joined Higgins and Winters in plant hunting and soon inundated the explorers with their own collections. Photo by Joseph J. Higgins.

gold-mine diggings in that area in the next several days, including *R. gracilentum* (73571), *R. herzogii* (871095), and *R. macgregoriae* (73574).

For their next foray, Higgins and Winters, accompanied by Millar, ventured into the backcountry between Lae and Wau. "Andrée obtained permission from the elders of Patep II, a village about midway between these two towns, to utilize their coffee warehouse area as a camp," remembers Winters. "Luckily, it was not harvest season for coffee. Andrée proved a master at organizing a camp. She had brought along two young men from the Botanical Garden crew to assist in collecting plants as well as her own cook, and we had our mid-morning tea in short order."

Patep II was the explorers' first experience living in a native village. "For three days we collected in all directions, spending the nights in our mummy sleeping bags in a native hut," wrote Higgins (1970). "Each trip into the bush four to six natives followed along to carry our bundles and scamper up trees and through heavy bush to get plants for us." Being near sea level, Patep II area was heavily forested. As Higgins remembers, "The exotic distractions of the jungle whetted my interest in tropical ferns while Harold was enamored of the flowering material. Interested indigenous natives began to catch on to what we were doing. They proceeded in nearly inundating us with their own collections so that we were busy curating this appreciated bonus. We paid them 10 cents for each armload."

The environs of Patep II turned out to be very rich floristically and yielded many discoveries. Among them

were numerous orchids, such as *Acanthephippium papuanum* (701191), *Coelogyne pustulosa* (701214), and *Grammatophyllum papuanum* (70851); ferns, including *Drynaria sparsisora* (701265); and gingers, such as *Curcuma longa* (72686). After ten days of what Winters (1970b) described as "frantic collecting" in the Wau area, the explorers had gathered two hundred plants.

Little tree with flowers

On 2 February the expedition headed northwest from Lae up the Markham Valley, through the Kassam Pass, to the eastern highlands. There Higgins and Winters worked for several days around Kainantu, Aiyura, and Arona. On Kassam Pass and along the road from Aiyura to Arona they collected a couple of undetermined *Impatiens* with flowers ranging in color from rose to creamy white (71223–4). In the hills above Aiyura, Higgins and Winters found blue-flowered *Dianella ensifolia* (7360), an imposing flax-lily, and *Rhododendron macgregoriae* (73575–6), along with several other rhododendrons of uncertain identity (871120–2). Near Kainantu they found a single small plant of a particularly attractive form of *R. zoelleri* (871118), which had flowers with a broad golden throat and petal tips marked with dark salmon, and a form of *R. macgregoriae* (73577) with rose-pink flowers, larger than typical for this species.

Upon their return from the highlands, Higgins and Winters scheduled a charter flight for 9 February that would take them south to Woitape; from there, they planned to walk up Mount Albert Edward, 3993 m, in the Owen Stanley Range. At the last minute, however, they had to change plans. "Our trip to Mount Albert Edward fell through because of continued bad weather there," explained Winters (1970c). "As an alternate plan we chartered a plane to take us to Mindik Village, north of here [Lae] in the Saruwaged Range."

Upon landing in Mindik, a Swiss Lutheran missionary station, on a narrow grass strip, the explorers hired a dozen bearers to carry 500 kg of gear to the village of Aregenang, 20 km away. "After a half day's hike up and down and around many mountains we reached the village and were abandoned immediately by our bearers after receiving each of their seven shillings," recalled Higgins (1970). "Our new natives gave us one of their village huts to stay in for the next several days. Here, again, in all directions we struck out to gather all the plants we could. The hut was quite a dwelling to behold, naturally a thatched hut.

Higgins washes his hands with water brought to Aregenang in bamboo poles. The villagers called him *Masta Mausgras,* Mister Mouth Grass, for the bushy beard he had developed by that time. Photo by Harold F. Winters.

Winters and the native bearers return to Aregenang after a day of collecting in the surrounding hills. Photo by Joseph J. Higgins.

The walls and floor, however, were fashioned by hand hewn boards which were flat only in a general way! Our air mattresses and mummy bags gave us excellent sleeping quarters in the rear half of the native dwelling. One man from the Lae Botany Division accompanied us, who was pretty good with his Pidgin English. In the front half by the door the cooking and eating took place, while one-third of the native village stood outside by the door watching our every move. We got to know quite well several of the natives who went out in the bush with us each day."

Winters remembers how over the course of the next couple days they became acquainted with the villagers: "We purchased excellent pineapples and papayas from the natives who were generous with what they had. One evening they built a fire on the ground in front of our hut and roasted sweet potatoes for our dinner. Unfortunately, there were so many natives that we could not reciprocate with food, our supplies were too limited. However, they seemed pleased with a few sheets of newspaper from our supply for plant pressing. These they cut into strips and rolled cigarettes using home-grown or crumblings from stick tobacco."

This daily going out "in the bush" around Aregenang resulted in numerous valuable collections, including orchids such as *Dendrobium neo-guineense* (701222), ferns such as *Blechnum dentatum* (701204) and *Marattia brassii* (701269), aroids such as *Holochlamys beccarii* (701242), and several undetermined species of *Impatiens* (71229–31). But they had not found any rhododendrons.

"Searching for rhododendrons during our first two days at Aregenang had been disappointing," recalls Winters. "It was difficult to make the natives understand what our priorities were. None of the natives spoke English but most spoke and understood Pidgin. None of our party was really proficient in that *lingua franca* of the islands, so I drew a picture of an arborescent rhododendron, showed it to the usual evening assembly in front of our house and using the few words of Pidgin that I knew, told them that we wanted to find a *lik-lik dewai im e gat powers,* meaning little tree with flowers, such as I had drawn. One dignified older man evidently of some standing in the village nodded his head and indicated that he knew where to find these plants. We arranged for him to guide us there the next morning."

Higgins describes that memorable day: "From our thatched home at about 3000 m, we hiked down the steep trail through spectacular scenery to stride a razorback ridge. Heavily forested peaks rose above our curving, twisting footpath as we progressed through the great diversity of flora. Lush isolated valleys fell away before us." Following a rather torturous hike, the older guide led the explorers to the top of a narrow ridge. "There he pointed to a spectacular clump of *Rhododendron zoelleri* (73579), just what we hoped to find," remembers Winters. "Some plants were 3 m tall, in full bloom with clusters of magnificent flowers each 8 cm in diameter with butter yellow throats and bright salmon limbs of five petals. If this were the end of our expedition, I think we would have been happy."

Winters takes cuttings from *Rhododendron zoelleri* (73579) found growing near Aregenang. Photo by Joseph J. Higgins.

The lower of two glacial lakes on Mount Wilhelm, where Higgins and Winters camped for several days. Photo by Joseph J. Higgins.

Thrilled by this discovery, Higgins and Winters rushed to gather the seeds and cuttings, and to prepare herbarium specimens and photographic documentation. "It became a Hollywood production considering all the color shots we took at different distances and angles, Harold and I exchanging places for 'human interest.' It was one great day," remembers Higgins.

Western highlands

In late February, Higgins and Winters returned to the highlands, this time the western part. They began with exploring areas around Kundiawa, a town built on an old Lutheran mission site. "After spending several days going out from our motel in Kundiawa into very rugged and beautiful mountains," wrote Higgins (1970) to Seibert, "we began one of our grandest ventures." This started

with a half day's drive on one of the most daring roads of New Guinea to Keglsugl. Their destination was Mount Wilhelm, 4509 m, the tallest peak in Papua New Guinea.

"Our carriers were waiting at Keglsugl so we started right off, 6.5 miles [10.5 km], mostly up," recorded Winters (1970d). "We must have crossed the same stream fifteen times and for part of the way the stream was the trail. After a few times of jumping from rock to rock you give up and slosh through as do the barefoot natives. It rained most of the way but we arrived at the camp, 11,800 feet [3600 m], about 5:20 p.m. Since it was too late for them to return, all the natives stayed with us the first night. It is a dramatic setting. The camp is located near the lower of two glacial lakes. The water cascades down Mount Wilhelm into the upper [lake], falls to the second, then another series of rapids and falls below the

Porters who accompanied Higgins and Winters on their hike down from Mount Wilhelm to Keglsugl. Photo by Joseph J. Higgins.

One of the unidentified *Impatiens* (71233) collected by Higgins and Winters along the road from Mount Hagen to Mount Kum. This clone was later distributed as a cultivar, 'Mt. Kum'. Photo by Joseph J. Higgins.

lower lake. Finally it flattens out and flows through a beautiful alpine meadow for 1.5 miles [2.4 km] before entering the forested area below. The mountain rises stark and bare behind the lakes."

Despite frequent rain, the exploration of the flora on the mountain continued. "One native man was in our company from the Lae Botanical Division who took care of the language problem and stayed with us to help collect and carry during our several days' stay on Mount Wilhelm," recalled Higgins (1970). "A wood stove in the house kept fired most of the time chased away the 48°F [9°C] recorded in the a.m. inside as we got up each morning. Although fog and rain were much more on hand than we would like to remember in the afternoon and evening, we did manage to get several different species of *Rhododendron* from the surrounding hills as well as a number of others."

One of the rhododendrons collected on Mount Wilhelm was *R. gaultheriifolium* (871094), a small, dense shrub with dark purple-red flowers. Among other plants found there was an orange-flowered orchid, *Dendrobium flammula* (70837), forming dense mats on tree branches, and *Dimorphanthera leucostoma* (701234), an ericaceous vine with tubular, 5 cm long, red flowers, which Winters later called "one of the most showy species we saw on the entire trip" (1970g).

On the morning of 5 March the porters returned and the whole group hiked down, taking longer on the return trip because they collected along the way. By previous arrangement they were met by a single-engine plane at a small landing strip in Keglsugl, which at 2445 m in ele-vation is the highest in New Guinea, and flew back to Kundiawa. Their work in the highlands continued for several more days in the area around Mount Hagen, 4000 m, west of Mount Wilhelm, and in the Chimbu and Waghi valleys.

It was in this area that Winters noticed that "the highland peoples of New Guinea have a great appreciation for flowers, particularly in the Chimbu and Mount Hagen areas. Here roadsides and gardens often are bordered with such introduced flowers as cosmos, dahlias, and marigolds. Numerous native varieties of *Impatiens* are cultivated, also" (1970f). In fact, the western highlands turned out to be the most fruitful grounds for collecting impatiens. Of the fourteen collections made near Mount Hagen, all but two were from cultivated plants. Some were recognized as forms of *I. schlechteri* (71236–7, 71240) and *I. linearifolia* (71220–2); others remained unidentified (71232–5, 71238–9, 71241–2). Their flowers were exceptionally large and in various shades of salmon, pink, red, and orange. Many also had foliage variegated with tones of yellow, pink, or red. This area was also rich in rhododendrons. Pink-flowered *Rhododendron dielsianum* (73569–70) was collected along the road from Goroka to Kundiawa, while red-flowered *R. rarum* (871100) was seen in several locations in the highlands. Returning from the highlands on 17 March, the explorers added a few hundred plants to their collections. "We did pretty well collecting in the highlands and these represent some of the best rhododendron materials assembled to date," wrote Winters from Lae (1970d).

The impatiens collected in New Guinea, first placed in quarantine at the USDA Plant Introduction Station in Glenn Dale, Maryland, were sent to Longwood Gardens in March of 1971. They exhibited great genetic variability with respect to growth habit, leaf size, shape, and color. Since little was known about breeding New Guinea impatiens, Robert J. Armstrong, Longwood's geneticist, began crossing the plants in every possible combination. By the summer of 1972, seven hundred first-generation hybrid seedlings had been raised. By intercrossing among these, an additional three thousand seedlings were available the following year. From among these, the ten best plants were selected for naming and introduction. This first set, released in 1974, was called the Circus Series and included 'Carousel' shown here. Armstrong continued his breeding work on impatiens during the 1970s. Ten more cultivars were released in 1977 and an additional six in 1979. Photo by Robert J. Armstrong.

Wild lime discovered

On 22 March, Higgins and Winters departed Lae for the last time and flew south to Port Moresby, the capital of Papua New Guinea, built on several hills surrounding a natural harbor opening to the Coral Sea. Much of their collecting around Port Moresby concentrated near Itikinumu Hill, east of the city, and along Brown River to the north.

"Even though this is the hot, dry side of the island it has rained every day since we have been here," recorded Winters (1970e). "Here in Port Moresby I am giving emphasis to the request for citrus relatives. So far I have not found *Microcitrus warburgiana,* but did find one wild lime (budwood), a *Microcitrus* or *Eremocitrus* with leaves like the latter and fruits like the former, and another with foliage as in *Atalantia* but fruits as in *Triphasia.* We found

only a few fruits of the last but will try to return to Brown River again if the rain lets up. We were rained out yesterday and left shortly after noon before the road became completely impassable."

The unknown wild lime found by the explorers on one of their scoutings near Brown River turned out later to be a new species and was named by Winters *Microcitrus papuana.* "The existence of *Microcitrus* population at Brown River has been known to local botanists for some years," recalled Winters (1976), "but it was thought to be a variant of *Microcitrus warburgiana . . .* the only other species of *Microcitrus* known from Papua New Guinea. The collection site for *M. warburgiana* was Milne Bay, approximately 364 km southeast of the Brown River site."

On 1 April, Higgins and Winters shipped the last of their New Guinea collections from Port Moresby. Before returning to the United States they stopped in both Manila and Jakarta to pick up additional plants. In the end the expedition brought back 868 collections, which included 140 Vireya rhododendrons. "The rhododendrons were later distributed to various botanical gardens, arboreta, and individual collectors around the country," recalls Winters. "They seemed to perform best in the San Francisco Bay area of California, probably because of frequent fogs and low night temperatures. But even there the outdoor plantings were eventually damaged by an unusual cold spell. Although some of the collections were from near or even above the frost line in New Guinea, they proved not to be sufficiently hardy. However, Vireya rhododendrons from New Guinea can be grown indoors

Petunia integrifolia (871181) collected by Armstrong and Lawson at Chiba University. Photo by Tomasz Aniśko.

Lawson, left, and Wong in the Singapore Botanic Gardens. Photo by Robert J. Armstrong.

with special attention to control of shade, humidity and temperature as for tropical orchids throughout the United States."

Among Higgins and Winters's collections were also twenty-five impatiens. Little did the explorers anticipate that this modest representation of impatiens from New Guinea would give rise to a whole new group of summer bedding plants. The early indications of what would become of these plants appeared two years after the expedition. "*Impatiens* has really become a popular item," wrote Winters (1972) to Seibert. "To date the New Guinea impatiens collections have created more excitement than any of our other groups of introductions from there." And this was only the beginning. In 1974, Longwood Gardens released the first generation of ten hybrids called Circus Series, developed by intercrossing the New Guinea collections. These were followed soon by an avalanche of introductions from breeders at other organizations. Fifteen years later New Guinea impatiens matured into an industry producing millions of plants annually in the United States and Europe and, together with Sultana impatiens, became the number one bedding plant.

AROUND THE PACIFIC

In 1987, Longwood and USDA personnel joined together on a month-long trip around the Pacific that provided an opportunity to observe ornamental plants cultivated in several countries and to procure the most promising ones for introduction into the United States.

The team included Dr. Roger H. Lawson, research leader at the USDA Florist and Nursery Crops Laboratory, and Dr. Robert J. Armstrong, research horticulturist at Longwood Gardens. "The overall goal of this trip was to find and collect plants that would have potential as florist crops," explains Armstrong. "I, of course, would be on the lookout for plants that I thought might be useful in Longwood Gardens displays. We visited mostly nurseries, gardens, some universities, and private individuals in five countries: Japan, Singapore, Indonesia, Australia, and New Zealand."

Chiba's petunia

After arriving in Tokyo on 9 August, Armstrong and Lawson paid a visit to Chiba University, where they met with researchers from the Faculty of Horticulture and later toured the nursery. "In Japan we visited many nurseries and seed companies," recollects Armstrong, "but I think the most significant place visited was Chiba University where we collected *Petunia integrifolia* (871181) which had been collected by Professor Toshio Ando in Argentina. In the trial garden at Chiba University this petunia did not exhibit, to me at least, any particularly outstanding qualities, but our hosts wanted us to take something along with us and it was a nice looking petunia. This species was later to exhibit remarkable resistance to drought, and was distributed by Longwood Gardens in its plant exchange program where it was picked up by breeders and used to develop drought resistant hybrid petunias. It was also used extensively in its original state in outdoor displays at Longwood."

Aquatic collection at the Bogor Botanic Garden. Photo by Robert J. Armstrong.

Another plant spotted at Chiba University that later turned out to be a very successful introduction was *Lantana trifolia* (881224), a small shrub native to Central America that produces a beautiful combination of lavender flowers and lavender fruits. This plant later became a permanent feature of various display areas at Longwood Gardens.

Armstrong and Lawson spent the following two days in the Yokohama area visiting nurseries and various establishments of Sakata Seed Corporation, including Sakata Garden Center, Chogo Research, and Chigasaki Breeding Station. "Sakata is the largest producer of flower seeds in the world," explains Lawson. "At the company's breeding station in Chigasaki we were shown many new pot plants including dwarf *Clematis,* such as *C.* 'Hakuba' (93227) and *C.* 'Misette Blue' (93228). These dwarf cultivars are the result of more than thirty years of breeding at Sakata.

In addition to being grown as pot plants with multiple flowers, they are also trained to a single stem and sold as cut flowers."

On 15 August, Armstrong and Lawson departed for a short visit to Singapore. Located only a couple of degrees north of the equator, Singapore welcomed the explorers with oppressively hot and humid weather. At the airport they were greeted by Dr. Seth M. Wong of the National University of Singapore. Wong arranged for Armstrong and Lawson to tour the Singapore Botanic Gardens and a number of nurseries, including Plantek International and Multico Orchids.

Adventuresome Java

On 19 August, Armstrong and Lawson left for Java, Indonesia. "Java turned out to be quite an experience," remembers Armstrong. "The number of plants collected

Robby Kerst and his wife shared with Armstrong and Lawson several plants from Kerst's nursery at Cikopo Selatan. Photo by Roger H. Lawson.

Succulent house at the Cibodas Botanic Garden. Photo by Robert J. Armstrong.

Heterocentron macrostachyum 'Nanum' (871166) collected by Armstrong and Lawson at the Cibodas Botanic Garden. Photo by Robert J. Armstrong.

was modest, but Java did prove to be the most adventuresome part of the trip." Upon their arrival in Jakarta, the travelers headed south for Bogor. There they checked into a hotel and the next morning "set out on foot to find the Bogor Botanic Garden," remembers Armstrong. "We sort of had a map, but not a good one. We found what we thought was the entrance to the garden, but as we walked in we were suddenly surrounded by armed soldiers. There was a certain amount of consternation, and we eventually figured out we were in the presidential palace grounds which were adjacent to the botanic garden. We eventually did find the administrative offices of the gardens where we met the director Dr. Sampurno Kadarsan who introduced us to Baskoro who was to be our guide. We were shown around the gardens and after that Baskoro hired a

taxi for us and we drove up to Robby Kerst's nursery at Cikopo Selatan. This was a very nice nursery with a lot of interesting plant materials. We collected there *Heliconia wagneriana* (871167), *Pteris quadriaurita* (871175), and noted several other plants we would like to obtain, especially a dwarf lavender *Anthurium* (900914)."

After lunch the explorers drove with the Kersts up the mountain to the Cibodas Botanic Garden. "This was a very pleasant place," recalls Armstrong. "We collected there seeds of several Mexican *Cuphea* species, including *C. micropetala* (871168) and various color selections of *C. procumbens* (871170–2), and *Heterocentron macrostachyum* 'Nanum' (871166), shrub of Melastomataceae, also native to Mexico."

Poinsettias, *Euphorbia pulcherrima,* grown at the Horticulture Experiment Station in Cipanas. Photo by Robert J. Armstrong.

Bush in the Brisbane Water National Park near Gosford. Photo by Robert J. Armstrong.

"On 21 August Baskoro picked us up at the inn in a four-wheel-drive Toyota and we drove up the mountain to Cipanas to visit the Horticulture Experiment Station," remembers Armstrong. "There was interesting work going on there and some interesting plants. We were shown poinsettias, *Euphorbia pulcherrima,* unlike any I had ever seen before. These plants had many layers of bracts and came in several different colors. We collected seed from several promising plants around the experiment station, including *Browallia americana* (871176), covered with small blue flowers, and *Pitcairnia punicea* (871173), a red-flowered bromeliad."

Armstrong and Lawson dedicated their last day in Java to making the final inspection of the collections at the Bogor Botanic Garden. It resulted in a number of seed collections. Among them were an undetermined species of *Abutilon* (871163) with small yellow flowers, *Hibiscus acetosella* (871162), a native of Africa, and *Oxalis corniculata* var. *atropurpurea* (871177), with small orange flowers.

Golden air

"We flew to Sydney in the morning of 23 August when spring flowering was at its height," remembers Lawson, "and we were introduced to Australia's flora even before we landed. As the airplane descended, bright yellow patches within the city beneath us resolved into masses of flowering acacias, one of the dominant trees on the Australian east coast. So colorful and profuse were the flowers that the air was golden with their reflected color."

After going through customs and securing a rental car, the explorers proceeded up the coast to Gosford where they were to meet with Angus Stewart and his wife Jennie. "Angus is a keen Australian naturalist who lives about 60 km north of Sydney where he operates a tissue culture laboratory specializing in Australian native plants," explains Lawson. "By previous agreement, Angus had put into tissue culture a number of Australian plants that were thought to have potential as florist crops," adds Armstrong. "Bringing plants back in tissue culture was ideal since they were easily transported in this condition. Among these were *Philotheca myoporoides* (88697) and *Philotheca* 'Stardust' (88696)."

The next day Armstrong and Lawson paid a visit to Bryan Parry's Nursery, a commercial tissue culture facility in the Gosford area, where they acquired a number of tissue cultured *Grevillea,* including *G. dallachiana* (88681), *G. lanigera* (88698), and *G.* 'Poorinda Tranquility' (88679). Later that day the explorers made their way to the Brisbane Water National Park to see the native flora. "Here the ridges of the Hawkesbury Sandstones soar dramatically above tidal mudflats, waterways, and mangrove stands," Lawson recalls. "Curious honeycomb-like formations reflect centuries of extensive weathering. Despite shallow soil, a rich variety of flora occurs in the park. Many of the plants grow in crevices and indentations in the rocks, supported only by wind-blown soil or loose rocks that have eroded from larger outcrop formations. Aboriginal carvings of birds, animals, and human figures adorn broad expanses of sandstone, adding to the wild and primitive atmosphere."

Botanizing in the Brisbane Water National Park, Armstrong and Lawson marveled at the diversity in plant

Beds of South African *Leucadendron orientale* grow at Proteaflora. Mathews, shown, founded the company. Photo by Robert J. Armstrong.

A dark blue selection of *Lechenaultia biloba* 'Moora' (881155) procured by Armstrong and Lawson from Plant Growers Australia in Park Orchards. Photo by Robert J. Armstrong.

height, flower size, form, and color within a single genus. "We observed several of these natural variants in the Hawkesbury Sandstones," remembers Lawson. "Within a few hundred meters of one another we saw *Eriostemon australasius* ranging from dark to light pink, to nearly white. A few kilometers distant we saw red-flowered and pink-flowered *Grevillea* growing within a couple of meters of each other. Mixed in this prolific population was the single bright red pink flower of a natural hybrid. Many of the popular plants sold in the Australian nurseries represent careful selection from these populations."

On 26 August, Armstrong and Lawson left the Gosford area to head back to Sydney, and flew to Melbourne the next day. From Melbourne they drove east to Monbulk. "We made our way to Bush Gems Garden Nursery, where we were met and entertained by Mervyn Turner and his wife Nyare," recalls Armstrong. "Turner was responsible for the development of the Bush Gems series of hybrid kangaroo-paws, *Anigozanthos*. One of his selections called 'Baby Roo' (90913) has become a regular feature of Longwood's Mediterranean House display."

The following day the explorers drove down to Longford to visit James Frew at his nursery. "The diversity and uniqueness of the plant material in Frew's nursery was almost unbelievable," explains Armstrong. "Frew is a real plant collector and lover. He spends his holidays in the bush looking for new and better plants and then the rest of the time working his nursery and harvesting the plants for cut flowers. We were indeed privileged to see this nursery, since Frew is very protective of his material and does not wish other nurserymen to know what he has. He

gave us a number of South African *Erica,* including *E. cerinthoides* (881213), *E. persoluta* (881215), and *E. perspicua* (881216)."

On 29 August, Armstrong and Lawson drove to Proteaflora near Monbulk, where they met Peter Mathews, founder of the company, who gave them a tour and shared a number of plants. From there they drove to Plant Growers Australia in Park Orchards, owned by Rodger and Natalie Peate. There the explorers were again given a number of plants, the most notable of which were *Lechenaultia biloba* (88686) and its superior dark blue selection 'Moora' (881155).

The explorers' next stop was in Montrose at Austraflora. "This is the nursery that was originally started by the well known authors Rodger and Gwen Elliot," explains Armstrong. "This nursery had an incredible variety of plant materials. A number of these were given to us to take back with us. By this time we were developing quite a collection of plant materials, both in tissue culture and plants mostly in tubes. The tissue culture tubes we carried in our suitcases. These were taken out each night and placed under a light in the motel room in order to help keep the material in good condition."

Jury on magnolias

On 30 August, Armstrong and Lawson flew from Melbourne to Sydney and then on to Auckland, New Zealand. They began their exploration in the Auckland area, where they visited several nurseries. At Dawn Nurseries, Armstrong collected seeds of *Sophora tetraptera* (871164) "covered with yellow flowers." Then, on 2 Sep-

New Zealand is situated in the Pacific Ocean more than 1600 km southeast of Australia. It comprises two main islands—North Island and South Island—as well as a number of small islands. The combined area of the islands making up New Zealand exceeds 270,000 km². Both North and South islands are bisected by mountains and hills. The tallest of them, the Southern Alps, with the highest peak Mount Cook, 3764 m, form a nearly 500 km long mountain chain on the South Island. Because the mountains obstruct the prevailing westerly winds, the contrast in climate from west to east is more pronounced than that from north to south. The rainfall ranges from 330 mm east of the Southern Alps to 7600 mm on the western slopes of the mountains. Temperatures are moderated by the surrounding ocean, and their annual mean values decrease from 15°C in the far north to 9°C in the far south. For its size, New Zealand has a relatively small flora of about two thousand species of vascular plants, but some 84 percent of them are endemic to these islands. The prolonged isolation of the country has led to the development of such a unique flora. The indigenous vegetation consisted mostly of mixed evergreen forest of predominantly *Nothofagus* species, remnants of which can be seen only in areas unsuitable for development or protected as national parks.

tember, the explorers flew south to New Plymouth. There they visited the nursery of Ted and Nolene Roberts, "a remarkable couple," according to Armstrong, specializing in growing bulbs, mostly of Amaryllidaceae, and later that day went to Duncan and Davies nursery to see New Zealand native foliage plants.

"While in New Zealand we toured many nurseries, garden centers, and gardens," recalls Armstrong. "Many of these had wonderful collections of plants. Probably the most notable of these places visited was the Felix and Mark Jury Garden in Tokorangi near Palmerston North. The collections of bulbs, camellias, Vireya rhododendrons, and magnolias were really quite good. The magnolias developed by Felix were nothing short of spectacular, and they were being grown in the middle of a sheep paddock! After much discussion Roger was able to convince Mark Jury that he should send some of his magnolias with us to see what they would do in the United States (900572–9). Unfortunately, these magnolias

Mark Jury presents one of his spectacular hybrid magnolias. Photo by Roger H. Lawson.

Rugged shores of Lake Taupo, New Zealand's largest lake, located in the center of the North Island. Photo by Robert J. Armstrong.

turned out not to be hardy in the climate of Longwood Gardens."

On 5 September the explorers drove north to Taupo, on the shore of Lake Taupo, located in the center of New Zealand's North Island in the midst of remarkable hot-springs country. "The lake is very beautiful," comments Armstrong. "It is said to be 2000 feet [600 m] deep shortly from shore. It is a drowned volcanic crater. Earthquakes are said to occur almost constantly in the area." The reason for their visit was the Geotherm Exports, a company specializing in *Phalaenopsis* orchids. "The greenhouses at the Geotherm Exports are heated by volcanic steam," explains Lawson. "Ground vents occur all over this area to relieve the underground pressure. Because of the advantage of the natural source of heat, there are many specialty growers in the vicinity who produce high value crops such as orchids."

Two days later Armstrong and Lawson drove north from Taupo to the coast of Bay of Plenty to visit several nurseries. The next day they closed the loop and returned to Auckland, stopping at the Auckland Regional Botanic Garden, where they met George Rainey, past president of the New Zealand Nurserymen's Association. "Rainey led us all around Auckland showing us various plants before he finally led us to his house, garden, and nursery," recalls

Armstrong. "It was a very special house and garden. The nursery had some neat things also. Rainey gave us a number of plants to take back with us, including *Virgilia divaricata* (871176), a South African shrub with very fragrant rose-colored flowers." The visit to Rainey's garden concluded the expedition. Later that day Armstrong and Lawson left New Zealand and returned to the east coast of the United States, with Armstrong making short stops to pick up plants in Hawaii and California.

AUSTRALIA'S DRIVE-BY FLORA

The increasing use of Australian plants in Longwood's conservatories led to yet another plant exploration trip, only four years after Armstrong and Lawson visited that continent. In 1991 Rick Darke, curator of plants at Longwood, and Kathy Musial, curator at the Huntington Gardens in San Marino, California, teamed up for a four-week trip that would take them across Australia, from Perth to Sydney. Since there were many restrictions on collecting Australian plants in the wild, the trip was planned to allow the collectors to acquire choice plants from botanical gardens and nurseries specializing in native plants.

Hardenbergia comptoniana (911101), a vine acquired by Darke and Musial at the Lullfitz Nursery. Photo by Rick Darke.

Agrostocrinum scabrum was among the plants Darke and Musial encountered growing on the sandplains of the Chittering Valley. Photo by Kathy Musial.

Sandplains and the wheatbelt

Darke and Musial arrived in Perth on 5 September. They decided to follow a route that would give them an opportunity to see several types of vegetation, including sandplain (known as *kwongan*), wheatbelt, mallee-heath, *jarrah* forest, and *karri* forest. "Wildflower viewing is a major tourist attraction in Western Australia, and readily available locally produced brochures describe driving routes for prime wildflower sightings," explains Musial. "Western Australia has pretty much a 'drive-by' flora, as most can be seen right from the roads, and indeed in many areas the only native bush is in roadside verges, the rest having been cleared for agriculture. In some cases, these roadside verges are the last habitats of critically endangered species."

First the explorers set out on 7 September heading north to Wanneroo, some 20 km from Perth. They stopped at Lullfitz Nursery, which sold Australian native plants and was surrounded by a demonstration garden. "Later continuing north just a short distance, we spotted along the road a nice stand of *Xanthorrhoea preissii*, *Anigozanthos humilis*, and *A. manglesii*," remembers Musial. "Driving up the Chittering Valley, we came upon another open sandplain with *Agrostocrinum scabrum*, *Lechenaultia biloba*, and *Diuris* orchids. Our next stop was at a rare *Hibbertia miniata* population, one of the few orange-flowered species in that genus. A little further on was a large stand of *Dryandra polycephala* and *D. carduacea*, species popular for cut flowers. Wild populations of many Western Australia plants have been damaged by

A colony of sky-blue *Lechenaultia biloba* was seen in the Chittering Valley north of Perth. Photo by Rick Darke.

Eucalyptus pyriformis trees with flowers ranging in color from cream to red were observed in the Alexander Morrison National Park located southwest of Three Springs. Photo by Kathy Musial.

cutting for the flower trade but cut flower farms are now reducing this problem."

The following morning Darke and Musial stopped along the coast at Nambung National Park, famed for its stark landscape of thousands of limestone pillars. From there they headed to the South Eneabba Nature Reserve, where they observed many fire followers, including *Verreauxia reinwardtii*, blooming after a recent burn. On 9 September the team detoured east off the Brand Highway to see the Howatharra Hills Reserve, abloom with *Verticordia chrysantha*. Then they continued to the Kalbarri National Park, about 160 km north of Geraldton, where they studied extensive northern sandplain vegetation, including *Geleznowia verrucosa*, *Grevillea dielsiana*, and several smokebushes, *Conospermum* spp.

"The next day on our way back south along the Brand Highway, we again detoured inland at Northamp-

ton toward Mullewa via Yuna," says Musial. "Near Yuna we saw spectacular carpets of annual *Helipterum splendidum* and *Podolepis canescens*, but the main objective this day was to find *Lechenaultia macrantha* between Mullewa and Morawa. Before the trip I recorded collecting localities for this species from herbarium specimens held at the Royal Botanic Garden in Melbourne. Despite this detailed information it still took us driving up and down the Mullewa–Morawa road a few times before we spotted an excellent stand late in the day."

On 11 September the collectors botanized along the unpaved roads southward between Three Springs and York, stopping at several national parks and reserves in the heart of the wheatbelt. "We found a number of *Hakea* species with interesting foliage as well as an excellent stand of *Eucalyptus pyriformis*, with individual trees

East Mount Barren is the dominating landform in the eastern end of the Fitzgerald River National Park. Photo by Rick Darke.

Banksia repens was among the species inhabiting mallee-heath just east of Esperance on the south coast of Western Australia. Photo by Kathy Musial.

Eucalyptus preissiana is a prominent species of mallee-heath in the Fitzgerald River National Park. Photo by Rick Darke.

with a range of flower colors from cream to red," recalls Musial. "Armed with locality details gleaned from herbarium sheets, I was thrilled to spot the highly endangered *Grevillea dryandroides* growing in a small roadside reserve near the town of Ballidu."

The next day they continued southeast from York to the town of Esperance on the south coast of Western Australia. "Driving through the Lake Grace and Lake King regions—which are lakes in name only, nearly always being dry—we observed much salt-damaged land," recalls Musial. "The damage was caused when land was cleared of native vegetation and irrigated for agricultural crops. Irrigation water evaporating from the soils exposed to direct sun carried salts to the surface, while the rainfall was too low to leach them out, raising salt concentration to toxic levels. South of Lake King we started to see the

southern sandplain vegetation, with distinctly different species composition than the northern sandplain."

Eucalyptus heaths and forests

The main destination for 13 September was the Fitzgerald River National Park, southwest of Ravensthorpe, a World Biosphere Reserve noted for its unique flora and fauna. "While we were driving south toward Hopetoun, East Mount Barren, 299 m, came into view, one of the quartzite coastal hills and the main landform at this end of the national park," remembers Musial. "The region encompassing the national park is known as the barrens, with vegetation primarily of mallee-heath, with mallee or *Eucalyptus* densely scattered throughout the heath, low shrub vegetation morphologically similar to the heaths of Europe, but made up of plants from different families.

Darke and Musial spotted *Adenanthos obovatus* in Torndirrup National Park, south of Albany. Photo by Kathy Musial.

Kingia australis flowers following a recent fire in the Stirling Range National Park, north of Albany. Photo by Kathy Musial.

Darke and Musial encountered *Acacia drummondii* ssp. *elegans* while botanizing at the foot of Mount Toolbrunup in the Stirling Range National Park. Photo by Rick Darke.

Isopogon latifolius flowering in the flats surrounding Mount Toolbrunup in the Stirling Range National Park. Photo by Kathy Musial.

The most noticeable species of mallee were *E. preissiana* and *E. tetragona,* but in the east end of the barrens we found the rare endemic *E. sepulcralis.*"

Darke and Musial made Albany, the main city on the south coast of Western Australia, their base for the following several days. On 16 September they went to the Stirling Range National Park, north of Albany, featuring the only significant mountains in the otherwise flat landscape of Western Australia. "Bluff Knoll, at 1073 m the highest peak in southern Western Australia, is home to some of Australia's rarest plants," explains Musial. "As it came into view on our drive into the park from the south, I was dismayed to see that there had been a very recent and devastating-looking fire. All of Bluff Knoll, clearly visible as we approached, as well as the surrounding area, had been torched. On the flat terrain along the road, *Kingia australis,* which typically flower only after a fire, were in bloom everywhere. So were many other plants including *Acacia drummondii* ssp. *elegans, Hakea cucullata,* and *Isopogon latifolius.*"

The following day the pair left the Stirlings and drove west to Northcliffe. "This part of Western Australia is the realm of *Eucalyptus diversicolor,* known as *karri,* one of the world's tallest trees and an important timber tree," says Musial. "Typical associates of *karri* are *Acacia pentadenia, Banksia grandis,* and *Casuarina decussata,* with *Hardenbergia comptoniana* and *Kennedia coccinea* found in the understory. This area, just on the southwest tip of Australia, receives 1000 mm of rain per year, supporting the luxuriant forest of giant eucalypts."

On their way north back to Perth, Darke and Musial drove through the *jarrah* forests. "Adjacent and inland from *karri* forest, is *jarrah* or *Eucalyptus marginata* forest," notes Musial. "Receiving about 750 mm of rain per year, *jarrah* is not as tall as *karri* but is also prized for its timber, especially for furniture. Today, much of the *jarrah* forest is closed to entry to prevent the spread of *Phytophthora cinnamomi,* a soil-borne fungal pathogen introduced from Asia in the early part of the twentieth century and wreaking havoc on the vegetation of Western Australia." Darke and Musial dedicated their last two days in Western Australia to purchasing and shipping plants. On 21 September they flew to Adelaide.

Silver goes to Longwood

In Adelaide, Darke and Musial were joined by Claire Sawyers, director of Scott Arboretum in Swarthmore,

Collection of South African *Erica* species at the Wittunga Botanic Garden near Adelaide. Photo by Rick Darke.

Pennsylvania. Together they visited several gardens in the area. "We started with a visit to the Wittunga Botanic Garden, one of the annex gardens of the Adelaide Botanic Garden," remembers Musial. "In a hot, dry, low elevation of the Adelaide Hills, Wittunga features Western Australian and South African plants, and is noted for its collection of South African *Erica,* said to be one of the finest outside of South Africa. Then we went to Mount Lofty Botanic Garden, another of the annex gardens, located in the Mount Lofty Ranges east of Adelaide. At 200 m elevation with annual rainfall of 1000 mm, this garden has a cool temperate climate and features plants such as magnolias and rhododendrons, as well as an excellent collection of South African Proteaceae. Finally, we visited the Adelaide Botanic Gardens in downtown Adelaide. Walking around the gardens, we spotted a fabulous silver-

Banksia dryandroides (911120) was obtained from White Gums Nursery in Stawell. Photo by Kathy Musial.

Dampiera linearis (911110) seen by Darke and Musial near Albany was later purchased from White Gums Nursery in Stawell. Photo by Rick Darke.

leaved plant, *Plectranthus argentatus,* growing under a tree in the shade. We all marveled at the plant, and vowed to seek it out and bring one back to the United States."

Later that day the group headed east to Pinaroo, some 240 km east of Adelaide. "We crossed into Victoria via the Big Desert Wilderness, Ngarkat Conservation Park, and Little Desert National Park," remembers Musial. "Some of the interesting plants seen were *Callitris preissii* ssp. *verrucosa* and *Carpobrotus modestus,* one of the few succulent plants in Australia. The next day we visited the Grampians National Park. The Grampians, a series of north–south parallel mountain ranges in western Victoria, are home to many interesting plants, including *Eucalyptus alpina,* one of the smallest species, and *Restio tetraphyllus.* We stayed in Stawell that night for our visit the next day to Neil Marriott's White Gums Nursery, spe-

cializing in *Grevillea.* Neil's nursery and lovely garden surrounded his home. The garden was built on low raised mounds and featured many plants we had not seen elsewhere. We took the opportunity to purchase plants from the nursery, *Banksia dryandroides* (911120), *Grevillea victoriae* (911121), and *Dampiera linearis* (911110) among them."

The group's travels in Australia ended with a drive to Melbourne. There they were invited to stay with Rodger and Gwen Elliot in their home in the outer suburbs of the city. The next day Darke shipped to Longwood sixty-one plants he had procured from the nurseries along the way. On 29 September he and Sawyers departed for New Zealand, while Musial stayed behind in Melbourne. In New Zealand, Darke and Sawyers traveled for ten days, stopping in Christchurch, Dunedin, and Auckland, adding another twelve choice plants to their collections. A visit to the Titoki Point Garden and Nursery operated by Gordon and Annette Collier in Taihape on the North Island, resulted in a collection of the much desired silver-leaved *Plectranthus argentatus* (92275), seen previously in Adelaide Botanic Garden. This plant was later widely distributed in the United States, gained popularity among the gardening public, and has since been offered by some nurseries under the name 'Longwood Silver'.

Plectranthus argentatus 'Longwood Silver' (92275), spotted by Darke and Sawyers in Titoki Point Garden, is frequently featured in Longwood's seasonal plantings. Photo by Tomasz Aniśko.

Rodger and Gwen Elliot, Darke, and Musial, left to right, at the Elliots' house in the Melbourne suburbs. Photo by Rick Darke.

AFRICA

PLANTSMAN'S SAFARI

"Charming hosts, tremendous eaters, energetic conservationists, enthusiastic about their indigenous plants, with a wonderful sense of humor, extreme segregationists, rapidly industrializing their country, with excellent landscaped highways, an abundance of cars, rapidly expanding suburbs, with a stable economy, excellent standard of living, with little inflation (less than 2 percent since 1958), with shark infested beaches, and a tremendous capacity to consume the results of a large and growing wine industry." This is how Dr. Russell J. Seibert (1963e), Longwood's director, described his hosts in South Africa after returning from a five-week tour of that country. An invitation to visit had come in 1963 from Professor H. Brian Rycroft, director of Kirstenbosch National Botanical Garden, at the foot of Table Mountain near Cape Town. That year the garden and the Botanical Society of South Africa celebrated their Golden Jubilee. To mark the occasion, Rycroft invited fifty prominent botanists from twenty-one countries to participate in the celebration from mid-September through October. The celebrations included two busy weeks of lectures and symposia held at the University of Cape Town, followed by an extensive botanical tour of the country.

Seibert saw this as an opportunity to become acquainted with the botanical riches of the African continent and to acquire new plants for Longwood. "South Africa has many interesting flowering plants," he wrote,

"the majority of which are rarely seen in America because their requirements are so different from the conditions under which we are accustomed to grow plants. Take *Alberta magna* of the Rubiaceae—it is seldom seen even in California. We finally flowered it once at Longwood Gardens. Many have tried and as many have failed to grow South Africa's most beautiful and most frustrating orchid, *Disa uniflora*. However, a few South African plants are among some of our favorites for Longwood's horticultural exhibits: *Veltheimia viridifolia,* nemesia hybrids, freesias, clivias, pelargoniums, gladiolus species and hybrids, and *Gerbera jamesonii*" (Seibert 1965d).

Bougainvillea street trees

On his way to South Africa, Seibert stopped for a couple of days in Nairobi, Kenya, arriving on 14 September. In Nairobi he was greeted by Peter Greensmith, parks superintendent, who gave him a grand tour of the city's parks. Seibert also paid a visit to the Nairobi Arboretum and to the private garden of George Classen, vice president of the Kenya Horticultural Society, who had assembled an extensive collection of succulents, one of the best in East Africa.

Seibert was clearly taken by the selection of plants cultivated in Nairobi, as indicated by the long litany of plants he requested from Greensmith. Writing back to Longwood, Seibert exclaimed, "What a wonderful collection of plants here!" and "This place is the most amazing source of good ornamentals!" (1963b).

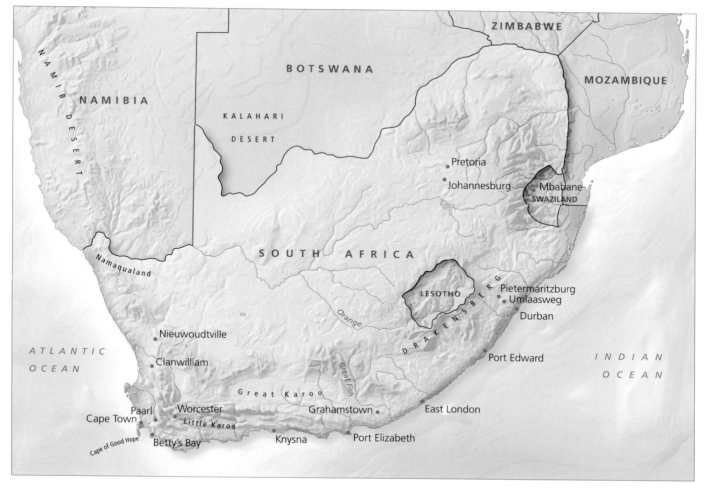

South Africa has a flora of more than twenty-four thousand species. Climates range from the extremes of the Kalahari Desert in the north, through the vast expanses of plateau grassland (high-veld), unique bushland (fynbos), the semidesert of the Karoo tableland, the alpine regions of the Drakensberg mountains, and the coastal forest in the south. Colorful fynbos, with some seven thousand species, is the key element of Cape Province in the south. This region receives between 400 and 1500 mm of rain each year. Regular fires are essential to the existence of this unique flora. North of the Cape lies the Karoo, where an open bushland is interspersed with a few scattered trees and more common succulents. This area receives only 200 to 450 mm of rain annually. The Great Karoo in the northeast receives most of its rain in summer and is dominated by small trees, shrubs, and long-lived grasses. The Little Karoo to the south and Namaqualand to the west receive rain primarily during the winter months. This gives rise to flora of mostly stemless rosette plants and succulents. Namaqua-

land is rich with bulbous and rhizomatous plants, which immerse the landscape in a sea of color in early spring. Further north, in the Namib Desert, where less than 100 mm of rain falls each year, even succulents are smaller and sparser. Fires are a rare phenomenon here. Highveld covers the high interior plateau of South Africa, from the eastern Cape to the Drakensberg mountains. Most of the rainfall here, 600 to 800 mm, occurs during summer. Grasses dominate, but bulbous and rhizomatous plants are abundant. Savanna of the lowveld and Kalahari basin occupies more than a third of the area of South Africa. It receives on average 250 mm of rain annually, mainly in summer. It is characterized by a ground layer of grasses and an upper layer of shrubs or trees. Forests in South Africa are fragmented, occurring only in small patches in areas that burn rarely and receive at least 800 mm of rain. The last remaining strip of indigenous forest is found in the center of the long southern coastline between the Knysna and Tsitsikamma regions.

Lush meadows dotted with white blooms of calla-lily, *Zantedeschia aethiopica,* at the foot of Table Mountain, 1086 m, south of Cape Town. Photo by Walter H. Hodge.

Greensmith later sent to Longwood twenty-four of the ornamentals requested by Seibert. Among them were eleven varieties of *Bougainvillea.* The collection of these spectacular vines developed in Nairobi by Greensmith was considered among the finest in existence. "I have never seen anything like the varieties or the way they are grown here," admitted Seibert (1963b) in a letter sent back to Longwood. His praise for the skills of Kenyan gardeners was inspired by the unusual techniques employed in growing a bewildering array of bougainvilleas around the city. In addition to enveloping all sorts of structures, as one would expect vines to do, bougainvilleas in Nairobi grew as ground covers, creating massive floral carpets. Living fences, dazzling with vibrant colors, were fashioned out of them, too. Most remarkable, however, were the bougainvilleas trained as 4 m high street trees, truly stunning when in full bloom.

Many of the bougainvilleas received from Nairobi were later exhibited in Longwood's Rose House, although limited space prevented Longwood's gardeners from displaying the vines in a manner that would rival those seen by Seibert in Nairobi. Nevertheless, these Kenyan bougainvilleas formed a cascading backdrop in the Rose House for some thirty-five years.

Pride of Table Mountain

Upon arriving in Cape Town, South Africa, on 18 September, Seibert was quickly immersed in an intense program of Golden Jubilee symposia held at the University of Cape Town. The symposia were interspersed with short excursions within Cape Province. Among them was an "exhilarating trip" to Table Mountain and a tour of a "marvelous" spring wildflower show at Goodwood (Seibert 1964f). Other destinations included the Cape of

Cape of Good Hope, south of Cape Town, was a destination for one of Seibert's field excursions. Photo by Rick Darke.

Good Hope Nature Reserve, the Harold Porter Botanic Reserve, the Karoo Garden in Worcester, and the Paarl Nature Reserve.

While visiting the Bolus Herbarium at the University of Cape Town, Seibert met with the herbarium curator, Professor Edward A. Schelpe. This meeting made possible a collaboration between Seibert and Schelpe, which led to the most significant introduction resulting from the South African trip, that of *Disa uniflora,* commonly called the Pride of Table Mountain.

Disa is invariably considered the most beautiful and spectacular of all wildflowers of South Africa. In the past it had a reputation for being impossible to maintain in cultivation; with few exceptions, even experienced orchid growers gave up in despair. Although introduced to Europe as early as 1825, *Disa uniflora* did not become firmly established in cultivation outside its country of origin. Writing in 1967, Kenneth Johnson, who pioneered work on growing this orchid in South Africa, described the success thus far as "spasmodic and transitory." On many occasions he had been told of someone growing *Disa,* but whenever he tried to follow up on the information, he "invariably received the depressing news that whilst they did once grow a few, unfortunately they all died!"

Lack of success in growing this orchid and indiscriminate collecting in the wild led to its relative obscurity. Johnson was alarmed by the dwindling of the wild *Disa* population: "In the short space of one hundred years this wonderful flower has almost disappeared from the nearby haunts where it once flowered so prolifically. . . . It is both a pressing need and at the same time a great challenge to horticultural ingenuity to evolve simple methods of cultivation and so make possible the propagation of this

Seibert in the Cape of Good Hope Nature Reserve. Photo by Russell J. Seibert.

Seibert considered *Disa uniflora* (64900), acquired from the University of Cape Town, the most significant introduction from his trip to South Africa. Photo by Rondel G. Peirson.

superb indigenous orchid on the widest possible scale" (1967).

Was it the unmatched beauty of *Disa* or the frequent failures of others who tried to grow it that motivated Seibert to take on the challenge? We do not know. He did, however, with help from Schelpe, procure a dozen small offshoots of this rare orchid (64900). They arrived at Longwood in June of 1964, and in September of 1965 Seibert proudly reported back to Schelpe: "Through the use of great T.L.C. (tender loving care) and our facilities for growing in a mechanically air-conditioned greenhouse, thus compensating for our naturally hot, humid summer nights, we have now flowered *Disa uniflora*" (1965a). Schelpe instructed Seibert about the main points of growing *Disa,* including "maintaining moist and cool conditions during the summer, watering by cap-

illarity from below during the spring and summer, and [overcoming] their extreme susceptibility to fungal attack, especially just prior to flowering" (1963). Of the original twelve offshoots, four survived under the watchful eye of Clarence Deckman, Longwood's orchid grower. Although the future of this orchid still remained uncertain, Seibert was cautiously optimistic: "There is good reason for feeling that cool night conditions, brisk air movement and low-pH growing media, are helpful factors for *Disa*'s successful growth. . . . With present-day modern techniques of artificial climate control, this plant should receive added cultural attention and should be induced to produce viable seeds" (1966a).

Three years later Lois W. Paul (1969), Longwood's supervisor of education, reported on the progress made with *Disa*: "From this shaky start, Mr. Deckman flowered four plants, pollinated them and collected the seeds. He now has close to three hundred plants from this first generation. A second and third generation are being produced. Through experimentation the dreaded fungus on the soft stem has been eliminated. Thanks to up-to-date air-conditioning, a moist, cool atmosphere is maintained during the hot summer months." In 1969 all this work finally paid off. In May and June of that year, visitors to Longwood Gardens could view possibly the grandest, showiest terrestrial orchid as a mass display. As Paul noted, it was "a first in this country."

Cadillac of proteas

Seibert compared his South African experience to a "plantsman's safari" and later reminisced about "trophies" he hoped to acquire: "I am sure that everyone on the trip had different primary interests and was impressed with different plants—for there were thousands of them of interest. For my own part, three groups seemed to stand out as special. The ericas, or South African heaths; blood-lilies in the genus *Haemanthus* (Amaryllidaceae); and the family Proteaceae, with particular emphasis on the genera *Protea* and *Leucospermum* because of their spectacular flower heads" (1964f).

Of all the plants of South Africa, Seibert was most impressed with Proteaceae, some of which have been tried at Longwood Gardens since 1956 but with only limited success. "A number of them have been flowered and an occasional one exhibited," recalled Seibert (1965d). "Proteas require nearly four to five years before they begin flowering. The big problem is to keep them growing that long (since their growing requirements are very exacting) and that is just the opposite from our natural as well as most of our greenhouse conditions." After the first round of trials Seibert admitted that proteas "have proved to be a challenge as conservatory plants—usually dying considerably prior to their four–five year maturing period for flower expectation" (1964f).

He was, however, determined to continue experimenting with this group of plants to overcome "the innumerable problems with which the American horticulturist is faced in attempting to grow them" (Seibert 1965d). There could be no better opportunity to study conditions under which these plants flourish than to observe them in their natural environment in South Africa. Visits to Kirstenbosch National Botanical Garden, renowned for its collection of Proteaceae, allowed Seibert

Seibert acquired giant protea, *Protea cynaroides* (631272), from the Municipal Arboretum in Paarl. Photo by Walter H. Hodge.

to see these plants at their best. A tour of a botanical reserve on Paarl Mountain, northeast of Cape Town, led Seibert to believe that proteas can be "well grown under cool, dry nights and constant breezes, and in acid soil."

Seibert was encouraged by what he learned in the field in Kirstenbosch and Paarl. He later wrote to Rycroft about his hopes related to proteas: "They are indeed a very challenging group and one with which I think we can have a certain amount of success" (1964b). On Seibert's request, Rycroft sent seeds of thirteen species of *Protea* along with fifty-five species of other South African plants.

This generous offering from Kirstenbosch inspired frequent correspondence, in which Seibert brought Rycroft up to date with regard to proteas: "Since last writing you, we now have several additional species of

Leucadendron discolor (64726) was among the many South African plants procured by Seibert from Kirstenbosch National Botanical Garden. Photo by Walter H. Hodge.

Silver trees, *Leucadendron argenteum* (631271), are among the most recognizable trees of South Africa. Photo by Walter H. Hodge.

Protea which have come into bloom; namely, *P. compacta, P. susannae,* and *P. obtusifolia.* Our problem, of course, is that we have usually only one plant or very few seedlings to germinate and experiment with, so we do hope that before too long, we can germinate sufficient plants of each species to allow us to do a bit of experimental comparative growing of the various species" (Seibert 1964a). Longwood growers hoped to receive from Rycroft hints on the cultivation of these plants. However, Rycroft could not offer much help, since, as he noted, "We have never grown proteas in pots under glass and, therefore, have no experience of this type of culture" (Rycroft 1964).

Seibert observed numerous species of proteas in South Africa but was especially impressed by *Protea aristata*: "The finest of all, *P. aristata,* has been almost annihilated in nature, but it is hoped that this species can be successfully grown and saved. The beauty of its buds is outstanding in the genus" (1965d). He considered this species to be the "Cadillac of proteas" (1963c) and exalted its qualities: "I think that is one of the most magnificent things I have ever seen" (1964b). Seibert eagerly requested the seeds of *P. aristata* from Rycroft, but Kirstenbosch at that time had only three plants in its collection, and these seldom produced seeds. Rycroft did not know when he would be able to send a few seeds to Seibert.

Horticultural virtues of this family are not limited to *Protea* alone. Upon his return from South Africa, Seibert shared his impressions on some of the other proteaceous plants he acquired for Longwood: "One of the most publicized trees of that far-off part of the world is the 'silver tree,' *Leucadendron argenteum* [631271]. It really does appear to be of silver, leaves flashing in the sun and wind. Unfortunately, the tree has all but disappeared in the wild; however, it is being planted wherever it can be cultivated successfully. The Proteaceae include the silver tree and the very interesting *Leucospermum reflexum* [631106, 631150–1] and *L. nutans* [631148–9, 631195]. The leucospermums or 'pincushions' are among the favorites of the family. *L. reflexum* has great possibilities for use in arrangements, since it will last for a month as a cut flower. *L. nutans* is planted a great deal along the landscaped modern highways of South Africa" (1965d).

Once Seibert had brought the wealth of both plants and firsthand field observations back from South Africa, the experimentation being conducted at Longwood on

The stunning inflorescence of *Leucospermum reflexum* (631106, 631150–1) has a most unusual architecture and makes a long-lasting cut flower. Photo by Walter H. Hodge.

Leucospermum nutans (631148–9, 631195) was among Seibert's favorite proteaceous plants. Photo by Walter H. Hodge.

growing proteas, leucodendrons, and leucospermums gained new momentum. "Gradually, at Longwood Gardens," recalled Seibert (1964f), "we have been able to simulate conditions which appear to allow an ever-increasing amount of success and, at least, the enjoyment of seeing a few of the protea species flower. Essential to the growth of *Protea* and *Leucospermum* would seem to be a well drained acid soil. Conditions of their indigenous South African climate indicates that they will not tolerate warm, humid nights. Of equal importance, is their requirement to grow in moving air. Our mechanically air-conditioned Experimental Greenhouse appears to supply some of the basic requirements for their growth." That work was to continue for another thirty years, culminating with the opening of Longwood's Mediterranean

House, where proteas, their relatives, and other South African plants formed the core of a permanent exhibit.

Cross-country escapade

Having two weeks of symposia behind him, Seibert and many of the other Golden Jubilee participants embarked on a grand tour of some of the most botanically interesting sites in South Africa. This month-long tour took them across the country, from Cape Town to Johannesburg.

During the first three days the group went through the dry tableland region of Karoo along the south coast. Turning south allowed them, after crossing Outeniqua Pass, to reach Knysna, a small town on the coast of the Indian Ocean. Vegetation around Knysna could not be more different from that seen in Karoo. Here lush temperate rain forest thrived and provided home to many tree ferns. On 4 October, driving from Knysna to Port Elizabeth, further east, the group stopped to explore the vegetation at the foot of Tsitsikamma Mountain. There Seibert collected seeds of *Protea latifolia* (631111). The following day was dedicated to visiting the parks of Port Elizabeth, said to be the very finest in South Africa. Seibert acquired seeds of several species from Saint George's Park. Among them was *Jubaeopsis caffra,* which he described as "one of the really rare South African botanical treasures" (Seibert 1964c). This palm, related to the coconut, is found only at the mouths of the Umsikaba and Umtentu rivers and at Mkambati in Pondoland.

On 6 October the group continued their drive eastward through Grahamstown and Great Fish River valley to the coastal town of East London. Before reaching the

Seibert considered *Aloe ferox* (631145), which he had collected near the Great Fish River, to be one of the best in the genus. Photo by Walter H. Hodge.

Seibert collected *Encephalartos villosus* (631240) near Port Saint Johns in Pondoland. Photo by Gottlieb A. Hampfler.

Great Fish River valley, Seibert collected *Aloe ferox* (631145), which he praised: "Of the hundreds of species, I still think *A. ferox* is one of the best" (1965d). In the Great Fish River Valley he collected *Senecio herreianus* (631146), a desert ground cover. After spending a day visiting sites around East London, the group continued traveling along the coast to Port Saint Johns in Pondoland. There Seibert collected seeds of *Encephalartos villosus* (631240) and *Clivia miniata* (631245–6). Further north, after crossing the Umtamvuna River into Natal Province, they reached Port Edward, where Seibert collected bulbs of *Lachenalia tricolor* var. *aurea* (631239). Later, on 10 October, the group arrived in Durban.

The two days spent in Durban allowed for a visit to the Bews Botanical Laboratory of the University of Natal in Pietermaritzburg and to the Durban Botanic Garden.

With help from Dr. K. D. Gordon-Gray and Olive Hilliard of the Bews Botanical Laboratory, Seibert was able to procure seeds of several species of *Acacia* and many other plants. When visiting the Durban Botanic Garden, Seibert noted the remarkable selection of *Canna* grown there. Upon his return to Longwood, he wrote to F. W. Thorns, director of Durban Botanic Garden: "While there, I was quite impressed with your collection of cannas and wonder if it would be possible for you to send a start of the cream colored canna as well as your best yellow, neither of which do we seem to have in this country" (1963d). Ernest Thorp, curator of the garden, sent rhizomes of three varieties: 'Ambassadour' (642), 'Banner' (64934), and 'King Midas' (641). Three years later crosses made between 'Ambassadour' and 'Banner' (as well as 'Lunniy Svet', received from the Nikitsky

On occasion the muddy roads of Zululand became impassable for the bus carrying the group of botanists. Photo by Russell J. Seibert.

Seibert collected *Mussaenda erythrophylla* (641299), a native of tropical West Africa, at the Holy Cross Mission in Kolahun. Photo by Walter H. Hodge.

Botanical Garden in Yalta, Ukraine) marked the beginning of a canna breeding program at Longwood that was to continue for some twenty years, ultimately producing eighteen new selections.

On 13 October the group left Durban to travel north through Zululand to Mbabane in Swaziland. From Mbabane they continued north to Kruger National Park in Transvaal on the border with Mozambique. After spending four days botanizing and collecting plants in the park, the group arrived in Pretoria, the capital of South Africa, on 20 October.

While in Pretoria, Seibert visited the Botanical Research Institute, the National Herbarium, and the Botanical Gardens, where he acquired bulbs and seeds of several plants, including *Haemanthus magnificus* (64262), *Protea caffra* (641093), and *Vellozia retinervis* (64263). The following couple of days were dedicated to visiting places of botanical interest around Pretoria. The most memorable for Seibert was The Wilds, a South African wildflower garden developed in Johannesburg. In The Wilds, many indigenous plants from all over South Africa and Namibia (formerly South-West Africa) have been introduced and cultivated successfully in spite of the fact that the Transvaal climate is quite different from other parts of the country. In the garden, Seibert especially admired an extensive collection of proteas, ericas, and cycads.

In the next few days the tour was to continue through the Orange Free State back to Cape Town, but Seibert decided instead to leave South Africa. On 24 October he flew to Monrovia in Liberia. Because of his previous research on the rubber tree, he knew about the Firestone Company's immense rubber plantations in Liberia and wanted to see the botanical garden associated with the plantations in Harbel and other sites of horticultural interest in the area. Seibert was especially interested in observing which native and introduced plants were being used there as ornamentals. Dr. Ger Verhaar, director of research, took Seibert in tow, showing him the botanical garden, the 32,0000-hectare rubber plantation, some of the forest edges, and the Holy Cross Mission in Kolahun, before letting him depart for Philadelphia on 27 October.

Among the most remarkable trees Seibert saw in Harbel was the West African native *Erythrina altissima* (66100), a truly magnificent sight when in flower. This tree is deciduous, opening dusty pink flowers after the leaves fall. Verhaar later forwarded to Longwood seeds of *Erythrina* as well as several other large trees from Harbel. Seibert, thrilled with the prospect of growing it at Longwood, wrote back to Verhaar: "It is always interesting trying these unknown quantities for their adaptability to greenhouse conditions. . . . It may well be necessary to raise the roof in our hothouse prior to having it flower. We are just completing the new conservatory in which we will be featuring the palm family. Among other things in that house, it may be possible to grow and flower a few of these very rare, spectacular, tropical trees" (1966b).

Darke, left, and McGregor among orange blooms of *Bulbinella floribunda* near Nieuwoudtville. Photo by Rick Darke.

TAKING CUES FROM MOTHER NATURE

"Anyone sensitive to landscapes and plants of extraordinary beauty should experience spring in South Africa. It blew me away!" remembers Landon Scarlett, planning and design manager at Longwood Gardens, who, together with Rick Darke, Longwood's curator of plants, embarked on a plant-collecting trip to South Africa in 1986.

"Early in 1986 Frederick E. Roberts, Longwood's director, proposed a collecting trip to South Africa and asked me to join that endeavor," recalls Scarlett. "He saw a value in having a designer as part of the team. One of Longwood's greatest strengths is that the displays for which it is so well known are the result of a dynamic collaboration of plantsman, grower, and designer utilizing plant materials from around the world, and the 1986 expedition was a great example of that collaboration. For both myself and Rick it was also an opportunity to see Mother Nature in the roles of chief designer, plantsman, and grower. We were inspired!"

As Darke explains, "At the time, Roberts was leading the initiative to reduce Longwood's dependence on fossil fuels required to heat conservatories to temperatures required to sustain tropical plant displays. The goal for the South Africa trip was to replace tropical plants displayed in some of the conservatories with species that would thrive at lower temperatures."

Darke and Scarlett prepared an itinerary for a six-week trip that would allow them to sample the floristic richness of the diverse South African landscapes. Their plan included visits to the Cape, Little Karoo, Great Karoo, and Natal, each region with a distinct flora.

Gardening Mother Nature's way

Darke and Scarlett arrived in Cape Town, the capital of Cape Province, in mid-August, just in time to watch the spring floral spectacle unfold. They started off by joining a tour with the Botanical Society of South Africa, which soon brought them to northern Cape Province, into the heart of the area where one of South Africa's floral gems, *Bulbinella floribunda*, occurs naturally. "We were stunned by countless acres brightened by the sturdy, candle-like clusters of yellow *Bulbinella* flowers," wrote Darke (1987a). "The local naturalist surprised us by saying that we were a little early, and that the display would be even more spectacular two weeks later. The flowers of *Bulbinella* open gradually, from bottom to top, a process that takes more than a month."

Before the tour ended, Darke and Scarlett were taken to a private wildflower reserve set up by Neil McGregor on his farm Glenlyon near Nieuwoudtville in the northern Cape, where a strikingly attractive orange form of *Bulbinella floribunda* occurred. "Mother Nature, with the help of a determined farmer and his sheep, created there an astonishing display of *Bulbinella floribunda*," recalls Scarlett. "Always appreciative and supportive of the natural *Bulbinella* display, McGregor explained that originally he had prevented his sheep from grazing there and found the display diminished a little each year. Figuring that herds of bok, indigenous antelope, had migrated freely over his farm in pursuit of food for millennia before the coming of farm fences, he adjusted his management approach, letting his sheep graze on the bulbs after the current year's seed had ripened. Gradually the *Bulbinella* population increased. McGregor's theory was that like the hooves of the bok, the sheep's hooves helped plant the seeds at the optimal depth for their survival and subsequent germination. The sheep's droppings probably helped too. To my mind, this was gardening of the highest order."

Cape gardens

Back in Cape Town, Darke and Scarlett dedicated several days to visiting places of horticultural interest in and around the city. Time spent at the world-renowned Kirstenbosch National Botanical Garden resulted in more than a hundred new plants obtained from this garden's vast collections. "We were blessed with good advice in planning this trip that led us to people in South Africa who helped us in immeasurable ways," remembers

This particularly silver form of *Athanasia parviflora* (861310), which Darke and Scarlett collected in Kirstenbosch National Botanical Garden, has become an important feature of Longwood's indoor Silver Garden. Photo by Rick Darke.

Old Nectar, home and garden of van der Spuy near Stellenbosch, east of Cape Town. Photo by Rick Darke.

Protea cynaroides was among the species flowering in Rustenberg's reserve for proteaceous plants. Photo by Landon Scarlett.

Scarlett. "I will always treasure the cups of tea and great conversation on the front porch of the van der Spuy's Cape Dutch home Old Nectar near Stellenbosch, 20 km outside Cape Town. Una van der Spuy, one of South Africa's top plant experts, would pack the trunk of her car with picnic food and take us around. One day she took us to Rustenberg, the home and garden of Peter and Pamela Barlow, makers of the famous Rustenberg wines."

"The design inspiration for Rustenberg's garden appeared to have come from the early twentieth century British examples," recalls Scarlett. "The garden was embellished with some of the showier South African native plants, but mostly contained non-native imports to simulate the British style. There was an impressive, but totally separate from the English-styled garden, reserve area for proteaceous plants. Although they were not considered compatible with the English garden aesthetic, the Barlows felt they were just too good to resist!" At Rustenberg the group was met by Jim Holmes, manager of the gardens and reserve. While touring the garden, Holmes showed the collectors some of his botanical treasures, which included a yellow-flowered *Veltheimia bracteata* (861011).

Silver of Little Karoo

On 14 September, Darke and Scarlett traveled east from Cape Town to the tableland region of Little Karoo paralleling the south coast. "My lasting impression of Little Karoo was of a magnificent, empty, open space filled with stop-you-in-your-tracks plants, where once or twice a day

From left to right, Holmes, Darke, and van der Spuy admire a yellow-flowered plant of *Veltheimia bracteata* (861011). Photo by Landon Scarlett.

Bayer and Forrester at the Karoo Desert National Botanical Garden in Worcester. Photo by Landon Scarlett.

The yellow-flowered *Veltheimia bracteata* obtained by Darke and Scarlett became one of the most successful South African plants displayed in Longwood's conservatories. Photo by Larry Albee.

Little Karoo is an arid tableland region with an elevation of 300 to 600 m along the south coast of Cape Province. Photo by Landon Scarlett.

Silver-leaved plants fill rock crevices in mountain passes of Little Karoo. Photo by Landon Scarlett.

The Indian Ocean coast of South Africa east of Knysna. Photo by Landon Scarlett.

Pamela Barlow, left, and van der Spuy in Barlow's garden at Rustenberg. Photo by Landon Scarlett.

we might pass another car," says Scarlett. "We visited with Bruce Bayer, curator, and Jane Forrester, horticulturist, at the Karoo National Botanical Garden in Worcester, some 60 km east of Cape Town, with its display of aloes and other succulents for which South Africa is famous. Some of the plants Bayer and Forrester shared with us included *Aloe ciliaris* (861260), *Cyphostemma juttae* (861258), and *Erythrina humeana* (861259)."

The native vegetation of Little Karoo convinced Darke and Scarlett that South Africa had more to offer than just the brightly colored bulbous plants and pelargoniums for which it was, and is, so famous. "My awareness of the aesthetic possibilities of gray and silver foliaged plants blossomed in South Africa," recalls Scarlett. "Such plants flourish in Mediterranean and desert regions around the world with low rainfall and intense sunlight, where gray and silver serve to reflect the sun and thus preserve moisture. Prior to this trip, I had thought of silver and gray plants as texturally interesting, but dull. Mother Nature in South Africa changed that. The mountainous, folded rock passes in Little Karoo were stuffed with stunning silver foliaged plants. The impression these plants made on me there, along with the powerful image of succulents growing in a northwestern Great Karoo landscape, eventually led to the creation of Longwood's Silver Garden."

Traveling along the south coast, Darke and Scarlett arrived in Knysna, where some vestiges of native South African forest can be seen. "We tracked down centuries old *Podocarpus latifolius* and *Ocotea bullata* near Knysna," Scarlett remembers. "Both were fenced off for their own protection. The indigenous forests had been seriously over-timbered by 1815 and were replaced over time with plantations of fast growing trees like pine which we see today."

This *Echium simplex* (87126) brought Darke and Scarlett to "a squealing stop" while traveling to Knysna. Photo by Rick Darke.

Darke and Scarlett's discoveries on the trip were not limited to indigenous plants. "A long tradition of gardening in South Africa was obvious," Scarlett explains. "On roadsides, non-native plants seeded themselves. Some of them, such as *Echium,* were strikingly beautiful. One particular *Echium simplex* (87126), a species introduced from Madeira and the Canary Islands, flowering near Knysna with its 2 m tall white flower spikes, brought us to a squealing stop for an ogle."

The *Echium* plant that impressed Scarlett so much was growing in a private garden. "The owner was not home; therefore, we obtained his address and wrote him for seed upon our return," reported Darke (1987b). "He kindly replied that he would collect seed when ripe. We eventually received a copious quantity—neatly stuffed into two old socks! Apparently, the socks, which were in

A wide variety of American cacti and succulents grew at Giddy's Nursery in Umlaasweg, Natal. Photo by Landon Scarlett.

turn enclosed in old cigar boxes, met all USDA requirements for approved packaging."

This memorable encounter with such a fine example of the *Echium* tribe later led to many other species of the genus being incorporated in Longwood's conservatory displays. "From that moment on, *Echium* of many sorts would get major attention when foreign seed lists circulated at Longwood," explains Scarlett.

Reunion in Durban

From Knysna, Darke and Scarlett continued east to Port Elizabeth, where they flew 700 km northeast to Durban, the largest city of Natal Province. "We were greeted there by a group of former students trained at Longwood Gardens," remembers Scarlett. "They looked after us in Durban and organized a small reunion party. Then we visited the famous specimen of *Encephalartos woodii* at the Durban Botanic Garden. This lovely cycad has not been seen in the wild since 1916, and only male forms exist." An offset from Durban obtained by Seibert following his trip to South Africa in 1963 still grows at Longwood (69941).

"Next we accompanied one of the former Longwood students, Trevor Hornby, on a jaunt to Giant's Castle Reserve, a stunning combination of rugged mountains and rolling grassland in the Drakensberg on the border of Natal and Lesotho," remembers Scarlett. "Getting there was the longest, dustiest ride of my life to date. Being there was worth every mile. We then made a stop to see Giddy's Cactus and Cycad Nursery in the town of Umlaasweg in Natal where we were surprised to find a

Rolling grasslands in the Giant's Castle Reserve in the northern end of Drakensberg. Photo by Landon Scarlett.

large selection of American cacti and succulents. There we were, Americans seeking exotic plants in South Africa visiting South Africans who were seeking exotic plants from America." The most significant acquisition from Giddy's Nursery, however, was a native South African plant, another yellow-flowered form of *Veltheimia bracteata* (861075–7).

On 22 September, Darke and Scarlett flew from Durban to Johannesburg, South Africa's largest city, in Transvaal Province. "In Johannesburg we saw more private gardens, including Brenthurst, the garden of Harry Oppenheimer, one of South Africa's leading industrialists," remembers Scarlett. "Dick Scott, estate manager at Brenthurst, was justly proud of his native cycads and the blaze of color provided by various South African bulbs and annuals. Scott shared with us several plants from Brenthurst's collections, including *Athanasia*

parviflora (861271), *Scilla natalensis* (861269), and *Wachendorfia thyrsiflora* (861270)."

A few days later Darke and Scarlett departed for the United States, carrying with them more than 135 collections. In addition they established links with top horticulturists in that country that would result in many more South African plants being sent to Longwood in the years that followed. "The South Africans were wonderful hosts," says Scarlett, looking back at the trip. "They exhibited intense botanical curiosity which has resulted in a wealth of publications and information on South Africa's native flora. Fine local institutions and individuals actively and willingly shared with us their enthusiasm for their plants."

"In my first job at Longwood," adds Scarlett, "I grew proteaceous plants brought from South Africa in 1963 by Dr. Seibert. But it was seeing these and other South

Scarlett, left, and Darke with some of the plants they brought from South Africa, here growing in Longwood's experimental greenhouses. Photo by Rick Darke.

African plants growing and thriving in their natural habitat that convinced me of their immense display possibilities. This trip gained Longwood the inspiration for its new indoor Silver Garden, and a fresh look at ways to grow and display plants taking cues from Mother Nature."

SOUTH AFRICA REVISITED

The next chapter of exploration in South Africa involved Darke and Dr. James R. Ault, plant physiologist at Longwood Gardens, who together traveled to that country in early September of 1993. The purpose for their trip was to continue the investigations began in 1986, but this time to observe plants that bloomed later in the spring.

Also more emphasis was to be placed on trees and shrubs, as opposed to the bulbous plants that dominated the earlier trip.

Ault and Darke were joined in South Africa by Melinda Zoehrer, horticulturist for the Delaware Center for Horticulture in Wilmington. They intended to revisit many of the sites included in the 1986 trip, but started off by traveling on 7 September to a new location at the Ramskop Nature Reserve near Clanwilliam, about 200 km north of Cape Town. Since they arrived as most wildflowers were in their peak bloom, the explorers were able to select twenty of the showiest species, including many brightly colored perennials such as red- and orange-flowered *Arctotis gumbletoni* (93873–4), red-flowered *Gazania krebsiana* (93879), and yellow- to orange-flowered *Ursinia cakilefolia* (93886).

During the following couple of days, Ault and Darke visited two more nature reserves, one in Calvinia, about 120 km northeast of Clanwilliam, and another in Nieuwoudtville, 60 km west of Calvinia. From Nieuwoudtville they returned to Cape Town, where Kirstenbosch National Botanical Garden served as their base. From here they arranged excursions to places such as the nearby Table Mountain, Hottentots-Holland Nature Reserve, and Karoo Desert National Botanical Garden in Worcester, considered to have the best collection of succulents in the Southern Hemisphere.

On 19 September, Ault flew to Durban on the coast of the Indian Ocean, while Darke and Zoehrer stayed in Cape Town. In Durban, Ault spent a day studying plant collections at the Durban Botanic Garden. In the gardens he spotted a number of promising plants, including shrubs such as silver-leaved *Barleria albostellata* (93940), which flowers all summer long; *Combretum kraussii* (93941), with leaves that change from white to green and, in fall, to red; and *Polygala virgata* (93944), which produces a profusion of purple-pink flowers in winter and spring. Another day spent in the Fern Valley Botanical Garden in the town of Kloof, 15 km outside Durban, resulted in the collection of two showy shrubs: white-fruited *Ardisia crenata* 'Alba' (93945) and blue-fruited *Dichroa febrifuga* (93946), both introduced from Asia.

Back in Cape Town on 27 September, Ault and Darke continued visiting places of botanical and horticultural interest in their search for superior ornamental plants. Kirstenbosch National Botanical Garden, which has the most comprehensive collection of South African plants, offered the explorers an opportunity to observe and study the wealth of the country's flora under cultivated conditions. In the end they procured nearly eighty of the most promising plants for trial at Longwood.

Day-trips out of Cape Town took Ault and Darke to several nature reserves in the area, including the Cape of Good Hope, Fernkloof near Hermanus, and Paarl Mountain. These trips were then supplemented with visits to Harold Porter National Botanical Garden in Betty's Bay and Cape Seed and Bulbs in Stellenbosch, a nursery owned by Jim and Anne Holmes. This nursery developed a reputation as a source of some of the most unusual South African bulbous plants. Holmes shared with the collectors several of his plants, *Dierama medium* (9418), *Oxalis palmifrons* (9421), and *Watsonia humilis* (9420), bringing the total number of plants collected to 120. In Cape Town, Ault and Darke concluded their four-week trip and returned to Philadelphia.

Ramskop Nature Reserve near Clanwilliam, north of Cape Town, welcomed Ault and Darke with a profusion of spring flowers. Photo by James R. Ault.

A bizarre *Cyphostemma juttae,* prominently featured at the Karoo Desert National Botanical Garden in Worcester, has also been exhibited in Longwood's Silver Garden. Photo by James R. Ault.

Ault observed the show of *Greyia sutherlandii* (931063) flowers in Drakensberg, a mountain chain along the border between Natal and Lesotho. Photo by James R. Ault.

Eulophia speciosa (94610), a terrestrial orchid with fragrant flowers, was among the plants Ault acquired from the Durban Botanic Garden. Photo by James R. Ault.

Graham Duncan, left, of Kirstenbosch National Botanical Garden, converses with Zoehrer and Ault during their 1993 visit. Photo by Rick Darke.

A yellow-flowered selection of *Strelitzia reginae* 'Kirstenbosch Gold' (93612) was among nearly eighty plants Ault and Darke acquired from Kirstenbosch National Botanical Garden in Cape Town. Photo by James R. Ault.

Holmes with rare yellow-flowered *Clivia miniata* in his Stellenbosch nursery, Cape Seed and Bulbs. Photo by James R. Ault.

The lush vegetation of the Fern Valley Botanical Garden, situated in the town of Kloof, near Durban, on the coast of the Indian Ocean, contrasted dramatically with xerophytic flora of the Cape region. Photo by James R. Ault.

REVIVING CORNFLOWER BLUE

Since their opening in 1921, Longwood conservatories featured a mass display of florist's cineraria, *Pericallis* ×*hybrida,* every spring. In later years a blue-flowered strain known as 'Cornflower Blue' was chosen for this purpose. "Seed of this strain for years was obtained from a breeder in Germany who in early 1990s discontinued it," remembers Dr. Robert J. Armstrong, research horticulturist at Longwood Gardens. "Since this was the only source, it fell upon Longwood to maintain its own seed supply if it wanted to continue to exhibit this plant. At first seed was produced by simply self pollinating the plants and collecting the seed. Unfortunately, it was soon discovered that the vigor of the resulting plants was being rapidly reduced with each generation. This kind of loss of vigor is known as inbreeding depression which often results when normally highly out-crossed species are continually self-pollinated. It was decided that if this crop were to continue at Longwood, drastic measures would need to be taken. To remedy the situation the most desirable plants were

selected as seed parents and then crosses were made among these plants. As the result 'Cornflower Blue' cineraria began to be stabilized again, but it was thought that this strain could be improved if the plants were more vigorous, more upright, and more open in habit."

Florist's cineraria is a hybrid that originated through crossing among several species of *Pericallis* native to the Canary Islands, but its exact parentage is not known. In 1995 Roberts suggested that a trip be organized in order to collect some of the species that could be crossed with 'Cornflower Blue' to improve its vigor.

Darke and Gary R. Keim, indoor display specialist, were asked to take part in the endeavor. The main purpose for the trip was to find the wild relatives of the florist's cineraria, but Darke and Keim intended to be on the lookout for other ornamental plants as well, especially the many *Echium* species native to the Canaries.

They started off on 31 May on the island of La Palma. Over the course of five days of collecting, Darke and Keim found what they were looking for: *Pericallis appendiculata* (95506) and *P. papyracea* (95507), two of

Visitors to Longwood conservatories admire a display of florist's cinerarias, *Pericallis × hybrida,* in 1958. Photo by Gottlieb A. Hampfler.

Darke, left, and Keim began their exploration of the Canaries on the island of La Palma. Photo by Rick Darke.

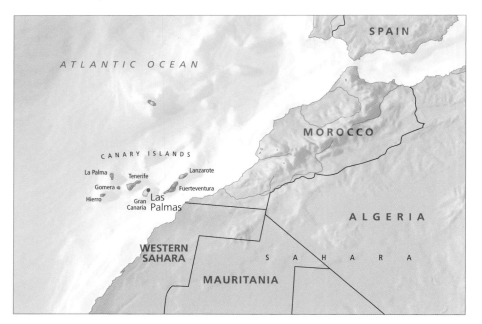

The Canary Islands, an archipelago of the northwest coast of Africa with an area of more than 7200 km², comprises a western and an eastern group. The western group, consisting of Tenerife, Gran Canaria, La Palma, Gomera, and Hierro islands, features tall mountain peaks rising directly from the ocean floor, with Pico de Teide, 3718 m, the tallest among them. The eastern group, consisting of Lanzarote, Fuerteventura, and several smaller islets, surmounts a submarine plateau rising to about 500 m above sea level. The rich volcanic soils and mild climate of the Canaries support a diverse vegetation, including about two thousand species, of which 25 percent are endemic to the islands. The Mediterranean climate of hot, dry summers and warm, wet winters is influenced by the close proximity of the Sahara Desert, rain-bearing north–west trade winds, and the high altitude of the mountains of the western islands. While the trade winds may bring 800 to 1500 mm of precipitation to the highest peaks of the western islands, the eastern Canaries experience extreme dryness due to hot Saharan winds. The main types of vegetation are distributed in altitudinal zones. Xerophytic scrub occupies lower slopes up to 700 m; at its upper limit, it merges into a woodland. Evergreen forest, dominated by various species of laurels, is found in the wetter areas of the western islands between 400 and 1500 m. From 1200 to 2000 m is an open, savannalike pine forest, while above 1900 m the montane scrub vegetation features many of the islands' endemic species.

the possible wild ancestors of florist's cineraria, as well as several species of *Echium,* including *E. brevirame* (95496), *E. gentianoides* (95806), and *E. webbii* (95498).

On 5 June the travelers made a brief stop on the island of Gran Canaria with the purpose of visiting Jardín Botánico Viera y Clavijo in Las Palmas. From Gran Canaria they relocated to Tenerife to spend five days exploring the island's flora. They began on Monte de las Mercedes, just north of Santa Cruz, the island's largest city. Among the plants collected in the area were *Isoplexis canariensis* (95503) and *Ranunculus cortusifolius* (95504). Hiking along the cliffs near Puenta de Teno, the western-

Mauve-flowered *Pericallis papyracea* (95507) growing in its native habitat on La Palma. Photo by Rick Darke.

The taller, more open, vigorous cinerarias resulted from crossing *Pericallis ×hybrida* 'Cornflower Blue' with *P. papyracea* (95507). Photo by Robert J. Armstrong.

Echium gentianoides (95806), found on La Palma, is claimed to have the deepest gentian-blue flowers of all *Echium*. Photo by Rick Darke.

Improved blue cinerarias, *Pericallis ×hybrida,* can be admired in Longwood's conservatories in early spring. Photo by Tomasz Aniśko.

most point of Tenerife, Darke and Keim found *Euphorbia canariensis* (95499), *Lavandula buchii* (95501), and *Vieraea laevigata* (95511). Another day on the island's north coast, between Puenta del Hidalgo and Puenta de Anaga, resulted in collections of *Lavandula buchii* (95502) and *Sideritis macrostachys* (95508).

Returning to Philadelphia after two weeks in the Canaries, Darke and Keim carried with them two species of *Pericallis* so eagerly awaited at Longwood, along with collections of twenty-two other plants native to the islands. Out of the two species of *Pericallis, P. papyracea* turned out to be more useful in restoring vigor to the blue cinerarias. "It was a very tall plant with small rose-colored flowers," remembers Armstrong, who directed the breeding of cinerarias. "This species was crossed with the 'Cornflower Blue' strain, with the first generation being intermediate between the parents. Selected plants from this first population were back-crossed to the 'Cornflower Blue' several times. The resulting plants were then crossed among themselves, which resulted in a new and improved blue cineraria that can be now admired in Longwood's conservatories."

RUSSIA AND
ITS NEIGHBORS

Conservatory in the Botanical Garden of the Komarov Botanical Institute in Leningrad (Saint Petersburg). Photo by Russell J. Seibert.

A cascade of fountains in front of the Grand Palace of Peterhof in Leningrad (Saint Petersburg). Photo by John L. Creech.

WORLD'S LARGEST COUNTRY

Following a high-level official visit to the Union of Soviet Socialist Republics (USSR) by Orville L. Freeman, secretary of the USDA, in 1962, an opportunity came about to send to that country a team of American plant collectors. Longwood's director, Dr. Russell J. Seibert, was eager to see that the USDA-Longwood plant exploration program took advantage of this possibility to gain access to the vast territory of the USSR. "We, of course, are especially pleased that this trip has promise of producing plants of considerably more hardiness than a number of the other trips," wrote Seibert (1963a) to Dr. Carl O. Erlanson of the USDA New Crops Research Branch.

Two USDA explorers were asked to undertake the mission, Dr. John L. Creech, assistant chief of the New Crops Research Branch, and Dr. Donald H. Scott, leader of the Small Fruit and Grape Investigations. On rather short notice an ambitious program was drafted for a six-week trip starting in late August 1963. "The Soviet Union is a country rich in potential ornamental plants," Creech later wrote (1988). "Many have not entered our gardens because collectors have limited access. But the Soviets have a great love of flowers and an exceptional awareness of the importance of plants in their society." The trip was to take Creech and Scott to Moscow, Leningrad (Saint Petersburg), and locations in the southern USSR, from Tashkent in Uzbekistan to Kishinev in Moldavia.

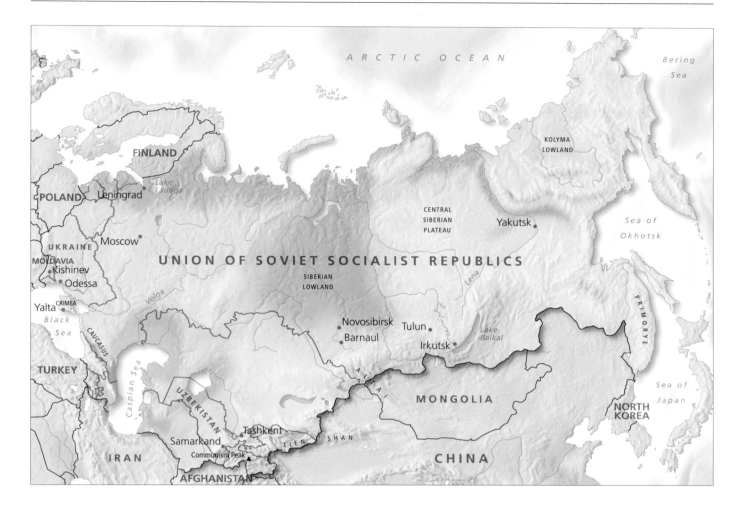

With an area of 22.4 million km², the USSR was the world's largest country, covering a sixth of the planet's land surface. About a quarter of its territory lay in eastern Europe, while the rest lay in northern Asia. Founded in 1922, the USSR comprised fifteen republics, of which Russia was the largest with more than 17 million km². Corresponding with such enormous territory was a great variety of natural landscapes, complexity of relief, and large climatic differences between the regions. Vast plains occupy the western part of the former USSR, while plateaus and high mountain ranges prevail in the east. The highest mountains are found along the southern border, with Communism Peak at 7495 m in the Pamirs in what is now Tajikistan. Vast latitudinal climatic zones stretch from the arctic above latitude 70° north, the subarctic between 60° north and 70° north, and the temperate zone between 40° north and 60° north, to the subtropics in parts of Transcaucasia and south-central Asia. Most of the territory has a climate that is distinctly continental and marked with large temperature differences between summer and winter. The regions along the coast of the Black Sea are subject to a milder, maritime climate, while those in the southern Far East, influenced by the Pacific Ocean, have a monsoon climate. About seventeen thousand species of plants native to the region of the former USSR are distributed in clearly defined latitudinal vegetation zones, ranging from the arctic waste and tundra in the north, through forest and steppe, to semideserts and deserts in the south. In mountainous regions, especially those of the Caucasus, the Carpathians, and the Primorye, vegetation types are arranged in altitudinal zones. In addition, the humid subtropical climate of Kolkhida and Lenkoran in Transcaucasia supports lush broad-leaved forests with an undergrowth of evergreen plants and lianas, while Mediterranean vegetation is found along the coast of the Black Sea.

Sulfuring grapes for raisin production near Samarkand in Uzbekistan. Photo by John L. Creech.

Creech and Scott arrived in Moscow in mid-August and a few days later continued on to Leningrad. There they spent three days touring the Botanical Garden of the Komarov Botanical Institute, the Vavilov Institute of Plant Industry, a fruit experiment station in Pavlovsk, and Peterhof, a residence of Peter the Great founded in the eighteenth century. "The main purpose of visiting Leningrad was to work out our field schedule with the staff of the Vavilov Institute," explains Creech. "All plant exchanges as well as field exploration in the USSR emanated from that organization. It was here that the famous plant explorer Dr. Nikolai I. Vavilov established in the first half of the twentieth century the concept of geographical centers of crop diversity on which all modern plant exploration depends." Following a memorable visit to Peterhof, Creech wrote to Seibert: "The evidence of sophistication in ornamental horticulture reflects the grand days of Czarist Russia. . . . The fountains of Peterhof were beautifully done and far exceeded what I saw at Versailles" (1963c).

Melons in the tub

On 29 August, Creech and Scott, accompanied by Dr. K. Pekhoto of the Vavilov Institute, departed for Tashkent, the capital of Uzbekistan, where they planned to spend two weeks. Most of this central Asian republic is occupied by dry, sun-baked plains, with uplands and mountain ranges dominating the landscape in the east. Uzbekistan is among the world's largest producers of cotton but is also renowned for its orchards and vineyards.

"Uzbekistan has an arid climate where summer temperatures reach 45°C, while in winter they drop to -25°C," recalls Creech. "It is a vast region of collective and state farms involving 45 million hectares of cultivated land. Apples, pears, and nut crops are grown around Tashkent, raisins and fresh grapes dominate in the Samarkand area, whereas peaches and apricots in the Fergana Valley."

Touring research institutes, experiment stations, and horticultural enterprises, Creech and Scott saw a number of promising fruits and some ornamentals, but they were especially impressed with hardy drought-resistant *Hibiscus* hybrids. "Because it is a major cotton growing area, there was an ongoing program of breeding closely related *Hibiscus* as ornamentals," explains Creech. "This involved *H. coccineus* and *H. moscheutos*. There were several outstanding dwarf varieties, of which we requested seeds from the best ones, 'Taj Mahal' and 'Shaliapin'."

Visits to the R. R. Shreder Horticultural Institute in Tashkent and to that city's bazaar allowed them to sample a variety of local produce, including watermelons, *Citrullus lanatus*. "We have been promised anything we want in the way of plant materials and have said we would like to collect their best melons, onions, certain of the grapes and some wild species," Creech reported to Erlanson (1963a). "As a matter of fact we just made a melon collection—with Dr. Pekhoto of Leningrad, we finished off a fine round watermelon in our bathroom, collecting the seeds in the tub. It is a 10 inch [25 cm] melon, quite round, and very high density. So we kept the seed."

An excursion to Bostandek in the Chirchik Mountains provided the explorers with their first opportunity to make collections of plants growing in the wild. "We went into the mountains at Bostandek which is the western end of the Tien Shan range and it is a barren, dry mountain with mostly wild apples, *Crataegus,* and *Prunus* in several sorts, especially almonds," recorded Creech (1963b). "Everyone has tried their best to be helpful and in general it has been an interesting stay. We have a large sample of *Prunus mahaleb* from the mountains where it grows on barren hillsides with a rainfall of 300 mm and that in winter." The overall impression of the region was, however, rather discouraging for plant collectors: "The land was barren, dry, and devoid of extensive forests. It suggested a sustained depleting of forests and over-grazing of pastures by sheep and goats" (Creech and Scott 1963).

A road leading to Bostandek in the Chirchik Mountains in the western end of the Tien Shan range, Uzbekistan. Photo by John L. Creech.

Creech, Scott, and their colleagues from the Nikitsky Botanical Garden collect on the dry, open hillsides above Yalta. Photo by John L. Creech.

Wild apple trees, *Malus sylvestris* and *M. pumila* var. *paradisiaca,* grow on the barren slopes of the Chirchik Mountains, one of the centers of origin for cultivated apples. Photo by John L. Creech.

Nikitsky's goodly share

On 14 September, Creech and Scott boarded a plane in Tashkent and flew west over the Caspian and Black seas to Simferopol on the Ukraine's Crimean Peninsula. The Nikitsky Botanical Garden in Yalta, on the coast of the Black Sea, was to serve as their base during the five-day stay in the Crimea. "In ornamental horticulture the Nikitsky Botanic Garden at Yalta is on a par with any arboretum in the United States or western Europe except for Kew Gardens," wrote Creech and Scott (1963). "It is now 151 years old and is a leading institution in fruit breeding, introduction, and testing ornamentals and breeding of new woody and herbaceous garden plants.

Creech and Scott found *Hedera helix* var. *taurica* (65125), later named 'Yalta', in moist riverside forest above Yalta. Photo by Tomasz Aniśko.

Nelumbo caspica (631268) grown from seeds procured by Creech and Scott from the Nikitsky Botanical Garden. Photo by John L. Creech.

Canna 'Lunniy Svet' (64292), brought by Creech and Scott from the Nikitsky Botanical Garden, was used in 1967 by Robert J. Armstrong, Longwood's geneticist, in the first series of crosses which eventually led to the development of eighteen new cultivars released to the public. Photo by Robert J. Armstrong.

Their breeding program in cannas is excellent. It is apparent from conversations and the condition that Nikitsky is an institution with status and unlimited financial support."

Staff from the Nikitsky assisted Creech and Scott in their travels throughout the Krymskiye Mountains, a mountain chain along the coast of the southern Crimea, with the highest peak being Chatyr Dag at 1525 m. There they collected a number of wild apple and pear species, as well as ornamentals. In moist riverside forest above Yalta they found *Acer campestre* (65111), coloring bright yellow in fall; *Cornus mas* (66125), with large, sweet fruits; and a form of *Hedera helix* var. *taurica* (65125) later named 'Yalta'. On drier, open hillsides and exposed cliffs, the explorers collected *A. tataricum* ssp. *semenovii* (65414), a shrubby form with small leaves; purple-flowered *Crocus speciosus* (631267); and *Pinus pallasiana* (65127), Crimean pine with dense crowns and ascending branches.

"In our short sojourn, I collected enough interesting ornamental material to justify our effort," wrote Creech (1963c) to Seibert. "As a matter of fact, some of our collections such as *Crataegus microphylla* and *Acer stevenii* are not in cultivation. We gathered a number of collections of *Cornus mas* which if hardier than current forms, would 'pay for the trip' according to Don Wyman [at Arnold Arboretum of Harvard University]."

At the Nikitsky Botanical Garden, Creech and Scott were invited to take cuttings or plants of any material desired. "Of immediate interest to Longwood are two items," noted Creech (1963c), "a cream-colored *Canna* hybrid called 'Moonlight' ['Lunniy Svet' 64292] and the rare *Nelumbo caspica* [631268] which comes from the mouth of the Volga river and is quite an attractive plant. It is prohibited to collect this plant under ordinary circumstances but my new friends at the Nikitsky Botanic Garden furnished me with a goodly share of seed they had just collected." In addition, from the vast collection in the garden, the explorers procured, among others, *Exochorda tianschanica* (65113), a spring-flowering shrub originally from the Tien Shan; *Pinus stankewiczii* (65128), a pine species native to Crimea and noted for its drought tolerance; and *Buxus sempervirens* (67872), an especially hardy form of boxwood from the Caucasus.

Meandering through Moldavia

From Yalta, Creech and Scott departed for Kishinev, capital of Moldavia, on 21 September. Moldavia, the second smallest of the fifteen republics, occupies about 33,700 km² between the meandering rivers of the Prut and the Dnestr along the border with Romania. Thanks to its warm climate, with mild winters, sufficient rainfall, and very fertile soils, Moldavia developed a sizeable horticultural industry. It became one of the main suppliers of wine, fruits, and vegetables for the entire USSR.

Creech and Scott intended to spend a week there touring experiment stations and collecting plants in the foothills of the Carpathians. Although this region was less varied botanically than the Crimea, the explorers found interesting apples, pears, and cherries. Traveling northwest from Kishinev, they explored native flora at several locations. Near Strasheny, about 20 km from Kishinev, they collected *Juglans regia* (6459), a local selection with large, thin-shelled fruits, growing near a farmhouse. In the surrounding forest they found *Quercus robur* (64303), a good form of English oak with a tall, straight trunk. The next stop was near Kalarash, another 20 km further to the northwest, where Creech and Scott collected two dogwoods, *Cornus mas* (66126), with large sweet fruits, and *Cornus sanguinea* (66250), with reddish stems and purple-black fruits. Finally the explorers reached Yedintsy, some 200 km north of Kishinev. There, on a dry, exposed hill, they collected black-fruited *Viburnum lantana* (65116).

With September coming to a close, Creech and Scott returned to Moscow and three days later left for Washington. "True to their word, when we were about to depart, we received a large package of plants and cuttings from each of the various locations we visited," remembers Creech. "In all, our trip resulted in 140 collections of wild and cultivated plants including fruits and ornamentals. In addition, 53 items we had requested were shipped later following an approval by plant quarantine officials in Leningrad. This is an important point because a successful collecting trip does not end with the field activity but creates the opportunity for continued plant exchange in the future."

FROM SIBERIA WITH PLANTS

Several years passed before a new round of negotiations on the scientific exchange between the United States and the USSR allowed for another plant-collecting expedition to return to that country. It was agreed that Creech would again undertake an expedition in 1971, this time centered primarily on Siberia. "This is an extremely important area from which to collect and introduce hardy plant materials into this country," emphasized Seibert (1970b).

The trip was planned and conducted in cooperation with the Vavilov Institute of Plant Industry in Leningrad. In 1969, Creech and Seibert hosted the director of the institute, Professor D. D. Brezhnev, during his visit to the United States. In return, Brezhnev offered his assistance in organizing the expedition. He assigned two scientists from the institute, Dr. G. Shmaraev and Dr. N. Korsokov, to accompany Creech on the trip, each for about a month.

The goals for the expedition were "to collect native plants from Siberian regions of the Soviet Union, particularly those of value as ornamentals and as shrubs for stabilizing areas denuded by road and other construction activities, mining, and other factors destructive of natural vegetation," wrote Creech (1970b). "Also, to locate germplasm useful in developing disease, cold, drought, and pollution resistant varieties of ornamental plants." Seibert saw the potential for acquisition of cold- and drought-hardy Siberian plants as an important aspect of the expedition: "The prospects for new and improved types of ornamentals for the United States drought areas with extremes of summer heat and winter cold look very encouraging!" (1971).

The Siberian cities of Novosibirsk, Irkutsk, Barnaul, and Yakutsk were chosen as centers from which local excursions were to be made. Because of the short growing season in Siberia, the trip was planned for the summer months of July and August.

Self-pruning willows

Creech arrived in Leningrad on 28 June. He spent the first couple of days finalizing details of the expedition with the staff of the Vavilov Institute. Then he visited other leading botanical institutions, including the garden of the Komarov Botanical Institute and the dendrarium of the Academy of Forestry.

Creech's first plant-collecting trip took him north of Leningrad to the forests of the Karelian Isthmus, a strip

A self-pruning form of *Salix fragilis* that Creech collected in the Karelian Isthmus, north of Leningrad (Saint Petersburg). Photo by John L. Creech.

Field trials of new cultivars of *Phlox paniculata* developed by breeders working at the Central Siberian Botanical Garden in Akademgorodok near Novosibirsk. Photo by John L. Creech.

of land between the western shores of Lake Ladoga and the Gulf of Finland. "I was up north of Leningrad during the week collecting in the forest that was once Finnish territory and have been able to take what I desired from both the garden of the Komarov Botanic Institute and the Institute of Forestry," Creech recorded (1970a). "There are some quite interesting forms and species, all of which are among the hardiest here in Leningrad." One of the plants he collected in the Karelian Isthmus was a curious form of a willow: "*Salix fragilis* but of a subglobose kind that the Russians call 'self-pruning' and it looks just like that. It has a completely sheared look but it is the natural form."

Back in Leningrad, in the hotel where he was assembling all of his collections, Creech was pleased with the results: "All in all, it is a quite useful selection of plant material and as it stands right now, in my bathtub, all are in excellent condition" (1970a). A few days later all the living plants collected on this phase of the trip were shipped via air pouch, and on 11 July, Creech, accompanied by Shmaraev, departed Leningrad for Siberia.

Heavenly blue alliums

Creech's first stop was Novosibirsk, a major cultural and industrial center of western Siberia. Just south of Novosibirsk, Creech visited Akademgorodok, an academic city, where he toured the Central Siberian Botanical Garden. "By far, one of the most interesting of institutions that collectors can visit in the USSR is Akademgorodok," wrote Creech (1988). "Created in 1957, Akademgorodok includes most of the Soviet Union's basic scientific institutes. Among the other sciences, researchers there are

studying various aspects of biology, including genetics. Horticulturists and botanists are assembling a vast germplasm repository of Siberia's native plants."

Creech thought very highly of the scope of the collections at Akademgorodok: "[This] is one of the finest botanic gardens of its type I have seen," he wrote (1971c). "The garden is organized into a series of separate sections, one in which native plants have been assembled on a taxonomic basis, a medicinal plant garden of excellent quality, a garden of forage and pasture grass species, a fruit tree garden, a collection of trees and shrubs in a very informal park-like arrangement, and a large collection of ornamentals—particularly bulbs, ground covers, and cutflower species" (1972).

Creech was thrilled by this opportunity to study the extensive collections and trials of ornamental plants, including many species native to Siberia. "The grasses are just ripening, as well as the perennials and legumes," he noted (1971c). "These are the major components of the Siberian flora and certainly a beautiful array of species they are. There are alliums of the clearest blue I have seen and many ground covering species." Creech acquired from the collections and the trial plots numerous showy grasses, bulbs, and hardy perennials, including bright crimson-flowered *Paeonia anomala* (7264) and yellow-flowered *Papaver alpinum* (7269).

Taiga's ghostly birches

Three days later Creech flew east to Irkutsk, situated some 70 km from the shores of Lake Baikal. Founded in

Creech collects seeds of *Vaccinium* in the Siberian taiga near Tulun. Photo by John L. Creech.

A typical association of white-barked *Betula verrucosa* and stately *Pinus sibirica,* prominent trees of the Siberian taiga. Photo by John L. Creech.

1652 as an outpost for trading with China, Irkutsk later became one of the chief cities on the Trans-Siberian Railroad. "The weather is bright and hot," noted Creech (1971c). "But this is the height of the season. Here the last frost is mid-June and the first one is in mid to late August, so the growing season is only about sixty days. Can't do much with that! . . . Among the trees, poplars and Siberian elm are the most common. The streets of Irkutsk are lined with allées of *Populus laurifolia,* a very dense upright smallish tree. Avenues of them run literally for miles, planted so close as to form shaded walkways. We certainly can make use of this tree in a similar manner for our colder regions."

After visits to local institutions in Irkutsk, Creech traveled about 350 km northwest on the Trans-Siberian Railroad to Tulun. "At the small experiment station near Tulun," he recorded (1972), "in a region of dark, heavy soils, the wooded areas in some places are largely mixtures of pine and larch. The forest floor is hummocked with sphagnum mounds and in this bog-like condition vacciniums, spireas, alders, and small birches flourish. To my surprise a rhododendron also occurs in considerable quantity. This is *Rhododendron ledebourii* Pojark., a close relative of *R. dauricum,* from which it differs by its more evergreen habit in winter."

Creech marveled at the seemingly endless taiga with prominent birches, *Betula verrucosa,* and pines, *Pinus sibirica,* describing "a mixture of white ghostly birch trunks in fog bound green forests. There are taiga meadows everywhere in full bloom, a vast array of blue and pink *Trollius,* gentians, *Dianthus superbus, Veronica,*

Geranium, and *Linaria.* I also found *Lilium martagon,* a frequent plant in the birch forests" (1971d).

Altai crabapples

Back in Irkutsk, Creech and Shmaraev prepared for their next excursion, this time to Barnaul, situated in the steppe region some 180 km south of Novosibirsk. Their main destination was the Altai Fruit and Decorative Plant Station, located in the foothills of the Altai mountains near Barnaul. "A fruit-breeding station at Barnaul has a collection of trees, shrubs, and herbaceous plants from the Altai mountains, including 25 acres [10 hectares] of more than 1500 species of ornamental plants" (Creech 1988).

Creech was especially impressed with an excellent collection of the wild forms of crabapple, *Malus pallasiana.* In addition to its extensive representation of Altai plants, the station maintained smaller collections of plants from China and the Far East. "It was here that I collected *Rhododendron adamsii,* a dwarf compact species with white to pink flowers, several species of *Actinidia,* the unusual large-leaved plant, *Echinopanax elatus,* and *Microbiota decussata,* a curious juvenile-leaved conifer," wrote Creech (1972). One selection that held much promise as a cold- and drought-resistant plant was *Salix ledebouriana* 'Kuraika', a selection of the local wild willow. "A handsome species making tall arching hedges of silvery-grey," noted Creech (1971d). "I hope it survives."

From Barnaul, Creech and Shmaraev returned to Novosibirsk and on 23 July flew to Moscow. "I am very pleased with the range of materials I am collecting, as it represents some rather interesting Siberian plants,"

The Altai Fruit and Decorative Plant Station near Barnaul in the foothills of the Altai mountains. In the background is a row of silver-leaved *Salix ledebouriana* 'Kuraika'. Photo by John L. Creech.

The laboratory and administration building at the Main Botanic Garden of the Academy of Sciences in Moscow. Photo by Russell J. Seibert.

Creech reported (1971d). "Two of the rhododendrons will be new to us but more important is the fact that we are dealing with plants that grow under the greatest range of high and low temperatures for plants of this nature. Because of this reason, I made a first swing around southern Siberia and will go back to the best area in about two weeks when the grasses and legumes will be ripe."

Gardens of Moscow

During a week-long stay in Moscow, Creech arranged for another shipment of plants to be dispatched to the United States and made visits for collecting purposes to several gardens in the Moscow area. "In Moscow several institutions feature trees, shrubs, and herbaceous plants that will interest the horticultural visitor," he noted (1972). "In most such places, emphasis is on the native plants of the USSR, and nowadays it is fashionable to collect and display Siberian species."

Creech's itinerary included the Main Botanic Garden of the Academy of Sciences, the University of Moscow Botanic Garden, the Shreder Botanical Garden of the Timirazov Agricultural Institute, and the Forestry Institute at Pushkino. "The Main Botanic Garden includes display beds of horticultural varieties of annuals and perennials, large collections of trees and shrubs arranged on a systematic basis, and greenhouses with exotic species," he noted (1972). "The University of Moscow Botanic Garden features 40 hectares of native plants arranged on a geographical basis; and one can visit an alpine flora, a steppe collection, plants from the Far East,

the Caucasus region, or the Crimea. Much of this garden is based on domestic explorations by the staff of the Garden." Among the plants Creech acquired from this garden were several species of peonies, including *Paeonia caucasica* (7265), *P. kavachensis* (7266), *P. tenuifolia* (7267), and *P. triternata* (7268).

Creech described the Shreder Botanical Garden as "considerably smaller, less than 12 hectares, and perhaps the least likely to be encountered. The small herbaceous garden is devoted to economic plants mainly used for teaching purposes, but nearby is the dendrarium with a rather interesting collection of trees and shrubs" (1972). Among Creech's collections from the garden were a pink-flowered hybrid of *Cornus alba* crossed with an unknown parent (74238); *Prunus maackii,* with rich red exfoliating bark, frequently used as a street tree; and *Acer tegmentosum,* a striped-bark species, heavy with bright yellow fruits and, according to Creech, "most attractive."

Quite a place

In Moscow, Creech said farewell to Shmaraev, who had to return to Leningrad. Korsokov took his place, joining Creech for the remainder of the trip. Together they departed Moscow for Yalta in the Crimea on 30 July. In Yalta, Creech collected native Crimean plants on Ai Petri, 1233 m, which towered over the city, and on the steppe plateau to the north. "So it has been a worthwhile excursion," he commented upon returning from Ai Petri. "Here *Carpinus orientalis, Acer stevenii, Taxus baccata,* and *Pinus pallasiana* are the main ravine plants. A prostrate

The Krymskiye Mountains, including Ai Petri, 1233 m, rise above Yalta and separate the city from the steppe plateau to the north. Photo by John L. Creech.

Juniperus is scattered on the edges of the steppe cliff and the steppe itself is largely *Poa pratensis.* . . . Quite a place" (1971e).

In addition to the maples, junipers, yews, grasses, and herbaceous ornamentals he collected in the wild, Creech obtained a number of choice garden plants from the Nikitsky Botanical Garden, which he had visited during his 1963 trip. "The Nikitsky Botanic Garden has a fine collection of forms of *Cedrus* and other rare ornamentals. There is an intensive breeding of cannas and several new varieties have been named. Grafting material of *Cedrus* [711021–7] and roots of the new canna varieties [7249–7250] were made available to me, as well as other ornamentals I selected in their collections and nurseries" (Creech 1971b).

The ultimate

From Yalta, Creech and Korsokov flew to Novosibirsk, where Creech revisited the Central Siberian Botanical Garden in Akademgorodok with the intention of collecting some of the plants that had not gone to seed when he had visited the garden in July. "The local botanists, as in every other case, were most helpful and generous," he noted (1971b). "Grasses, herbaceous plants, and some trees were seeding, and I was permitted to go through the collections of native species to gather seed."

From Novosibirsk, Creech and Korsakov continued to Yakutsk, the main city of Yakutia in eastern Siberia, which had profited from gold mining and fur trading since its founding in 1632. "There is no means of travel to Yakutsk except by airplane," wrote Creech (1971b).

Creech in the Yakut village of Berdigestyakh, 300 km from Yakutsk. Photo by John L. Creech.

Creech found *Potentilla fruticosa* blooming profusely in the open meadows in the permafrost region near Berdigestyakh. Photo by John L. Creech.

"Here in the permafrost taiga, a small botanic garden is devoted to plants of eastern Siberia." Despite fiercely cold winters with temperatures dropping below -50ºC, this garden appeared to thrive. "At this time it consists of only 10–12 hectares containing some 120 species in demonstration plots. About thirty native species are useful decorative plants. *Pinus sibirica, Larix sibirica, Betula verrucosa,* and several spruce species frequent the permafrost bogs. They do not grow tall because the ground is frozen solid from about three feet [90 cm] below the surface. But this solid base helps contain moisture during the growing season, and it is said that without the permafrost, Siberia would be a vast arctic desert" (Creech 1972).

With the help of the garden staff, Creech made a journey to a Yakut village, Berdigestyakh, some 300 km from Yakutsk. He was the first foreigner to reach the remote community. "The route to Berdigestyakh is generously called a corduroy road in parts, elsewhere it is up to the driver to find the route," Creech explained (1971b). "But the experience was not regretted in the least." While admiring surprisingly rich vegetation of wild potentillas, birches, dwarf willows, and other subarctic plants, Creech noted that the road, where it existed, was little more than "a dirt track with sections of log roads leading through the swamps. Forest fires were often smoldering along the route. And, on occasion, there were grave markers for truck drivers who, stranded alone during winter, had died" (1988).

Arriving in Berdigestyakh, Creech experienced a delightfully cordial welcome on the part of the villagers, who were genuinely concerned for his welfare. "The village consisted of some 3500 Yakuts mainly occupied in

trapping fur-bearing mink and sable, herding reindeer and pursuing similar limited agricultural pursuits. In the conifer forests there, subarctic plants inhabit the meadows and other open areas. Potentillas are numerous. I also saw dwarf *Lonicera* with edible fruit, *Vaccinium* and wild roses. *Rosa acicularis,* with its many small thorns and pendant pear-shaped fruits, was particularly handsome. I was particularly delighted to see the neat, compact *Spiraea betulifolia,* which I have often encountered in the mountains of Japan" (Creech 1988).

Creech remembered that staying late one evening in Berdigestyakh, satisfied by bountiful collecting and contemplating his experience in this remote and desolate outpost, he looked down at the timeless village and, thinking about where else plant collecting could take him, said to himself, "Well, this is the ultimate" (1971a).

Upon their return to Yakutsk, Creech and Korsakov boarded a plane on 19 August and flew to Moscow. Several days later, after some last-minute collecting in the Moscow gardens, Creech left for the United States. The 290 lots of seeds and plants that resulted from this expedition contained, in Creech's words, "a sufficient number of surprises for me to make the journey well worthwhile" (1972).

Of his two trips to the USSR, Creech concluded: "The Soviet Union has an excellent chain of botanic gardens and plant evaluation centers, which have historically demonstrated an expertise in distributing the wild plants of the USSR. Couple that with its great climatic variation and the vast array of species suitable to the coldest regions of America's midsection, and this country should be high among our priorities for future collecting sites" (1988).

Georgia occupies an area of 69,500 km² in the central and western parts of Transcaucasia. In the west it reaches the Black Sea, in the east the Transcaucasian depression. The northern border follows the high mountain ranges of the Greater Caucasus, with the tallest peak, Mount Elbrus, rising to 5633 m; the southern border crosses the Lesser Caucasus, where the tallest peaks reach about 3300 m. The intermountain region of Georgia is divided into the western part, the ancient kingdom of Colchis, and the eastern part, the ancient kingdom of Iberia, by the Likhi Ridge, which connects the Greater

Caucasus to the north with the Lesser Caucasus to the south. Despite its small area, Georgia has exceptionally diverse plant communities, from desert and semidesert in the eastern part of the country, to lush Colchic forests of moist subtropical climate in the west, to high-mountain vegetation in the north and south. This diversity of plant communities is reflected in the forty-two hundred vascular plants found here.

RETURN OF THE ARGONAUTS

Thirty years passed before the next expedition would continue plant exploration in that region. In the meantime, historical changes took place: the USSR was replaced by the Commonwealth of Independent States (CIS). In 2001 an expedition was organized to Georgia, one of the republics in the Caucasus and a member state of the CIS. The main purpose for the expedition was to collect new germplasm of common boxwood, *Buxus sempervirens,* from areas where it grows wild in Georgia and also from locations where it was introduced centuries or possibly millennia earlier.

The expedition was organized in collaboration with the Georgian Academy of Sciences, Institute of Botany. The institute's director, Professor Giorgi Nakhutsrishvili, agreed to host the group of plant explorers and assigned two scientists, Dr. Maia Akhalkatsi and Dr. Marina Mosulishvili, to participate in the expedition. I compiled a team of several boxwood experts from the United States, including Charles T. Fooks, owner of Woodland Nursery in Salisbury, Maryland; Todd Lasseigne, assistant director of the J. C. Raulston Arboretum in Raleigh, North Carolina; Tatum N. and Paul M. Saunders, owners of Saunders Brothers Nursery in Piney River, Virginia; Frederick R. Spicer, manager of horticulture for Morris County, New Jersey; and Dr. Robert D. Wright, profes-

Standing between boxwoods at the entrance to the Institute of Botany in Tbilisi are, left to right, the author, Otar Abdaladze, Mosulishvili, Nakhutsrishvili, and Akhalkatsi. Photo by Tomasz Aniśko.

sor of the Virginia Polytechnic Institute and State University in Blacksburg.

Sacred tree

Our search began on 9 June in the area 60 km northwest of Tbilisi, the capital of Georgia. In this part of the country boxwood is not considered to be indigenous. Numerous established populations found in eastern Georgia are believed to be remnants of intentional introductions that took place in the remote past. Boxwood has been considered a sacred tree since antiquity by the

Around a small church of Saint George near the village of Navdaraant Kari, many boxwoods were planted for ceremonial purposes. Photo by Tomasz Aniśko.

woods (011280–1) grew throughout this site. "The three of us roamed through this small stand of *Buxus,* at Saint George's, excited as kids in a candy store," recalled Fooks (2002). "We noted two variations in the leaves of what we saw. One type was a rather narrow, lighter green leaf, and some having larger, wider, rounder leaves that were somewhat glaucous."

The site near Choporta very much resembled the one near Navdaraant Kari, but only the ruins of the church remained. Despite this fact, villagers continue to visit the site, light candles, and leave coins between stones as small offerings. Boxwoods growing around the ruins had attained almost treelike size; after centuries of self-seeding, they had spread far beyond the original site and established a population covering almost an entire hillside. Browsing through an undergrowth of small seedlings gave us a taste for what amazing variability can be found in such populations (011282–4).

The following day we visited Shio-Mgvime Monastery located near Mtskheta, 30 km west of Tbilisi, founded in the sixth century. It was built into a picturesque hillside, steep cliffs providing a dramatic backdrop for two churches and the monk's living quarters. The grounds of the monastery were shaded by large trees, but old boxwoods were planted near the churches. Most of them were densely planted as a tall hedge separating the lower and upper levels of the monastery (011286–8). Variability of plants in the hedge confirmed our earlier observation that planted boxwoods in Georgia are usually seed-grown and most likely transplanted from the wild. "All of the boxwood we saw planted in eastern Georgia appeared to be collected plants as no two were alike, even in hedges," commented Fooks (2002). "Of course, this was in our favor as it gave us much more to select from."

people of this region. Many Christian churches were built in places that had been sacred to the local people for millennia. Boxwoods growing in these sites were adopted in Christian religious ceremonies. A tradition of bringing boxwood twigs to a church on Palm Sunday continues even today. These twigs are later taken home, where they are believed to offer protection to the house and good fortune to the family.

We were able to travel back in time and immerse ourselves in this world of ancient myths on the first day of our expedition, when we visited two sacred places of worship, one near the village of Navdaraant Kari and another near the village of Choporta.

The site near Navdaraant Kari included a small church of Saint George sheltered by a grove of trees. Inside the church, which dated back to the Middle Ages, were signs of worship—small pictures, burnt candles, and coins inserted into cracks in the walls. Here we met with our first wish-tree, its branches clad with ribbonlike pieces of cloth. A person wanting a wish or prayer to come true would tear a piece of cloth from his or her dress or shirt and tie it to the tree while making the wish. To complete our transcendental experience, we proceeded to a spot near the church where there were tables at which villagers feasted following the sacrifice of a lamb. Numerous box-

its eastern limits just west of Tbilisi. As we gained elevation, the forests of *Pinus kochiana* gave way to broadleaved forests and vast expanses of meadows thick with a dazzling diversity of flowers. At one point our van came to a sudden stop when a fenced-in, ungrazed meadow appeared before us. Despite loud protests from a donkey tied to a post, we climbed the fence and found ourselves surrounded by lush grasses and flowers of all colors: blue *Vicia* and *Galega,* purple *Onobrychis* and *Dactylorhiza,* yellow *Hieracium* and *Pedicularis,* red *Papaver,* and pink *Orobus*—a stunning floral spectacle kept in constant motion by the wind. Unafraid of deer ticks and poison ivy, neither of which existed there, several of us dropped to our knees, overpowered by the beauty of the place and eager to take a few close-up photographs.

Mount Didgori was a site of the battle between Georgian and Turkish troops that occurred in 1121. The battlefield, which extends for several kilometers, is mostly covered by lush subalpine meadows. The top of Mount Didgori is marked with a monument consisting of dozens of massive swords pushed into the ground and posing as crosses. Colossal sculptures of dismembered bodies of warriors are scattered in the meadows around the crosses. Truly monumental in scale, the memorial, surrounded by the serene Trialeti Range, makes a powerful impression.

In the afternoon, continuing north from Didgori toward Nichbisi, we again entered a broad-leaved forest. At one of the stops, we wandered into a small ravine where a small relict population of *Taxus baccata* (011278) managed to survive outside its continuous range to the north and west. As we descended from Trialeti Range to the valley of the Mtkvari River, the forest was gradually replaced by so-called *shibliak* vegetation, consisting of drought-resistant plants. This bleak landscape of limestone, bleached by scorching sun and sparsely inhabited by xeric vegetation, did not entice prolonged botanizing. With no tree tall enough to offer shade in sight, and with our supply of water already exhausted, we were soon back on the road to Tbilisi.

Having been told by a botanist working at the Institute of Botany about a large boxwood tree growing in the Kvatakhevi Monastery, we decided to add this destination to our plan. On 13 June we traveled west on the main highway connecting Tbilisi with the Black Sea coast. In Mtskheta we turned onto a local road leading to Nichbisi. A couple of kilometers past Nichbisi we turned again, this time onto a dirt road heading north toward a remote

A lonely boxwood tree stands at the entrance to a church in Shio-Mgvime Monastery, which dates back to the sixth century. Photo by Tomasz Aniśko.

One impressively large boxwood tree stood alone, guarding the entrance to the church. Its dark evergreen foliage was in stark contrast to the subdued, faded, pale colors of the xeric vegetation covering the surrounding hills. Clearly the tree was not meant to be mere ornamentation but had acquired powerful spiritual significance as an arboreal embodiment of the promise of eternal life. Underneath the tree, cracks in the wall of the church's bell tower were filled with hundreds of boxwood seedlings. Trying to be discreet in such a sacred site, we left the seedlings undisturbed.

Trialeti Range

Our next destination was Mount Didgori, 1800 m, situated some 40 km west of Tbilisi in the Trialeti Range, which is part of the Lesser Caucasus. The range reaches

The open woodland of Vashlovani in eastern Georgia combines xerophytic trees and shrubs with drought-resistant grass cover. Photo by Tomasz Aniśko.

protect the unique, savannalike, open woodland and steppe vegetation of far eastern Georgia. The climate of the reserve is dry, with annual precipitation of only 470 mm. The reserve is cut by a maze of ravines 60 to 70 m deep. The Tbilisi Institute of Botany has a field station there. Merab Khachidze, who is in charge of the station, guided us through the reserve. Khachidze planted several boxwoods on the grounds of the station forty years ago. Despite a harsh climate and an exposed site, these shrubs appeared to be in good health and provided us with an abundant crop of cuttings (011292).

forested gorge cut by a stream in the northern slopes of the Trialeti Range. The Kvatakhevi Monastery was situated near the end of the gorge, protected on three sides by the steep mountain slopes.

There indeed was a very large, multitrunked boxwood tucked against the inside of the monastery wall. This magnificent specimen had even its lowest branches beyond the reach of someone standing on the ground. A monk, who appeared to be the only person living in the monastery and taking care of the church, shook his head when we asked about a ladder. Fortunately the tree was growing close enough to the wall that its branches could be reached from the top of it. Thus climbing the wall allowed us to collect plenty of cuttings (011291). Fruits, however, were very sparse, and those found were mostly devoid of seeds. After much picking, only three seeds were recovered (011290). Inside the church we noticed little bundles of boxwood branches laying around. We were told that these were placed there on Palm Sunday and would remain there until the next year.

Eastern steppe

On the morning of 14 June we headed east to the Vashlovani Nature Reserve, 200 km from Tbilisi, located in the Dedoplis Tskaro district. The reserve was established to

Upon entering the reserve, we saw vast expanses of steppe overflowing the undulating hills of the Shiraki plateau, stretching all the way to the horizon. The steppe was broken only by a single thin line of dirt track marked by the vehicle we were traveling in. Having been warned about poisonous snakes, we did not dare to step too far into the waist-deep ocean of grass. The open woodlands are communities of xerophytic woody plants combined with drought-resistant grass cover.

Kasristskali was the nearest village, some 10 km north of Vashlovani Nature Reserve. It is primarily inhabited by shepherds and their families, who utilize vast expanses of steppe for grazing sheep and cattle. Driving through the village, we noticed young boys armed with an air-gun and shooting birds. Their hiding place turned out to be a large group of boxwoods, planted seemingly as a hedge but long since neglected and forgotten. In this group we found two plants with exceptionally glaucous foliage, each differing in leaf size (011294–5).

Lagodekhi

On 15 June we traveled east from Tbilisi to the Greater Caucasus. We set up our base in Shilda, a village in the district of Lagodekhi. Our first destination was an arbore-

The valley of the river Chelti near Shilda supports a lush deciduous forest of wingnuts, oaks, hornbeams, and hawthorns. Photo by Tomasz Aniśko.

Pontic azaleas, *Rhododendron luteum,* grow in the subalpine meadows of the Lagodekhi Nature Reserve. Photo by Tomasz Aniśko.

tum of the Lagodekhi Nature Reserve. The arboretum was established at the end of the nineteenth century by Ludwik Młokosiewicz, a Polish botanist serving as an officer in the Russian Army, best remembered for his discovery of a new species of peony, later named after him, *Paeonia mlokosewitschii.* Despite its small area of only 2 hectares, the arboretum has an array of magnificent tree specimens, including a large boxwood tree more than a hundred years old (011297–8).

At the headquarters of the Lagodekhi Nature Reserve we were met by Gogi Mamukelashvili, vice-director of scientific affairs. The reserve's administration buildings are surrounded by a small park where many exotic trees and shrubs were planted in the past. Among the most intriguing specimens was a weeping form of *Magnolia*

grandiflora (011279). Several low-growing boxwoods were also noticed near the entrance to one of the guest-houses (011299). After having lunch on the side of a stream near the reserve's headquarters, Mamukelashvili led us through a forest of predominantly *Fagus orientalis.* In the afternoon we reached a place where a colony of *Paeonia mlokosewitschii* is known to flower every spring. Unfortunately, our desperate efforts to find fruiting plants were unsuccessful.

On 16 June we reached Bzatagora, or Boxwood Hill, located outside Kvareli, 160 km northeast of Tbilisi. This was once the site of an ancient temple or sacred grove. It is believed that the boxwood population in Bzatagora resulted from an introduction from the western part of the country. Since then the population in Bzatagora has grown to cover an entire hillside. Mature boxwood trees formed a very dense canopy that excluded much of the light from reaching the forest floor. Little vegetation of any sort was present under the boxwoods. However, in places where an opening in the canopy was caused by a falling tree, hundreds of small boxwood seedlings were growing and competing with each other. It was among these seedlings that we observed the greatest diversity. Within a relatively small area we found plants with pendulous (011305–6) and prostrate (011307) branching habits, plants with very glossy, dark green leaves (011310), and plants with strongly glaucous leaves (011309). One seedling even had variegated foliage (011308).

In the afternoon we hiked in the valley of the river Chelti near Shilda, known for its *Pterocarya pterocarpa* forest. Picturesque willows and poplars grew closer to the river. Higher up, large wingnuts, oaks, hornbeams, and hawthorns created a patchwork of different textures and shades of green on the hillsides. Flocks of sheep strolled casually along the edges of the forest. Our hike ended when two big sheepdogs blocked our path, leaving no doubt as to what they intended to do should we decide to proceed.

The following morning we returned to the Lagodekhi Nature Reserve to undertake, with Mamukelashvili as our guide, a 14 km hike to reach the subalpine meadows at about 2500 m. Upon emerging from the forest above the timberline, we were immediately surrounded by the overpowering scent of Pontic azalea, *Rhododendron luteum*. The azaleas were in full bloom and scattered in large numbers in the meadows. Several megaforbs, or tall herbs, still in their vegetative stage, were pointed out to us. Unlike many other mountain systems, the Caucasus has tall herbaceous vegetation well represented in its subalpine zone. Megaforbs are mainly dicots, characterized by rosetteless shoots, short tap roots, and rhizomes. They develop on rich soils under conditions of high humidity, high solar radiation, and negligible daily fluctuations of temperature.

Floristic junction

On 21 June we reversed our course and headed west from Tbilisi to Algeti Nature Reserve, in the Tetritskaro district. It was established in 1965 on the southern slopes of the East Trialeti Range, which is a part of the Lesser Caucasus. The administration of the reserve is in the village of Manglisi. Malkhaz Kavteladze, director, and Khatuna

Tsiklauri, doctoral candidate at the Tbilisi State University, welcomed us and guided us in the reserve.

The main purpose for the reserve is to protect forests of *Abies nordmanniana* and *Picea orientalis* in the eastern part of the Lesser Caucasus. The climate is transitional between moderate subtropical-continental and humid-marine. The reserve has a rich and diverse flora of more than a thousand vascular plants. Botanists consider the southern slopes of the East Trialeti a floristic junction, where elements of Colchic, Hyrcanian, Caucasian, Middle Eastern, and Persian floras meet.

After hiking through the spruce forest, we descended to a small hamlet. Shepherds who spend summer there while their sheep graze in the surrounding hills treated us to a meal. It was served under an oak tree on the site of a ruined medieval church.

That evening, while returning to Tbilisi, we stopped at a roadside vendor selling plants. "We purchased a boxwood, which had been hacked on quite a bit, but got our interest," remembered Fooks (2002). "It was one perfectly straight pole with all of the branches perpendicular to the trunk. It seemed to have great promise as a fastigiate plant. We purchased it for 10 lari, trimmed the cuttings [011313] and later planted it in the Tbilisi Botanical Garden."

Kazbegi

On 23 June we headed north to Kazbegi in the Greater Caucasus, 160 km from Tbilisi. The Georgia Military Road, which leads to Kazbegi, is the only major road that crosses the Caucasus and connects Georgia with Russia. First it follows the river Aragvi to the Cross Pass, and from there it follows the river Tergi flowing north to Russia. It is an ancient trading route that the Russians converted into a carriage road during the nineteenth century. The town of Kazbegi, elevation 1797 m, is situated on the banks of the river Tergi in Phansheti Valley, overshadowed by the mighty Mount Kazbeg, 5047 m. The town and the mountain were named after Alexander Kazbegi, a local noble and much-loved poet who lived in the nineteenth century.

The next day we drove to the village of Phansheti, located in the Tergi River valley, about 4 km south of Kazbegi. Steep slopes there are largely covered by scree, which provides habitat to mountain xerophytes. Numerous mineral springs created small marshes in the valley, which at the time of our visit, when several species of

A narrow ribbon of the Georgia Military Road. This is the only major road crossing the Greater Caucasus and connecting Georgia with Russia. Photo by Tomasz Aniśko.

Ranunculus were in bloom, appeared from a distance to be dusted with gold. Villagers in Phansheti channeled one of the springs into a large outdoor swimming pool, the last thing we expected to see in these rugged mountains. The pool was constantly filled by gushing water from a mountain spring on one end and overflowing on the other. Set in the middle of a vast meadow, against a backdrop of magnificent Mount Kazbeg, it appeared almost surreal.

Gveleti Gorge, located near the village Gveleti, just a few kilometers north of Kazbegi, was our destination for the afternoon. It follows Tibaistskali, a tributary of Tergi, fed by glaciers on Mount Kazbeg. Upon entering the gorge, the recognizable trail soon disappeared among lush grasses and herbs, forcing us to carefully navigate our way among rocks and follow the course of the Tibaistskali upstream. Along the stream many herbaceous plants were

in full bloom, including *Caltha polypetala* (011052), *Filipendula vulgaris* (011051), and *Linum catharticum,* but most enchanting was the profusion of *Campanula* and *Geranium* species. Some of the individual *Geranium* plants identified as *G. sylvaticum* (011049) and *G. ibericum* (011050) stood out from the crowd because of their exceptionally rich bluish purple flowers. Our progress was eventually halted by a waterfall and the unclimbable, vertical rock face some 30 m high surrounding it.

On 25 June, in order to reach Truso Gorge, 40 km south of Kazbegi, we turned off the Georgia Military Road in the village of Almasiani. A dirt track allowed us to drive as far as the tiny settlement, Zemo-Okrokana, where a medieval defensive tower guarded the entrance to the gorge. From the village we continued hiking west, following a track along the river Tergi until we reached a wide-open valley where numerous mineral springs

The austere landscape of Truso Gorge is filled with scree covered by sparse vegetation.
Photo by Tomasz Aniśko.

A medieval watchtower in Sno Gorge, where watchmen warned the inhabitants of the mountains against advancing invaders.
Photo by Tomasz Aniśko.

created striking creamy pink deposits along the river. Interestingly, at one point along the trail we saw a wish-tree, this time a juniper, decorated with pieces of cloth. It was growing out of a rock above the trail, its branches hanging low enough for people to reach them. Under the tree was a large pail of empty bottles, indicating that the trail might have been traveled more frequently than we thought. As with the churches we had visited earlier, small coins were placed in the crevices in the rock.

After lunch we headed to the Sno Gorge. A dirt track leading to the gorge begins on the east side of the Georgia Military Road, about 5 km south of Kazbebi, near the village of Arsha. The Sno Gorge starts as a wide-open valley with picturesque emerald green fields and pastures. Past the village of Sno, some 2.5 km into the valley, the road enters a narrow canyon and climbs gradually for 18 km to the village of Juta. Built at an elevation of 2200 m, this is among the highest permanently settled villages in the Caucasus. A horse track, which we took, leads north from the village toward Russia. Above the trail a vast colony of *Rhododendron caucasicum, Daphne glomerata,* and *Vaccinium myrtillus* smothered the whole hillside, while the meadows along the river were filled with orchids and sporadically accented with statuesque *Heracleum sosnowskyi.* Glistening in the afternoon sun were silver-leaved willows, *Salix kusnetzowii,* which occupied little nooks between rocks near the river.

On 26 June we made a daring attempt to climb Mount Kazbeg to reach the subnival vegetation at the base of the Gergeti Glacier. Mount Kazbeg is a long-extinct

Holy Trinity Church rises above the clouds. It was built in the fourteenth century on a ridge near Kazbegi at 2216 m. Photo by Tomasz Aniśko.

volcano and the highest peak in the central Caucasus. It is believed to be the place where Amirani, the Georgian archetype of Prometheus, was chained to the mountain. The morning began with a brisk hike to the Gergeti Holy Trinity Church, built in the fourteenth century on a ridge, 2216 m, opposite the town of Kazbegi and silhouetted against the impressive, overpowering Mount Kazbeg. The trail started just above the village of Gergeti on the left bank of the Tergi River. Led by two local guides, we quickly entered a forest of predominantly *Betula litwinowii* only to emerge from it on the top of the ridge with alpine meadows extending as far as the eye could see.

The Holy Trinity Church, barely visible in the clouds, appeared to float in the air. Heading in the direction of the church, we were quickly engulfed by thick fog. A herd of cows leisurely stood on the hills around the church. They were almost motionless, as if awaiting church bells to break the silence. Wishing to avoid disturbing the tranquility of the scene, we lowered our voices and proceeded slowly to the church. The building was locked and appeared deserted except for a couple of dogs and a lonely herdsman standing on top of the wall watching his cows.

Spicer, Wright, and I took on the challenge of reaching Gergeti Glacier at 3045 m and seeing subnival vegetation, which can be found just below the permanent snow cover. Despite the extreme conditions, more than three hundred species of plants occur in the subnival belt, about a third of which are unique to this ecosystem. These plants developed morphological adaptations allowing them to cope with high solar radiation, temperature fluctuations, and desiccating winds during the growing season, while allowing for hibernation under the snow during the winter.

At about 2300 m, Spicer began feeling the effects of the thin air and decided to turn back and return to the church. Wright chose to do the same at about 2600 m. To make things more difficult, it started to rain. As my two guides did not seem to be bothered in the least by the low oxygen, the steep climb, and the rain, we continued our hike to the glacier. Thick clouds reduced visibility to between 10 and 20 m and made it impossible to gauge our progress or have a sense of the distance from the glacier. Changes in vegetation and the first patches of snow indicated, however, that we were approaching it. Finally, an opening in the clouds made it possible to see the glacier, 8 km long and 7 km wide, down below our feet.

On the morning of 27 June we hiked on Mount Kuro, 4071 m. This mountain had appeared to us in its full glory the first evening we came to Kazbegi as we sat in the dining room of the Kazbegi Ecological Center, where we were staying. The windows there looked out to the east, and suddenly someone pointed to the view outside. There it was: Mount Kuro, gloriously illuminated by the sun setting on the opposite side of the valley. Since that moment we had admired it every day—slate-gray and gloomy at breakfast, glistening as if gold-plated at suppertime. On our last day in Kazbegi, we were finally able to explore its slopes.

Meadows on Mount Kuro, immediately above Kazbegi, were grazed, so that only individual rock outcrops, beyond the reach of sheep, were richly encrusted with floral jewels, *Campanula* species in particular. Only upon reaching a very steep rocky ridge at about 2000 m did we discover the plant diversity of this mountain in its full. There, along the edge of the forest of crooked-stem birch, *Betula litwinowii,* and mountain-ash, *Sorbus caucasigena,* we found a lush meadow that had escaped grazing and bore a lavish vegetation dazzling with color. Golden *Inula orientalis* (011054) and *Ranunculus caucasicus,* blue *Myosotis alpestris* and several species of *Campanula,* lavender *Linum hypericifolium,* pink and rose *Pyrethrum roseum,* purple *Stachys macrantha,* and chartreuse *Alchemilla oligotricha* lured us higher and higher. The colors seemed exceptionally brilliant and intense, perhaps because of the sheer rock cliffs of Mount Kuro, which dropped like a slate-gray curtain behind them. The air was perfumed by a diminutive rose, probably *Rosa pimpinellifolia,* and by the even smaller *Daphne glomerata.*

If not for Mosulishvili, we might have forgotten about the whole world there, savoring the beauty of the Caucasian flora, inhaling the oxygen-deficient mountain air, and absorbing the UV-rich sun rays. All these things can lead to a strange state of euphoria known to affect plant collectors around the world. Mosulishvili brought us back to reality, reminding us of the need to return to the Kazbegi Ecological Center. We had to prepare for the next day's departure and the travel to Bakuriani in the Lesser Caucasus.

Lesser Caucasus

On the evening of 28 June, after an all-day drive from Kazbegi, we arrived in Bakuriani, 1700 m, located in the northern slopes of the West Trialeti Range in the Lesser Caucasus. Bakuriani was established in the 1930s as a ski resort, but despite its popularity it retained much of the atmosphere of a small mountain village, with its traditional wooden cottages. The snow cover in this area lasts from November to March, and occasionally until May. Our home for the next couple of days was the Ecological Center in the Bakuriani Botanical Garden, where we were welcomed by Dr. Nukri Sikharulidze, director of the garden.

In order to reach our destination for the day, Lake Tabatskuri, south of Bakuriani, we had to take a dirt road up through the Trialeti Range. Sikharulidze arranged for two UAZ jeeps to take us on a strenuous road through the mountains. Upon reaching the Tskhra-Tskaro Pass at 2454 m, a spectacular view opened before us of highland pastures and mountain ranges stretching south into Armenia. As the road we traveled on descended from the pass on the south side of Trialeti Range, it became less like a road and more like an obstacle course, sometimes disappearing altogether. Our admiration for the rugged UAZs and their skillful drivers grew by the minute. By the early afternoon we reached Lake Tabatskuri, backed by a couple of extinct volcanoes. The lake provides enough fish to support two small villages on its shores, which are settled mostly by the Armenian minority. "About fifty families lived here," remembers Paul Saunders. "No supermarket, hospital, or short-order food stops here. Only a jeep road into this secluded village in the mountains at 2000 m connects it to the world beyond. Similar to the early American Indian practices using buffalo patties on the treeless prairie as fuel for campsites, the villagers were drying cow dung into foot square slabs for fuel for winter."

Standing in front of a variegated boxwood (011323) in a formal park surrounding Romanov's palace in Borjomi are, left to right, Paul M. Saunders, Likhovtschenko, and Fooks. Photo by Tomasz Aniśko.

Romanov's retreat

Our next destination was Borjomi-Kharagauli National Park, located northwest of Bakuriani, on the northern and southern slopes of the eastern Adjara-Imereti mountain range. The northern end of the park merges into the Likhi Ridge, which divides Georgia into eastern and western parts. The northern boundary coincides with the river Chkherimela, while the southwestern boundary follows the river Mtkvari. The national park covers more than 68,000 hectares, which places it among the largest parks in Europe.

Borjomi, one of the oldest health resorts in Georgia, was built in the gorge of the river Mtkvari, which boasts springs of mineral water with exceptional medicinal qualities. The park began in the second half of the nineteenth century when Mikhail Romanov, brother of the ruling Russian czar, was appointed viceroy of the Russian Empire to Transcaucasia and decided to build a summer residence in Borjomi. The former Romanov estate was declared a nature reserve in 1935, after the fall of the Russian Empire and the accession of Georgia to the USSR. The formal park surrounding Romanov's palace was developed into a health resort.

"On entering the resort we saw a nice little variegated boxwood," recalled Fooks (2002). "However, since the guards at the gates only a few yards away were armed with submachine guns, we felt intimidated in spite of having our Georgian guides and passed it by." Fortunately, a little while later we met Levan Likhovtschenko, who had been a horticulturist at the resort for more than forty

A fallen tree halted progress in Baniskhevi Gorge in the Borjomi-Kharagauli National Park. Photo by Tomasz Aniśko.

years. Likhovtschenko graciously shared with us some of the boxwoods he had brought to Borjomi from western Georgia forty years earlier, including the variegated one we saw at the gate (011322–3).

Our destination for the afternoon was Baniskhevi Gorge on the southern side of the Adjara-Imereti mountain range. In this gorge many plants typical for the Colchic forest of western Georgia can be found growing together with plants characteristic of the drier eastern Georgia. Colchic plants in the gorge are found primarily in the understory of *Fagus orientalis* forest between 800 and 1300 m and include many broad-leaved evergreen shrubs such as *Ilex colchica* (011277), *Prunus laurocerasus,* and *Rhododendron ponticum*. At the elevation of 1350 to 1400 m, beech forest is replaced by *Abies nordmanniana* forest with undergrowth of *Rhododendron ponticum*. Above 1800 m, the forest gradually gives way to sub-alpine herbaceous vegetation. Thanks to UAZ jeeps and their amazing drivers, we were able to cross the stream several times, and we drove deep into the gorge until a fallen tree blocked our path. From this point on we continued on foot, hoping to find our first wild population of boxwood. This was not to be, however. Having been warned about Baniskhevi being a brown bear habitat, we proceeded cautiously. After seeing fresh bear tracks and bear dung on the trail, the group decided to return to the vehicles.

On our way back to Bakuriani, we stopped at what used to be the first botanical garden in this mountain resort. We were told that Lavrenty Beria, the infamous chief of Joseph Stalin's secret police, was so overtaken by the beauty of this site that he decided to turn the botanical

A twelfth-century stone bridge spans the sides of the Kintrishi Gorge, one of many such structures still standing in Adjara. Photo by Tomasz Aniśko.

garden into his summer residence. Indeed, the botanical garden was relocated to its present site at the Ecological Station, while the old one functioned as Beria's summer retreat. Extensive plantings of boxwood surrounded Beria's house; one unusually low-growing plant near steps leading to the lower level of the house caught our attention (011324).

Colchis

On 1 July we were to cross the Adjara-Imereti mountains and enter the historical Colchis of western Georgia. After traveling north out of the Borjomi Gorge, we turned west onto a main road between Tbilisi and the coast. The road crossed the mountains through a long tunnel under the Rikoti pass. Some 20 km further west, we turned onto a road leading to the gorge of the river Chkherimela. We

traveled along the river as far as the village of Kharagauli, which placed us near the northern boundary of the Borjomi-Kharagauli National Park, on the northern slopes of the Adjara-Imereti mountains. Upon reaching the vicinity of Kharagauli we found ourselves surrounded by slopes covered with boxwood groves. Steep slopes of loose, crumbled rock made maneuvering difficult, but the profusion of boxwoods and their diversity lured us higher and higher. The site appeared to have been forested in the past, with boxwood growing as the understory. Now grazing by domestic animals prevented regeneration of the trees, while boxwood, unpalatable to the animals, flourished in the site despite full exposure to sun. The diversity of forms, colors, sizes, and shapes of the boxwood growing here held up our group much longer than initially planned (011326–36). "Our guides and driver practically had to pry us away from there," remembered Fooks (2002). Kharagauli is believed to be the easternmost natural population of boxwood in the Adjara-Imereti mountains.

Loaded with boxwood cuttings and seeds, we returned to the main road and continued west through Kutaisi to the coastal city of Poti. Kutaisi was the capital of the ancient kingdom of Colchis and the destination of the legendary Argonauts' expedition led by Jason in pursuit of the Golden Fleece. After reaching the coast of Colchis near Poti, the Argonauts sailed up the Rioni River to Kutaisi. In Poti we changed directions and drove south along the Black Sea coast toward Batumi. Plantations of tea and citrus signaled that we were to enjoy a balmy, subtropical climate. Upon reaching Batumi we were met by Dr. Zurab Manvelidze, head of the plant conservation department of the Batumi Botanical Garden, who would not only be our guide in and around Batumi but who also wholeheartedly opened his home to us, a group of strangers from the United States.

Our first excursion out of Batumi on 2 July took us to Kintrishi Nature Reserve, about 50 km northeast of the city, a sanctuary for chestnut and beech forests in the gorge of the Kintrishi River. Because of its location between the Black Sea and the mountains of Adjara-Imereti, the nature reserve receives very high precipitation—nearly 4000 mm annually on average. The terrain in the park is very rugged, with high peaks, steep slopes, and several river gorges.

Kintrishi Gorge was mostly covered by a lush deciduous forest with rich undergrowth, which included dense thickets of boxwood (011337–42). "These natural thickets of boxwood contain thousands, even millions, of plants growing in some of the most rugged country imaginable," remembers Paul Saunders. "Gorge after gorge of boxwood, often growing along with rhododendron and holly, on nearly vertical slopes made green with the varying shapes and shades of these seedlings. Truly a boxwood heaven!"

Independence Day

Our last day of collecting was to be 4 July, when we paid a visit to the Batumi Botanical Garden, located some 9 km north of the city. The garden was founded in 1912 and now belongs to the Georgian Academy of Sciences. It covers an area of 113 hectares and features more than five thousand species of plants from around the world, representing temperate, Mediterranean, and subtropical climates.

The unique climate of Batumi allows for cultivation of frost-sensitive subtropical plants next to hardy plants from northern temperate climates. The garden design is based on geographical regions representing floristic zones of North America, Japan, the Far East, South America, Australia, and New Zealand. A formal garden called Primorsky Park offers a spectacular vista opening to the Black Sea and is lined with boxwood hedges (011350), clipped *Laurus nobilis* and *Prunus laurocerasus,* as well as stately *Cryptomeria japonica, Phoenix canariensis,* and *Pinus taeda.*

Before we departed Batumi to return to the United States with more than eighty collections of boxwoods and more than 180 collections of other plants, an unexpected grand finale to this expedition awaited us in Manvelidze's house. "Zura and his family were the most gracious hosts," remembered Fooks (2002). "His daughter and some neighbor girls assisted his wife in preparing and serving the meals. They played the piano and sang for us after the evening meal. They surprised us with a fantastic Fourth of July celebration. When we came back from our day trip we found balloons tied to the stair railings. Inside, the table was set with red, white, and blue napkins in each glass and a large cake at the head of the table with an American flag. We were very touched. Many of their friends and relatives had gathered. The ladies outdid themselves. The dinner was superb. After dinner there was the usual singing with a little different twist tonight. We sang the *Star Spangled Banner* and some other patri-

otic songs for them. It was hilarious. I must say I spent my most memorable Fourth of July in a foreign country."

FROM THE CASPIAN TO THE BLACK SEA

The results of the 2001 expedition opened our eyes to the floristic wealth of Transcaucasia. The diversity of boxwood, in particular, far exceeded our expectations. Participants of the 2001 trip came to the realization that boxwood exploration in that region should continue. With this goal in mind, in 2002 preparations began for another trip that would allow for additional collections of boxwood to be made across the region, from the Talish Mountains on the border between Azerbaijan and Iran, through Georgia, along Russia's Black Sea coast, and finally to the Crimean Peninsula in Ukraine.

The team this time included Lynn R. Batdorf, curator of the National Boxwood Collection at the U.S. National Arboretum in Washington; Dr. Henry F. Frierson, Jr., professor at the University of Virginia in Charlottesville; David J. Williams, production manager of Woodland Nursery in Salisbury, Maryland; and me. While we were helped by many botanists along the way, Mosulishvili accompanied us on the entire trip and played a pivotal role in organizing it.

Hyrcanian boxwood

On 6 June the team assembled in Baku, the capital of Azerbaijan, sited along the coast of the Caspian Sea. We were greeted by Mosulishvili, along with Professor Vagid D. Gadjiev, director of the Institute of Botany in Baku, and Professor Valida Ali-zade, the institute's deputy director. On our first day, accompanied by Gadjiev, we traveled south to the Talish Mountains, along the border with Iran, and part of the ancient Persian province of Hyrcania. "Our ride from Baku along the central Caspian coast was largely through barren semi-desert until we reached the fertile Talish region where the climate became almost subtropical," recalls Frierson. "The Talish Mountains contain small stands of *Buxus hyrcana,* also classified as a subspecies of *Buxus sempervirens,* which has a geographic range extending to the neighboring part of northern Iran."

Our destination was Lenkoran, renowned for its tea plantations. A few kilometers south of Lenkoran we stayed in a guesthouse built on the picturesque Lake Xanbulaq, in close proximity to the Hyrcanian Nature

Azerbaijan's southernmost town, Astara, is nestled at the foot of the Talish Mountains, which are home to *Buxus hyrcana*. Photo by Tomasz Aniśko.

An Azeri boy guided us through the marshes of the river Akusha-chay to this population of *Nelumbo caspica* (02614). Photo by Tomasz Aniśko.

Reserve. The next day, thanks to a four-wheel-drive military truck that was arranged for our group by Hadji Saa-farov, vice-director of the reserve, we penetrated deep into the reserve. There we were led by Saafarov to a couple of wild boxwood populations (02594–602). Some of the boxwoods in these sites were 10 m tall and estimated to be 250 years old. We speculated that one of the sites could actually be an ancient burial site, because it had a fairly regular mounded shape rising above the surrounding area and contained a large number of rocks scattered on the surface. Interestingly, boxwoods were confined only to the mound and did not spread into the adjacent forest.

On 9 June we traveled on the road along the valley of the Lenkoran River, heading west to Lerik, where, as we ascended into the Talish Mountains, we came upon groves of boxwood surrounding a mosque and nearby cemetery. The following day we collected in the hills just northwest of Astara, the southernmost town in Azerbaijan, which is nestled along the Caspian Sea at the border with Iran (02605–13). The boxwood forest there shared a southeast-facing slope with a cemetery and mausoleum.

"It was clear that the populations of *B. hyrcana* in the Talish region were centered around Moslem cemeteries and that the species was considered to be sacred," wrote Frierson (2003). "The finding of stands of *B. hyrcana* at religious sites led to the question of whether they had been planted there or whether they arose naturally and were therefore protected as holy sites. We surmised that the populations of boxwood at some of these sites were so extensive that it was likely that they were native to these specific areas."

On 11 June we departed Astara to return to Baku. Along the way we stopped in the marshes along the river Akusha-chay, about 50 km south of Salyany, to look for *Nelumbo caspica,* Caspian lotus, which had been acquired by Creech during his 1963 visit to the Nikitsky Botanical Garden in Yalta. Thanks to help from a local boy, who guided us through a maze of narrow dikes, we eventually came upon a small colony of *N. caspica* (02614). As there were no seeds available, we collected shallowly rooted rhizomes. In the evening we reached Baku, said farewells to Gadjiev and Ali-zade, and boarded a night train that took us through the broad dry steppe of central Azerbaijan and on to Tbilisi, Georgia.

Georgia's river gorges

Upon our arrival in Tbilisi we headed east to the town of Signakhi. Knowing that boxwoods are not native in that part of Georgia and that they are typically found growing only around places of worship, we wanted to visit a monastery near the town. "One of the most spectacular boxwoods we found on this trip," recalls Frierson, "was planted at the Monastery of Saint Nino, Convent of Bodbe near the town of Signakhi, where we discovered a unique single small dense plant whose new foliage was sky blue, beautifully contrasting with the dark green of the mature leaves (02615). Fortunately, we were granted permission to take cuttings, but we received no information about the origin of this plant." We were fascinated by an old allée of boxwood (02616–7) in the monastery's vegetable garden; maintained through coppicing, it pro-

Resting at a stop along the road through the Lesser Caucasus to Batumi are, left to right, Mosulishvili, Williams, Manvelidze, Frierson, and Batdorf. Photo by Tomasz Anaśko.

The valley of the river Adjaris Tskali in Adjara was a fruitful ground for boxwood hunting. Photo by Tomasz Anaśko.

vided the monks with material from which to carve little crosses.

"It quickly became apparent to us that boxwood possesses important religious significance," explains Batdorf. "The Georgian Bible states that Jesus entered Jerusalem on branches of boxwood meant to rid the way of evil spirits. It was believed that evil spirits could not penetrate the hard, dense wood of the boxwood, thus areas near boxwood were considered purified. Today the wood of boxwood is carved into small crosses and other religious symbols to wear as necklaces."

Returning to Tbilisi, we visited the Institute of Botany and the Botanical Garden. On 16 June we headed west over the mountains of the Lesser Caucasus to Batumi on the Black Sea coast. In the evening we reached Akhaltsikhe, a small town in southern Georgia near the border with Turkey, where we were met by Manvelidze, who arrived from Batumi with two UAZ jeeps to take our group over the most strenuous part of the road through the mountains. As he had done a year earlier, he also graciously offered us room and board in his home during our several days in Batumi.

The following day we continued driving west while the road gradually climbed the increasingly rugged mountains. Once we surmounted the crest of the Lesser Caucasus and began to descend to the valley of Adjaris Tskali on the west side, boxwoods became quite prevalent, and we made several stops to collect seeds and cuttings.

"In the evening we stopped near the small village of Dologani where we found masses of boxwoods growing along both banks of a small river, Dologanis Tskali,"

Williams, left, and Frierson collect boxwood cuttings at a church in Skhalta, west of Tsabliana in Adjara. Photo by Tomasz Anaśko.

remembers Frierson. "As we would observe at many other locations, the plants grew directly along the water. Here, we saw perhaps the greatest diversity of boxwoods, whose leaves varied greatly in size and shape. We gathered seeds and cuttings from many specimens until darkness inhibited further collecting (02620)."

Batumi welcomed us with persistent rain. "Despite the downpour, we drove to the mountains east of Chakvi, a small coastal town north of Batumi," recalls Frierson. "There we explored in a torrential rain a protected area of boxwood forest in a gorge traversed by rivers and streams and laden with waterfalls. Here boxwoods draped the steep slopes, forming a canopy."

Still harassed by rain, on 19 June we left Batumi for Kutaisi. There we were met by Dr. Shamil Shetekauri, plant taxonomist at the Institute of Botany in Tbilisi,

Steep banks of Dologanis Tskali in Adjara revealed perhaps the greatest diversity of boxwoods seen during the expedition. Photo by Tomasz Aniśko.

Lush forests along the turbulent river Tsachkhura sheltered a plethora of boxwoods. Photo by Tomasz Aniśko.

who helped guide us through the provinces of Samegrelo and Racha. "Near the village Inchkhuri, we found *Buxus* (02621–2) growing along the small river Abasha and on steep limestone slopes adjacent to an abandoned limestone quarry and kiln," wrote Frierson (2003). "We next traveled a short distance to a site along the river Tsachkhura, which was an extremely scenic environment, as the fantastic river gorge was filled with limestone and *Buxus*. The loud rushing of water was assisted by days of heavy rain. Disappointingly, our trekking here was cut short due to downpour and the perception that the area might be unsafe." The only shelter we could find was a tiny roadside cabin checkpoint. "Men were stationed there to prevent illegal logging," recalls Frierson. "We met at the cabin several very hospitable Georgians who shared their potent homemade spirit *chacha* with us over lunch. Unfortunately, with no end to the rain in sight, we had to turn back to Kutaisi."

On 21 June we headed northeast from Kutaisi to the Racha region in the Greater Caucasus. Upon reaching Nakerala Pass, 1217 m, separating Imereti from Racha, we discovered a population of boxwoods growing at the highest elevation seen during the trip (02623–4, 02627). At the same site potentially more cold-hardy forms of *Prunus laurocerasus* (02625) and *Ilex colchica* (02626) were collected.

From the Nakerala Pass, we continued to Nikortsminda in Racha. "Our most remarkable discovery of boxwood was near the village of Nikortsminda," explains Batdorf. "In the nearby gorge of the Sharaula River, adja-

cent to an old hydroelectric plant, we found thousands of boxwood growing in a very wet and shaded environment. They exhibited a wide variety of unique characteristics." As Frierson remembers, "The plants grew along the river and even on limestone rocks within the river. Some boxwoods in this damp and dark environment had branches that were covered with moss. Remarkably, some plants, varying in height up to about 3 m tall, were distinguished by having flaking bark, a striking and unique appearance, which had never been seen by any of us before. We wondered if this exfoliation was due to the moist environmental conditions or whether it was a natural characteristic of the plants. Cuttings from these and other unusual specimens were taken with the hope that they might result in new cultivars of boxwood in future years

Exfoliating bark of *Buxus sempervirens* (02629) found in the gorge of the Sharaula River near Nikortsminda in Racha. Photo by Tomasz Aniśko.

The dark interior of a boxwood forest in the Sataplia Ecological Reserve near Kutaisi. Photo by Tomasz Aniśko.

harvest of timber, we satisfied our appetite for boxwoods with a limited collection of cuttings (02636–7). The boxwood forest in Sataplia, with its eerie atmosphere, dinosaur footprints, and proximity to Kutaisi, seemed just the place at which the legendary Jason of the Argonauts might have found the Golden Fleece, guarded by a sleepless dragon.

Two days later we drove back to Batumi. The following day Batdorf returned to the United States, and the rest of us boarded a hydrofoil that took us to Sochi in Russia. This allowed us to avoid Abkhazya, the breakaway region of Georgia in the northwestern part of the country, bordering Russia.

Russia's boxwood reserves

In Sochi we were met by Professor Mikhail V. Pridnya, researcher at the Research Institute of Mountain Forestry and Forest Ecology, based at the Sochi Dendrarium. "Our first excursion was south of Sochi in the Greater Caucasus, where we observed *Buxus sempervirens* (02642–3) growing on limestone along and above the river Mzymta, 16 km north of Adler district," recalls Frierson. "Upon returning to Sochi, we toured the spectacular Yew and Boxwood Reserve, a protected environment of about 300 hectares, located some 3 km from the coast on the southeastern slope of Ahun's range. Here we saw the tallest boxwood specimens, with some over 15 m in height. The boxwood canopy in the reserve was dense, and there was little growth of other plants below in the warm and moist environment. The trees grew straight

(02628–34)." Batdorf was equally intrigued by specimens with exfoliating bark, a previously unknown attribute for any boxwood: "It is discoveries such as this that make plant exploration so important."

On 23 June we traveled to the Sataplia Ecological Reserve located several kilometers west of Kutaisi. "It had been created about 1935, and contained a 70 hectare boxwood forest, a stone outcropping with dinosaur footprints from 120 million years ago, and caves," explains Frierson. "Formerly, the forest here had been damaged by limestone mining, and boxwood timber had been harvested in the nineteenth century to be used as wooden parts in the textile industry. Tons of Caucasian boxwood had been cut during this time period for use in European, especially British, industry." In contrast to the historical

Old growth of boxwoods in the Yew and Boxwood Reserve near Sochi. Photo by Tomasz Aniśko.

The Livadia Palace, site of the 1945 Yalta Conference, features clipped *Buxus balearica* (02648) along its main façade. Photo by Tomasz Aniśko.

with relatively few branches. It was readily conceived how simple the harvest of such plants would have been in the nineteenth century. There had been great harvests of boxwood until the time of the Russian revolution, after which its cutting had been severely limited by the new government. Today, the harvest of boxwood timber is prohibited, but it is likely that there is still some illegal harvesting in the national parks. In one forest that we visited, we found a group of boxwood logs along the road, which we surmised might be evidence of poaching. We collected seeds from trees along a steep cliff at a remarkable lookout above a gorge containing the river Khosta (02641–2)."

The next day we toured the Sochi Dendrarium, a 110-year-old park and arboretum showcasing plants that thrive in the warm climate of the Black Sea coast. "We took cuttings from two interesting boxwood plants (02644–5)," wrote Frierson (2002), "one of which was a variegated form that I had never seen before, having occasional, slightly irregular leaf margins and distinct lime green leaf variegation of the new shoots."

The following day was spent at another reserve, north of Sochi, where we collected seeds (02646) along the Dagomys River, 4 km above the village Baranovka. As Frierson recalls, "Pridnya speculated that there might be boxwood trees as old as 1000 years but admitted that he had not seen them and that a dendrochronological study of purported ancient trees would be of interest. He gave us a map detailing the specific locations of boxwood forests within the Russian portion of the Greater Caucasus, including those on the northern side of the mountain

range, which we did not know existed. Indeed, seeing this precise map stimulated the thought for the need of future exploration in that region along the northern limit of boxwood distribution."

Yalta's palaces

After an entire day of bus and ferry riding, on 29 June we arrived in Yalta. Our botanist guide was Professor Vladislav V. Korzhenewskiy, head of the flora and vegetation department of the Nikitsky Botanical Garden. Yalta has long been a Russian vacation spot, ever since its development following the annexation of the Crimea by Catherine the Great in the eighteenth century. Because of the city's balmy Mediterranean climate and spectacular scenery, likened to that of the French Riviera, Russian aristocracy built their elaborate residences and estates there, many of which survive today as museums and public parks. As boxwood was not to be found in the wild in Crimea, our search was centered on plants growing in historic parks, botanical gardens, and old cemeteries.

We first toured the Italian Renaissance–style palace at Livadia, constructed as a summer residence for Czar Nicholas II and Queen Alexandra, and the 1945 site of the Yalta Conference attended by Franklin Roosevelt, Winston Churchill, and Joseph Stalin. The present Livadia Palace was built in 1911, but the surrounding park was laid down in the 1830s. In the park we saw tall clipped hedges of *Buxus balearica*, with neatly trimmed specimen plants along the front of the palace (02648). Later we headed to the nearby Vorontsov Park surrounding Alupka Palace, which dates back to 1846. There we

Yalta, situated near the southern end of the Crimean Peninsula, enjoys a balmy Mediterranean climate and spectacular scenery.

observed large specimens of *B. balearica* and collected seeds and cuttings of *B. sempervirens* (02647, 02649). "The most notable boxwood plantings in Crimea were those seen in the Nikitsky Botanical Garden," stresses Frierson. "We made there many collections of seeds and cuttings of *Buxus sempervirens* that included several variegated and pendulous forms (02650–60)."

Upon completion of our work in Crimea, we drove to Odessa, and there we concluded our journey from the Caspian Sea to the Black Sea. On 5 July, after a long month of plant hunting, we said farewells to Mosulishvili and departed for the United States.

A total of seventy collections made on this trip, including sixty-two boxwoods, were successfully introduced into the United States and later distributed among the participating parties. As Frierson concludes, "This expedition assembled a comprehensive collection of Cau-

casian boxwood, which has the potential to greatly augment the expanding list of cultivars that adorn the gardens." Batdorf adds: "To specialize in boxwood as I have done for nearly three decades, leads one to believe to have seen it all. Thus, imagine the excitement and thrill when one discovers an important, previously unknown plant. This is the reward that keeps us searching for the plant material that just might be the next popular cultivated boxwood."

EUROPE

FROM THE MEDITERRANEAN TO THE NORTH SEA

In 1956, while contemplating strategic goals for Longwood's plant exploration, Dr. Russell J. Seibert, Longwood's director, recognized that the collections of plants maintained in European gardens were unmatched by any others. He saw a need for "an exploratory survey of plant materials in southern European nurseries and botanical gardens, to look for and send back plants of potential use to American ornamental horticulture which are not in this country and which are not normally available through other channels" (Seibert 1956b).

Soon after, Seibert and Dr. Walter H. Hodge, head of education and research at Longwood, as well as various colleagues from the USDA, began planning a trip that would concentrate on the southern areas of Europe, in particular southern France, Italy, Portugal, and Spain, with a short detour through Great Britain. They expected "that much of the material brought in may be of interest to Longwood" (Hodge 1956d). Yet the whole basis of backing the exploration was "to help out ornamental horticulture in the United States in general."

Dr. Frederick G. Meyer, at that time dendrologist at the Missouri Botanical Garden in Saint Louis, later a botanist for the USDA, was asked to lead this expedition in the spring of 1957. In Meyer's view the time was right for such an undertaking: "In the United States, we are now in the midst of a great Renaissance of interest in

At 10.6 million km², Europe (right) is the second smallest continent after Australia. More than half of Europe's territory consists of lowlands, beginning with the most extensive Great Russian Plain westward to the North European Lowland. The central uplands and plateaus form distinctive landscapes of regions such as Bohemia, Massif Central, or Iberian Meseta. The northwest highlands dominate much of Iceland, Ireland, Britain, and Scandinavia. High mountains are found in the south of Europe; the Alps include Mont Blanc, Europe's highest peak, rising to 4807 m. The western part of the continent, from Norway to northern Spain, is exposed to Atlantic air masses and subject to maritime climate, with mild winters, cool summers, and abundant precipitation (more than 1000 mm) year-round. In contrast, eastern Europe is influenced by continental climate, with cold winters, hot summers, and only moderate rainfall (600 mm or less). Central Europe has transitional climate resulting from the interaction of maritime and continental air masses. The Mediterranean climate of southern Europe is characterized by mild, wet winters and hot, dry summers. Vegetation zones transition from tundra in the extreme north of Russia and Scandinavia, through the boreal forest of predominantly conifers and mixed forest of evergreen and deciduous trees, to Mediterranean vegetation in the south, steppe in the southeast, and semidesert around the northern shores of the Caspian Sea.

ornamentals, in fact, the greatest in the history of our country" (1959e).

Expecting to find an immense wealth of plants growing in various European collections, Meyer was concerned about establishing a priority basis for the selection of plants and cuttings to keep reintroductions to a

Meyer, dendrologist at the Missouri Botanical Garden in Saint Louis, was selected to conduct the 1957 plant-collecting expedition to Europe. Photo by Gottlieb A. Hampfler.

minimum. To ease Meyer's apprehension, Hodge offered these comments: "It is always better to bring in a thing that is questionable and then throw it out after it has been brought in rather than assume that we have it in this country and then later find that it is not true in the sense that it is not available. In other words, lots of things have to be re-introduced several times before they take on" (Hodge 1957a). Meyer agreed: "If a plant is not generally known or occurs in one botanical garden or some other out-of-the-way corner, the plant might as well be back in its native habitat or in Madrid, Lisbon, or some other place. Even though here, it is not doing what an introduced plant might be expected to do" (Meyer 1957a).

An American in Paris

Accompanied by his wife, Jean, Meyer traveled to Europe on a steamer bound for the French port of Le Havre. Upon their arrival in France on 4 March, the couple headed to Paris and rented a car, a little Renault, which, as Meyer pointed out, was "going to work out splendidly for getting around!" (1957b). Having Jean at his side during the entire trip allowed Meyer to devote all his attention to plants: "She is always full of encouragement and is a true Spartan in all matters that count. She is an excellent wrapper-upper and has taken over the packing of all the material I send. . . . I could hardly operate without Jean" (1957c).

Meyer's first stop in Paris on 6 March was the Jardin Kahn, located on the banks of the Seine at Saint Cloud. The garden was founded by Albert Kahn, a prosperous Paris banker of the late 1890s. A most unusual form of

Ginkgo biloba, with strongly divaricate branches that give it a skeletal appearance, originated here and is named 'St. Cloud'. The next day Meyer headed to Grand Trianon à Chateau Neuf, an extensive arboretum adjacent to the Palace of Versailles, which contained "a notable collection of trees maintained in the great tradition of French arboriculture" (Meyer 1959e). Later that day he visited the Arboretum Vilmorin-Andrieux at Verrières-le-Buisson near Paris, established by Philippe-André de Vilmorin in 1815, an important repository of woody plants introduced into France.

On 11 and 12 March, the Meyers stayed in Orléans, south of Paris, in the valley of the Loire River, counted among the largest nursery production areas of northern France. One of the places he visited was the Chenault nursery, founded by Léon Chenault in 1895 and perpetuated by his son Raymond. "A short stop at Orléans and a visit with Monsieur Raymond Chenault was productive," wrote Meyer (1957c). "He is a well-known and ardent plantsman, and is one of the most knowledgeable plantsmen for cultivated plants in France. The original specimen of *Berberis ×chenaultii* is now very large in his garden." Meyer acquired from Chenault a number of shrubs of outstanding merit, including a dwarf form of the Austrian pine, *Pinus nigra* (591632).

Narcissi of northern Spain

From Orléans the Meyers continued southwest to Biarritz, which brought them near France's southern border with Spain. Driving through the northwestern part of Spain, Meyer observed that "the native flora is full of interesting plants with horticultural merit. At San Sebastián, *Narcissus bulbocodium* var. *citrinus* [581608] was common on the grassy, steep, north slopes above the sea. This form of the species has lemon yellow flowers and occurs only in this part of Spain" (1957c).

After spending a night near Santander, the couple left the coast and took the road along Río Esla. "The mountain scenery became quite wild further on as we approached the mountain range of the Picos de Europa which is the highest mountain range in the north of Spain," recorded Meyer (1957c). "An interesting rock plant, *Globularia willkommii* brought our little French Renault car to a sudden halt. It was making large patches of blue on the rock cliffs above the river. Near the summit of the Picos de Europa the road rises to 1670 m and the snow-capped peaks rise still higher. The crowning triumph at this point

A 6 m tall camellia hedge surrounds a formal garden of clipped boxwood and tulip beds in Porto's Jardim Botânico. Photo by Frederick G. Meyer.

was *Narcissus asturiensis* [581630] which dotted the moist slopes near the melting snow by the thousands. This beautiful miniature daffodil looks exactly like the larger trumpet daffodil everyone knows, except that *N. asturiensis* is only 3–4 inches [7.5–10 cm] tall. . . . Along the river in the adjoining meadows at Riaño, *Narcissus bulbocodium* var. *monophyllus* actually caused the meadows to be completely yellow. This Hoop-Petticoat daffodil was at its height. We were awed to see it growing in an absolutely soppy wet meadow. Also at Riaño, the giant form of the trumpet daffodil *Narcissus pseudonarcissus* var. *nobilis* also occurred in some abundance."

From Riaño, the road led the Meyers out of the mountains and onto the flat plains of New Castile toward León. "Beyond León, the country is less flat and becomes mountainous again westward towards the Portuguese frontier," wrote Meyer (1957c). "In the Province of Orense, Spain, we saw *Narcissus triandrus* for the first time in great profusion on the decomposed granitic rocks which is the common native rock throughout the north of Portugal and this part of Spain. . . . Wherever this sort of rock occurs, it is safe to judge that daffodils are in the vicinity and only a tour reconnaissance is needed to find them. Such was our luck wherever we went. This is the wettest portion of Spain, and certainly the vegetation was the most verdant we have seen anywhere in that country."

Renaissance camellias

The Meyers entered Portugal from Spain after crossing the river Minho between Tuy and Valença. After a few hours they reached Porto on the Atlantic coast at the mouth of the river Douro. "In spring," Meyer reported (1959e), "few areas of western Europe can compare with northern Portugal. The mild, relatively moist belt around

Jardim Botânico Coimbra is the oldest botanical garden in Portugal. Photo by Walter H. Hodge.

Formal plantings in the Jardim Botânico of the University of Lisbon. Photo by Frederick G. Meyer.

Cyathea and *Dicksonia* tree ferns in Parque de Montserrate flourish in the mild climate of Sintra. Photo by Walter H. Hodge.

Oporto [Porto] receives a rainfall of approximately 35 to 40 inches [900–1000 mm] per year. As a result, northern coastal Portugal remains perpetually green. In March and April native species of heather and numerous species of Leguminosae carpet the northern Portuguese hills in a kaleidoscopic riot of color."

Porto is the major center of the nursery industry in Portugal. The city, recognized as the home of the oldest camellias cultivated in Europe, made a lasting impression on Meyer: "A glorious, unforgettable two weeks where every single dewy morning we walked through thousands of fallen camellia blossoms and kicked them up with our feet as we kick up dried leaves in October in the Missouri woods" (1957c).

The oldest specimens of camellia grow at Villa Nova de Gaya. "The old family archives of the Conde de Campo Bello, present owner of the villa, indicate that three living plants of *C. japonica* from Japan were planted in the garden about the middle of the sixteenth century," wrote Meyer (1959e). "This is not impossible, since early Portuguese traders in the Orient first made contact with Japan in 1542. . . . The oldest trees in question are now about 18 to 24 inches [45–60 cm] in diameter at the base and nearly 30 feet [9 m] tall at a reputed four hundred years of age. The flowers are single rose-pink."

On 21 March, Meyer toured Porto's Jardim Botânico, established in the 1930s on a 12-hectare site of an old private estate. From Jardim Botânico's collections, Meyer procured many plants, including *Camellia japonica* 'Mathotiana' (65132), the most outstanding cultivar grown there as a hedge; *Narcissus rupicola* (581634), a dwarf native Portuguese species; and *Romulea bulbocodium* (591633), a native species of southern Portugal, with grasslike leaves and blue flowers.

The next stop on Meyer's route, Coimbra, is home to the oldest and largest botanical garden in Portugal. "It is really full of most interesting plants," wrote Meyer (1957c) to Seibert, "and its site is, I would say, unique for a botanical garden. It is terraced in the Italian fashion because it lies on a side hill overlooking the Rio Mondego which flows past the town." In Coimbra, Meyer teamed up with Professor Francisco J. Fernandes Casas, director of the botanical garden and the leading authority on *Narcissus*—"most charming and most helpful"—to do botanizing and plant collecting around the city.

In early April the Meyers arrived in Lisbon. "Climatically, Lisbon and the area to the west around Sintra are unlike other areas of southern Europe. Extremes of temperature and aridity are less severe than in comparable areas of the Mediterranean. In summer, cloudy and foggy days are not uncommon in Lisbon, and extreme heat is rare. Frost occurs infrequently. Palms flourish and subtropical plants are commonly grown in parks and gardens in this area" (Meyer 1959e).

Lisbon has many botanical and horticultural institutions. During his visit, Meyer toured several of them, including the Jardim Botânico of the University of Lisbon, which dates back to 1839. Among the many plants collected at this garden was the Brazilian soap-bark tree, *Quillaja brasiliensis* (581704).

Meyer also visited the Estufa Fria in Lisbon's Edward VII Park, among the more unusual horticultural attractions of southern Europe. "This lath house 'conservatory' is without artificial heat and covers nearly 2 acres [0.8 hectare]. Many tender tropical plants that otherwise would not thrive without protection are grown in the Estufa Fria. A rock embankment on one side provides a natural habitat for growing subtropical vines, ferns, begonias, saintpaulias, aroids, and other species that prefer the environment of a humid tropical forest. Clambering lianas are planted on concrete pillars made to simulate tree trunks that support the superstructure of the Estufa Fria" (Meyer 1959e).

Meyer inspects a dragon's blood tree, *Dracaena draco,* nearly 12 m wide, planted during the seventeenth century in the royal Ajuda Park, Lisbon. Photo by Frederick G. Meyer.

Lisbon's Estufa Fria displays plants in a colossal lath house covering 0.8 hectare. Photo by Walter H. Hodge.

Holy Week in Madrid

After three weeks in Portugal, the Meyers headed back to Spain: "From Lisbon we took the ferry boat and crossed the River Tagus and drove beyond towards Spain to the southeast. Southern Portugal is the cork growing center. There are miles and acres of cork trees. The brick red of the freshly peeled ones give the orchards a weird, but beautiful aspect. . . . Olives also grow here in great profu-

sion. Portuguese olives are consumed almost entirely within Portugal. The Portuguese literally bathe themselves in the olive oil. The roadsides in southern Portugal are lined with the ice-plant, *Mesembryanthemum,* that South African plant so widely distributed now in all regions with a Mediterranean climate. Also, the large, white-flowered *Cistus ladanifer* was beginning to make quite a splash on the hills. Towards the Spanish frontier, the country becomes considerably more rugged in aspect

Kalanchoe rosei var. *seyringii* (572879), displayed in Longwood's indoor Silver Garden, was among more than fifty *Kalanchoe* obtained by Meyer at Les Cedres. Photo by Tomasz Aniśko.

and here lies one of the areas important for the cultivation of the Spanish chestnut. The wild peony, *Paeonia officinalis,* was beginning to flower in the chestnut groves" (Meyer 1957c).

Several days later the couple reached Madrid. "Good Friday imposed an enforced holiday for us at the end of Holy Week in this sunny, dry land of festivals," wrote Meyer (1957c). "We were without money, package material, or gasoline; and all banks, embassies, American Express, gas stations, even the museums were closed in commemoration. . . . Easter-time in Spain is the most colorful time of the year and everyone makes quite the most of it. Spanish ladies with flowing mantillas were quite the fashion in Madrid. We had to leave Spain before the fetes and festivals that followed Holy Week in order to get to the French Riviera before the season became any further advanced."

Côte d'Azur

Before reaching the French Riviera or Côte d'Azur, the Meyers stopped in Montpellier to visit the Jardin des Plantes, established by Henry V in 1594. "The Mediterranean climate of Montpellier is considerably more severe in winter than the area farther east along the French Riviera," reported Meyer (1959e). "The tenor of the climate is indicated by the plantings which consist largely of temperate species tolerant of some yearly frost. Of palms, for example, only *Chamaerops humilis* and *Trachycarpus fortunei* thrive at Montpellier." Among the more unusual species Meyer spotted growing at Montpellier was *Mahonia moranensis* (591324), a rare holly-grape native to Mexico, reaching 2.5 m in height and laden with clusters of blue berries in July.

The next day the Meyers arrived at Menton, the easternmost coastal town of the French Riviera at the Italian frontier. As a geographical province, the French Riviera extends along the Mediterranean coast from Hyères in the west to Menton in the east. "The mildest area of all, 'La Petit Afrique,' begins just east of Nice and extends eastward to Menton and beyond to the Italian Riviera for a few miles," noted Meyer (1959e). "The Maritime Alps rise for several thousand feet almost directly from the sea and thus effectively shelter the coastal region against the cold northerly winds. . . . In the mild arid climate cacti are widely grown and have naturalized throughout the area in a latitude comparable to that of southern Newfoundland."

Among the first gardens visited by Meyer (1959e) in Menton were Villa Casa Rossa, "a modern French garden in Provençal taste," and Serra de la Madone Val, one of the finest collections of subtropical plants on the Riviera, assembled over a period of forty years by Major Lawrence Johnston, who traveled around the world in his quest for unusual plants. From the latter garden Meyer procured an array of choice plants, including *Mahonia lomariifolia* (58450), "a striking arborescent species" introduced by Johnston from Upper Myanmar; *Sarcococca ruscifolia* (58488), "perhaps the showiest species of the genus with clusters of dark red fleshy fruit"; and *Nerium oleander* 'Aurantiacum' (5892), "the most attractive" oleander with orange-yellow flowers.

On Cap Ferrat, east of Nice, Meyer paid a visit to Les Cedres, the garden of Julian Marnier-Lapostolle. "Mr. Marnier is, of course, present head of the firm which makes 'Grand Marnier' [a prestigious French liqueur]," explained Meyer (1957e) in a letter to Hodge. "The man, though, has a passion for plants, and has brought together certainly the largest collection of ornamental plants on the Mediterranean. Although he specializes in succulents, his collections of woody plants and also herbaceous material is really quite fabulous. He has tried to bring the tropics to his garden, and he has created the most realistic jungle I have seen down this way. . . . The nice thing about Marnier's garden is that he has given me complete freedom to have anything he has, so long as there is a piece large enough for us to have."

Gardens at Villa Taranto near Pallanza benefit from the dramatic backdrop of the snow-capped peaks of the Alps. Photo by Walter H. Hodge.

Les Cedres offered Meyer a unique opportunity to acquire an extensive collection of plants not seen elsewhere, especially succulents. "The collections comprise about ten thousand kinds of plants—wild species and horticultural forms combined. . . . The collection of *Kalanchoe* is one of the most comprehensive at Les Cedres. This genus offers promise for hybridization because of the wide diversity in shape and color of the flowers. Some species are not showy even though others are very much so. *K. pumila* (572873) with orchid-colored flowers, and *K. manginii* (572860) with scarlet tubular flowers are two species of unusual merit in the collection" (Meyer 1959e). Along with these two plants, Meyer sent Longwood Gardens more than fifty other species and forms of *Kalanchoe* as well as several hundred other succulents obtained at Les Cedres.

World's oldest botanical gardens

At the end of April, the Meyers left the French Riviera and traveled to Italy. "The gardens of Italy bring to mind formal gardens of clipped hedges, topiaries, fountains, and statuary," recorded Meyer (1959e). "Foliage plants rather than flowers overshadow the basic requirements of plantings in the traditional Italian gardens. . . . Modern

Meyer was impressed with the extensive collections of unusual plants at Palermo's Orto Botanico, describing it as "a veritable gold-mine." Photo by Walter H. Hodge.

Italian gardens are strongly influenced by the style of the classical period but they are becoming modernized to the extent of using colored foliage plants, such as *Teucrium, Santolina, Echeveria, Coleus,* and *Alternanthera* to supplement the traditional woody species."

Meyer's first stop in Italy was La Mortola, near Ventimiglia on the Italian Riviera. Founded in 1867, La Mortola occupies a picturesque site overlooking the

The world's second oldest botanical garden, located in Padua. Inside the glass house is *Chamaerops humilis,* which was planted in 1585 and two centuries later was studied by Wolfgang von Goethe while preparing *Die Metamorphose der Pflanzen.* Photo by Russell J. Seibert.

but more as a horticultural collection with the best to be obtained in flowers, shrubs, and trees" (Meyer 1959e).

From the Riviera, the Meyers headed north to Lake Maggiore, where they spent several days near Pallanza. On 4 May, Meyer paid a visit to the gardens of Villa Taranto. "The site of the garden relies upon fine scenery as an outstanding natural asset along the shores of Lake Maggiore at Pallanza within sight of the snow-capped peaks of the Simplon Pass of Switzerland. Climatically, the garden is favored by a high rainfall of about 90 inches [2300 mm] a year. Relatively little frost occurs, but some freezing is to be expected each winter. Camellias, tree ferns, palms, rhododendrons, magnolias, hollies, and conifers are abundantly represented" (Meyer 1959e).

In Pallanza the couple reversed their course and traveled south to Sicily. Tempered by the Mediterranean, Sicily enjoys one of the most southerly geographical positions of Europe, with a mild, arid, nearly frost-free climate along coastal areas. Palermo's Orto Botanico surprised Meyer with a rich assortment of unusual plants: "That was a veritable gold-mine. I believe I collected more things at that one spot than I have anyplace on the trip thus far—over eighty collections. The climate of Sicily permits growing quite a lot of tropical plants that one does not see elsewhere out of doors in Europe. . . . I still can not imagine why such a good collection of plants should exist at Palermo midst such a poverty stricken population, but it does nevertheless" (Meyer 1957d). Among the eighty collections procured from Orto Botanico was *Brexia madagascariensis* (5851), a small evergreen tree from Madagascar.

On 20 May the Meyers were back on Italy's mainland and two days later the couple reached Rome. There they toured two sites of horticultural interest: Orto Botanico of

An eighteenth-century orangery in Florence's Orto Botanico. Photo by Frederick G. Meyer.

Mediterranean on La Punta della Mortola, named for the many native myrtles, *Myrtus communis,* growing there. "Horticulturists know La Mortola not only for the large and varied plant collections but also as an architectural gem of the gardener's art. Few private gardens in Europe have attained the breadth and scope of La Mortola. Architecturally, the garden is designed in Anglo-Italian taste partly as a botanical garden in the traditional sense

A broad avenue in Florence's Orto Botanico is lined with evergreen azaleas. Photo by Walter H. Hodge.

the University of Rome and Roseto di Roma. "The botanical garden of the University of Rome was formed on a portion of the eighteenth century garden adjacent to the Villa Corsini," noted Meyer (1959e). "Located on the slopes of one of Rome's famous seven hills, the garden enjoys a choice site in one of the most historical parts of the Eternal City." The Roseto di Roma, designated as one of Europe's official rose test gardens, was built after World War II on a site facing the Palatine Hill and the Temple of Constantine. Designed in the form of an amphitheater, "the collection of roses, apart from the comprehensive array of modern hybrid teas and climbers, includes a good assortment of shrub roses and early hybrids to illustrate the evolution of the garden rose over the past 150 years."

Continuing their drive northward, the Meyers arrived in Florence on 26 May. They spent the next couple of days studying the collections of this city's Orto Botanico, the world's third oldest garden, dating back to 1545. This allowed Meyer to select forty plants for introduction to the United States. "The garden of about 5 acres [2 hectares] occupies the original site near the heart of the city," noted Meyer (1959e). "Designed originally as a 'garden of simples' (a garden for growing medicinal plants), an arboretum now covers about four-fifths of the total area. Several broad tree-lined avenues bisect the garden at right angles. A pool in the center is the focal point for the outlying features of the garden. A large cork oak, *Quercus suber,* over 100 feet [30 m] tall, and a twisted olive tree, *Olea europaea,* 40 feet [12 m] tall, date from plantings in the sixteenth century."

Driving west following the river Arno, the Meyers reached Pisa on 1 June. "Luca Ghini, father of botanical gardens and one of the first great Renaissance teachers of plant science, is said to have brought plants from the hills near Pisa to grow 'for the utility of students,'" noted Meyer (1959e). "Thus the first of the world's botanical gardens was born at Pisa in 1543." Some fifty years later the garden was transferred to its present location, where it occupies about 3 hectares. Among Meyer's introductions from Pisa were *Eryngium pandanifolium* (58434), "perhaps the largest species in the genus," and many variants of *Narcissus tazetta,* including 'Aureus' (581643), 'Italicus' (581648), and 'Papyraceus' (581646).

After visiting the world's oldest botanical garden, the Meyers traveled to Padua to see the second oldest garden, younger than the garden in Pisa by only two years. "A well preserved sixteenth century stone wall, 15 feet [4.5 m] high, completely encircles the original garden of about 4 acres [1.6 hectares]," recorded Meyer (1959e). "A balustrade atop the wall is studded with marble busts of former directors and garden curators. Inflorescences of *Yucca* sculptured in wrought iron atop the garden gates complete the ornamentation of the ancient garden wall." Many plants now widespread in cultivation in Europe—such as lilacs, sunflowers, or potatoes—first were grown in Padua. The oldest plant in the collection was a chaste-tree, *Vitex agnus-castus,* planted in 1550. Among the old plantings in the garden, of special interest to Meyer was a group of Mediterranean fan palms, *Chamaerops humilis,* planted in 1585 and studied by Johann Wolfgang von Goethe on his visit to Padua in 1787 in preparation for his classical treatise on plant morphogenesis, *Die Metamorphose der Pflanzen.*

Hanging gardens of Monaco

By 10 June the Meyers were back on the Italian Riviera and driving west along the coast of the Mediterranean. They arrived in Monaco. "If ever there was a modern hanging garden, it exists in Monaco at the Jardin Exotique," recorded Meyer (1957f). "The garden lies on a cliff 100 m above the sea overlooking the palace of Monaco and the Mediterranean. The garden is traversed by switch-back pathways, rustic and very artistically done bridges, valleys of kleinias, archways of pachycereus, with grotesque euphorbias, crassulas and other cacti on a scale unapproachable by any succulent garden I know."

Monaco's Jardin Exotique was founded on approximately 1 hectare on the edge of a jagged precipice in 1913. "The inventory of species cultivated of succulent genera is indeed extensive," commented Meyer (1959e), "but the grouping of the species in the spectacular location manifestly is of greater interest to most visitors. Construction problems and maintenance of the collection bring forth a host of problems unique to this garden. All soil for growing the plants, for example, must be carried by hand."

Jardin Exotique—which, according to Meyer, "must be seen to be appreciated fully"—was a source of more than three hundred introductions, mostly succulents, sent to Longwood. The explorer must have been greatly inspired and enthused by these "hanging gardens," as he humbly admitted in a letter, "I have never seen succulents so beautifully displayed as they are at the Jardin Exotique" (1957e).

The Meyers complemented their stay in Monaco with visits to two gardens, beginning with the Casino Gardens at Monte Carlo. In the Casino Gardens, the largest public garden in Monaco, dating from the latter part of the nineteenth century, "palms, cacti, water gardens, flowering trees, and large well-kept flower beds in the sunken garden form the principal features" (Meyer 1959e). Among the plants Meyer acquired there was *Oreopanax capitatus* (591598), a small evergreen tree of "outstanding merit" with handsome lustrous foliage. The couple also got a firsthand look at Princess Grace's palace garden. "We were obliged to have a special invitation from the Prince himself, which seemed to make the visit all the more special," wrote Meyer (1957f) to Hodge. "The garden is small with orange trees, palms, a few nice statues and a brazier for the prince and princess to do their own steaks on in the garden. I have never seen roses being grown in such curious fashion—grass between all the bushes in a rather shaded spot."

Iberian summer

After leaving Monaco, the Meyers stayed in the French Riviera for another three weeks to revisit some of the gardens they had seen in April. Continuing west along the Mediterranean coast, they returned to Spain in late July and headed for Madrid. "The botanical garden in Madrid long has stood among the well-known botanical institutions of Europe," recorded Meyer (1959e). "Founded in 1781, this garden developed rapidly at the end of the eighteenth century and early part of the nineteenth as new plants were brought to Spain from the colonies in the New World. The *Dahlia,* for example, first entered Europe in 1789 via the botanical garden in Madrid."

Meyer found that despite its luminous past, Madrid's botanical garden has a relatively small collection of plants: "At an altitude of 2000 feet [600 m], the climate of Madrid is not the most propitious for growing plants. Extremes of temperature are commonplace. Strong winds that sweep across the arid plains of New Castile bring biting cold in winter and torrid blasts in midsummer" (1959e). He did, however, spot a few greenhouse plants worthy of introduction. Among them were *Achimenes lanata* (581322), with "small light blue flowers and white-woolly leaves"; *Piper ornatum* (58497), a climbing pepper with "lustrous green leaves mottled pink with pink veins"; and *Vellozia elegans* (58124), with "white flowers that turn green with age."

It was early August when the Meyers reached southern Spain. "I am enjoying very much the short stay here at Granada," wrote Meyer (1957g) to Hodge. "There are some interesting plants, especially rock garden subjects in the Sierra Nevada Mountains which rise to 10,000 feet [3050 m] above the city." From Granada the Meyers drove west toward Portugal, making stops in Málaga and Seville. Spending a little over a week in Portugal, they retraced their route from Lisbon through Coimbra to Porto, visiting many of the sites seen in spring: "I am now speeding my little Renault towards England as fast as I can. The re-do through Spain and Portugal has, I think, been most worthwhile, as it has made it possible to see plants during the height of summer under quite different conditions from the early spring months. I do think this is a wise procedure in collecting, especially for seeing the wide range of plant materials which exist here on the Mediterranean" (Meyer 1957h).

By late August the Meyers arrived back in Paris, thus closing the main loop of their European exploration. "This tour of the Mediterranean has been a big order," wrote Meyer (1957g) to Hodge. "I believe that I shall have sampled the best collections of plants in the areas visited, but I lament the fact, somewhat having to cut short seed collecting which could be profitably pursued from this time on. . . . However, I am anxious to get on to England and sample the hollies at Edinburgh, the Java rhododendrons at Kew, as well as other plants and places."

Britain's vast archives

After stopping briefly in London, the Meyers headed north to Edinburgh, on the shore of the Firth of Forth, on the Scottish coast of the North Sea, to "sample" collections of the Royal Botanic Garden there. Founded in 1670, the Edinburgh garden is the second oldest in Great Britain. "The garden is widely known for the collections of Chinese plants," noted Meyer (1959e). "Beginning about 1900, introductions from south central and southwestern China continued to pour into the botanic garden for the next quarter century. . . . As a source of new germplasm, the Chinese collections at Edinburgh are of inestimable value to ornamental horticulture."

The three weeks spent at Edinburgh were "most productive," as Meyer wrote in a letter to Hodge (1957i). "I wish I could say I had time to finish looking and collecting all they have of interest. Time just will not permit it." Despite time constraints, Meyer managed to collect and send back to the United States three hundred new introductions. One of the more notable plants acquired was *Agapetes serpens* (591599), a tender ericaceous shrub from the Himalaya, with lanternlike red and green flowers.

A day-trip to nearby Glasgow allowed Meyer to visit that city's botanic garden, which dates from 1817. He returned with a number of interesting plants, including *Cochliostema jacobianum* (58415), with bright blue flowers on long peduncles, native to Ecuador; *Marcgravia umbellata* (591595), a climber from tropical America, with flowers pollinated by hummingbirds; and *Phyllagathis rotundifolia* (591328), from Sumatra, with leaves a unique iridescent blue.

Upon their return to England the Meyers spent the last days of September in Norfolk and Cambridge. "The subtropical and tropical collections at Talbot Manor in Norfolk probably cannot be duplicated elsewhere among the private exhibitions of these plants in Great Britain," noted Meyer (1959e). "With insatiable energy, Mr. L. Maurice Mason, owner of the garden, has traveled in recent years to Borneo, Malaya, New Guinea, South Africa, Tanganyika, Madagascar, British Guiana, and Costa Rica in search of new ornamental plants for his collections." Among some 225 plants procured from Mason's collection were *Episcia lilacina* (58432) from Costa Rica, *Hoya imperialis* (58440) from New Guinea, and *Impatiens repens* (58444) from Sri Lanka. Meyer's next destination was Cambridge University Botanic Garden, one of the leading centers of botanical and horticultural research in Great Britain. "To the Cambridge Botanic Garden goes the credit for having produced, nearly sixty years ago, some of the first *Gerbera* hybrids

Massive tree ferns, *Dicksonia antarctica,* grow in the Kibble Palace of the Glasgow Botanic Gardens. Photo by Russell J. Seibert.

Golden-rain tree, *Laburnum ×watereri* 'Vossii', trained onto a pergola in the Royal Botanic Gardens, Kew, near London. Photo by Russell J. Seibert.

known to horticulture," wrote Meyer. "Original plants still exist in the Cambridge collections."

Meyer spent early October studying plant collections of the renowned Royal Botanic Gardens, Kew, in the suburbs of London. "It stands today among the most comprehensive botanical institutions in existence," he commented (1959e). "The plant collections are truly remarkable in scope. Basically, Kew Gardens is a research institution and for this reason the living collections are devoted especially to species of botanical interest. Ornamental plants, though, are abundantly represented in the extensive collections." Meyer's introductions from Kew were limited to special groups, chiefly broad-leaved evergreens. Among others, he procured more than sixty cultivars of hollies, including *Ilex ×altaclarensis* 'Smithiana' (611477) and *I. aquifolium* 'Flavescens' (611472).

On 13 October, Meyer paid a visit to Chelsea Physic Garden, the second oldest garden in England, founded in 1683. "The garden stands on the original 4 acres [1.6 hectares] adjacent to the River Thames. In the center, a statue of Sir Hans Sloane reminds the visitor that this eighteenth century physician-naturalist was the great benefactor of the Chelsea garden. . . . The collections consist mostly of herbaceous species grown in narrow beds divided by verdant grass pathways in the style of an eighteenth century herb garden" (Meyer 1959e). The following morning he visited the Royal Horticultural Society's Garden at Wisley on the outskirts of London. He was especially impressed with what were then new hybrid gazanias, ranking them "among the outstanding herbaceous ornamentals of recent origin."

The Meyers spent the last week of October in Cornwall, visiting gardens at Penjerrick near Falmouth, Trewithen at Truro, and Caerhays Castle. "Geographically, few British gardens are more favorably situated than the Cornish garden of Caerhays Castle, located at the head of a protected cove near Saint Austell on the eastern shore of the Cornish peninsula," noted Meyer (1959e). "The collections are particularly rich in Chinese species of *Camellia, Magnolia, Rhododendron, Ilex, Acer,* and *Quercus.* Thickets of the wild form of *Camellia reticulata* (581685), *C. saluenensis,* and small forests of rhododendrons form the understory beneath towering evergreen Chinese oaks."

Back in England in early November, Meyer revisited some of the gardens in and around London, including Wisley, Chelsea, and Kew. As a result of his ventures in Scotland and England, he was able to ship more than a thousand introductions to the United States. "As a source of ornamental plants, British gardens are unrivaled among the gardens of Europe," Meyer commented (1959e). "British plant explorers, perhaps more than any other, have pioneered in the field of plant introduction intensively for two centuries. Horticulture and gardening have become a part of a great British tradition." Writing to Hodge, Meyer described Britain as "a vast archive of ornamental plants" (1957i).

Meyer's nine-month, 24,000 km journey concluded on 14 November when he and Jean sailed out from Southampton. After visiting more than eighty public and private gardens, arboreta, experiment stations, and nurseries, he was returning home having collected a staggering number of plants, about twenty-eight hundred in all. As Meyer himself noted, "Never before has any American had the opportunity of doing this sort of project on this scale for the Mediterranean region" (1957e).

LEARNING FROM EUROPE

Meyer's immensely productive 1957 trip to southern Europe and Great Britain reinforced the idea that there was a need to continue exploring the collections of ornamental plants in Europe. Three countries with strong horticultural traditions, the Netherlands, Belgium, and Germany, were chosen as destinations for Meyer's next expedition, scheduled for 1959.

Considering the flourishing nursery industry in all three countries, Meyer planned to devote more time to visiting nurseries, in addition to touring botanical gardens and private collections: "This trip is going to be rather different from the last. I shall be purchasing much more material this time and I hope our losses will be nil" (Meyer 1959a).

One Boskoop in the world

Arriving in the Netherlands in early July 1959, Meyer made Boskoop his headquarters for seven weeks. This was the most practical location from which to undertake exploration work in the western part of the country. "The Boskoop nursery area near Leiden and Rotterdam," Meyer commented (1963), "is a classic example of the efficient management of land by the Dutch. Indeed, Boskoop is unique among areas devoted to nursery crops. Most impressive are the neatly tended nursery plots, the innumerable canals, and the colorful houses of the nursery owners."

"The indefatigable industry of the Dutch people to recover land from the sea is a source of constant inspiration to all visitors of the Netherlands," Meyer remarked (1963). "The best agricultural soils lie on reclaimed land below sea level. In fact, more than one-third of the country lies below the level of the sea. It is in these areas that the finest horticultural crops are produced. . . . Horticulture and gardening at the local level in the Netherlands is not so well developed as one might expect in a country with a rich heritage in these pursuits covering nearly four centuries. In Great Britain, France, Italy, and other European countries, commercial horticulture traditionally is the servant of gardening. In the Netherlands, where the opposite situation prevails, the tradition of commercial horticulture takes precedence over developments in home gardening."

After barely two weeks of going through the Boskoop nurseries "with a fine tooth comb," Meyer reported enthusiastically to Hodge: "I am making slow progress through these little Dutch nurseries at Boskoop. What a place! Six hundred nurseries on 2000 acres [800 hectares]. The water table is only 12–14 inches [30–35 cm] below the surface. You have never seen such plants. It looks as though I will find quite a lot of conifers of interest to us—dwarf types. Only a few of the nurseries have collections, the bulk are only plant factories for

Fargesia murielae was first brought to the Arnold Arboretum of Harvard University by Ernest H. Wilson, who collected it in 1907 in China. Only a single plant survived the long journey, and it was sent in 1913 to Kew Gardens in England, where it was propagated and distributed throughout Europe. It was not until 1959 that this bamboo was reintroduced successfully into United States, when Meyer acquired it from the Royal Moerheim Nurseries in Dedemsvaart. Photo by Frederick G. Meyer.

export purposes. Certainly there is only one Boskoop in the world!" (Meyer 1959b).

Lost bamboo found

After an exceptionally productive time in the Boskoop area, Meyer relocated to the northeastern part of the Netherlands. One of the nurseries he visited there was the Royal Moerheim Nurseries near Dedemsvaart, regarded as a leading producer of perennials and deciduous shrubs. "For more than sixty years, Messrs. Ruys, owners of the firm, have produced a host of new ornamental plants, both herbaceous and woody, many of which are now widely grown in gardens of Europe and America. Among the plants that originated in this nursery, the Moerheim blue spruce, *Picea pungens* Engelm. 'Moerheimii', is perhaps the most widely known. This selection, introduced in 1912, long has been a favorite in Europe and in the United States" (Meyer 1963).

Among the plants Meyer procured from the Royal Moerheim Nurseries were *Buddleja crispa* var. *farreri* (60428), a low-growing butterfly bush; *Kolkwitzia amabilis* 'Rosea' (60454), a superior form of beauty bush; and *Fargesia murielae* (601632), a clump-forming bamboo from China. Meyer ultimately considered the bamboo to be "one of the most important introductions of the 1959 exploration trip." Although it was first brought from China to the Arnold Arboretum in Jamaica Plain, Massachusetts, as early as 1907, it was then forwarded to

Europe without ever having been distributed in the United States.

Meyer later described the Ruys' *Fargesia murielae*: "A handsome plant, more than fifty years old, in the nursery [it] forms a solid clump about 10 feet [3 m] in diameter with hundreds of culms 10 feet [3 m] tall with a graceful arching habit. If this bamboo proves to be fully hardy in the latitude of Washington, D.C., we shall have for the first time a nonrunning bamboo for gardens and for potential economic use in middle latitudes of the United States" (1963).

You should see Pfitzers

In early August, Meyer paid a visit to the Trompenburg Arboretum, developed on a 4-hectare site on the outskirts of Rotterdam by J. R. P. van Hoey Smith. "I spent a most interesting Saturday afternoon and evening with Mr. Smith and wife," wrote Meyer (1959c). "He has the necessary capital (shipping and brokerage) and has an avid interest in plants. His garden goes back 150 years. His newer introductions are really quite interesting. The one conifer he has we must keep an eye on is *Picea omorica* 'Expansa' (61840). As the name suggests, it is a spreading type, something like a spreading Pfitzers but even lower and with lovely pendulous habit of the Serbian spruce."

In spite of a relatively high water table, averaging from 60 to 90 cm over most of the property, about a thousand kinds of trees and shrubs thrived in the peaty

The conifer collection in Trompenburg Arboretum on the outskirts of Rotterdam. Photo by Frederick G. Meyer.

soils of Trompenburg. Especially well represented in the arboretum were oaks—about eighty different kinds—"a specialty of the present owner" (Meyer 1963). One that caught Meyer's attention was *Quercus pontica* (60761), a handsome low-growing species from the Caucasus.

Meyer was taken by the vigor of the many conifers grown at Trompenburg. Following his visit, he wrote to Hodge: "You should see Pfitzers [*Juniperus* ×*media* 'Pfitzeriana'] growing on this peat soil! Quite something. In a private garden in Rotterdam, I saw one with a 30 foot [9 m] spread. Where in the States they would grow this well I would not know" (1959c).

Meyer did not miss out on the opportunity to visit several of the most respectable botanical gardens in the Netherlands, including the oldest, the Hortus Botanicus at Leiden, founded in 1587. "When Carolus Clusius assumed the first professorship in 1594, this was a tiny garden of only 45 by 35 yards [41 by 32 m]," Meyer

remarked (1963). "With an apothecary assistant, Clusius planted more than 1000 species and varieties of plants, predominantly medicinal. From the original garden only one plant remains, a golden-chain tree (*Laburnum anagyroides* Med.) which flowers profusely every May in the place it has stood since it was planted in the Hortus in 1601."

Over time the garden increased in size to 6 hectares, with boundaries defined by canals on two sides. "The Leiden garden is so very nice," wrote Meyer (1959d), "small, but very well kept and old trees are wonderful. Some plants in the greenhouses are of interest to us, including the true variegated umbrella plant, *Cyperus alternifolius* 'Variegatus' [592563]." Besides *Cyperus*, nearly fifty other plants in Leiden's collections stimulated enough interest to be acquired by Meyer.

Leaving the Netherlands after nearly two months of browsing through its best collections of ornamental plants, Meyer secured a sizeable bounty of several

A 30 m tall windbreak of noble fir, *Abies procera*, in the nursery of G. D. Böhlje near Westerstede. Photo by Frederick G. Meyer.

hundred species and cultivars to be shipped to the United States. In a letter to Hodge, he remarked, "Holland is a wonderful place for plants, and Dutchmen who know how to grow them" (1959c).

Grown to perfection
Crossing the border from the Netherlands to Germany, Meyer found himself in East Friesland. The Oldenburg area of East Friesland ranks second, after the Pinneberg area north of Hamburg, among the most important nursery centers in the country. "Many first-rate nurseries are located in this intensely farmed area of deep fertile soil and moist cool-temperate climate," noted Meyer (1963). "The sandy acidic soils with relatively high organic content are suited for growing nursery crops, especially ericaceous plants and conifers. The climate is strongly influenced by the proximity of the North Sea which lies only a few miles to the north."

Meyer visited many top nurseries around Oldenburg. One was the nursery of Herman A. Hesse in Weener on the river Ems. Founded at the beginning of the twentieth century, this nursery has long maintained a plant-breeding program, resulting in numerous selections and hybrids.

Meyer acquired from Hesse nearly three hundred plants, including many of Hesse's introductions, such as *Fraxinus excelsior* 'Hessei' (61805).

Several other nurseries in the region were noted by Meyer (1963) as outstanding. The nursery of G. D. Böhlje near Westerstede, where "hardy shrubs are grown to perfection," supplied about a dozen introductions. H. Bruns's nursery, also near Westerstede, impressed Meyer as "a first-rate collection of unusual hardy trees and shrubs." The rhododendron nursery of Dietrich Hobbie at Linswege represented "an unbroken effort of more than twenty years to produce a new race of hardy plants for the often inclement climate of Germany."

Hamburg's oasis
From East Friesland, Meyer traveled south to Dortmund, the site of the 1959 Bundesgartenschau, or the Federal Horticultural Exhibition. "The Germans have the best idea," wrote Meyer (1959b) to Hodge. "Every two years they put on a horticultural fair lasting from May to October. Instead of sheep, goats and horses, it's all plants, growing in permanent positions and put on by nursery-men. Following these shows, the plant material becomes

A Baroque garden, enclosed by a hedge of *Carpinus betulus,* in the Royal Garden of Herrenhausen in Hannover. Photo by Frederick G. Meyer.

Pleached lindens, *Tilia,* and African lilies, *Agapanthus,* at the Royal Garden of Herrenhausen. Photo by Frederick G. Meyer.

the property of the local botanic garden in the town—the material includes new stuff and is, of course, worth a great deal of money. It is not a bad idea that does not seem to have been thought of in America."

After Dortmund, Meyer turned his attention to the Pinneberg-Elmshorn-Rellingen area of Holstein, located just north of Hamburg on the main route north to Denmark, which, he said, "comprises the largest nursery region of Europe, larger and with more nurseries than the Boskoop area in the Netherlands. The fertile soils, a mild climate, and a well-distributed rainfall favor the growing of superior nursery stock relatively quickly and cheaply" (1963). There Meyer toured a number of nurseries, including those of Rudolf Schmidt in Rellingen, W. Kordes and Son in Elmshorn, and Timm and Company, also in Elmshorn, prime examples of Germany's "thriving nursery industry."

Near Ahrensburg, northeast of Hamburg, Meyer visited Tannenhoft Arboretum in the village of Schmalenbeck. Developed in the early 1900s as a private country estate, Tannenhoft Arboretum later became associated with the Institut für Forstgenetik und Forstpflanzenzüchtung, a government organization devoted to studies in the breeding of forest trees. Among the plants Meyer procured there were several oaks, such as *Quercus petraea* 'Giesleri' (61383), with long, narrow, yellowish green leaves; *Q. petraea* 'Muscaviensis' (61384), with mostly entire, unlobed leaves; and *Q. robur* 'Cucullata' (61387), with smaller, hood-shaped leaves.

Hamburg's Botanic Garden impressed Meyer as "a welcome oasis for thousands of busy city people who use the garden daily for relaxation and inspiration about plants" (1963). Founded in 1810, the garden features a lake, a rock garden, and conservatories full of tropical plants, all amidst a "verdant green canopy of large trees and pleasant walks." One of the more unusual plants spotted in Hamburg was *Fagus sylvatica* 'Ansorgei' (602379), considered the rarest of the named selections of European beech. This slow-growing selection—found in 1891 in the nursery of C. Ansorge near Hamburg—has deep bronze-green, linear to lanceolate leaves.

A sizable segment of the earth's flora

Traveling south from Hamburg, Meyer stopped in Hannover, where he toured the Royal Garden of Herrenhausen and the Berggarten, both dating back to the seventeenth century, when Hannover was an independent German state and a center of cultural life. While the spacious and elaborately ornamented Herrenhausen was designed for court functions, the nearby Berggarten was developed as a botanic garden for scientific purposes.

Continuing south from Hannover, Meyer arrived in Frankfurt am Main in early October. He spent some time there exploring collections growing in the Palmengarten and at the Botanical Garden of the University of Frankfurt. The Palmengarten, which began as a small planting undertaken by the citizens of Frankfurt in 1869, has grown into a major botanic garden of international repute. Meyer took special note of a series of large conservatories, where, he said, "Fritz Encke, director, has brought together a first-rate collection of tropical plants admirably grown and splendidly displayed" (1963).

One glasshouse of the Palmengarten in Frankfurt am Main features *Victoria amazonica* and other aquatic plants. Photo by Russell J. Seibert.

The large palm house of the Palmengarten in Frankfurt am Main dates back to 1869. Photo by Russell J. Seibert.

Adjacent to the Palmengarten was the Botanical Garden of the University of Frankfurt, a relatively new garden spread on 8 hectares and constructed primarily for academic use. Among the plants Meyer acquired from these two collections were *Erica* 'Evening Glow' (611387), with flowers that open white and change to rose as they age; *Nepenthes×dormanniana* (611388), with pitchers heavily spotted with red blotches; and *Selaginella patula* (601417), a club-moss native to Jamaica.

After touring several of Germany's botanical gardens, Meyer commented that in Germany, like in other parts of Europe, "the botanic garden carries with it a time-honored tradition in university life dating from the Italian gardens, first at Padua in 1545. . . . Germany long has remained in the forefront in matters horticultural with a heritage in this field quite as old as that of the Netherlands. Elaborate gardens were traditional among the wealthy before World War II, when it was possible to maintain a large estate. Since the last war the small home garden has come into prominence. A horticultural elite long has existed in Germany at a level unknown in the United States" (1963).

Leaving Germany for Belgium, Meyer had this to offer in retrospect: "To a botanist, horticulturist, or serious amateur, a visit to a German botanic garden, either municipally or university operated, can be a rewarding experience, if for no other reason than exposure to a sizable segment of the earth's flora in so small a space" (1963).

Traditional pursuit

Belgium was Meyer's next and last stop. "In Belgium," he remarked, "horticulture is a traditional pursuit" (1963). The country "long has maintained an enviable position in the production of ornamental plant crops, dating back to the early years of the nineteenth century when Louis van Houtte, Ambroise Verschaffelt, and J. J. Linden were leading names in the horticulture of this country with headquarters in Ghent. Belgium still ranks among the most important centers on the Continent for the commercial production of ornamental plants."

Meyer's tour of Belgian nurseries concentrated around Brugge, northwest of Brussels, a city known for its canals and bridges. There he visited a number of growers, including Sander and Fils, long dedicated to growing orchids, bromeliads, and other greenhouse plants, and Horticulture Flandria, also devoted to greenhouse plants, particularly bromeliads, ferns, and aroids.

North of Antwerp, Meyer toured the Kalmthout Arboretum, which in his view "stands among the most important private establishments of its kind in Europe. The older part of the collection dates from 1857, when Charles van Geert acquired the property for nursery purposes. For nearly a half century thereafter, this nursery was renowned in Europe as a source of exotic trees, shrubs, and selections of Indian azaleas (*Rhododendron indicum* Sweet), known as van Geert azaleas. . . . The de Belder family acquired the property in 1951 and quickly restored the derelict nursery of about 20 acres [8 hectares]. Many old specimen trees exist throughout the property; around these, new introductions are constantly being added. . . . Some of the woody collections reputably originated from introductions brought from Japan, about 1860, by the German-Dutch botanist and plant explorer, Philipp Franz von Siebold" (Meyer 1963). Two witch-hazels acquired by Meyer, *Hamamelis* ×*intermedia* 'Jelena' (60451) and *H.* ×*intermedia* 'Ruby Glow' (60714), were originally raised at Kalmthout.

Next, Meyer visited the Royal Botanic Garden of Belgium in Meise, about 8 km north of Brussels. "The spacious grounds at Meise covering 225 acres [90 hectares] were given by the royal family of Belgium for a national botanic garden. It is an imposing site where large specimen trees abound and verdant lawns provide sweeping vistas for some distance. . . . An extensive range of tropical conservatories called the Palais des Plantes will include separate departments for plants of Africa, Asia, America, and Australia" (Meyer 1963). Among the plants Meyer procured were *Chlorophytum alismifolium* (611625), with densely tufted leaves and lax racemes of white flowers; *Eugenia guilleminiana* (611661), an evergreen shrub with gracefully arching, fernlike branches; and *Eulophia horsfallii* (611662), a terrestrial orchid with giant leaves 2 m long. His bounty complemented twenty-three cultivars of croton, *Codiaeum variegatum* var. *pictum*. Many of these, including 'Baronne James de Rothschild' (611630), 'Benoît Comte' (611629), and 'British Empire' (611631), were later displayed in Longwood's conservatories, where they can still be seen.

Meyer's trip ended on 14 November. His collections in Belgium, added to those from the Netherlands and

Laurus nobilis specially trained at the Sander and Fils nursery in Brugge. Photo by Frederick G. Meyer.

Germany, exceeded twelve hundred plants. Looking back at his two European trips, he concluded, "Europe still is a potent source of ornamentals and probably will continue to be, especially if one is willing to make a systematic survey . . . of places where collections of these plants exist. Much may be learned from Europe where the importance of gardening and horticulture long have been recognized in the development of 'pure' agriculture" (1963).

EUROPE'S GARDEN FLORA

Meyer's two European trips in the 1950s led to the introduction of a staggering amount of material, about four thousand new plants in all. This collection of the best of what Europe had to offer continued to enrich American horticulture for many years. During the following quarter century, the attention of Longwood explorers turned to other regions of the world, but by the 1980s it became clear that the time had come to return to some of Europe's most active horticultural centers. With its flourishing nursery industry and ever-expanding interest in gardening, Europe continued to be, as Meyer put it, "a potent source of ornamentals."

The Kingdom's floral treasury

Rather than trying to repeat Meyer's expeditions, which lasted many months and covered several countries, Longwood envisioned a series of shorter, more focused trips. The United Kingdom, one of the epicenters of horticultural activities in Europe, was chosen as the destination for the first trip. In 1987, Dr. Darrel A. Apps, head of Longwood's education division, teamed up with Sylvester G. March, chief horticulturist at the U.S. National Arboretum, for a five-week trip that would take them through Scotland, England, and Wales.

Apps and March headed first to Scotland. On 20 September they arrived in Edinburgh, where they began the exploration of Britain's cultivated flora by touring the renowned Royal Botanic Garden, home to one of the largest living plant collections in the world. Two days later they traveled north to Glendoick Gardens near Perth, some 60 km away, a nursery owned by Peter Cox, a veteran plant explorer and leading rhododendron expert. Having procured from Cox a selection of rhododendrons and other ericaceous plants, Apps and March continued north to the Highlands, where they stopped at the Inshriach Alpine Nursery in Aviemore, a small town surrounded by the picturesque Cairngorm Mountains and claimed to be the coldest place in the British Isles. At the Inshriach they picked up an assortment of more than thirty of the most interesting perennials, including *Codonopsis ovata* (88809), *Podophyllum hexandrum* (88862), and *Astilbe* 'Inshriach Pink' (88777), a hybrid selected at that nursery.

Apps and March concluded their stay in Scotland on 25 September with a visit to Threave Gardens near Castle Douglas, about 130 km south of Edinburgh. From there they headed west to Morpeth in Northumberland, England's northernmost county. Their destination was Herterton House Garden Nursery, where they stocked up on a number of perennials, among them *Achillea* 'Taygetea' (88760) and *Campanula trachelium* 'Bernice' (88795). From Northumberland they traveled south and two days later arrived in Colchester in Essex County,

some 80 km northeast of London. There they toured Beth Chatto's garden, famed for its stunning compositions of drought-tolerant plants growing in an impoverished gravelly soil. Among thirty plants Apps and March procured there were *Alchemilla erythropoda* (88763), *Crambe koktebelica* (88814), and *Strobilanthes atropurpureus* (88870).

A few days later, after visiting nurseries in Norfolk and Suffolk County, the explorers relocated to Cornwall, on the island's southwestern tip. In Madron near Penzance, Apps and March toured Trengwainton Garden, set up in a valley overlooking Mount's Bay. In the nearby Redruth, they stopped at the Burncoose and South Down Nurseries, where they obtained *Aesculus wilsonii* (92680) raised from seeds collected from trees growing at Caerhays Castle and introduced from China by Ernest H. Wilson in 1908.

From Burncoose the team continued traveling east and, on 7 October, arrived in Yelverton in Devon, just north of Plymouth. Their destination was the Garden House in the nearby Buckland Monachorum, a small but highly admired naturalistic garden situated on the edge of the scenic Dartmoor National Park. From its diverse collections, Apps and March selected a number of rarities, such as *Daphne* ×*burkwoodii* 'G. K. Argles' (89501), *Edgeworthia papyrifera* (88822), and *Helleborus niger* 'White Magic' (88833).

From Devon the team headed east to London, stopping along the way in specialty nurseries and picking up more plants. On 11 October they paid a visit to the RHS Garden Wisley, just south of London. In Wisley's well-stocked garden center they found a number of interesting plants, including *Aster* ×*frikartii* 'Jungfrau' (88776), *Bergenia* 'Pugsley's Pink' (88782), and *Hypericum androsaemum* 'Albury Purple' (88835). Then a visit to Hilliers Nurseries, among England's most distinguished nurseries, located in Romsey just north of Southampton, turned out to be even more fruitful. After spending a day browsing, Apps and March selected twenty-five plants from Hilliers' extensive collections, among them *Cotinus* 'Grace' (88813), *Viburnum* ×*bodnantense* 'Deben' (88877), and *Tetracentron sinense* (88871).

During the next two weeks, Apps and March continued their forays to the leading nurseries and private collections of southern England and Wales, tirelessly looking for new and interesting plants worthy of introduction to the United States. From Bressingham Gardens in Norfolk

The Palm House at the Royal Botanic Gardens, Kew, where Darrel A. Apps and Sylvester G. March made their final stop during their 1987 trip. Photo by Tomasz Aniśko.

they procured a wide assortment of well more than a hundred choice trees, shrubs, and perennials. In Notcutts Nursery in Suffolk they found a number of unique trees, such as *Aesculus indica* 'Sydney Pearce' (92678), and shrubs, such as *Staphylea holocarpa* 'Rosea' (88868). While at the Fibrex Nurseries near Stratford-on-Avon, south of Birmingham, they obtained a collection of new cultivars of *Pelargonium* ×*domesticum* (88845–51). From John T. Gallagher of Verwood in Dorset, an accomplished breeder and collector, they acquired an assortment of rare cultivars of *Magnolia* and *Nerine*.

The trip that began at the Royal Botanic Garden Edinburgh ended on 30 October with a visit to the Royal Botanic Gardens, Kew, an unquestionable horticultural mecca, situated on the banks of the river Thames on the outskirts of London. Here the five-week plant-hunting expedition through some of Britain's finest gardens and nurseries, which resulted in more than five hundred collections, concluded with a very modest acquisition, despite Kew's enormous holdings. Apps and March chose only two old but little-known selections of common boxwood, *Buxus sempervirens* 'Pendula' (88785) and *B. sempervirens* 'Prostrata' (88786). Perhaps by this point they felt overwhelmed with the diversity of plants in British gardens and were unable to absorb in such a short time Kew's seemingly inexhaustible collections.

Nursery escapade continues

It was at the Royal Botanic Gardens, Kew, the end point of Apps and March's 1987 trip, that the next team of explorers began five years later. In June of 1991, Dr. James R. Ault, Longwood's plant physiologist, and R. William Thomas, head of Longwood's education divi-

The Temple of Aeolus overlooks Kew's extensive Order Beds. From the vast collections of the Royal Botanic Gardens, Kew, Ault and Thomas selected thirty-three plants for use in Longwood's cool conservatories. Photo by Tomasz Aniśko.

Astrantia 'Hadspen Blood' (92711), a hybrid between *A. maxima* and *A. major,* was among the plants Ault and Thomas acquired from Hadspen Garden in Castle Cary. Photo by Tomasz Aniśko.

sion, traveled to the United Kingdom to continue the work of their predecessors, Apps, March, and Meyer. This time Ault and Thomas did sift through the Kew's collections, selecting a wide range of plants suitable for Longwood's cool conservatories, including *Asteriscus maritimus* (92692), *Fabiana imbricata* f. *violacea* (92688), and *Helichrysum sibthorpii* (92693).

Ault and Thomas's nursery tour focused on southern England, from Somerset County in the southwest to Hertford County north of London. In Somerset in the town of Castle Cary, they visited Hadspen Garden and Nursery, of Nori and Sandra Pope, widely acclaimed for an unorthodox use of color in the garden. Among the ten plants Ault and Thomas acquired at Hadspen were *Astrantia* 'Hadspen Blood' (92711), a hybrid between *A. maxima* and *A. major* developed by the Popes; *Rodgersia* 'Parasol' (92780), a hardy perennial notable for its bold, reddish foliage; and *Euphorbia characias* ssp. *wulfenii* 'Lambrook Gold' (92738), a selection found by Margery Fish of East Lambrook Manor, only 25 km from Castle Cary.

The story of 'Lambrook Gold' inspired the explorers to pay a visit to the garden established by Fish, one of the great divas of the English cottage garden style. The gardens, which slid into neglect after Fish's death in 1969, have since been restored. In the small specialty nursery there, which offers a wide selection of unusual plants, Ault and Thomas found a few rarities such as *Geranium macrorrhizum* 'Czakor' (92744), ×*Halimiocistus* 'Ingwersenii' (92746), and *Argyranthemum* 'Mrs. F. Sander' (92707).

In Hampshire, southwest of London, Ault and Thomas toured two nurseries near Southampton. In the town of Boldre, 20 km south of Southampton, they visited Spinners Nursery, specializing in rare, hardy plants. Then in Kilmeston, some 25 km northeast of the city, they stopped at the Blackthorn Nursery of Robin and Sue White, famed for its hellebores, several of which Ault and Thomas obtained for trialing at Longwood, including outstanding selections of *Helleborus niger* (92750–1) and *H.* ×*sternii* (92752).

A visit to Hopleys Plants in Much Hadham, Hertfordshire, just north of London, turned out to be the most

Darke, Pagels, and Anke Mattern, left to right, in Pagels's nursery in Leer. Photo by Rick Darke.

Ault and Thomas acquired *Cercidiphyllum japonicum* 'Rotfuchs' (92716), a German selection with purple foliage, from the Spinners Nursery in Boldre. Photo by Tomasz Aniśko.

fruitful stop. This nursery's claim to fame was the introduction in the 1970s of the first red-flowered cultivar of *Potentilla fruticosa,* named 'Red Ace'. Among the nearly fifty plants acquired from Hopleys were some of this nursery's other introductions, such as *Potentilla fruticosa* 'Hopley's Orange' (92776), *Prostanthera* 'Poorinda Ballerina' (92777), and *Salvia patens* 'Chilcombe' (92782), as well as an assortment of *Nerine* cultivars and species (92760–7). With this visit, Ault and Thomas concluded their nursery escapade and in mid-June returned to the United States with a hefty bounty of 127 choice plants.

Innovative perennials

Germany, Europe's horticultural powerhouse and the birthplace of many an innovative idea on plants and gardens, was understandably chosen as another destina-

Hans Simon in his garden in Marktheidenfeld, where Darke procured *Carex morrowii* 'Gilt' (89921). Photo by Rick Darke.

The nursery of Gräfin von Zeppelin in Sulzburg was Darke's southernmost destination during his 1989 trip to Germany. Photo by Rick Darke.

tion for the European plant exploration. In August of 1989, Rick Darke, Longwood's curator of plants, traveled to West Germany with the primary goal of acquiring new perennials. Over the course of a couple of weeks he visited nurseries from Ostfriesland in the north to Schwarzwald in the south.

In Ostfriesland, Darke stopped in the town of Leer near the Dutch border to visit the nursery of Ernst Pagels, one of Germany's foremost breeders of perennial plants. Among the plants he obtained from Pagels were *Astilbe chinensis* var. *taquetii* 'Purpurlanze' (89911), *Lamium galeobdolon* 'Silberteppich' (89919), and *Symphytum grandiflorum* 'Blaue Glocken' (89920).

In Schwarmstedt, about 30 km north of Hannover, Darke toured the nursery of Ruth and Wilfried Siebler.

Here he spotted *Saponaria* ×*lempergii* (89909) and ×*Solidaster luteus* (89923). Further south, in the nursery of Heinz Klose in Lohfelden near Kassel, he found *Cortaderia dioica* (89927). Continuing south from Kassel, he reached Marktheidenfeld, about 70 km southeast of Frankfurt, where he visited the nursery of Dr. Hans and Helga Simon and procured *Carex morrowii* 'Gilt' (89921).

Darke's southernmost destination was the nursery of Gräfin von Zeppelin in Sulzburg, Schwarzwald, one of Germany's leading nurseries specializing in perennials. From their extensive offerings, Darke selected a number of plants, including *Phlomis chrysophylla* (89898), *Origanum laevigatum* 'Herrenhausen' (89906), and *Centaurea cheiranthifolia* (89901).

Hugin with his best-known introduction, *Sedum* 'Matrona' (93537), valued for its deep wine-colored stems, purple-tinted leaves, and pink flowers. Photo by Rick Darke.

Gräfin von Zeppelin with *Salvia officinalis* 'Berggarten' (93543), which Darke later procured from the nursery Haussermann Stauden und Geholze in Stuttgart. Photo by Rick Darke.

Four years later, Darke returned to Germany and to the nursery of Gräfin von Zeppelin. This time he picked twenty-seven of their new introductions, including *Clematis heracleifolia* 'Cassandra' (93535), notable for its exceptionally clear deep blue flowers. In Freiburg, 20 km north of Sulzburg, Darke visited the nursery of Ewald Hugin, best known for introducing *Sedum* 'Matrona' (93537), a putative hybrid between *S. maximum* and *S. spectabile,* which later gained widespread recognition and acclaim in both Europe and North America. Another German selection that has since become popular in the United States was *Salvia officinalis* 'Berggarten' (93543), a form with large, rounded, gray-green leaves, which Darke obtained in Stuttgart from the nursery Haussermann Stauden und Geholze.

These two trips to Germany resulted in more than seventy new perennials being brought back to the United States. Many of these plants can still be viewed at Longwood, proof that German plant breeders deserve their reputation for selecting outstanding garden plants.

AROUND
THE CARIBBEAN

DOMINICA ROOTS

The island chain of the West Indies extends from Cuba and the Bahamas in the north to Trinidad and Aruba in the south. It may be divided into three groups: the Bahamas, the Greater Antilles, and the Lesser Antilles. It comprises islands of greatly contrasting size, geologic origin, and topography. The islands are surrounded by warm oceanic waters and swept by predominantly easterly trade winds. The resulting moderately high temperatures and abundant rainfall support the luxuriant and rich flora of the islands, which includes about twelve thousand species and is characterized by a high rate of endemism.

The need for Longwood to explore these islands for new ornamental plants was very apparent to Dr. Walter H. Hodge, Longwood's head of education and research. While working as a predoctoral student at the Gray Herbarium of Harvard University in the late 1930s, he had conducted plant-collecting and floristic studies on Dominica in the Lesser Antilles. During a discussion in 1958 with Dr. Russell J. Seibert, Longwood's director, regarding future plant explorations, Hodge remembers asking, "How about my going back to my roots, that is to what started me in tropical botany of which I became a specialist all my life and particularly of the New World tropics? Why don't we go and stop at all the islands that have botanical gardens all the way down to Trinidad and then come back?"

Seibert concurred, thus the planning for the trip to the West Indies began. It was not until three years later, however, that the execution of this plan became possible and Hodge made arrangements to depart on a three-week trip in late January of 1961. "The purpose was to visit public and private gardens of certain of the West Indies and British Guiana [Guyana]," he recorded, "particularly those gardens with which we have had established plant exchange relations and with the idea of becoming personally familiar with the materials grown at the present time and with the officials in charge, and to make collections of native plants of potential ornamental value observed in the wild, especially on the Lesser Antillean island of Dominica. . . . On this trip I was accompanied by my wife Bobbie [Barbara T. Hodge] who served in an unofficial capacity as an efficient field aid helping in the keeping of notes, the cleaning and packing of plant materials, etc." (Hodge 1961b).

British possessions

"This trip in 1961 brought back very many memories of my early work in the tropics," recalls Hodge. "It was in this area back in 1937, while a new botany staff member of the Massachusetts State College, that I and my wife-to-be, Bobbie, took the first trip to see the Lesser Antilles and especially Dominica. My purpose was to collect material for a new course in economic botany. A year later, as a doctoral candidate at Harvard University I began floristic work on Dominica which was to develop into my doctoral

The Lesser Antilles are a chain of islands disposed in an arc about 800 km long, extending from Puerto Rico, the smallest and easternmost of the Greater Antilles, to Trinidad, off the northeastern corner of Venezuela. Geologically the Lesser Antilles can be divided into islands of volcanic origin, such as Dominica, Grenada, and Saint Lucia, and those of limestone origin, like Barbados and Saint Croix. The climate of these islands is tropical, although the fairly constant northeastern trade winds lower the prevailing temperatures. The mountainous islands have very mild

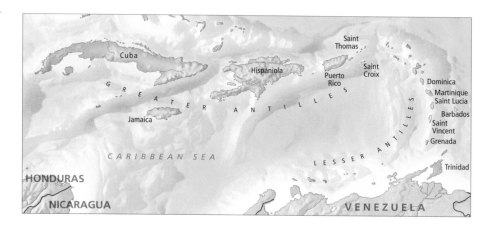

weather year-round, especially at higher elevations and on the windward coast. The rainfall is abundant in the wet season, from June to December, with an annual average of about 1000 mm. Higher mountain peaks receive much higher rainfall, on some islands to well more than 6000 mm, and are frequently clad in dense clouds. Vegetation at elevations below 450 m is xerophytic, especially on the west coast. Mountain rain forest with luxuriant, high-stemmed, broad-leaved trees is found between 450 and 750 m. Mossy forest of dwarf, wind-twisted trees is found above 750 m; this region, known as elfin woodland or cloud forest, is subjected to almost constant mist or rain.

thesis on the flora of this interesting island. Of all the Lesser Antilles it was the most rugged, least populated, and with pristine mountains attaining nearly 1500 m in elevation. The island was precipitous and heavily covered with the finest rain forests still extant in the Lesser Antilles, if not in the whole West Indian area."

Returning to the West Indies in 1961, the Hodges left Philadelphia on 20 January. Before reaching Dominica they spent several days in British Guiana and Trinidad—at that time, like Dominica, British possessions. "Our tour was to stop at any major botanic gardens en route to Georgetown, British Guiana, and back to Dominica," explains Hodge. "We hoped to find new outstanding ornamental plants with the aid of visitations to botanic gardens, where we could see what actual plants were being grown and which ones might be of use in Longwood conservatories or that could be grown in the outdoor gardens during the summertime."

The Hodges arrived in Georgetown on 30 January. There they visited the Botanic Garden, where Hodge was especially interested to see the outstanding collection of palms: "As the current president of the recently established Palm Society at that time, I was looking not only for palms which we could grow indoors at Longwood but also those that might interest gardeners living in Florida, southern California, or Hawaii."

On the way to Dominica, the Hodges stopped at the Botanic Garden in Georgetown, known for its extensive palm collection. Photo by Walter H. Hodge.

Steep volcanic slopes meet the Caribbean Sea along Dominica's west coast. Morne Anglais, 1123 m, is seen in the distance. Photo by Walter H. Hodge.

Two days later the Hodges flew to Trinidad. There they toured the Botanic Garden in Port of Spain, Saint Augustine Nurseries, several private gardens, and especially the ornamental and economic plantings at the Imperial College of Tropical Agriculture at Saint Augustine. "The College," Hodge explains, "was the main British institution for training botanists, horticulturists, and the like, for Britain's possessions in the tropics back before World War II. People who had received training at Kew Gardens in England could then go and study at the Imperial College in Trinidad. At the time of our visit it had become a unit of the new University of the West Indies, which is based in Jamaica. At Saint Augustine we met with an old friend Dr. John Purseglove, dean of the college, who showed us around."

From the collections maintained at the Imperial College, Hodge picked a few choice plants, including an undetermined species of *Clitoria* (61210), a herbaceous vine with attractive, deep blue, double flowers; selections of *Ixora* (61211–3) with yellow, pink, and dark red flowers; and *Pachyrhizus erosus* (61214), the yam-bean, an annual legume with an edible tuber, grown in Central America since pre-Columbian times, which he intended to grow in Longwood's economic plants garden.

Lofty island

"And then on 3 February we went on to Dominica," remembers Hodge. "Of course it was quite a different landing than in the 1930s. Back then we arrived by ship, which anchored offshore thus requiring a launch to take passengers to a jetty. This time we flew to the northwest coast, where it was remarkable that they found a spot for a new little airport."

Dominica, located between Guadeloupe and Martinique, is about 45 km long and 24 km wide with a total area of about 780 km². The island's rugged mountain ranges run north to south and have numerous precipitous peaks, the highest of them Morne Diablotin, 1447 m. The west-flowing Layou, Dominica's largest river, ties in with the headwaters of the east-flowing Pegoua and Castle Bruce rivers to form the main east–west valley system separating the northern and southern peaks.

The remarkable feature of Dominica is its

Roseau, Dominica's capital, viewed from Morne Bruce. Photo by Walter H. Hodge.

forests: "This forest area remains intact, for, although the companion Antillean islands, because of their comparative lowness and accessibility, have lost much of their original stands, Dominica alone has retained them. Her loftiness has been at once her savior and the millstone around her neck, for, although her beauty has never aged, she has had to sacrifice riches for it since economically speaking Dominica is poor. Her soil is rich, but the difficulty is to cultivate soil which is situated on what are for all intents and purposes ninety degree slopes and which when cleared of forest become sterile and eroded away by landslides caused by incessant rain" (Hodge 1944).

Near Roseau the Hodges found a place to stay at one of the old estates and rented a jeep, the best kind of vehicle to have on the narrow roads of Dominica. "Roseau," noted Hodge (1944), "the chief town of the island, which is little more than an overgrown village, is tightly jammed upon the only available level ground bordering the rugged Dominica coastline–a small delta hewn from the very mountains and tumbled down to the sea margin by the actions of Roseau's lusty little river."

The Hodges began the exploration of the island with a visit to the Botanic Garden at Roseau. "Tiny Roseau has but one real attraction–her botanic gardens," wrote Hodge (1944). "In the beauty of this well-kept English

park, which complements rather than vies with the natural vegetation of the surrounding mountains, one can find growing nearly all the outstanding representatives of the world's tropical flora. Indeed, the Roseau Gardens are famed as among the best in the West Indies; they possess particularly one of the finest palm collections in the Western Hemisphere." From the garden's collection, Hodge selected a number of plants, including *Barleria barbata* (61303), *Psychotria ipecacuanha* (61317), and *Poitea carinalis* (61291), the national flower of Dominica, a small endemic tree or shrub with very handsome, red, pealike blooms.

The leaf green of the forest

Hodge spent most of his time in Dominica collecting wild plants from the wet mountain forests of the island's interior. "In such a forest almost every tree seems to be different," he wrote (1944). "Boles ten feet [3 m] in diameter are common, and many of the trunks of these giants are thrust two hundred feet [60 m] into the air from bases that flare like the flying buttresses of continental cathedrals. Arboreal foliage is so high above one's head as to defy recognition, but from this canopy drop the cord-like roots of *kaklin* (*Clusia*), a common strangling arborescent epiphyte. On the trees appear numerous

The Imperial Road was one of the few paved roads that provided access to the interior of Dominica. Bobbie Hodge, pictured, is looking towards Morne Grand Bois, 910 m. Photo by Walter H. Hodge.

Collecting *Glomeropitcairnia penduliflora* (61325), one of the largest known epiphytic bromeliads, near the summit of Morne Plat Pays. Photo by Walter H. Hodge.

vines, such as marcgravias, *zelle mouche* (*Carludovica*), which lift their festooning cables to the sunlight, while lower down are aroids and ferns clutching at every foothold. Beneath the trees the light is dim and ground vegetation is never dense. A rubiaceous shrub (*Cephaelis*), with tiny white flowers surrounded by waxy blue bracts, is most common living among colonies of low ferns, feathery selaginellas, or occasionally with various rare terrestrial orchids. But colorful plants are few and over all is just the leaf green of the forest."

At higher elevations the rain forest is replaced by elfin or mossy forest. "One has to become an acrobat on the uppermost grueling slopes of Dominica's mountains," warned Hodge (1944), "for here the constant trade-wind causes the forest aspect to change. The trees are of different species and are dwarfed, twisted, and massed in impenetrable and grotesque fashion upon the steeply pitching slopes in such a way that one can only make progress by clambering hand over hand through the appressed, dripping, wind-blown treetops. Rain here, except on rare occasions, is almost incessant, with the result that mosses are everywhere, covering the limbs like cushions and spilling out water at every touch; their presence in such numbers gives to this upper region the name mossy-forest."

Exploring the interior

Using Roseau as his base, Hodge undertook several excursions into the interior of the island. Following Roseau River upstream, he reached the settlement of Laudat,

northeast of the capital. There he collected *Didymopanax attenuatum* (61219), *Charianthus purpureus* var. *rugosus* (61215), and *C. corymbosus* (61216). Then, east of Laudat, on the southern flanks of Morne Micotrin, 1221 m, he botanized near Freshwater Lake, one of only two small bodies of fresh water on the island. Among the plants collected were *Dryopteris consanguinea* (61232), a terrestrial fern; and *Guzmania megastachya* (61299), a bromeliad. North of Morne Micotrin, Hodge botanized on Morne Trois Pitons, 1387 m, the area where he thought "the best pickings" on the islands could be made. Among the plants he found was *Renealmia racemosa* (61220), a tall herb of the rain forest floor.

"When I was collecting plants on Dominica in the 1930s as a systematic botanist I was not concerned about

Bobbie Hodge holds an impressive specimen of *Aechmea smithiorum* (61297) collected near Laudat. Photo by Walter H. Hodge.

Heliconia caribaea (61224–6), one of the two species native to Dominica, was collected by Hodge at Mount Joy estate. Photo by Walter H. Hodge.

their possibilities as horticultural subjects," recalls Hodge, "but of course I still thought they were pretty neat so I had remembrances of certain exceptional plants. One of the species I wanted to get for Longwood was a giant 'tank' bromeliad, *Glomeropitcairnia penduliflora* (61325), common in the edge of elfin forests in the mountains from about 1000 m up to the summits. I thought that, although we may not have a greenhouse big enough to bring this bromeliad to maturity, because its inflorescence gets to be about 4.5 m tall, and it must be 2 m or more in diameter, it would be a remarkable plant to display even in its vegetative stage with a 'tank,' one of which is recorded to have held up to 20 liters of water. I knew the easiest place to find it so went to the site on Morne Plat Pays, 943 m, located near the southern end of the island."

Other bromeliads collected in Dominica included *Thecophyllum urbanianum* (61296) and *Aechmea smithiorum* (61297). Hodge described the latter in his field notes: "Leaves produced are up to 1 m long and the flower spikes are 30–40 cm long with very attractive inflorescences with pink scape bracts and floral bracts varying from lilac to orchid in color; plants readily sucker; a good species for the Longwood collection and also a rare one, probably never brought into cultivation before."

"Then we collected heliconias," remembers Hodge. "There are only two species of *Heliconia* native to Dominica, *H. caribaea* and *H. bihai,* but they are both attractive ones. Dominica is where the first heliconia, that is *H. bihai,* was described in the eighteenth century. At Mount Joy estate I collected rhizomes of several forms of

Cyathea arborea and other tree ferns are a prominent element of Dominica's forests and clearings. Photo by Walter H. Hodge.

Carib Indians of Dominica use the aerial roots of *Anthurium palmatum* (61306–7) in basket weaving. Photo by Walter H. Hodge.

Heliconia caribaea (61224–6) reaching over 3 m high and producing inflorescences with red or yellow bracts."

Being blessed with abundant rainfall and a gentle climate, Dominica is home to many ferns. "Tree ferns, as only Dominica can produce them, predominated," wrote Hodge (1944), "arching over the roadway and filtering motes of sunlight through a filigree of fronds. There are five kinds of tree ferns on this little island [including a rare endemic *Cyathea hodgeana* discovered by Hodge in the 1930s] plus about two hundred other fern species, which vary from thirty-foot [9 m] arborescent giants to tiny filmy epiphytes scarcely a quarter of an inch [6 mm] high. Real variety when one considers that so-called ferny New England can boast of a mere sixty odd species!" With such a wealth of ferns inhabit-

ing the forests, Hodge had no difficulty assembling an impressive representation, which included a tree fern, *Trichipteris aspera* (61267); terrestrial species of *Dicranopteris* (61266), *Polybotrya* (61261), and *Tectaria* (61236); and many epiphytes. Of special note were many collections of filmy ferns, such as *Trichomanes* (61231, 61233, 61248, 61256–7) and *Hymenophyllum* (61237, 61241, 61258).

In the same habitats where ferns flourished, Hodge encountered interesting orchids such as *Jacquiniella globosa* (61270) and *Maxillaria coccinea* (61275), often growing in mats of moss covering tree limbs, and anthuriums such as *Anthurium cordifolium* (61308), *A. dominicense* (61305, 61312), *A. lucidum* (61309–10), and *A. palmatum* (61306–7). The decorticated, dyed aerial roots

Hodge and George J. W. Ford, gardener at Longwood, inspect bromeliads brought back from Dominica. Photo by Gottlieb A. Hampfler.

of *A. palmatum* have been used by Dominica's Carib Indians in basket weaving.

After ten days of exploring Dominica, Hodge's collections exceeded one hundred. With plants, rhizomes, and seeds carefully cleaned and packed, the Hodges left Dominica on 13 February and returned to the United States. They made a brief stop in Miami to visit the Fairchild Tropical Garden, hoping to pick up a few palms. One of them, *Chamaedorea ernesti-augusti* (61302), is still displayed in Longwood's conservatories.

NOT ENOUGH TIME HERE

The islands of Lesser Antilles support floristic diversity beyond what could be expected on such small landmasses. Plants of the Lesser Antilles have affinities with those in the Greater Antilles, Central America, and northern South America. Seibert was well acquainted with flora of Hispaniola in the Greater Antilles through his work in 1940 on the USDA's rubber survey, intended to identify areas suitable for rubber production in the Caribbean and in Central and South America. He was acutely aware of the richness of the Caribbean flora and its potential usefulness for Longwood's conservatory exhibits. Therefore, six years after Hodge's expedition to Dominica, Seibert planned another trip to explore several other Antillean islands.

Bearded island

The island of Barbados was originally named Los Barbados by Spanish sailors, in reference to the "bearded" aerial roots of *Ficus citrifolia* commonly seen there. It is a coral island, some 34 km long by 20 km wide, generally level

This bouquet of *Ixora macrothyrsa* was presented to the Seiberts upon their landing in Bridgetown. Photo by Russell J. Seibert.

Iris and John Bannochie hosted the Seiberts at the Andromeda Gardens in Barbados. Photo by Russell J. Seibert.

Standing under trees of *Tabebuia leucoxylon* in Welchman Hall Gully in Barbados are, left to right, Peter Webster, Iris Bannochie, Isabelle Seibert, and John Bannochie. Photo by Russell J. Seibert.

but with small hills in the central part, the highest point of which is Mount Hillaby, 336 m. Seibert, accompanied by his wife, Isabelle, arrived in Barbados on 27 December 1967. Upon landing in Bridgetown, the two were greeted by Anthony Hunte, president of the Barbados Horticultural Society, with a huge bouquet of *Ixora macrothyrsa*. *Ixora* enjoys great popularity among gardeners in the southern Caribbean, and many selections have been developed there from wild plants brought from Southeast Asia.

On 28 December the Seiberts drove to Bathsheba on the windward east coast of Barbados. As they traveled along the coast, Russell Seibert observed the regeneration of the West Indian mahogany, *Swietenia mahogani,* on steep hills where it was exposed to strong winds and subjected to rapid erosion. This was part of the soil conservation efforts on the island. In Bathsheba they visited Andromeda Gardens, the private garden and nursery of Iris and John Bannochie. Andromeda contains what is, in Barbados, by far the largest collection of tropical plants from around the world, assembled over many years through the efforts of the Bannochies.

Seibert explained to his hosts at Andromeda that his interest was primarily in "ornamental plants, but also such plants as have both ornamental and other usefulness to man, whether it be agricultural, horticultural, or medicinal" (R. J. Seibert 1967b). He was convinced that "plants with interesting stories and background of historical interest are always of interest to the public and worthy of display in our horticultural displays at Longwood Gardens." Iris Bannochie suggested he explore Welchman Hall Gully. Created by collapsed limestone caverns, the gully is a cool, lush ravine receiving dense fog due to its topographic orientation. Preserved by the Barbados National Trust, this densely wooded area, filled with a tremendous variety of plants, represents what Barbados looked like before settlers arrived on the island in 1627. In Welchman Hall Gully, the Seiberts were shown breadfruit trees, *Artocarpus altilis,* introduced to the New World from Polynesia by the French before 1790. Although this tree never fulfilled the original hopes of becoming a major food source, its fruits are still eaten on Barbados and other Antillean islands. After an eventful day, Seibert found time to scribble back to Longwood only a brief note: "Too many things of interest—not enough time here" (1967c).

Breadfruit, *Artocarpus altilis,* bears round, chartreuse fruits, warty in appearance and up to 20 cm in diameter, throughout the year. Breadfruit trees have been grown in various greenhouses in the United States for many years, but it was not until 1970 that the first of them, planted in Longwood's Palm House ten years earlier, bore fruits. The fruit set was so heavy that one witness compared them to "ornaments on a Christmas tree." Photo by Russell J. Seibert.

The Spice Island

The following morning the Seiberts had to depart Barbados on a flight southeast to Grenville, Grenada. Although similar in size to Barbados—34 km long by 20 km wide—Grenada is in other ways quite different. This is a heavily wooded, volcanic island, largely mountainous, with the highest point being Mount Saint Catherine, 840 m. Plantations on the island are conglomerates of banana, cocoa, and breadfruit. Widely cultivated nutmeg, cloves, ginger, and cinnamon earned Grenada its status as the Spice Island. To reach Saint George's, the capital on the

Burris welcomed the Seiberts to Saint George's Botanic Garden, Grenada. Photo by Russell J. Seibert.

west side of the island, the Seiberts took a road that, after a curvy and steep climb, led them over a volcanic crest and through a lush forest filled with tree ferns.

In Saint George's the Seiberts were greeted by Neville Burris of the local Botanic Garden, who over the next two days showed them around the island. While botanizing in coastal plant communities they stopped near Grande Anse Beach, south of the capital, where Seibert collected seeds of two small trees, a yellow-flowered *Suriana maritima* (68115) of "excellent landscape value," as he recorded in the field notes, and *Agati grandiflora* (68111), with showy, pendant, pink flowers. On 31 December, Burris took the Seiberts to the Botanic Garden, which covered three verdant hectares in Saint George's. The visitors were enticed with what Isabelle Seibert (1968) described as the garden's "impressive" entrance. Burris also accompanied the couple to several fine private gardens laid out in the hills above the town.

Oldest in the hemisphere

Two days later the couple left Grenada for Saint Vincent, a little more than 100 km to the north. This volcanic and mountainous island is slightly smaller than Grenada and Barbados, 30 km in length and 18 km in width, but it exceeds both in altitude, with its highest point, Soufrière, reaching 1234 m. It is noted for its Botanic Garden in Kingstown, a well-planted 8 hectares with beautiful views of the sea. Founded in 1765, this garden is the oldest in the Western Hemisphere.

The garden's director, Con de Freitas, characterized by Isabelle Seibert (1968) as a "perpetual conversant," was exceptionally helpful in assisting the Seiberts in their

Purchas and his anthurium-growing establishment at Morne Grande in Saint Lucia. Photo by Russell J. Seibert.

The Seiberts in Saint Thomas. Photo by Russell J. Seibert.

There are more than a hundred species of *Mucuna,* both in the Old World and the New World, and many have beautiful flowers. *Mucuna bennettii* from New Guinea, shown here, is reputed to be the showiest of all tropical climbers. Photo by Walter H. Hodge.

botanizing on the island. "We certainly had a marvelous opportunity of seeing Saint Vincent through Con de Freitas," reminisced Russell Seibert (1968a). A terrific travel companion, de Freitas generously shared many plants from the Botanic Garden. Among them were *Heliconia bihai* (68765), a form with bracts entirely yellow rather than the typical scarlet; *Quamoclit coccinea* (68112), with scarlet salverform flowers; and *Petrea volubilis* var. *albiflora* (69591), producing starlike white flowers borne in erect racemes some 30 cm long. One plant, however, the elusive *Mucuna rostrata* (69527), captivated Seibert more than others. This large woody climber, native to Trinidad, Panama, and northern South America, blooms with spectacular flame-colored flowers that resemble enormous sweet peas arranged in hanging racemes some 20 cm long. The plant is reputed to be very shy about fruiting and producing seeds. It is easy to imagine, therefore, how thrilled Seibert was when several months later he received a packet containing six seeds and a letter from de Freitas: "The *Mucuna,* much to my surprise, fruited. I was told that it never did in Trinidad, but it produced about four pods here" (1969).

On 9 January the Seiberts said their farewells to de Freitas and flew to Saint Lucia. There they visited Guy and Mary Purchas at Morne Grande, who grew *Anthurium* on 16 hectares and shipped cut flowers to England and Canada. They also toured George V Park, which in 1936 replaced a former botanical garden. Two days later the couple left Saint Lucia for Fort-de-France in Martinique, about 50 km to the north. The island's

Looking out to Buck's Island from the eastern point of Saint Croix. Photo by Russell J. Seibert.

scenery is dominated by Montagne Pelée, a volcano 1397 m above sea level. Martinique does not have a botanical garden, but the Seiberts decided to pay a visit to Trois Ilets, birthplace of French Empress Josephine.

Virgin Islands

Several days later the Seiberts found themselves in Saint Croix, an island only 32 km long and 8 km wide and yet the largest of the Virgin Islands. At the airport a plant inspector gave Seibert a hard time with his plant press and luggage filled with cuttings and seeds. Luckily, Seibert's Longwood card "turned the trick," as Isabelle Seibert (1968) recalled, so the couple could continue with their visit as planned.

Saint Croix is largely level, with only small hills stretching along its north coast, of which the highest is Mount Eagle at 345 m. These hills are not high enough

above sea level to cool and condense the atmospheric moisture brought on by the trade wind; therefore they receive a comparatively smaller amount of rain than the volcanic islands to the south. One day the couple chartered a launch to go to Buck's Island, only a few kilometers off the north coast of Saint Croix, the site of a reef national monument. On the morning of 16 January, the Seiberts started with a brief flight to Saint Thomas, an island some 60 km north of Saint Croix. In the afternoon they continued to San Juan, Puerto Rico, and then to Mayagüez on the west end of the island, where a USDA research station is situated, to present a seminar there.

Two days later the couple returned to San Juan to stop at Pennock Gardens, a well-established nursery run by Charles F. Pennock, where Seibert acquired an undetermined *Tillandsia* (68107) and *Dioscorea bulbifera* (68114), "a curiosity vine with small 'potatoes' develop-

A Mexican species, *Chodanthus puberulus* (58159), named by Seibert in 1940, was grown in Longwood's conservatories for nearly thirty years. Photo by Gottlieb A. Hampfler.

In the 1930s, Seibert was a young aspiring botanist studying at Washington University in Saint Louis. Bignoniaceae, comprising more than a hundred genera and seven hundred species, appealed to him as a subject of taxonomic studies. Once armed with a master's degree in botany, Seibert accepted a fellowship at the Arnold Arboretum of Harvard University and chose this family as his topic of investigation. The result was the publication in 1940 of "The Bignoniaceae of the Maya Area," in which Seibert proposed a new genus, *Scobinaria,* and two new species, *Cydista heterophylla* and *Chodanthus puberulus.*

All squared and planted

Seibert's extensive knowledge of Bignoniaceae found a new application in 1955 when he took on the role of director at Longwood Gardens. Over the years, Seibert, impressed by the beauty of these plants, acquired many of the most decorative species for trial and use in the garden's conservatories. As part of this effort, in February of 1967 he organized a brief excursion to collect Bignoniaceae in Yucatán, Mexico's Maya area, the very same area he had focused on in the article he wrote twenty-seven years before.

On the early morning of 8 February, Seibert, accompanied by Isabelle, rented a taxi in McAllen, Texas, and crossed the Rio Grande to reach the town of Reynosa on the Mexican side. A two-hour flight took the couple over the Gulf of Mexico from Reynosa to Mérida in Yucatán. From the air Yucatán seemed "all squared and planted to corn and wheat" (I. L. Seibert 1967), but soon the Seiberts noticed countless yellow *Tabebuia chrysantha,* a tree native to mountain forests from Mexico to Venezuela, "a conspicuous and brilliant bloomer, flowering before the leaves" (R. J. Seibert 1940).

Before long they were on the road heading out of Mérida east to Chichén Itzá, a site of Mayan ruins. The couple was enthralled to see along the road pink *Tabebuia pentaphylla.* "So gorgeous," Isabelle Seibert said of the tree in full bloom (1967). "Being one of the best known and useful trees in Central America," wrote Russell Seibert in his 1940 article, "*T. pentaphylla* presents an unrivaled beauty in the spring months when the trees are covered with their pale pinkish purple to almost white flowers." Before reaching Chichén Itzá, Russell Seibert spotted blazing orange-red flowers of *Spathodea campanulata,* another arboreal member of Bignoniaceae, native

ing along the climbing stems," as he recorded in his field notes. The Seiberts returned to Philadelphia on 21 January after a nearly month-long trip, bringing back treasured suitcases full of herbarium specimens, live plants, and seeds, but also their unforgettable memories. "What more could we ask?" wrote Isabelle Seibert after the trip (1968).

PLANT HUNTING ON MAYAN GROUNDS

It is easy to understand why one might have a lifelong admiration for the many plants of the family Bignoniaceae. Writing in 1948, Seibert noted that several genera of this family "are important in the lumber industry of tropical regions," while "many others hold unlimited horticultural possibilities." In the neotropics, many species of *Tabebuia* are considered among the most important timber trees. South American *Jacaranda mimosifolia* may well be the world's most widely planted ornamental tropical tree. *Spathodea campanulata,* native to tropical Africa, follows closely in popularity. *Podranea ricasoliana* and *Pyrostegia venusta,* both from Africa, are among the most widely cultivated vines. The same could be said about *Campsis radicans* in temperate regions. The popularity of several species of *Tabebuia* led to their election in many Latin American countries as their national tree or national flower: *T. rosea* in El Salvador, *T. billbergii* in Venezuela, *T. serratifolia* in Brazil, and *T. chrysantha* in Ecuador.

Yucatán belongs floristically to the Caribbean region of the Neotropical kingdom. It is subject to a warm, humid climate that supports very rich plant life. The territory of the peninsula comprises the Mexican states of Campeche, Yucatán, and Quintana Roo, as well as Belize and the northern section of Guatemala. It separates the Gulf of Mexico from the Caribbean Sea. The northern part of the peninsula is a uniform, almost level plain, but further south the terrain undulates, alternating between depressions and low hills of less than 300 m in elevation. In the north the average rainfall is about 800 mm. The wet months are June to October, followed by a prolonged dry season. The southern part of the peninsula receives substantially higher rainfall. Among the

most striking features of Yucatán is the absence of surface streams. The limestone forming most of the Yucatán is so porous and the surface so level that rainwater sinks below the surface, where it forms underground reservoirs called cenotes. In the northern plains, the land, where not under cultivation, is covered with bush and scrubby woods, with only sporadic large trees or palms. Many plants are spiny and deciduous during the dry season. In the central and southern parts of the peninsula, the heavier rainfall supports extensive dense forests. By its floristic features, Yucatán is sharply differentiated from the rest of Central America and more closely related to Cuba and other islands of the Antilles. The number of species indigenous to Yucatán, some twelve hundred, is relatively low when compared to other parts of Central America, but it has a surprisingly large number of endemic species, estimated at about 17 percent.

to tropical Africa but extensively planted throughout the tropics as an ornamental and a shade tree.

Climbers of the Mayan ruins

The next morning the couple went to the site of the Chichén Itzá ruins by way of an ancient Mayan road, which stretched between a massive pyramid, called El Castillo, and a large sinkhole used in sacrificial ceremonies, called Cenote-Sagrado. Along this road Seibert found a whole wealth of botanical treasures belonging to the Bignoniaceae and offering flowers in shades of purple, rose, lavender, and pink: *Amphilophium paniculatum* (6781), *Arrabidaea chica* (6775), *A. floribunda* (6782), *Cydista diversifolia* (6786), and *Neomacfadya podopogon* (6779–80), all woody vines. *Cydista diversifolia*, widespread in thickets and forests from Mexico to Venezuela and the West Indies, is closely related to *C. heterophylla*, a species named by Seibert in 1940.

On 13 February the Seiberts drove from Chichén Itzá back to Mérida and, after a brief stop to replace a flat tire,

Seibert spotted blazing orange-red flowers of *Spathodea campanulata* near Chichén Itzá in Yucatán. Photo by Russell J. Seibert.

Around Cenote-Sagrado, a large sinkhole used for sacrificial ceremonies in Chichén Itzá, Seibert found a number of woody vines of the family Bignoniaceae. Photo by Walter H. Hodge.

A typical Mayan homestead on the plains around Muna. Photo by Walter H. Hodge.

Among the Mayan ruins at Uxmal, Seibert found *Onohualcoa fissa* (6784) and *Amphilophium paniculatum* (6774), woody bignoniaceous vines. Photo by Walter H. Hodge.

continued north to Dzibilchaltún, a site of one of the main Mayan settlements on the Yucatán Peninsula. In Dzibilchaltún, in dry, rocky scrub forest, Russell Seibert found an undetermined species of *Cassia* (6777), a small tree about 8 m tall, covered abundantly with attractive yellow flowers. In the afternoon the couple set a course for Uxmal, south of Mérida. The apparent monotony of the plains stretching along the road was broken only

once, as they drove over "one low mountain range that juts up from the flatness around Muna" (I. L. Seibert 1967).

The following morning, in Uxmal, the Seiberts explored the ruins of one of the largest Mayan cities. Along the edge of the bush surrounding the ruins, Russell Seibert collected two members of Bignoniaceae, both woody climbers some 8 to 10 m tall. One was *Onohualcoa fissa*

Bordered to the north by Nicaragua and to the east by Panama, Costa Rica has both Caribbean and Pacific coasts and is split down the center by a volcanic mountain chain of the Continental Divide. The highest point is Chirripó Grande, 3819 m, in the Cordillera de Talamanca. With a little more than 50,000 km², Costa Rica covers only 0.03 percent of the earth's surface, but it contains approximately 6 percent of the world's biodiversity. Its flora is estimated to include more than nine thousand species of flowering plants and eight hundred ferns. Most of Costa Rica's land area was once covered by forest vegetation. The savannalike areas seen today resulted from clear-cuttings for farming and cattle ranching. The types of forest found throughout the country are determined by the amount of rainfall and its distribution, and by changes in temperature associated with elevation. They range from the dry, deciduous, scrubby forest in the northwest to the constantly wet, lowland rain forest of the eastern shore and lowlands, to the oak-dominated cloud forest of the high Cordillera de Talamanca.

(6784), producing lavender flowers marked by white throats, an "excellent subject for conservatory display—spectacular!" as Seibert recorded in his field notes. The other was *Amphilophium paniculatum* (6774), seen previously in Chichén Itzá. He also found *Petrea arborea,* a woody vine with light blue flowers, and *Erythrina americana* (6778), a small tree with soft pink flowers, growing on rocky limestone rubble. Further south from Uxmal was yet another ancient Mayan settlement, Kabáh, which the couple reached in the afternoon. Seibert browsed through the scrub forest surrounding the ruins to find again two examples of bignoniaceous vines: *Cydista diversifolia* (6787) and *Arrabidaea floribunda* (6785).

Back in Uxmal, Seibert decided to continue botanizing in the nearby dense scrub woods the next morning. He returned from this plant hunt with several trophies. Among them were two bignoniaceous climbers seen previously, *Arrabidaea floribunda* (6776) and *Onohualcoa fissa* (6773). He also found *Pithecoctenium echinatum,* a white-flowered vine, for which the local inhabitants found a multitude of applications. "The spiny valves of the capsules are used as combs," recorded Seibert (1940). "The slender, long branches are very strong and are used for tying braces, etc., in the construction of huts. It is reported that the Maya use the seeds as a remedy for headache by moistening and applying them to the forehead or temples." Having gathered enough seeds and filled the herbarium press with specimens, Seibert left Uxmal with Isabelle and

headed north to Mérida. From Mérida the couple departed for Philadelphia on 18 February.

RETRACING COSTA RICAN TRAILS

"I really look forward to seeing some of the Costa Rican country and plant life which I never had a chance to see during our two years at Turrialba during 1948 and 1949 . . . just twenty years ago!" wrote Seibert (1968b) to Robert G. Wilson of San Vito de Java, his friend of many years, who established Jardín Botánico Wilson in Las Cruces, Costa Rica.

The two-year assignment to which he referred had begun in early December of 1947, when Seibert, at that time a geneticist for the USDA Office of Rubber Plant Investigations, arrived at a rubber station called La Hulera, situated outside the small village of Turrialba. At the station Seibert evaluated clonal rubber selections from outstanding trees that had been collected by various explorers in South America, including those he had discovered a few years earlier in the Peruvian region of Madre de Dios. The superior clones were ultimately transported to Africa to improve the large rubber plantation there.

The tropics in the scope
The years Seibert spent working in Central and South America helped him develop a deep appreciation for floras of tropical regions. Twenty years after his assign-

Robert and Catherine Wilson, founders of Jardín Botánico Wilson in Las Cruces near San Vito de Java. Photo by Russell J. Seibert.

Chamaedorea sp. (6952), a "very dwarf" palm collected by Seibert in Wilson's garden. Photo by Walter H. Hodge.

ment at La Hulera, while drafting a curriculum for the graduate program in public garden management initiated by Longwood Gardens and the University of Delaware—the first such program in the United States—he came to the conclusion that "no comprehensive advanced degree training program in horticulture and botanical garden management can afford to overlook the tropics in its scope" (Seibert 1968c).

With this in mind, Seibert decided to use his 1969 plant-collecting trip to Costa Rica as an opportunity to explore possibilities for providing Longwood students with experience in the tropics. He planned to meet in Costa Rica with Dr. Armando Samper, director of the Instituto Inter-Americano de Ciencias Agrícolas, and Jorge R. Campabadal, resident director of the Organization for Tropical Studies, to discuss arrangements that would provide an opportunity for Longwood graduate students and staff to undertake a tropical horticultural study tour in that country.

Seibert arrived in San José on 22 January and the same day met with Campabadal. The Organization for Tropical Studies, which Campabadal represented, is a consortium of universities and research institutions from the United States, Latin America, and Australia that in 1963 forged working relationships with colleagues in Costa Rica for the purpose of education and research in tropical biology. Among other functions, it provides opportunity for graduate and undergraduate education, facilitates research, and maintains biological stations in Costa Rica.

The Wilsons' garden

Seibert's primary destination for this trip was San Vito de Java, some 300 km southeast of San José near the border of Panama. A few kilometers south of this town was Las Cruces, where Robert and Catherine Wilson had developed their own private botanic garden. The Wilsons began creating their garden in 1961 on what used to be a cattle pasture and an abandoned coffee plantation. By the time of Seibert's visit, they had already managed to amass a very large and diverse collection of tropical plants from around the world, possibly the richest botanical collection of its kind in Central America. After a twelve-hour drive from San José, Seibert reached Las Cruces on the evening of 26 January.

Filled with excitement and armed with a field notebook and seed bags, Seibert rose early the next morning to begin exploring the Wilsons' collection. Among his long list of "trophies" were *Costus stenophyllus* (6955), native to Costa Rica, producing pale yellow flowers borne in bright red, conical inflorescences; *Columnea florida* (6954), with leaves marked by two red "eyes" underneath, which Seibert wanted to "grow in a basket and look up at"; *Piper auritum* (6959), known as *anisillo* because it "has odor of anise"; and *Coriaria thymifolia* (69726), a shrub with ferny foliage and long, pendant racemes tightly covered with tiny black

The valley of Río Reventazón near Paraíso, between Cartago and Turrialba. Photo by Russell J. Seibert.

berries, which, "although quite attractive, do not look in the least edible" (Wilson 1969).

In the garden Seibert also collected two good forms of *Calathea crotalifera,* native to Costa Rica (6950–1). The 3 m high *C. crotalifera* produces flowers hidden by large, brightly colored bracts, densely arranged and overlapping. The bracts are typically yellow, but green and bronze forms are known. Found from Mexico to Bolivia, this plant is commonly referred to as rattlesnake plant because its inflorescences resemble rattles.

Many plants growing in the Wilsons' garden were collected by Robert Wilson himself during his plant-hunting excursions throughout Costa Rica. Some of them were of undetermined identity, or possibly previously unknown. Those that interested Seibert particularly were orchids, *Calanthe* sp. (6949) with large, dark rose flowers, and *Sobralia* sp. (6948), a diminutive plant with unusually large flowers; as well as undetermined native palms, *Chamaedorea* sp. (6952), "very dwarf," one of the smallest palms, and *Euterpe* sp. (6956) once abundant but recently "being destroyed for use as palm heart salad," as Seibert recorded in his field notes.

En route to Turrialba

On 28 January, Seibert said farewells to his gracious and generous hosts in Las Cruces and departed for Golfito, a town on the coast of Golfo Dulce. There he stopped to

see banana plantations of the United Fruit Company. Near Golfito he found *Brownea macrophylla* (6948), a small leguminous tree producing large, pufflike, globose heads of scarlet flowers on the main trunk and branches, a phenomenon called cauliflory.

After spending a night in Golfito, Seibert set off on an eight-hour drive to Turrialba, situated in the valley of Río Reventazón, east of San José. While traveling on the Pan-American Highway between Buenos Aires and San Isidro de El General, in Puntarenas Province, Seibert made a stop to botanize on the surrounding hills. There he found *Socratea durissima* (6966), known as walking palm because of its prominent stilt roots.

In Turrialba, Seibert visited the Instituto Inter-Americano de Ciencias Agrícolas, where he consulted Samper about the planned study tour for Longwood graduate students. The institute, founded in 1942, has the main purpose of advancing agriculture in the region through research and modernization. Turrialba, strategically situated between South and North America, was chosen as its headquarters. Dr. Arnold L. Erickson, assistant coordinator, showed Seibert the research facilities and trial areas, including an extensive orchid collection. At the institute, Seibert collected an unusual small-leaved form of coffee bush, *Coffea arabica* var. *mirta* (6953), which he thought had possibilities as an ornamental plant for Longwood's conservatories. He also collected two palms: *Aiphanes*

Clusters of ripe fruits of *Bactris gasipaes* are offered for sale at a local market in Cartago. Photo by Walter H. Hodge.

Erickson showed Seibert a collection of orchids held at the Instituto Inter-Americano de Ciencias Agrícolas in Turrialba. Photo by Russell J. Seibert.

Slender trunks of *Bactris gasipaes* (6957) are prominently ringed and feature fearsome spines. Seibert collected seeds of this palm in Turrialba. Photo by Russell J. Seibert.

caryotaefolia (6958), a slender, spiny species producing fragrant flowers followed by brilliant red fruits, and *Bactris gasipaes* (6957), widely cultivated in tropical countries for its edible fruits.

A couple of days later, upon his return to San José, Seibert boarded a train for a six-hour ride to Puerto Limón on the Caribbean Sea coast of Costa Rica. In the swamps near Limón, Seibert spotted a palm, *Raphia taedigera,* locally known as *yolillo,* but he was unable to obtain its seeds at that time. *Raphia* is one of only two genera of palms, the other being *Elaeis,* that occurs in both the Americas and Africa. The leaves of *Raphia* are the longest of any flowering plant, and those of *R. regalis* can reach 25 m long. The Costa Rican *R. taedigera* has leaves only about half this size.

Back in San José on 3 February, Seibert met again with Campabadal to finalize details for the Longwood study tour. He also inquired about the possibility of finding a source for *Raphia taedigera* in Limón. Campabadal's response, which came a few months after Seibert's return to Longwood, was more than encouraging: "I have a good friend, Governor Solé of Limón, who is an ardent amateur horticulturist, and I am sure the Governor will cooperate" (Campabadal 1969). Indeed, thanks to the governor, in February of 1970, seeds of *Raphia* arrived at Longwood.

On his last day in Costa Rica, Seibert, accompanied by Campabadal and Dr. Rafael L. Rodriguez, head of the Biology Department at the Universidad de Costa Rica, visited several parks in San José and the garden of Charles H. Lankester in Cartago, outside San José. Don Carlos, as Lankester became known in Costa Rica, then ninety years old, showed the botanists around his garden and generously allowed Seibert to collect many plants, including *Anthurium subsignatum* (70760), *Begonia pustulata* (6947), and a couple of *Rhipsalis* species (6961–2).

On 5 February, Seibert departed for Philadelphia carrying with him twenty-eight new plants for Longwood's conservatories. In retrospect, however, more important was the fact that this trip set the stage for the launching of tropical internships in Costa Rica as an integral part of the Longwood Graduate Program, which over the course of more than thirty years trained many future leaders who shaped the field of public horticulture in the United States.

Lankester came to Costa Rica from England in early 1900 to work on coffee plantations. A few years later he turned his attention to collecting specimens of Costa Rican flora and fauna for some of the leading naturalists of that period. Lankester's contribution was recognized in 1923 when a newly discovered genus of orchids was named *Lankesterella*. In 1921, Lankester began to build a garden on 10 hectares of his Las Cóncavas property, which over the years grew to become one of the main destinations for all naturalists visiting Costa Rica. After Lankester's death in 1969, the garden was purchased by the American Orchid Society and the Stanley Smith Horticultural Trust, and donated to the Universidad de Costa Rica. Photo by Russell J. Seibert.

GRADUATES IN THE TROPICS

Four months after Seibert's reconnaissance trip, the first group of Longwood Program graduates—Ronald C. Bauman, William U. Massey, and Gary G. Gerlach—headed to Costa Rica, led by Dr. Donald G. Huttleston, Longwood's taxonomist, and Dr. Donald F. Crossan, professor of the University of Delaware. The group flew to San José on 11 June and the same day visited the Universidad de Costa Rica, where they met with Campabadal and Rodriguez.

Unbelievable epiphytes
With no time to spare, Crossan, Huttleston, and the students left the capital for San Vito de Java early the next morning. "We drove south through the mountains on so-called Pan-American Highway," noted Crossan (1969). "The road was very poor, mostly unpaved and often barely passable. We stopped over the course of the eleven-hour drive at various altitudes to botanize and collect soil and plant specimens." Despite countless potholes, mud,

Huttleston, Longwood's taxonomist, led the 1969 trip to Costa Rica. Photo by Gottlieb A. Hampfler.

The Wilsons' home on the hill at Las Cruces, seen through the fronds of tree ferns. Photo by Walter H. Hodge.

rock slides, and fords across turbulent streams, the team enjoyed the excellent weather and superb scenery. Some 300 km later they arrived at Las Cruces and the garden of Robert and Catherine Wilson.

"The next six days were spent botanizing in and around Las Cruces," reported Huttleston (1969b). "One walking trip was made to a cloud forest about 4 miles [6.5 km] distant, and on 15 June, we drove about 5 miles [8 km] north to Sabalito to see a large jungle logging operation owned by Vincent Lopez. We were somewhat encumbered during this period by heavy rains which began between one and two every afternoon and not infrequently continued into the night."

Las Cruces was the high point of the trip for all participants, but no one exalted the flora there more than Gerlach (1969): "Because of my interest in epiphytic plants, and more particularly orchids, the mountainous areas with heavy rainfall and the cloud forest were unbelievable. . . . The ecosystems that developed on the various trees were beyond my comprehension—the species of trees, varieties of mosses and lichens, and the plants of higher orders that were involved. . . . And what epiphytes! Never had I thought of an epiphyte as being another tree but we saw clusias that must have been 20 feet [6 m] tall and growing roots 40–60 feet [12–18 m] down to the soil."

From the Wilsons' garden, Huttleston procured a whole array of plants. Among them were bromeliads, including *Guzmania sanguinea* (69629) and *Orthophytum vagans* (69632); gesneriads, such as *Trichantha purpureovittata* (69628) and *Hypocyrta* sp. (69630); and an epiphytic cactus, *Rhipsalis pachyptera* (69635). In addition to plants from the Wilsons' collection, Huttleston himself collected a few around San Vito de Java, including *Gynandropsis pulcherrima* (69621) of Capparaceae and ferns such as *Gleichenia* sp. (69620) and *Pteris altissima* (69636).

Mystified by a parasite

On 19 June, after saying farewells to the Wilsons, "we drove down to the Pacific coast at Golfito," recorded Huttleston (1969b), "and were guided to Coto where we inspected banana plantations and a processing plant. In the afternoon we drove to Palmar Sur and were put up in United Fruit Company guest houses." The following morning the group took off on a long drive to Turrialba. On the way they stopped several times to collect plants

An undetermined *Bomarea* (69625) found by Huttleston on Cerro de la Muerte. Photo by Donald G. Huttleston.

Sugar cane delivered by a bullock cart to a mill near Turrialba. Photo by Walter H. Hodge.

and observe plant associations in San Isidro de El General Valley and the mountains of Cerro de la Muerte. Along the highest stretch of the road through the mountains, at about 3200 m, Huttleston collected seeds of undetermined species of *Bomarea* (69625) and *Oxalis* (69633).

The group reached the Instituto Inter-Americano de Ciencias Agrícolas in Turrialba in the evening. The next morning Erickson and Edilberto Camacho, horticulturist, showed them the grounds of the institute. Crossan (1969) recorded: "We spent the day in the plantings of cocoa, banana, macadamia nuts, palms, coffee, sugar cane, mangoes, and rubber trees, among many kinds of plants to be seen." While inspecting cocoa plantings, Huttleston collected *Oncidium pusillum* (69631), a diminutive epiphytic orchid that he spotted growing on one of the trees.

On 22 June, Huttleston, Crossan, and the graduate students went to Linda Vista, Captain Claude Hope's seed-production nursery at Dolce Nombre near Cartago. Huttleston was particularly impressed by a bright orange-flowered *Thunbergia gibsonii* (69724), which he later requested from Hope, along with twenty-four selections of *Solenostemon scutellarioides* (69803–18, 691004–11) and seven selections of *Browallia speciosa* (69819–25).

The next morning Erickson took the group to the top of Volcán Irazú. Crossan took an interest in observing "the cultivation of very steep hillsides without apparent erosion . . . and the re-colonization of the volcanic slopes by Ericaceae and Gramineae plant species" (Crossan 1969). It was, however, a very different plant that caused quite a stir among the team members.

Hope, founder of Linda Vista, became a leading producer of seeds of bedding plants. Hope came to Costa Rica during World War II to work on establishing plantations of *Cinchona* trees to provide the U.S. Army with quinine in the event that the main source of this drug, the Philippines, fell under Japanese control. Because of his affiliation with the Army, Hope became known in Costa Rica as Captain Hope, or El Capitán Hope. After the *Cinchona* project closed down, Hope remained in Costa Rica, established a program for breeding ornamental plants, and founded Linda Vista. Photo by Russell J. Seibert.

Gerlach remembered that encounter: "On Volcán Irazú it was shocking to find *Psittacanthus americanus,* a parasite, in flower and completely covering a number of oaks giving an appearance of being a totally new type of tree" (Gerlach 1969). Even Huttleston, an experienced botanist, admitted, "I was astounded and quite mystified for awhile by the spectacular parasite which was in full flower. I could not believe it was a mistletoe and parasitic since it dominated huge oaks" (Huttleston 1969a).

On 27 June the group departed San José for a short visit to Mexico City, where they planned to tour Jardín Botánico and other gardens. Three days later, as they flew back to Philadelphia, they were still reminiscing about Costa Rica. "Horticulturally the country seemed to be an oversized greenhouse," Gerlach later wrote (1969). "Windowsill plants suddenly covered acres or became huge specimens."

The slopes of Volcán Irazú east of San José. Photo by Russell J. Seibert.

COSTA RICAN AFFAIR CONTINUES

In 1973 yet another group of students who were enrolled in the Longwood Graduate Program headed south for a three-week study tour to Costa Rica. Six students—William Graham, Robert Haehle, Gary Koller, Herbert Orange, Herbert Plankinton, and Patrick Redding — were led by Dr. Richard W. Lighty, professor of the University of Delaware, and Patrick A. Nutt, Longwood's collections foreman. The group departed Philadelphia on 28 May and by way of Miami flew to San José. There they were met by Robert Wilson of the Jardín Botánico Wilson in Las Cruces, who would guide and assist the group for much of the trip.

Rainy afternoons in San José

"Our arrival coincided with the wet season," remembers Nutt. "In fact it rained nearly every day we were there, usually in the afternoon. During the dry winter months the clouds from the Caribbean are halted at the summits of the highest mountains but are driven down the Pacific slopes for a short distance. It is easy to see how the moisture is distributed in the mountains. On the lower slopes in winter, the fields are dry, but at a certain level the dust in the road disappears and the ground becomes progressively wetter and wetter. Immediately one notices that every tree is laden with orchids, bromeliads, and other

A parasitic *Psittacanthus americanus* was seen in full bloom on Volcán Irazú. Photo by Donald G. Huttleston.

epiphytes. It is to this line that the clouds and mist descend at night."

On the early morning of 30 May, Wilson led the group on their first excursion to explore the slopes of Volcán Irazú. Later, back in San José, the group met with Rodriguez at the Universidad de Costa Rica. "He was famous for his beautiful water color paintings of orchids," recalls Nutt, "and obviously a severe critic of indiscriminate collection, exploitation and sale of native orchids.

Lighty examines the huge leaves of a plant of *Gunnera insignis* encountered on the slopes of Volcán Irazú. Photo by Patrick A. Nutt.

A street vendor in San José sells *Oncidium* orchids. Photo by Patrick A. Nutt.

The turbulent waters of Río Reventazón, near Turrialba. Photo by Walter H. Hodge.

We actually saw evidence of this in San José, with street vendors offering bundles of bare-rooted orchids." Lighty was taken by Rodriguez's many talents: "He spent two hours grounding our group in the geological, biological, historical, and cultural characteristics of Costa Rica, which put much of what we were to experience into a solid context."

Seat of learning and research

The following morning, Lighty, Nutt, Wilson, and the students left for Turrialba to spend several days at the Instituto Inter-Americano de Ciencias Agrícolas. "This is an outstanding institution and seat of learning and research," remembers Nutt. "I was very impressed with the staff and the student body representing many nationalities. We had a gracious host in Erickson, who was of a

great assistance in guiding us around the huge institution and trial plots."

Nutt recalls also meeting with Camacho: "In 1970 we successfully fruited the breadfruit, *Artocarpus altilis,* in Longwood's conservatories, but I had failed in propagating it from regular stem cuttings; the tissue seeming too pithy. When I told Camacho about our lack of success with the breadfruit, he bravely donned his British Wellington rubber boots and we went out to one of the plots in the pouring rain where he skillfully demonstrated how to propagate it from root and then progressively stem cuttings. This acquired method was used successfully at Longwood later."

In the institute's cafeteria, which, in Nutt's words, "resembled a boot camp but offered much better food," the group met with Dr. Leslie R. Holdridge, the princi-

An imposing inflorescence of *Aechmea mariae-reginae,* found by Lighty and Nutt on Volcán Turrialba and in Las Cruces. Photo by Russell J. Seibert.

pal investigator on campus and a recognized authority on the forest vegetation of Central America. One of Holdridge's widely acclaimed accomplishments was devising a system for classifying vegetation types around the world, which became known as Holdridge life zones. He explained to the Longwood group how this life zone classification had found practical use in large-scale land-use development in Latin America, where more than a dozen countries, at the request of their governments, had been mapped in terms of Holdridge's system.

On 1 June, as Nutt recalls, "A group of us trekked down from the Instituto to the turbulent Río Reventazón, famous for white water rafting but also possessing a grim reputation for drownings. We were searching for a cycad, *Zamia skinneri,* and thanks mainly to Lighty's observation skills, we spotted a number of small plants and judiciously collected several (73860). One plant from this collection, by then a 120 cm specimen, was later donated to the Fairchild Tropical Garden in Miami, Florida, and planted in their rare plant house."

The next day the group climbed the nearby Volcán Turrialba, 3329 m, examined the Indian village ruins at Gyayaba, and collected a number of plants. "Only a few meters from the burial mounds were magnificent specimens of *Aechmea mariae-reginae,*" remembers Nutt. "Longwood had successfully grown this bromeliad but never so showy. I remember reading accounts from travelers flying over Costa Rica in the late 1920s and spotting colonies of this plant growing in the crown shafts of forest trees."

On 3 June the group said farewells to their hosts in Turrialba and headed back to San José. On the way they stopped in Cartago to pay a visit to Las Cóncavas, the garden estate of Charles H. Lankester, who had died in 1969. One of the plants received from Lankester's garden was *Dieffenbachia oerstedtii* (73809), notable for its leaves decorated with attractive lighter green markings. "Lankester was well loved by the Costa Ricans and he generously 'ploughed' back profits from his coffee plantation into his garden," recalls Nutt. "He possessed a wide knowledge of natural history. In botany, his special field has been orchids, which he hunted assiduously in the mountains and lowlands."

Forest in the clouds

The group's next destination was the Jardín Botánico Wilson, Wilson's garden at Las Cruces. As Nutt remembers, "the trip to San Vito was not without complications. The Pan-American Highway, although a good route, is not up to the standard of a North American turnpike! Our bus was held up for a considerable time by a rock slide, followed soon after by a blown tire. We took advantage of the delays to do some botanizing on the surrounding hills."

The group arrived in Las Cruces on 6 June. "After a most interesting tour of the gardens and propagation facilities," says Nutt, "we climbed to a nearby cloud forest in spite of rain. Thank goodness for light-weight rain gear! The head gardener, Bruce McAplin, was our guide. We collected some filmy ferns, *Heliconia tortuosa* (73816), and a superior form of *Guzmania angustifolia* (73813). We also collected a most unusual member of the gesneriad family, a remarkable *Columnea florida* (73861)."

Meticulously maintained gardens around houses of staff members of the United Fruit Company in Golfito. Photo by Patrick A. Nutt.

Unusual markings on the leaves of *Columnea florida* (73861), an epiphytic gesneriad found by Lighty and Nutt in the cloud forest above Las Cruces. Photo by Patrick A. Nutt.

A nursery of the United Fruit Company in Golfito, well stocked with ornamental plants. Photo by Patrick A. Nutt.

Lighty and Nutt's finds in the cloud forest were supplemented with many plants acquired from fabulously rich collections maintained at the Jardín Botánico Wilson. A wide array of plants procured there included many bromeliads, such as an imposing *Aechmea mariae-reginae* (73785), seen previously on Volcán Turrialba; *Guzmania sanguinea* (73815), with red leaves surrounding yellow flowers; and several neoregelias, including *Neoregelia* 'Catherine Wilson' (73826). Among the other plants acquired were ferns, *Diplazium atirrense* (73810), *Nephrolepis pendula* (73827), and *Odontosoria gymnogrammoides* (73829); orchids, *Lycaste macrophylla* ssp. *xanthocheila* (74600), *Oncidium cabagrae* (76107), and *O. globuliferum* (76108); and a couple of shrubs, including *Acnistus arborescens* (73783) of the family Solanaceae,

valued for its prolific honey-fragrant flowers and yellow-orange berries. Lighty recalls that *Acnistus* was noted "for its use seen in Las Cruces and Turrialba, where because of its thick, ridged, and spongy bark it proved an excellent substrate for epiphytic orchids. It was employed for this purpose either as cut limbs assembled as a supporting structure, or as a living small tree on which the orchids and bromeliads were tied with a bit of sphagnum moss. It was in the latter way that it was used at Longwood."

From Golfito to Cerro de la Muerte

On 8 June the group left Las Cruces and drove southwest to the coast of Golfo Dulce, where they stopped in Golfito at the headquarters of the United Fruit Company. "The highlight of our trip to Golfito was a tour with the highly skilled propagator of the nursery operated by the United Fruit Company," remembers Nutt. "The nursery

Fruits of mangosteen, *Garcinia mangostana* (73812), collected in Golfito. Photo by Patrick A. Nutt.

Blechnum buchtienii (73795), a dwarf tree fern resembling a cycad, was collected by Lighty and Nutt on Cerro de la Muerte. Photo by Patrick A. Nutt.

The misty habitat of *Puya dasylirioides* (73837) on Cerro de la Muerte. Photo by Patrick A. Nutt.

was established to provide lush plant material for the homes of staff members. Lavishly planted and very well landscaped, it featured most incredible hedges of uniform cycads, *Cycas revoluta*. We were also very impressed with the mature sealing wax palms, *Cyrtostachys lakka,* luring the passersby with their beautifully red-colored stems." From the nursery in Golfito, Lighty and Nutt obtained seeds of *Garcinia mangostana* (73812), mangosteen, a tree bearing fruits filled with delicious pulp.

During their journey back from Golfito to San José, the group stayed overnight at San Isidro de El General, described by Nutt as "a real ranching town." The next morning they set out for a hike on Cerro de la Muerte, 3491 m, in the mountains north of the town. As Nutt recalls, it was "considered the highlight of the whole trip. I was glad we brought suitable clothing. The fine mist is

described by the native very accurately as *pelo de gato* or cat fur. On Cerro de la Muerte, temperature may drop below freezing at night and thin ice may form, but snow is apparently rare. We botanized extensively, taking care not to fall into the wettest bog areas. Our search was rewarded finally by spotting the giant bromeliad *Puya dasylirioides* (73837) in full flower with some plants containing seed pods, and a dwarf tree fern, *Blechnum buchtienii* (73795), strongly resembling a cycad. We judiciously collected a little seed of *Puya* and pups of the fern. Unfortunately, neither fared too successfully at Longwood. I postulate that had we enjoyed air-conditioning plus a mist system, we may have been more successful. Other plants collected at this altitude often commence to wilt and suffer at sea level and higher temperatures."

Under Captain Hope's wing
Upon their return to San José on 10 June, the group visited Linda Vista, Captain Hope's seed-producing nursery. Hope shared with Lighty and Nutt cuttings of several plants, among them *Jacobinia umbrosa* (73818). One plant in particular caught Nutt's attention. "On entering the nursery," he remembers, "I spotted a superior red-flowered clone of *Pentas lanceolata* (73832), commonly called the Egyptian star cluster, probably a tetraploid form. Cuttings were taken and it proved to be a very successful pot plant subject for display at Longwood, both indoors and outdoors."

Hope's botanical interests went far beyond producing seeds of bedding plants. He led the group on a trip to a

The smallest of the Central American republics, just under 21,000 km², El Salvador is crossed from northwest to southeast by mountain ranges with many volcanic peaks, the highest being Monte Cristo, 2418 m. Between the mountain ranges is a semitropical plateau, averaging 600 m, broken by numerous fertile river valleys. Between the coastal mountain range and the Pacific is a narrow, low plain. With an area of more than 112,000 km², Honduras is the second largest country of Central America. Although it is the most mountainous country in Central America, it is also curiously the only one that has no volcanoes. The Central American Cordillera runs through the country from northwest to southeast. The tallest peaks—several exceeding 3000 m—are in the southern region. The broad northern coastal plain extends inland from the Caribbean Sea. Honduras has several large rivers, countless streams, and several coastal lakes. El Salvador and Honduras have a marked rainy season between May and October. During the dry season that follows, many trees lose their leaves, as much of the vegetation is deciduous. Evergreen forests are found at the higher elevation, where there is enough moisture year-round.

nearby nature preserve at Tapantí in the beautiful Orosi Valley, which, in Nutt's assessment, showed Hope's many virtues as "a master plantsman and ecologist." Lighty and Nutt naturally did not return from Tapantí empty-handed. Among the plants collected there were *Guzmania monostachya* (73814), a bromeliad with bright red bracts; *Ludwigia octovalvis* (73820), a yellow-flowered member of Onagraceae; and *Stachytarpheta frantzii* (73846) of Verbenaceae, producing spikes of dark purple flowers.

The following couple of days were dedicated to visits to a number of private gardens and nurseries in the vicinity of San José. The trip's final day was spent "thoroughly cleaning all the media from plants collected, in fact, anything questionable, and also cleaning the seed collected," recalls Nutt. "This was well worthwhile, as on 18 June, when we passed through the USDA inspection station in Miami, we were commended for cleanliness, and only two plants had to undergo quarantine." In addition to assuring that all the plant material was spotless, Lighty and Nutt employed various strategies to preserve the viability of cuttings and seeds. "Just before we got into the vehicle to take us to the airport," explains Lighty, "we ate the delicious pulp of the fruits of *Garcinia mangostana* collected at Golfito, and packaged the seeds in moist toweling. The care taken proved worthwhile because the seed germinated quickly when sown at Longwood."

EXPANDING THE SCOPE

Following the successful organization of tropical study tours in Costa Rica, Seibert envisioned expanding the scope of these tours by including other Central American countries. In 1971 he targeted El Salvador and Honduras, and planned a three-week trip that would allow him to combine plant collecting in these countries with arranging another tropical study tour for Longwood students.

Small marvel of El Salvador

Seibert and his wife, Isabelle, landed in San Salvador on 7 January. Dr. Ernest P. Imle, agricultural administrator at the American Embassy, welcomed them and assisted the Seiberts during their travels in El Salvador. The following morning, after paying a visit to the embassy, the Seiberts and Imle drove to Santa Tecla, some 13 km east of the city, to meet with the staff of the U.S. Agency for International Development and to tour the nurseries there.

On 9 January the Seiberts took a rocky road to the top of the volcano San Salvador, 1893 m. Coffee plantations covered the lower slopes of the volcano, while the roadsides were lined with "little shacks . . . made of cardboard boxes to house itinerant labor families picking coffee" (I. L. Seibert 1971). Upon reaching the top, the Seiberts descended the opposite side, over large, black lava beds, to the town of Quezaltepeque. On their return

Picturesque tree ferns surround the pools of Los Chorros near San Salvador. Photo by Russell J. Seibert.

Imle, left, and Vilanova admire *Platycerium* grown at Vilanova's nursery in Santa Tecla. Photo by Russell J. Seibert.

The lower slopes of San Vicente, east of San Salvador, are put into agricultural use, while the peak of the volcano is covered by cloud forest. Photo by Russell J. Seibert.

Loading mangrove firewood on oxcarts for transport to Los Jiotes, near La Unión on the coast of El Salvador. Photo by Russell J. Seibert.

to San Salvador, they stopped at Los Chorros to admire a series of spectacular, natural pools and waterfalls, fed by spring water from overhanging volcanic cliffs.

On 12 January, Seibert set off on an excursion to San Vicente, 2181 m, a volcano located about 60 km east of San Salvador, with a summit covered by dense cloud forest; and then south to the coastal town of La Libertad. He and Imle left on a trip to mangrove swamps along the coast. They first drove to La Unión, at the eastern tip of El Salvador, where they arranged for a boat that would take them on an all-day ride through the mangrove forests. The mangroves in El Salvador are so large that they even incited some interest as a source of valuable timber. Despite this use, these forests are still relatively well represented, as about 40 percent of their cover remains untouched.

Upon his return to San Salvador, Seibert went back to Santa Tecla and dedicated the next morning to examining plants grown in a nursery of Tomás Vilanova. He collected there an undetermined species of *Agave* (7154), a short, miniature type with yellow flowers, and *Aristolochia littoralis* (7155), a slender woody climber with flowers to 10 cm across, rich purple, marked with white veins, producing curious fruits that look like an "open parachute," as Seibert remarked in his field notes. The next day the Seiberts departed for Honduras.

Nature-lover's paradise

After landing in Tegucigalpa, the capital of Honduras, the Seiberts headed down a twisty, dusty gravel road to Zamorano, an hour's drive east, to the Escuela Agrícola Panamericana. This school offers three-year, high-school-level programs in all phases of agriculture. At Zamorano the Seiberts were welcomed by Robert P. Armour, director, who showed them the school's grounds and facilities. Russell Seibert expressed hope that a group of Longwood graduate students would be able to visit the Escuela Agrícola Panamericana during their tropical study tour in June of that year.

On 20 January, Seibert joined Antonio Molina, horticulturist at the Escuela, on an excursion to the nearby Montaña Uyuca, 2004 m, where a biological reserve had been set up to protect a tract of cloud forest. He spent the following day browsing through the collection of plants cultivated at the Escuela, while Isabelle set off for the hills, driving along a road that was "a narrow bed of ruts and boulders," as she explained (1971), to San Antonio de Oriente. "The little town used to mine silver and gold, and the hillsides were pitted with holes. The church dominated the red tile roofs clinging to the cliff. Little children led us around, providing a key to the church, which has a priest only once a year." In the cemetery next to the church, Isabelle found the grave of Paul C. Standley (1884–1963), a prominent American botanist and author of numerous Latin American floras. In 1950 Standley moved to the Escuela Agrícola Panamericana, where he worked until his retirement in 1957.

In the meantime, Seibert's hunt for interesting conservatory plants in Zamorano resulted in several collections. Among them were *Canarium ovatum* (7157), known as pili nut, native to the Philippines and the source of elemi oil; *Browallia speciosa* (7156), a shrubby member of Solanaceae with deep blue flowers; and *Lager-*

Molina, horticulturist at the Escuela Agrícola Panamericana in Zamorano, guided Seibert through a cloud forest reserve on Montaña Uyuca. Photo by Russell J. Seibert.

stroemia speciosa (7161), a tree native to tropical Asia, producing large panicles of purple or white flowers.

On 22 January the Seiberts returned to Tegucigalpa to catch a half-hour flight to San Pedro Sula, the second largest city of Honduras, situated near the border with Guatemala. Two days later they met John D. Dickson, plant pathologist at the Division of Tropical Research of the Tela Railroad Company, a subsidiary of United Fruit Company. Dickson offered to take the Seiberts to Lancetilla, a plant introduction garden of the United Fruit Company, near Tela, on the coast of the Gulf of Honduras. The ride to Tela turned out to be "a real disaster," noted Isabelle (1971), who "could not believe the road could be so bad." Tightly packed in Dickson's pickup truck, covered by "an inch thick" of dust, and feeling like "a milkshake," they reached Tela in late afternoon.

In order to reach Lancetilla, the Seiberts boarded a railroad car in Tela. Photo by Russell J. Seibert.

An avenue of Cuban royal palm, *Roystonea regia*, graces Jardín Botánico Lancetilla. Photo by Walter H. Hodge.

Their trip to Lancetilla continued the next morning. Since in those days the only way to the garden was "to walk or ride the tracks" (I. L. Seibert 1971), the Seiberts and Dickson boarded a little automobile modified with railroad-car-like wheels. Lancetilla, one of the United Fruit Company's experiment stations, was started in 1926 by Wilson Popenoe, an agricultural explorer specializing in Latin American neotropical crops, credited with introducing and popularizing the use of avocados in American kitchens. "Truly a magnificent collection of ornamentals," wrote Isabelle Seibert of Lancetilla. "But the Company lost interest and it is going down hill."

Fortunately the garden, which Isabelle considered "a nature-lover's paradise" (1971), was saved from neglect and is known today as Jardín Botánico Lancetilla. Located at the mouth of the river Lancetilla, only a few kilometers from Tela, Lancetilla is among the world's largest tropical botanical gardens. The word *Lancetilla* is derived from the local name of an indigenous palm, *Astrocaryum standleyanum*. The garden is known especially for its collection of tropical and subtropical fruit trees, said to be the largest in the Western Hemisphere.

Seibert was especially interested in some highly decorative heliconias grown at Lancetilla. He collected *Heliconia mariae* (7158), a large plant about 6 m tall, producing 1 m long pendant inflorescences with blood-red bracts. Among the other plants collected in the garden were *Aphelandra hartwegiana* (7164), native to Panama and Colombia, and *Clitoria fairchildiana,* native to Brazil.

The couple returned to Tela before dark. On the morning of 26 January they headed back—in the same,

much dreaded pickup truck—to San Pedro Sula, making a brief stop at La Lima. While at La Lima, Russell Seibert received an urgent phone call and was told his mother had suffered a stroke. He decided to cut the trip short and immediately returned to the United States. The Seiberts managed to catch a flight from San Pedro Sula to Belize, and from there to Saint Louis by way of Miami. On the early morning of 27 January, they reached Belleville, Illinois, to find Seibert's mother quite alert and fine.

CLOUDBERRIES AND THE CLOUD FOREST

Four months after Seibert's return, a group of Longwood Program graduates—Gordon E. Buswell, Edward Depoto, Loretta Hodyss, and Frederick E. Roberts—led by Lighty and Lois W. Paul, Longwood's education supervisor, traveled to Central America to retrace his steps.

The group left Philadelphia on 31 May 1971, stopping first in Miami for what Seibert called "a tropical plant indoctrination" (1970c). As Lighty explains, "The primary purpose of this trip was to expose Longwood graduate fellows to tropical agriculture, horticulture and human culture. To do this we began the trip with two days visiting horticultural facilities in the Miami area, principally Fairchild Tropical Garden and the USDA Plant Introduction Station. Fairchild Tropical Garden served as an introduction to important woody and herbaceous ornamentals in the pan-tropical plant palette, while the Plant Introduction Station exposed us to the wealth of tropical and subtropical economic plants we might see later."

A well thought-out institution

Unlike Seibert, who began his trip in El Salvador, Lighty's group flew first to Honduras. On 3 June their plane landed in Tegucigalpa. They were met by Armour, headmaster of the Escuela Agrícola Panamericana. "Armour saw us through customs, then put us in cars for a trip over dusty roads to Zamorano," remembers Lighty. "In the dry countryside along the way, we saw little agriculture, but noted the native pines were being tapped in the traditional destructive way, by periodic enlargement of notches, cut in the trunk with machetes, to renew the flow of resin. We noted a number of terrestrial xerophytic bromeliads and orchids in an otherwise barren landscape. Occasionally we passed coffee *fincas* where the coffee is grown by small landholders. These used orange trees and other fruits to provide the shade needed for the coffee plants."

The Escuela was founded by Wilson Popenoe, an American botanist, who earlier established and developed the introduction garden of the United Fruit Company at Lancetilla. "Popenoe spent a life in plant introduction, first as a protégé of the renowned explorer David G. Fairchild, and later as a research scientist for the United Fruit Company," explains Lighty. "Popenoe, a legend in his own time, died in 1975, and I have always regretted not meeting him on this trip. With regularity, our questions about how some plant had reached Central America, or how some important horticultural venture had begun was answered with 'Wilson Popenoe.' At Zamorano we stayed in Casa Popenoe, the Spanish colonial home Popenoe had occupied during his tenure as founding director."

Trekking through the cloud forest on Montaña Uyuca are, left to right, Lighty, Molina, Paul, Roberts, Buswell, Hodyss, and Depoto. Photo by Richard W. Lighty.

The days spent at Zamorano were filled with tours of the facilities and places of botanical, agricultural, and horticultural note. "The school is remote from any large towns, and was tightly run," recalls Lighty. "It is a self-sufficient operation with its own large generator to serve when outside power fails, a dairy, creamery, vegetable and agronomic crop production, slaughterhouse and other facilities which provide the practical experience to counter-balance the classroom training. Altogether a well thought-out institution."

The next day the group met Molina for a trip to a virgin cloud forest atop the nearby Montaña Uyuca. "A dark and misty trail passed through forests of enormous avocados, *Persea americana,* and oaks, hung with lianas, the tops of which were lost in the mist; where every surface was covered with mosses, lichens, filmy ferns, pepperomias, bromeliads, begonias and plants with no names we knew," remembers Lighty. "At the top, a caretaker lived and had a small plantation of cloudberry, *Rubus macrocarpus,* a most sweet and delicious fruit borne abundantly in the perpetual cool mist. Also found in this area were *Ostrya* sp. and *Carpinus caroliniana,* which we were told were native, and exotics planted for teaching purposes, such as apples, peaches, quince and *Pinus strobus.* Here, at 1500 m, we made our first collections, including several bromeliads and an orchid, *Pleurothallis grobyi* (71895)."

On 6 June, Lighty, Paul, and the students got an early start, going to the stables to mount ponies for the ride up to San Antonio de Oriente, a colonial village whose red

The village of San Antonio de Oriente, overlooking Zamorano Valley, Honduras. Photo by Richard W. Lighty.

Lighty found this diminutive orchid, *Oncidium pusillum* (71879), growing as an epiphyte in Jardín Botánico Lancetilla. Photo by Walter H. Hodge.

tile roofs were celebrated in the paintings of José Antonio Velásquez. One such painting was displayed at Casa Popenoe. "It was a rugged ride, but on horseback we had time to observe the age-old agriculture of small subsistence farms in what was an infertile and over-farmed landscape tended by impoverished people," remembers Lighty. "The village turned out to be as romantically beautiful as Velásquez' oil painting above the fireplace at Casa Popenoe had promised. Buswell collected an undetermined species of *Philodendron* (71881) here. The return was quicker than the journey out, as the ponies anticipated their feed and broke into an exhilarating gallop upon reaching the valley floor."

Another excursion with Molina took Lighty, Paul, and the students to the rim of the Zamorano Valley to view the typical landscape of the Honduran hinterland. "It was a dry countryside, sparsely treed with oaks and *Pinus caribaea*," remembers Lighty. "The oaks had a wonderful epiphytic flora of orchids and bromeliads, but the pines were being mutilated in the same way as those seen along the road from Tegucigalpa. We returned in time to go to a mid-day dinner at the home of a Peruvian instructor, Señor Julio Luga, for a 'typical meal' of several chicken dishes, peas, carrots, rice and beans, fresh tomatoes and lettuce, with beer as a beverage and topped off with cake for dessert. All the food was produced at the school. In the evening we were honored at dinner in Casa Popenoe—complete with after-dinner drinks. We reciprocated with gifts of good scotch whiskey we had brought for the purpose."

Keeping ahead of the dust

The next morning the group said good-byes to their generous hosts in Zamorano and headed to the airport to catch a flight to San Pedro Sula. "The trip was short and uneventful," remembers Lighty, "but the take-off was exciting. The runway was a narrow asphalt pad between sheer rock cliffs. Scattered along the base of each were the remains of many airplanes—engines, severed wings, pieces of fuselage, landing gears and propellers—enough to make several whole airplanes, we surmised. We speculated as to whether these were the result of the recent war between Honduras and El Salvador, or the poor judgment of pilots!"

Upon landing at San Pedro Sula, the group was met by Dickson, who had accompanied the Seiberts to Lancetilla earlier that year. Together they drove to La Lima, where they stopped for lunch at the United Fruit Company hotel. "It was like something out of a 1940's Humphrey Bogart movie," recalls Lighty. "Slowly revolving ceiling fans, narrow, natural-finish wainscoting, darkened by the years, and the close smell of perpetual humidity. We enjoyed a lunch of good seafood before setting off for Tela in Dickson's pickup. The women rode in the cab and men in the open bed. We traveled rapidly to keep ahead of the dust, and stopped only to buy some pineapples from a roadside vendor."

In Tela, Lighty, Paul, and the students checked into a motel, and the next day headed to the nearby Lancetilla. "The introduction garden in Lancetilla was the main research collection for the United Fruit Company in its heyday," explains Lighty. "Here research was carried out on new sorts of tropical economic crops which could be exploited by the Company. We traveled the short distance from Tela to the Lancetilla Valley by open work truck on a railroad spur. The tracks took us through thickets of *Heliconia* sp. and into an enormous tunnel formed by a grove of *Dendrocalamus giganteus.* As we came out of the tunnel, the arboretum lay around and ahead of us. At that time, the Company was pulling out of plantation agriculture, at least so far as banana production was concerned, and the arboretum was no longer important to it economically. It was still the largest collection of tropical economic plants in the Americas, but was being maintained largely by mowing. Pigs were running freely through the mature collections, while the forest had retaken much of the intensively cultivated experimental planting areas."

Having procured several plants from Lancetilla's enormous collection, among them orchids *Oncidium pusillum* (71879) and *Campylocentrum micranthum* (71899), Lighty and his group said goodbye to Dickson on 12 June. Following a swerving takeoff down a potholed runway, they flew the short distance back to San Pedro Sula. "We had most of the day to explore the city, its markets and suburbs and to get a feel for the life of a small city," recalls Lighty. "The next day we were driven to Copán de Maya, the enormous Mayan ruin that was in an early stage of excavation at that time. The three-hour trip took us through a mountainous agricultural region where we saw much overuse of the land through cropping of steep slopes and burning. Though only a small part of the center of Copán had been excavated, we were still impressed by the scale, the architecture, and its ornamentation."

Cloud forest of Monte Cristo

On 14 June the group departed San Pedro Sula and flew to San Salvador via Guatemala City. Direct flights were still prohibited in the wake of the conflict between Honduras and El Salvador. "Upon landing in San Salvador," remembers Lighty, "we were met by Gerald M. Garvey, an American forester who had come to El Salvador in the Peace Corps, married a Salvadoran and remained. He was our guide throughout our stay in El Salvador. We checked into a pension in a quiet and settled residential district of San Salvador, then went to hear a friend of Garvey's speak on the fauna of Central America. He painted a dim picture of devastation and extinction."

"On 16 June, taking a bare minimum of baggage, we set off at 5:30 a.m. for Metapán, a town in the north of

A restored section of Mayan ruins in Copán. Photo by Walter H. Hodge.

El Salvador," recalls Lighty. "On the way we passed many volcanoes and ancient cinder cones. After settling in at our accommodations, we met Garvey's wife, Chavah, and drove with her to her father's fruit farm. There we all piled into a four-wheel-drive truck and drove part way up the side of Monte Cristo, 2418 m, the highest mountain in El Salvador, to an old hacienda which had fallen into disrepair. It was a huge estate with extensive waterworks, and with many farmers now eking out a living as squatters. It had been self-sufficient to the point of having an iron foundry and a coffee *beneficio.* Growing on the place were a number of minor tropical fruits including *Spondias mombin* and several species of *Annona,* but by and large, nature had reclaimed much of the landscape. There we collected an undetermined species of *Euphorbia* (71872), planted as a hedge around the *beneficio* and which had persisted from the hacienda's heyday.

Huts of hacienda workers on Monte Cristo. Photo by Richard W. Lighty.

A run-down hacienda on the slopes of Monte Cristo. Photo by Richard W. Lighty.

In the mangroves along the shore of Bay of Jiquilisco are, clockwise from top, Buswell, Roberts, Paul, Depoto, and Hodyss. Photo by Richard W. Lighty.

"The next day we retraced our path to the hacienda where we transferred to a tougher vehicle suitable for the very rough and very winding dirt road to the summit of Monte Cristo, where Guatemala, Honduras and El Salvador come together. There we saw dramatic changes in the flora as we went up and down the mountain. At one point we saw trees that looked like *Liquidambar styraciflua*. They were, thereby, confirming the amazing distribution of this temperate tree—from the coast of Connecticut to the mountains of Central America."

Lighty collected a number of plants in the cloud forest around the summit of Monte Cristo. Among them were *Cavendishia guatemalensis* var. *chiapensis* (71878), *Roldana chapalensis* (71902), and a couple of orchids. Just below the summit he found several ferns, including *Pityrogramma dealbata* (71882), *P. triangularis* (71883), and *Polypodium pumilum* (71885).

Mangroves of the Bay of Jiquilisco

Upon returning from the escapade on Monte Cristo, the group changed vehicles and headed back to San Salvador. The following morning they met M. L. Rocher, a French forester who had spent his life working on mangroves in French Indochina, and who, when the French were forced out, had come to El Salvador to continue his work. "We drove with Rocher to the coast of the Bay of Jiquilisco," remembers Lighty, "where we rented a boat for a three-hour tour of black, white and red mangrove swamps—*Avicennia*, *Laguncularia*, and *Rhizophora*, respectively. The swamps, particularly those of the red mangrove, were not only highly productive in an ecological sense, but were most beautiful in their simplicity. At one point several of us volunteered to wade chest-deep in the dark water to push and guide the boat through the massive tangles of stilt roots. On our trip back we stopped at a Pacific Ocean beach for a swim and a taste of coconut jelly. We noted *Cocos nucifera* with double trunks, a rather rare occurrence. On the way back to San Salvador we collected several species of xerophytic, terrestrial bromeliads growing on an ancient lava flow, some of them showing off their orange or bright red bracts."

With only a couple of days remaining, the group stayed in and around San Salvador. "On 19 June we called on Tomás Vilanova in Santa Tecla," recalls Lighty. "Don Tomás was a manager of coffee plantations and a *beneficio* for TACA airline, and a wealthy patron of the arts, knowledgeable gardener, hybridizer, and nurseryman. He grew an enormous variety of tropical ornamentals including orchids, platyceriums, codiaeums and anthuriums. We were given cuttings of several of

A rare double-trunked *Cocos nucifera* in a coconut plantation along the Pacific coast of El Salvador. Photo by Richard W. Lighty.

One of the xerophytic, terrestrial bromeliads found growing on a seventy-year-old lava flow on the volcano San Salvador. Photo by Richard W. Lighty.

Vilanova's *Hibiscus rosa-sinensis* selections (71874) which had been requested by Seibert on his earlier visit in January."

On their last day in El Salvador, the group went to a beautifully landscaped resort on Cerro Verde where they observed a nearby active volcano, Izalco, 1950 m. "On the wooded slopes of Cerro Verde we found *Lopezia racemosa* (71876)," remembers Lighty. "We then visited a city park in San Salvador and climbed to a place called Puerto del Diablo where we had a grand view of the city and collected several gesneriads, including *Kohleria* sp. (71875) with yellow flowers, *Achimenes erecta* (71865) with red flowers, and another one with white flowers (71866)." Early next morning, while still reminiscing about the grand views from Puerto del Diablo and lush slopes of Cerro Verde, Lighty and his group arose early for a flight to Guatemala City. From there they flew to Philadelphia by way of Miami, returning home presumably feeling fully indoctrinated with regard to tropical plants.

Vilanova with his collection of rare anthuriums in Santa Tecla. Photo by Richard W. Lighty.

SOUTH AMERICA

DESIRE FOR DATURAS

From the very beginning, the focus for Longwood's exploration has been centered on bringing into the garden plants which might prove to be outstanding ornamentals. No wonder that when in 1956 Dr. Walter H. Hodge, Longwood's head of education and research, learned about taxonomical work on *Datura,* commonly known as angel's trumpets, being carried out in Colombia by Arthur S. Barclay, doctoral candidate, and Dr. Richard E. Schultes, professor, both from Harvard University, he wrote to them offering Longwood's support to collect seeds and cuttings of these plants.

Handsome reds wanted

Three species of *Datura, D. arborea, D. suaveolens,* and *D. versicolor,* as well as a closely related *Methysticodendron amesianum,* all currently classified as species of *Brugmansia,* were already successfully grown in Longwood's greenhouses. Hodge thought that a number of other shrubby and small tree types of *Datura* would make desirable conservatory plants: "Since this genus does so well here at Longwood under glass, we would like to have more variety if possible, and I know that the red-flowered species would be especially handsome if we could get the right clone" (1958a).

As he explained in a letter to Schultes, Longwood was not "anxious to become a repository for a complete *Datura* collection," yet it wanted all showy materials (Schultes 1956b). This posed a certain dilemma to the explorers in Colombia. "All daturas that I know in the Andes are showy, some extremely so," wrote Schultes. "I presume you will want them all." In response Hodge clarified Longwood's priorities, this time to Barclay: "Friend Schultes informs me that practically all the daturas are showy, and so I presume that we may expect materials of anything which you collect. I would like to emphasize that we are particularly interested in having material of any red-flowered items, since we do not have these at present in our conservatories" (Hodge 1956b).

In August of 1956, the news came from Schultes that Barclay's project in Colombia was going along well. After spending the whole of July searching for daturas between Bogotá, Colombia, and Tulcán, Ecuador, they had collected much material of *Datura* ×*candida* (561967, 562117), *D.* ×*dolichocarpa, D. sanguinea* (562120), and *Methysticodendron amesianum,* as well as several plants they could not assign to any known species. "One beautiful red coloured one, found on the slopes of one of the volcanoes, is, I think, a new species," wrote Schultes from Bogotá (1956a). "Different coloured variants of the common species are also turning up."

Anticipating that Barclay may have potential concerns about sharing collected plants, Hodge wrote to him: "I realize, of course, that some of this material you may wish to keep close in hand and not distribute widely until you have completed your studies upon it. On the other hand, I can assure you that here at Longwood none of this material would be in jeopardy if you saw fit to supply us with material for growing on for ornamental

Stretching from the Pacific Ocean to the Caribbean Sea, Colombia covers 1.14 million km², about 0.8 percent of the world's land surface, yet it is home to between forty-five thousand and fifty-one thousand species, or some 15 percent of all plant species. This makes Colombia one of the most biologically diverse regions in the world. One reason for this huge wealth of biological resources is the wide variety of landscapes across the country. The northern end of the Andes cuts through the western and central parts of Colombia, with the highest peak, Cristóbal Colón, reaching 5775 m. To the west of the Andes are the coastal lowlands, to the east the eastern plains. Colombia's climate varies primarily with elevation, the coastal lowlands and eastern plains being the warmest, and the high Andes being the coldest, whereas the seasonal temperature changes are very small. In contrast, the rainfall varies seasonally in most of the country, resulting in one or two wet seasons and one or two dry seasons during the year.

display. Also it would be another place where the species could be available to you for study or for obtaining further propagation material in the event that you lost some of your own" (Hodge 1956a).

Anything but fine red

Hodge was especially interested in receiving a red-flowered *Datura sanguinea*, which he had seen previously flowering in various parts of the Andes. In addition, he requested from Barclay propagation material and seeds of two hybrids, *D.* ×*candida* and *D.* ×*dolichocarpa,* as well as the new red-flowered species Barclay and Schultes discovered. He also urged Barclay not to miss on an opportunity of collecting "any colored variants of the common species which are especially attractive because of flower color" (Hodge 1956a). As a side note, Hodge asked Schultes to keep his "eyes open for any cultivated species of the genus *Anguloa*" (1956c), a Colombian orchid treasured for its unique, tulip-like, fragrant flowers, which Hodge had "been trying to get . . . but without any luck."

Barclay responded enthusiastically to Hodge's request: "I shall do all in my power to accommodate your request with cuttings and seeds of the various arboreal daturas that Dr. Schultes and I encounter" (Barclay 1956). Soon afterward, seeds and cuttings of daturas

The red-flowered *Datura sanguinea* (56121, 562120) collected by Barclay in Colombia turned out to be rather inferior forms of that species. Photo by Russell J. Seibert.

began arriving at Longwood, and a few months later Hodge was able to write to Barclay, "You will be interested to learn that several of your collections are turning out to be attractive additions to our *Datura* collection, and it is hoped that perhaps in the future someone will do a little work on hybridization and improvement, using these materials" (Hodge 1957c). Nevertheless, Hodge's desire for a good form of red-flowered *D. sanguinea* did

Anguloa clowesii (562115) collected by Barclay and Schultes in Colombia. It flowers in spring to early summer with fragrant, brilliant canary-yellow flowers up to 8 cm long on a 30 cm long scape. The flowers have strongly cupped tepals, which is why this plant is commonly called tulip orchid. Photo by Rondel G. Peirson.

Legacy continues

Barclay's research in Colombia came into fruition in 1959 when he published the results in Harvard University's *Botanical Museum Leaflets*. In this article, Barclay described three species of *Datura* new to science, among them the red-flowered beauty, which he found on the slopes of a volcano and named *D. vulcanicola*. "During my field studies of the tree daturas in the Colombian Andes," he wrote (1959), "I was surprised to find on the side of the famous and active Volcán de Puracé [4686 m] populations of what was at once distinguishable as a striking and beautiful new species of the genus." He offered an explanation for the occurrence of *D. vulcanicola* in this particular location: "I am of the opinion that the abundance of individuals at the type locality is probably the result of human activity. . . . We must not overlook the fact that for centuries this agriculturally rich volcanic area has been populated by advanced Indian peoples who are known to have employed daturas as narcotics in their magic and therapeutic practices."

It was not, however, until 1969 that Longwood was able to obtain this new *Datura* from Colombia. The opportunity came about when another of Schultes's graduate students, Tom E. Lockwood, was able to re-collect *D. vulcanicola* (6974) on the slopes of Volcán de Puracé, and sent cuttings and seeds of this species along with several others to Longwood. Three years later visitors at Longwood saw this rare plant displayed in the Rose House.

Hodge's hope for "a little work on hybridization" became reality in the late 1960s when Dr. Robert J. Armstrong, Longwood's geneticist, crossed the best forms of daturas collected by Barclay, *D. arborea* (562146), *D. aurea* (562122), and *D.* ×*candida* (562117), with a dozen of the plants acquired from California, England, and France. None of the progeny, however, surpassed the parent species, and the breeding ended in 1971. Barclay's three daturas, though, continued to be exhibited in the Rose House during the 1970s, the last of them, *D. aurea* (562122), dying in 1979. The legacy of Barclay's expedition remains at Longwood thanks to *Anguloa clowesii*, which appeared first as a digression in Hodge's letter. This orchid, brought back from Bogotá in 1956, can still be viewed in Longwood's conservatories.

not materialize at that time. "*Datura sanguinea* [56121, 562120], collected by you and growing here at Longwood," he wrote to Barclay, "are anything but the fine red color that I remember in plants growing at the Institute at Bogotá."

The disappointment caused by a meager performance of *Datura sanguinea* did not last long, as Schultes brought the good news about the much sought-after orchid: "I was able to get you some very healthy bulbs of *Anguloa clowesii* [562115] which are going to the quarantine people today. It is not uncommon here in Colombia. These I got from a friend's greenhouse" (Schultes 1956c).

Although the five southern states—Rio de Janeiro, São Paulo, Paraná, Santa Catarina, and Rio Grande do Sul—cover only about 10 percent of Brazil's territory, nearly half of the population lives there, and the core of the country's economic activities is concentrated within their boundaries. Most of this region is included within the Paraná plateau in the east and the seaward dissected edge of the Serra do Mar range, which rises steeply from the narrow coastal plain. Behind the northern end of Serra do Mar lies the valley of Paraíba, running parallel to the coast. Flanking the valley on the west is the highest mountain range of Brazil, Serra da Mantiqueira. Further west, the rolling, mountain-studded plateau gradually slopes and merges into the vast plain of the Paraná plateau. The rainfall in most of the upland region of the state of São Paulo ranges from 1000 to 2000 mm, falling mostly in the summer. Because of the dry winter season, much of the plateau is

covered by a tropical, semideciduous forest. The coastal lowlands and seaward slopes of Serra do Mar receive an annual rainfall of 1500 to 3250 mm, which supports a tropical rain forest. The southernmost region, including the states of Paraná, Santa Catarina, and Rio Grande do Sul, has a more temperate climate due to its elevation and latitude. While the coastal tropical forest reaches its southern end a little north of Pôrto Alegre in Rio Grande do Sul, more open stands of Paraná pine, *Araucaria angustifolia*, with an undergrowth of broad-leaved species, replace the tropical, semideciduous forests to the west. Savannas and tall-grass prairies predominate in the southernmost states of Santa Catarina and Rio Grande do Sul.

TRAVERSING THE SOUTHERN STATES OF BRAZIL

In 1957 a proposal was put forward for an expedition with the main purpose to "survey existing plant stocks held by government, private or commercial nurserymen in Argentina and Brazil and procure materials that appear to have promise for use in the United States, particularly species that may be adapted to the milder climates of this country" (Williams 1958). Drafting plans for collecting in Brazil, Dr. Russell J. Seibert, Longwood's director, noted that "of particular interest will be the species of *Tabebuia* and many Melastomataceae which in the southern part of Brazil and adjoining Argentina have sufficient frost tolerance to stand the conditions of southern California" (1958a). Seibert recalled his experience of growing these plants while he directed the Los Angeles

State and County Arboretum in the early 1950s: "The few that we tried in Los Angeles bloomed in containers at a very early age and I am convinced that they would make excellent tub subjects for conservatory work. In general, of very much interest, will be the whole field of brilliantly flowering trees."

Hardy, subtropical, flowering trees were thus chosen as the chief objects for this expedition, but other ornamental plants which could prove hardier than usual were also of great interest. Five southern states of Brazil, namely Rio de Janeiro, São Paulo, Paraná, Santa Catarina, and Rio Grande do Sul, were chosen as the target areas for collecting, with a possible reconnaissance mission to Argentina.

Seibert thought the best-suited candidate to undertake such an expedition would be Dr. Llewelyn Williams, a botanist employed by the USDA, who had "spent many

Williams, a botanist with extensive knowledge of the flora of South America, was selected to conduct the 1958 expedition to southern Brazil. Photo by Llewelyn Williams.

Dictyosperma album (58616) that was collected by Williams in Rio de Janeiro has been growing in Longwood's Palm House since its opening in 1966. Photo by Tomasz Aniśko.

years in Latin America having been with the Chicago Natural History Museum, during which time he prepared the *Woods of Northeastern Peru,* did considerable work with McBride's *Flora of Peru,* spent a great deal of time in Venezuela and, in addition to that, traveled pretty much of the warmer world in connection with the American Chicle Institute" (Seibert 1958b). Williams, an accomplished botanist and seasoned explorer, took on the challenge and prepared for departure in February of 1958.

Rio de Janeiro

The starting point for Williams's expedition was Rio de Janeiro, Brazil's capital until 1960. He arrived on 25 February. "The following morning I proceeded to the Botanical Garden," he recalled (1958). "This famous botanical institution, which will celebrate the 150th anniversary of its foundation next month, was selected as the most logical center to commence the collecting, as it possesses the largest and most varied collections of indigenous and exotic plants to be found anywhere in Latin America. Consent was kindly given by the director, Dr. Paulo

Campos Porto, to gather seed or fruit materials of selected ornamental trees, shrubs, vines, palms, and herbaceous species." A large number of collections, exceeding 230, were procured from the Botanical Garden, or Jardim Botânico. *Dictyosperma album* (58616), *Dypsis lutescens* (58617), and *Etlingera elatior* (581702) are but a few examples.

"On completing my work in Rio," recorded Williams (1958), "I then proceeded to Petrópolis and the surrounding highlands, where I had occasion to gather some fine materials in the private garden of Sr. Guilherme Guinle, an industrialist, who has probably the best and largest collection of *Anthurium* in Brazil or elsewhere. An inspection was also made of the series of orchids, and other ornamental plants, owned by Sr. Waldemar Silva, a short distance out of Petrópolis, and selections were made

Dypsis lutescens (58617), known in Brazil as *palmeira bambu,* was procured by Williams from Rio de Janeiro's Jardim Botânico. Photo by Tomasz Aniśko.

Philodendron verrucosum (581537) was among the many Amazonian plants obtained by Williams at Chácara Santa Rosa, a nursery in São Paulo. Photo by Tomasz Aniśko.

of certain desirable species. The surrounding hills, part of the classical collecting region of Serra dos Orgãos, are particularly rich in bromeliads, of which a number of species were gathered."

As a result of nearly three weeks of collecting in and around Rio, and in the uplands, two large shipments were dispatched. The second contained a wide array of anthuriums from Guinle, including such species as *Anthurium andraeanum* (591263) and *A. scherzerianum* (591277), as well as many of his hybrids (591265–75).

São Paulo and Paraná

Williams's next destination was São Paulo, the largest city in Brazil. "On Sunday, 16 March, I proceeded to São Paulo, and on the following day I visited several private and public gardens and nurseries in the city and neigh-

borhood, including that of Brandli's, Alberto Marques, Pollard's in Brooklyn-Paulista, and the Chácara Santa Rosa, owned by Nicolau Pepi, with a rich collection of indigenous plants, including some interesting species from the Brazilian Amazon region" (Williams 1958). From the garden of Robert L. Pollard in Brooklyn-Paulista, a suburb of São Paulo, Williams acquired *Alstroemeria caryophyllaea* (581468), with delightfully fragrant red-and-white flowers; *Petrea volubilis* (581528), a blue-flowered vine; and *Kohleria eriantha* (591609), a low shrub with attractive leaves marked with reddish brown border venation and large, drooping, cinnabar-red flowers.

"A large and interesting series of ornamental plants was also selected at the Horta da Prefeitura at Manequinho Lopes, under the direction of Sr. Arturo

In the garden of Robert L. Pollard in Brooklyn-Paulista, a suburb of São Paulo, Williams acquired *Alstroemeria caryophyllaea* (581468), which features delightfully fragrant red-and-white flowers. Photo by Tomasz Aniśko.

Etzel," noted Williams (1958). "This extensive nursery, covering about 30 acres [12 hectares], is a division of Parks and Gardens of the City of São Paulo, and specializes in particular in shrubs and small ornamentals." Among the many plants Williams acquired there were *Aglaia odorata* (581466), a tall shrub producing very fragrant flowers; *Cestrum nocturnum* (581486), a shrub valued for its ivory flowers with a cloverlike fragrance; and *Homalocladium platycladum* (581472), known as flatworm plant or ribbon-bush because of its unique flat stems.

Williams was especially pleased with several field trips around São Paulo. One "was made to the fine upland forest zone at Alta da Serra, above Paranapiaçaba, and located about halfway between São Paulo and Santos. This humid forest is composed of a large variety of woody species. Bromeliads are particularly common here also" (1958).

Another plant-collecting area judged by Williams as "outstanding" was in the highlands of the Serra da Bocaína, part of the Serra do Mar, about halfway between São Paulo and Rio, with an elevation ranging between 750 and 900 m. Most of the collecting there was done on the Fazenda Bonita, the property of William Roberto Marinho Lutz. The day at Fazenda Bonita permitted Williams to collect many epiphytes, including bromeliads such as *Billbergia amoena* (581482); orchids, among them *Epidendrum nutans* var. *dipus* (581499); and ferns, such as *Polypodium hirsutissimum* (581540) and *Vittaria pendula* (581571).

In early April, Williams proceeded to Curitiba, capital of the state of Paraná, southwest of São Paulo. The

Petrea volubilis (581528), a blue-flowered vine that Williams obtained from Pollard's garden, has graced Longwood's Rose House for more than forty years. Photo by Rondel G. Peirson.

city is situated on a vast plateau, which embraces nearly all of the states of Paraná and Santa Catarina, and the northern section of Rio Grande do Sul. Accompanied by Gert Hatschbach, "a capable amateur botanist," Williams undertook several excursions from Curitiba. "The first collecting trip," he noted, "was to the Serra São Luiz, with an elevation of about 3000 feet [900 m]. At the foot of and along its slopes the vegetation is composed in the main of thickets, where we encountered small trees and shrubs, such as *Prunus ulei*, *Tibouchina mutabilis* [581557], *Mimosa acerba*. . . . The most distinctive plant found at the summit of the Serra São Luiz was *Quesnelia imbricata* [581541] of the Bromeliaceae, with leaves in dense tufts and very attractive light to deep pinkish flowers. It grows usually in fairly deep shade among rocks" (Williams 1959).

Williams collects an undetermined *Hippeastrum* in the foothills of Serra do Mar near Piraquara, Paraná. Photo by Llewelyn Williams.

Philodendron renauxii (581532), collected by Williams near Corupá in Santa Catarina, is a characteristic plant of the littoral. Photo by Tomasz Aniśko.

Campyloneurum phyllitidis (581539), an epiphytic fern, was collected by Williams near Corupá. Photo by Tomasz Aniśko.

Santa Catarina

From Curitiba, Williams continued southward by road across Serra do Mar to the small coastal town of Itajaí, in the state of Santa Catarina, to visit the Herbarium Barbosa Rodrigues, which housed the most important representation of the flora of the state. Then he decided to proceed overland through Blumenau and Jaraguá do Sul to the little village of Corupá, at the foot of Serra do Mar. "At Corupá," Williams recorded (1959), "Senhor E. J. Eipper, a German immigrant, and his two sons operate a small private nursery with some interesting native plants from the surrounding forests, as well as some unusual exotic species. . . . An early German immigration to this region, as well as to the other areas in the south, has given rise to several distinctly European sections, where the German language and customs still prevail, and the majority of the people are distinctly of Nordic blood."

Accompanied by Eipper, Williams made several collecting excursions to the areas around Rio Paulo, Riberao do Rancho, and the dense, virgin cloud forest that clothes the seaward slope of Serra do Mar. An appreciable and varied collection of ornamental plants was collected there: orchids, including *Cyrtopodium verrucosum* (581523), *Huntleya meleagris* (581507), and *Oncidium flexuosum* (581522); bromeliads, such as *Aechmea calyculata* (581463), *Billbergia speciosa* (581476), and *Vriesea carinata* (581572b); gesneriads, such as *Corytholoma bulbosum* (581489) and *Hypocyrta perianthomega* (581566); and an epiphytic fern, *Campyloneurum phyllitidis* (581539).

Williams found rare *Gunnera manicata* (581431) at Boca da Serra near São Francisco de Paula, Rio Grande do Sul. Photo by Llewelyn Williams.

Rio Grande do Sul

From Corupá, Williams continued farther south, by road, through Joinville to Florianópolis, thence by air to Pôrto Alegre, in the state of Rio Grande do Sul. At the time, the leading authority on the flora of that state was Padre Balduino Rambo of the Colegio Anchieta in Pôrto Alegre. "Accompanied by Padre Rambo we explored the Fazenda Oroya, at Osório, about 100 miles [160 km] north of Pôrto Alegre, considered to be an area representative of the vegetation of the coastal or littoral zone," recorded Williams (1959). His finds there included *Wittrockia superba* (581574), a bromeliad with leaves pink at the tip; and *Ctenanthe muelleri* (581490), a member of Marantaceae inhabiting swamp forests around Osório.

"In addition to the fine cooperation extended by Padre Rambo," wrote Williams (1959), "appreciable assistance was received from Senhor Henrique Hanisch, and his wife, Dona Frida Schonwald Hanisch, who own a nursery on the outskirts of Pôrto Alegre." With Hanisch's help, Williams was able to continue his explorations northward to the plateau region of Serra Geral, reaching an elevation of about 1000 m. "From Pôrto Alegre," noted Williams, "the road leads through an extensive plain covered in great part by grassland mixed with low scrubby vegetation, until we reached Taquara. From there we begin a steady climb until the summit is reached at São Francisco de Paula. . . . At Boca da Serra, at an altitude of about 3500 feet [1050 m] and near the upper limit of the escarpment, we found a small clump of the somewhat rare *Gunnera manicata* [581431], of the

Cycas circinalis (581491), which Williams obtained in São Paulo, has been featured in Longwood's Palm House for forty years. Photo by Tomasz Aniśko.

family Haloragaceae. Its stems are thick and short, with large leaves forming a dense crown which may reach up to 25 feet [7.5 m] across. The leaf blades measure up to 5 feet [1.5 m] or more across, and the petioles are prickly, often 5 feet or more long. In Rio Grande do Sul this plant is limited to a few sites in the upper limit of the eastern escarpment, and grows best in deep shade, in the vicinity of waterfalls, bathed constantly by the spray."

Across the border

From Pôrto Alegre, Williams continued his journey south to Argentina. On 4 May he flew to Buenos Aires for a short visit there. "I had eagerly hoped to continue the collecting in the highland region of eastern Patagonia, in the Cordillera between Argentina and Chile. But it was then realized that the deadline set for my return to Beltsville,

15 May, was drawing close, and the considerable number of plants already collected in widely scattered zones in southern Brazil still remained to be assembled and made ready for shipment" (Williams 1958).

Running out of time, Williams decided to begin his orderly retreat northward. Upon arrival in São Paulo on 10 May, he collected additional materials from the Instituto de Botânica. "The entire collections," he remembered, "weighing close to 250 pounds [113 kg], were again repacked, wrapped in burlap, and delivered on 13 May to the air-cargo office of Panair in São Paulo, to be dispatched that evening or the following morning, and reached the Inspection House in Washington three or four days later" (1958).

The collections resulting from this expedition were truly impressive, not only when measured by their weight. Williams summed up the accomplishments: "In all, five shipments were made, comprising 1100 numbers, of which approximately one-half were seed samples and the remainder vegetative material. . . . Although many plants from low altitudes are represented in the collection, an effort was made to concentrate as much as possible on plants resistant to cold, growing in the higher altitudes, and which would be most adaptable to our own climate" (1958). Through his collecting, Williams showed that "south Brazil is a rich source of ornamentals. With a wide range of altitude and latitude there is a corresponding wide range of flora. Plants encountered in the tropical and subtropical regions of the States of Rio de Janeiro and São Paulo should be adaptable to Florida or the Southwest and California, while plants from the colder areas in the higher altitudes and the areas further south should be more readily adaptable to our northern regions" (Williams 1959).

EMISSARY TO SOUTH AMERICA

Trips to Colombia in 1956 and to Brazil and Argentina in 1958 revealed only a portion of the immense botanical wealth of South America. Seibert was acutely aware of the continent as an inexhaustible source of new ornamental plants worthy of introduction. Therefore, when making plans for acquisition of plants from many parts of South America, he realized that this could not be achieved in the course of a single expedition, no matter how ambitious. In 1959 Seibert designed a trip that in six weeks would allow

him to circle South America, making stops in Puerto Rico, Trinidad, Brazil, Argentina, Uruguay, Chile, Peru, Panama, and Costa Rica. Plant collecting was not the sole purpose of this trip, however. He hoped to establish lasting relationships with many botanical institutions in South America, with the idea that cooperation with these organizations would allow for future plant acquisition. Seibert filled his itinerary with visits to nature reserves, botanical gardens, research stations, universities, nurseries, and even private gardens. Often wearing a coat and tie instead of the more casual attire of a plant hunter, he scrutinized plant collections for new botanical gems while carrying out his assignment as Longwood's emissary.

Hopping the islands

The trip began with a brief stop in San Juan, Puerto Rico, where Seibert, accompanied by his wife, Isabelle, arrived the morning of 7 January. The Seiberts stopped in Carolina, a town southwest of San Juan, to pay a visit to Pennock Gardens, operated by Charles F. Pennock. There Seibert arranged for several plants to be shipped to Longwood, including *Coccoloba rugosa* (59748), a slender tree with diminutive bright red flowers borne in terminal racemes; and *Jasminum rex* (59749), an evergreen vine native to Thailand. The next day the couple drove to El Yunque, Caribbean National Forest, where they climbed in the rain through what Isabelle recalled as "the most lush growth we have ever experienced—handsome tree ferns, palms, lianas, so thick it was dark" (1959c). At El Yunque, at an elevation of about 300 m, Seibert collected spores of *Cyathea arborea* (59107), an imposing tree fern to 10 m tall. Before leaving Puerto Rico, he came across another interesting plant. This time it was a vine, *Sicana odorifera* (59108), known locally as *pepino angolo*. It is frequently cultivated in the vicinity of San Juan for its juicy fruits, looking "like a huge red sausage" (I. L. Seibert 1959a). Though wine-red on the outside, the fruits are orange inside with a star of black seeds in the center. The pulp is used to make a refreshing drink, while the dried rind is said to have medicinal value.

Two days later the Seiberts set a course for Trinidad. Their plane flew over the islands of the Lesser Antilles. By early afternoon they saw the island of Trinidad on the horizon. According to Isabelle, while descending toward Port of Spain, they "fairly shouted with glee looking down into a mossy panorama which looked splattered with orange paint. The island fairly blooms with *Eryth-*

Tree ferns, *Cyathea arborea,* in their natural habitat in the Maricao Forest, Puerto Rico. Photo by Walter H. Hodge.

The total number of plant species in South America (left) is unknown, as many have yet to be discovered, but conservative estimates range between seventy thousand and eighty thousand. The continent is split between two of the world's floristic kingdoms. The northern and central parts belong to the Neotropical kingdom, while the regions south of the 30º south parallel are part of the Holantarctic kingdom. The vast Amazonian region in the northeast includes the lowlands of the Amazon basin, French Guiana, Surinam, Guyana, and the coast of eastern Venezuela along with its adjacent islands, Trinidad and Tobago. This region is distinguished by its magnificent tropical rain forest, unmatched in the world with regard to its size and diversity of plant life. The Amazonian region surrounds a small but floristically unique region of the Guiana Highlands. Further south, the Brazilian region includes the Brazilian Highlands and the Gran Chaco region of Paraguay and Argentina. Its vegetative cover ranges from various

types of savanna, through arid tropical woodland and montane evergreen forest, to tropical rain forest along the Atlantic coast. To the west of the Amazonian and Brazilian regions is the Andean region, which encompasses coastal mountain ranges and the Pacific coast of South America from Venezuela south to northern Chile. The Andes obstruct the rain-bearing winds, giving rise to the Atacama Desert in northern Chile, and the arid Patagonian steppe in Argentina. The Chile-Patagonian region includes parts of South America that belong to the Holantarctic kingdom. Moving southward across Argentina, the subtropical forests give way to open grasslands, the pampas. Further south the arid Patagonian meseta is dominated by sparse grassland cohabiting with spiny xerophytic shrubs. In Chile the coastal areas transition from semi-desert in the north, through xerophytic shrub communities and forests of predominantly *Nothofagus,* to the sparse, tundralike vegetation of Tierra del Fuego in the extreme south.

Stifftia chrysantha (59144), a shrub producing bright orange flowers, was collected by Seibert at the Imperial College of Tropical Agriculture. Photo by Gottlieb A. Hampfler.

rina, a tall tree shading cocoa plantings" (1959c). At Port of Spain the couple was met by Dr. G. A. C. Herklots, principal of the Imperial College of Tropical Agriculture. Herklots showed the Seiberts college grounds landscaped with lush and verdant plantings. Among the most impressive plants was *Stifftia chrysantha* (59144), a beautiful orange-flowered shrub native to Brazil but also cultivated at the college.

From the equator to the Tropic of Capricorn

The Seiberts landed on the South American continent on 11 January, in Brazil's Belém, a city built near the mouth of the Amazon. "What a stunning sight to fly over the huge mouth of the Amazon River flowing out around many islands formed by the silt, and brown sediment

colored the Atlantic as far as you could see," remembered Isabelle (1999). Belém welcomed the Seiberts with unbearable heat and, to compensate for this, two botanical gardens. That same day the couple toured the botanical garden at the Museu Emílio Goeldi. The next morning they drove to the garden at the Bosque Rodrigo Alves and in the afternoon visited the Instituto Agronômico do Norte, which occupies some 2400 hectares along the Guama River. At the institute, Russell Seibert collected seeds of an unknown species of *Adenocalymna* (59281), a strong-growing vine embellished with large yellow flowers.

On 14 January the Seiberts left Belém for Rio de Janeiro, where they stayed for several days. One day the couple took a short excursion inland to Petrópolis, a former summer capital of Portuguese royalty, and continued on to Serra dos Orgãos National Park near Teresópolis. The park's montane scenery resembled "tremendous jagged fingers of black granite with green valleys softening the outline" (I. L. Seibert 1959b). There Russell Seibert collected seeds of *Paullinia cupana* (59286), with an intent to include the species in Longwood's display of economic plants. Known as *guarana,* this vine produces seeds from which a traditional beverage is prepared; it is considered to be the most stimulating of all caffeine beverages.

Seibert spent his last day in Rio de Janeiro at the Jardim Botânico, where he was shown around by the director, Campos Porto. This garden is known for its collection of palms, none of which is more widely recognized than the spectacular *Roystonea oleracea,* planted in double rows radiating from the entrance in three directions. It was another tree, however, that most enthralled Seibert: *Clusia grandiflora* (59282), native of Brazil but cultivated at the Jardim Botânico, with its stunning 12 cm wide white flowers, highlighted by pink blush and hovering gracefully at the ends of the branches. "Must be the finest of all clusias," recorded Seibert in his field notes.

Sailing across the Andes

A short flight on 20 January took the Seiberts south of Rio, over the Tropic of Capricorn, and into São Paulo. A few days later they continued their journey to neighboring Uruguay. In Montevideo they toured the Jardín y Museo Botánico, guided by Dr. Atilio Lombardo, and the Instituto Inter-Americano de Ciencias Agrícolas, where they were met by Dr. José Marull. While in the garden, Russell Seibert spotted *Phytolacca dioica* (59317), a strange tree frequently planted around Montevideo. This relative of the North American pokeweed has a very large, almost grotesque trunk base for water storage. Seibert planned to grow it in a tub to display as a "curiosity." While touring the garden's nursery, another plant caught his attention. It was *Stevia rebaudiana* (62652), a humble little shrub, traditionally used as a sweetener by Guarani Indians of Paraguay. Despite its modest floral presentation, the plant offered an overall very pleasing delicate texture. From the institute, Seibert also procured *Lagenaria siceraria* (59367), a vine cultivated in the vicinity of Montevideo. Small, bottlelike gourds of this plant, dried and decorated, served as the traditional cups for drinking yerba maté.

A flight over the Río de la Plata on 26 January brought the Seiberts for a brief visit to Buenos Aires. A day spent at the Jardín Botánico Carlos Thays provided Russell Seibert an opportunity to study an extensive collection of *Haworthia* held there. He requested several species of these rosettelike succulents indigenous to South Africa, including *H. cooperi* (591927), *H. laetevirens* (591928), and *H. rigida* (591931).

At La Plata Museum, part of the Universidad Nacional de La Plata, Seibert met with Dr. Humberto Fabris, an expert on the family Bignoniaceae. Seibert, who had been interested in Bignoniaceae since the days of his graduate research, was thrilled to discuss these plants with Fabris. He later requested from Fabris seeds of any Bignoniaceae "that might make worthwhile additions as ornamental plants to be grown in our large conservatory. I am especially interested in receiving seeds of the species *Tabebuia* from the southernmost geographical limits. The

Seibert admires a massive twenty-five-hundred-year-old stump of *alerce* or Patagonian cypress, *Fitzroya cupressoides,* standing near Puerto Montt. *Alerce,* once abundant in southern Chile and Argentina, is now threatened with extinction. Photo by Isabelle Seibert.

few which we have and which we have grown both in the west and southwestern United States in the Los Angeles area and here in the conservatories at Longwood Gardens, seem to prove excellent plants for growing in tubs. They are really magnificent ornamental plants" (Seibert 1959a).

On 1 February the Seiberts left Buenos Aires on a cross-country flight west to San Carlos de Bariloche, a small town at the foot of the Andes in the heart of Nahuel Huapí National Park. First they flew over a plain squared off into farmland, dotted by small patches of trees surrounding lonely houses, and later petering out into flat pampas with only scrub growth. After a little more than four hours, the Andes appeared, and finally Lake Nahuel Huapí, "unfolding like a mural . . . whose blue fingerlike extremities reach into virgin forest in a frame of frosted volcanoes" (D. Seibert 1962).

While in Bariloche, Seibert explored the surrounding forests dominated by *Nothofagus,* southern beech trees of

A white-flowered variety of Chile's national flower, *Lapageria rosea* var. *alba* (591670), was procured by Seibert from Jardín Suizo in Valparaíso. Photo by Gottlieb A. Hampfler.

escarpments. Upon docking at a lonely outpost, they disembarked to pass through the Argentinean border post. From there the couple continued on another bus across the Chilean border and into Puella on the bank of Lake Todos los Santos. After spending a night in a small lodge in Puella, the Seiberts boarded a steamboat that would take them on a half-day ride across the lake. Upon reaching Petrohué on the western tip of the lake, they exchanged the boat for a bus one last time. Following the shore of Lake Llanquihue to Puerto Varas, they left the Andes behind, while the environs turned into sprawling pasturelands dotted with stately Lombardy poplars.

Northbound

The day of 5 February was this trip's turning point. Puerto Varas was the southernmost location reached by the Seiberts in South America. In the morning they boarded a train to Santiago. After passing through a picturesque countryside of rolling pasturelands lined with rows of Lombardy poplars and Australian eucalyptus, the train entered Chile's Central Valley, enclosed between two mountain ranges—the snowcapped Andes to the east, the gentler Cordillera de la Costa to the west. The drier, flattened Central Valley was filled by vast expanses of wheat fields and orchards, and every now and then bisected by rivers rushing toward the ocean. Santiago was reached shortly before midnight.

In Santiago, Seibert hoped to meet with Chile's most prominent botanist, Dr. Carlos Muñoz Pizarro of the Ministerio de Agricultura. Unfortunately, Muñoz Pizarro was away. He arranged, however, for his friend Carlos G. Cariola to accompany the Seiberts during their visit. On 7 February, Cariola took the couple to the private garden of wealthy landowner Don Emilio Madrid. Madrid's estate, located near Maipú, south of Santiago, must have made a positive impression on Seibert, as he enthusiastically summed it up in his field notes, "It was a veritable botanic garden!" Among the plants Seibert requested from Madrid were a splendid red-flowered *Datura coccinea* (59413) and *Dendroseris litoralis* (59412), a small palmlike tree with very large heads of orange-yellow flowers, endemic to Juan Fernández Islands.

On 9 February the group drove to Valparaíso, south of Viña del Mar, to visit Jardín Suizo, a nursery run by Benjamín Pumpin. Seibert acquired there a species of *Alsophila* (59411), a tree fern native to Juan Fernández Islands, and an assortment of various selections of

"quite ethereal" appearance. On one of his outings he collected several species of *Lupinus* (59368) flowering in various colors and apparently cultivated in that area. A short boat ride took him to Bosque de Arrayanes near Puerto Quetri-Hué, a forest of ghostly *Luma apiculata*, twisted small trees of Myrtaceae with cinnamon-red bark.

Two days later the Seiberts began their journey across the Andes. First they boarded a boat to reach Puerto Blest on the west end of the lake, facing the border with Chile. From there a bus took them on a poor gravel road through the forest, bringing them to the point where "the road ends unceremoniously at the edge of the new lake where nothing but forest surrounds it" (D. Seibert 1962). There they changed to a small barge for a short ride across Laguna Fría, a diminutive lake enclosed by vertical

Lapageria rosea (59415–6, 591666–70), Chile's national flower. From Valparaíso the Seiberts rushed back to Santiago to catch a flight to Lima, Peru. They were leaving Chile inspired by its unique flora but also taken by the warmth with which they were met. "Of all the Latin American countries which I have visited," wrote Seibert upon his return to Longwood, "we have found the people of Chile the most *simpático*" (1959b).

The couple returned to Lima after a twelve-year absence. During World War II, Seibert had been recruited by the USDA as a botanist to survey rubber plants in Peru, and between 1943 and 1947 he and Isabelle had lived and worked in Tingo María, Iquitos, Cuzco, and finally Lima. The day after their arrival, Seibert paid a visit to Dr. Ramón Ferreyra, curator of the herbarium at the National Museum of Natural History and a leading Peruvian botanist. Later he toured Lima's Jardín Botánico, where he collected *Barnadesia lanceolata* (59409), a shrub with rose-pink flowers native to northern Peru.

It was the lush Panamanian vegetation, such as this coastal forest fringed by coconut palms near Portobelo, that swayed young Seibert in the 1930s toward a career in botany and plant exploration. Photo by Walter H. Hodge.

Homecoming to Panama

On 14 February the Seiberts departed Lima on a flight to Panama. For Russell Seibert this meant returning to a place where his career as a plant explorer had begun in 1935. That year, while studying botany under Dr. Robert Woodson at Washington University in Saint Louis, Seibert had been invited to go to Panama to help collect plants for the Missouri Botanical Garden. The experience of working at the field station set up by the Missouri Botanical Garden in the Canal Zone was thrilling enough to convince the twenty-one-year-old to change his major from geology to botany, and eventually to pursue a doctoral degree in the field.

After arriving in Panama, Seibert visited Summit Gardens, a 700-hectare park encompassing both botani-

Heliconia wagneriana (59419) was found by Seibert growing on the shores of Madden Lake in Panama. Photo by Walter H. Hodge.

cal and zoological gardens, located north of Panama City. In the gardens he collected seeds of a white-flowered *Lagerstroemia hirsuta* (59421), a small tree native to India. He then continued north to the shores of Madden Lake, a man-made reservoir supplying water for the Panama Canal. At the lake Seibert found *Heliconia wagneriana* (59419), its bracts brightly colored in red, pink, and yellow. The following day while botanizing on the

Cyrtostachys lakka (59928), or sealing-wax palm, valued for its deep red leaf sheaths, was procured by Seibert from a private garden in Balboa. Photo by Walter H. Hodge.

Norantea guianensis (59929) is a shrub producing curious, bright red, bladderlike bracts that function as nectar pouches. It was obtained by Seibert from a private garden in Balboa. Photo by Richard F. Keen.

Arpophyllum spicatum (61945), one of the orchids Seibert received from Lankester of Cartago. Photo by Richard F. Keen.

shores of the Gatún Lake he collected yet another *Heliconia* sp. (59420), this one with large red bracts.

The next couple of days spent in and around Balboa, just outside of Panama City, gave Seibert an opportunity to visit some of the private collections. There he acquired, among others, *Brownea macrophylla* (591940), a captivating shrub with large scarlet blossoms forming on the main trunk and limbs; *Cyrtostachys lakka* (59928), sealing-wax palm, rated among the most beautiful palms for its deep red leaf sheaths; and *Norantea guianensis* (59929), valued for its spectacular erect spikes of brilliant orange-red bracts forming nectar pouches.

On 18 February the Seiberts departed Panama and made a brief stop in Costa Rica to meet with Dr. Ralph

E. Allee, director of the Instituto Inter-Americano de Ciencias Agrícolas in Turrialba, and with Charles H. Lankester of Cartago, an orchid enthusiast and founder of the Lankester Botanical Garden. At the institute in Turrialba, Seibert collected *Solanum hyporhodium* (59430), which produces beautiful orange-red fruits used to make a preserve. From Lankester's collection, Seibert requested several orchids, including *Arpophyllum spicatum* (61945) and *Rossioglossum schlieperianum* (61947). Two days later the couple left Costa Rica and returned to Philadelphia, thus closing their circle around South America.

Peru, with an area of nearly 1.3 million km², extends from the equator to latitude 17º south. Altitudes range from sea level to the snow-covered summit of Huascarán, which, at 6768 m, is the tallest mountain in the tropics. Rainfall in Peru ranges from the extremely dry northern fringe of the Atacama Desert to cloud forests with more than 8000 mm of rain per year. The country is usually divided into three major floristic regions: the eastern Amazonian forest, the mountainous Andean region, and the narrow, mostly desert coastal region along the Pacific. The Amazonian forests are among the most biologically diverse on Earth. Many of these species of plants can also be found on the lower slopes of the Andean region, which is home to about a third of Peruvian flora. At the altitude of about 1500 m, the lower Andean forest is replaced by montane forest, which progressively decreases in diversity with altitude. Orchids and other epiphytes are an exception to this rule, being more prevalent and diverse in mid-elevation Andean forests than in other areas. Most of the Andean forests occur on the eastern slopes facing Amazonia. Above the timberline, at about 3500 m, this forest is replaced by high-montane flora composed mostly of herbaceous plants and shrubs. Flora of the coastal region is low in diversity, and the vegetation is sparse except in the condensation zones where winter fogs are intercepted by steep hills adjacent to the coast.

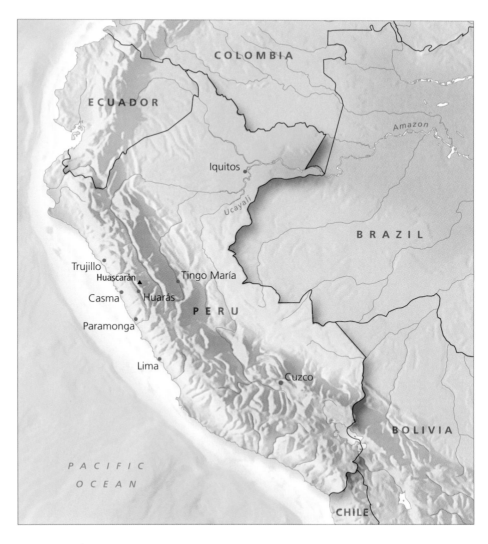

PERUVIAN ATTRACTION

"To see a fine new ornamental plant is exciting to me," wrote Seibert (1967a) after his return from the 1965 expedition to Peru. "However, to find such a plant in its natural local habitat is a memorable experience and probably explains why, for the past thirty years of my graduate student and professional life, plant exploration has attracted me to other parts of the world. This attraction, like a compatible marriage, does not wane with maturity. It becomes even more magnetic."

Return of the rubber-tree hunter

Seibert was not a novice to the Peruvian Amazonia and the Andes. His first assignment in Peru had come in 1943, when, after working for a couple of years for the USDA on their rubber plant survey in Costa Rica, Panama, Colombia, Venezuela, and Haiti, Seibert was asked, as part of a wartime effort, to search for high-producing, disease-resistant wild rubber in the Amazonian rain forest. In *One River* (1996), Wade Davis writes that Seibert "spent the first six months in Iquitos on the Ucayali river, nosing around the bars and waterfront

This leaf of *Victoria* 'Longwood Hybrid', measured in 1979 at Longwood's outdoor pools, reached 220 cm in diameter. The largest 'Longwood Hybrid' leaf on record, measured in 1995 at the Royal Botanic Gardens, Kew, was 259 cm in diameter. Photo by Richard F. Keen.

Victoria 'Longwood Hybrid' was raised at Longwood Gardens in 1961. That year Patrick A. Nutt made a cross between *V. cruziana* and *V. amazonica,* the only two species of giant water platters. Photo by Gottlieb A. Hampfler.

shanties, visiting the small farms where retired *seringueros* scratched a living from tired soil and old rubber trees swollen with wounds. Each of the rubber tappers had different memories of the boom, of the era when Iquitos came close to rivaling Manaus. . . . On one issue, however, Seibert found the rubber tappers in complete

agreement. To know the greatest of the trees—the *lecheros,* the real bleeders, as they put it—one had to travel upriver and beyond to the forests of Madre de Dios." After spending three years exploring the Madre de Dios region where Peru, Bolivia, and Brazil meet, Seibert successfully brought out superior rubber clones to plant in nurseries in Tingo María, on the east side of the Andes.

Years spent in Peru searching for rubber trees inspired Seibert with vivid images of fabulously rich flora and ancient culture, and allowed him to befriend many prominent botanists of that country. When contemplating a return to Peru nearly twenty years later, this time to search for ornamental plants, Seibert wrote to one of those botanists, Ferreyra in Lima: "For many years, it has been my desire to know more about the plants which were used as ornamentals by the ancient civilizations of Peru. Therefore, I hope to visit some of the older gardens which may be in existence in the ancient centers of the Peruvian civilizations such as Nazca, Cuzco, Ayacucho, Huancayo, Huánuco, Huarás, Trujillo, Lima, etc." (Seibert 1964e). In addition to exploring ancient centers of Peruvian civilization, Seibert decided to revisit the rain forest areas around Iquitos and Tingo María.

Meeting with giant water platters

Seibert was especially interested in studying *Victoria amazonica* in its natural habitat. By that time Longwood staff had mastered ways of growing both species of *Victoria, V. amazonica* and *V. cruziana,* in the heated water-lily pools outdoors. A hybrid between the species developed at Longwood in 1961 and named *V.* 'Longwood Hybrid' substantially improved the display value of *Victoria,* but Seibert was hoping for further improvements through breeding with new strains. He argued the

The Amazon riverfront in Iquitos, with river boats that ply rainforest waterways. Photo by Walter H. Hodge.

need for studying and introducing plants growing in Peru: "*V. amazonica* exists in the upper Amazon valley but seed of this strain has, to our knowledge, not been grown under cultivated conditions. It has not been adequately observed to see what differences might exist between this strain and that from the lower Amazon and Guianas from whence the cultivated species material has been derived" (R. J. Seibert 1965c).

"In going back over my notes of 1943–46, I find that the only place I actually noted it was on the Amazon below Iquitos in a slough on the south side of the river between Pepas and Transvaal," wrote Seibert (1964d) to Dr. Michael H. Langford at the American Embassy in Lima. He asked many of his correspondents in Peru if they had seen *Victoria amazonica*. One of them, Dr. Calaway H. Dodson of the Universidad Nacional de Amazonia Peruana, replied, "I have seen a *Victoria* which

I take to be *V. amazonica,* in the sloughs and backwashes of the Amazon just upriver from Iquitos while flying over. I don't know of any easy way to get to them but will have it arranged for you by the time that you get here" (Dodson 1964).

Filled with high expectations, Seibert arrived in Lima on 7 January and a couple of days later departed on a flight to Iquitos on the Amazon. In Iquitos, Dodson lived up to his promise and made arrangements for Seibert to travel to Ushpa Cocha, an oxbow lake about 30 km from Iquitos to observe *Victoria*. On 12 January, Seiberts and Dodson, accompanied by Guillermo Cetrado, ornithologist, and José Torres, herbarium assistant, both from the university, proceeded by launch upstream to a forest trail that led, after a three-hour overland hike, to Ushpa Cocha. There, on the far edge of the lake, they saw several plants of *Victoria*.

A Yagua Indian woman holds a bowl of gruel made from fruits of *Bactris gasipaes*. This will be used to make *chicha*. Photo by Walter H. Hodge.

Dimerocostus tessmannii (65847) was collected by Seibert at Ushpa Cocha, an oxbow lake near Iquitos. Photo by Tomasz Aniśko.

Fruits of peach palm, *Bactris gasipaes,* known only in cultivation in many parts of Central and South America, are eaten boiled or roasted. When dried and ground, the fruit pulp provides flour used for baking bread; when fermented, it provides an alcoholic beverage known as *chicha*. Photo by Walter H. Hodge.

As Seibert recalled (Anderson 1965b), "The partly Indian inhabitant on the bank of this lake told us that the new plants were only starting to grow as the rainy season was getting started. The plants, he said, would continue to come up and increase in size throughout the year until almost the entire shallow lake, a foot and a half to 3 feet [45–90 cm] deep at that time, would be covered with the large 6 foot [1.8 m] diameter leaves. Then, about October, and in the height of the dry season as the water level went down, plants would die back and disappear until the next rainy season."

As the plants were only beginning to flower, there were no maturing seed pods available for collecting.

"Since the plants are said to start here with the rainy season as the water in the lake or 'cocha' rises, one can only surmise that the platter petioles lengthen to accommodate the water depth," wrote Seibert (Anderson 1965b). "The plants, according to conversations, appear to be confined to some of the older shallow oxbow lakes. These appear to be filled by the rains, with clear run-off water rather than from the rising muddy waters of the Amazon spreading out into its lower flood plain in this general area."

Cetrado, who accompanied Seibert and Dodson to Ushpa Cocha, later collected seeds of *Victoria* at the height of the season and sent them to Longwood Gardens

Fruits of *Mauritia flexuosa* (65850) are sold in the market in Iquitos. The fruits are eaten fresh or used for extraction of cooking oil. Dried fruit pulp is ground into flour or used to make a fermented drink. Photo by Russell J. Seibert.

The Seiberts traveled on the Pan-American Highway through the coastal desert areas north of Lima. Photo by Walter H. Hodge.

in October of 1965. At Ushpa Cocha, Seibert collected several other plants, including the rare *Dimerocostus tessmannii* (65847), a member of the ginger family with very attractive yellow flowers; it was later planted in Longwood's Palm House, where it can still be admired.

Two days later Seibert made an excursion to Zungaro Cocha, another oxbow lake along Río Nanay, a tributary of the Amazon, some 25 km west of Iquitos. There he visited a 2000-hectare preserve of a virgin rain forest set aside for the Universidad Nacional de Amazonia Peruana. A 15 January excursion to Guayamba, west of Iquitos, resulted in the collection of several edible plants, including *Bactris gasipaes,* among the most desired cultivated palms in the area, which produces fruits that are edible after boiling in salt water; *Mauritia flexuosa* (65850), with striking, edible fruits, described as "almost an addiction to many"; and *Myrciaria paraensis* (65859), a shrubby tree with purplish fruits from which a refreshing drink is made.

Cojomaria—unexpected encounter

Upon his return to Lima on 16 January, Seibert spent a couple of days packing and shipping plants and seeds collected in the Iquitos area, and preparing for the next chapter of the expedition, which would take him into the high Andes. On 20 January the Seiberts left Lima for Huarás. Traveling in a rented car posed new challenges, since road signs, notorious for being stolen, were nowhere to be found. Asking strangers for directions became the only available alternative. The road north of Lima, which

first passed through stark, dry hills, was cut along fantastic sheer sand drops. From time to time green valleys formed by rivers rushing to the Pacific broke the monotony of the desertlike landscape.

After Paramonga, Seibert turned east onto a gravel road to Huarás. The valley lined with Lombardy poplars and eucalyptus gradually gave way to a moonlike scene of barren waste. Finally in this rugged terrain a few cacti appeared. After a long and steep climb, a mountain pass called Conococha opened at 4080 m onto a huge plain marked by a shallow lake of the same name which feeds a river. The plain is closed from the east by snowcapped mountain peaks, the tallest being Huascarán. By evening Seibert reached Huarás, a picturesque town with narrow cobblestone streets around the central square still showing scars from the 1941 rock avalanche that wiped out part of it.

The next day Seibert stopped at the Archeological Museum of Ancash, where he noticed an unusual form of *Cantua buxifolia* (6579), the national flower of Peru. Typically this shrub produces flowers with pink or purple floral tubes marked by yellow stripes and intensely red lobes. The specimen growing at the museum had flowers with yellowish floral tubes and white lobes. Dr. Mario Augusto Soriano Infante of the Archeological Museum graciously shared a number of seeds from this plant.

The Seiberts drove from Huarás to Trujillo via Sechín and Casma. The road out of Huarás ascended to reveal a magnificent view of the valley of Río Santa, filled with many cultivated, stone-lined fields of potatoes, beans,

Isabelle Seibert with children who are selling flowers of *Paramongaia weberbaueri* (65522) near Pariacoto. Photo by Russell J. Seibert.

Paramongaia weberbaueri (65522), first collected by Antonio Raimondi in 1874, was classified later by August Weberbauer as a species of *Ismene*. It was not until 1949 that Octavio Velarde-Núñez established genus *Paramongaia*, comprised of a single species, *P. weberbaueri*. Photo by Robert J. Armstrong.

and corn. Scattered about were tiny huts built with round stone bases and peaked thatched roofs. At 4225 m, the road reached a mountain pass at Punta de Callán, from where the view opened onto a tremendous valley. Its slopes were lined by a patchwork quilt of color produced by thousands of years of agricultural use and crisscrossed by centuries-old paths, Inca roads, and irrigation canals.

"One of the great thrills of plant collecting is to find an outstanding plant about which one was completely unaware," Seibert later wrote (1965c). "Such was the case on the trip to the Callejón de Huaylas and Trujillo. Peru has a phenomenal number of bulbous plants in the drier areas of desert, semidesert, and western Andean slopes. Most of these plants are very restrictive as to their habitat and remain in full bloom only a relatively short period of time. Only if one happens to be at the proper place at the proper time is one privileged to see some of these plants. The outstanding example of this type of occurrence took place as I was going from Huarás to Casma." At some point Seibert saw a lone Andean Indian on horseback carrying a sizeable bouquet of lovely yellow flowers. They were so huge that Seibert stopped his car and asked the man for their name. "The flowers, he said, were called 'cojomaria' and were found growing further down the road. A short drive and several high Andean switchbacks down, we encountered three children attending several bouquets of the same large, yellow amaryllidaceous flowers. Obviously, the bouquets were for sale but since the three children spoke no Spanish, our Quechua proved insufficient to communicate well. We surmised that the plants grew in an area further down the Andean slopes

and that for a 5-sole note, we could purchase a sizeable bundle of flowers. What remarkable blooms! At first sight, they remind one of giant daffodils, some 6 inches [15 cm] in diameter, butter yellow and very fragrant. Further down the Andes at somewhat less than 10,000 feet [3050 m] and along the steep slopes immediately above the village of Pariacoto, Department of Ancash, we suddenly observed huge quantities of the flowering bulbous plants growing within a rather restricted area of perhaps less than 1000 acres [400 hectares]. The soil appeared to be a decomposing granite. The natural vegetation was sparse scrub, almost chaparral-like. The plants were growing on extremely steep slopes which made their collection both difficult and precarious. With the aid of a car jack handle and digging to depths of 1 foot [30 cm], entire plants, including the bulbs, were recovered" (Seibert 1967a).

After climbing up and down the slope and nearly falling over a cliff, Seibert left the site with nine precious plants. Their incredible flowers were 15 cm in diameter, with one specimen reaching nearly 18 cm. Exhausted but thrilled with his rare find, Seibert reached the coastal city of Trujillo as the sun was setting over the ocean.

The flowers of *cojomaria* collected near Pariacoto were kept for a couple of days, and a few lasted until the Seiberts returned to Lima four days later. It was sometime afterward, while discussing the plant with Dr. Jorge León, a botanist with the Agency for International Development in Lima, that it was identified as *Paramongaia weberbaueri* (65522). This rare member of the amaryllis family was originally described from plants growing at the base of the Fortaleza Paramonga near the Pacific coast, hence the generic name. As Seibert recorded in his report, "Possibly, it can be surmised, this plant has survived as a former cultivated plant of the pre-Inca civilization occupying the Fortaleza. Actually, it is native near Pariacoto at about 8000 feet [2450 m] elevation where I was fortunate enough to find it flowering" (1965c). The relative obscurity in which this plant remained since its discovery can be explained by the fact that it is not well known even in Peru outside its natural habitat in the Department of Ancash. Seibert was determined to bring *Paramongaia* back to Longwood alive. In his field notes he described it as "a most striking flower like a giant narcissus and as fragrant. Keeps excellently as a cut flower. This is a prize collection—grow at all cost."

Sacred flowers of the Inca

On 29 January, Seibert flew from Lima to Tingo María, located on the eastern side of the Andes in the valley of Huallaga. Before coming to Peru, when planning this expedition, he had become intrigued by a rare fern, *Platycerium andinum* (6519, 6530, 65855). "Within the past few years, the only American representative of the 'staghorn fern' was rediscovered in Peru," wrote Seibert (1965c). "Originally, in the mid 1850s, Richard Spruce had discovered and collected the plant near Tarapoto, Peru. *Platycerium andinum* has particularly interesting and attractive spore-bearing fronds which are covered on the under surface with a silvery tomentum making them appear as spun-silver. Although I saw several plants growing in a primitive garden in Iquitos, the owner was out of the country and arrangements for its procural were not possible at the time. I was told of a young man in Tingo María who was reported to have collected plants of this species from the Province of San Martín. Contact was made with José Schunke in Tingo María and on my trip there, four plants were purchased." These plants were later sent to Longwood, where they were exhibited within conservatories for the next twenty-three years.

On 1 February, Seibert returned to Lima to prepare his collections from Tingo María for shipment to the United States. Four days later he was again on a plane, this time heading southeast to Cuzco. On the day of his arrival, Seibert visited the Museo Arqueológico. In the patio garden of this museum he spotted a weakly ascend-

Dodson stands beside *Platycerium andinum* (6519, 6530, 65855), a rare staghorn fern that Seibert procured in Tingo María. Photo by Russell J. Seibert.

ing shrub about 2.5 m tall growing into *Cantua buxifolia* for support. It had gracefully drooping, very long inflorescences. Individual flowers had dark purple calyces and 15 cm long, brilliant scarlet corollas. Upon closer inspection the plant turned out be *Salvia dombeyi* (65162, 65250), claimed to be one of the sacred flowers of the Inca.

That this *Salvia* made a great impression on Seibert is evident from his field notes: "One of the most spectacular inflorescences I have ever seen, should make a spectacular giant basket plant." The same level of fascination is reflected in the report he prepared upon his return to Longwood: "The most outstanding of all plants I had ever seen in Peru was 'the Sacred Flower of the Incas' *Salvia dombeyi*. The somewhat weakly growing shrub has remarkable drooping inflorescences about 16 inches [40 cm] long, made up of brilliant scarlet flowers 6–7 inches

Salvia dombeyi (65162, 65250) is a subshrubby climber up to 5 m tall. Its flowers appear later in summer and fall in conical racemes to 35 cm long. In Peru this plant can be found at altitudes of 3000 to 3600 m, between Cajamarca in the north and Cuzco in the south. Photo by Earl E. Smith.

In 1968, Armstrong made a cross between *Cantua cuzcoensis* (65164) with pale lavender flowers and *C. buxifolia* with purplish red flowers. One seedling, which produced an exceptional profusion of hot pink flowers, was selected from among the offspring and named 'Hot Pants'. Photo by Robert J. Armstrong.

[15–18 cm] long. The plant is used as adornment in the high elevations of southern Peru usually above 11,000 feet [3350 m]. There is question as to whether the plant exists in the wild. Presumably, it is only maintained as a relict plant under cultivation by the Indians. The flowers are used to decorate the altars of the Indian churches on feast days. It is well known to the Indians of the area by the Quechua name *nucchu*" (Seibert 1965c).

Seibert spent the next several days collecting plants from locations around Cuzco. In Urubamba he found *Cantua cuzcoensis* (65164), a 3 m tall shrub with drooping pink flowers, which Seibert considered more attractive than the better known *C. buxifolia.* Three years later

a cross made between *C. cuzcoensis* collected in Urubamba and *C. buxifolia,* performed at Longwood by Armstrong, led to a selection named 'Hot Pants'.

Despite chilly weather and continuous rain, which inflicted Seibert with an unrelenting cold, collecting continued in the Cuzco area for a few days, after which Seibert returned to Lima on 10 February. Several days passed during which Seibert prepared his botanical treasures for the trip back to the United States. He also used the time to visit outdoor markets in Lima. Such places, where countless local varieties of cultivated fruits, vegetables, and flowers are traded, are often ignored by plant explorers interested exclusively in wild plants. Seibert

Paramongaia weberbaueri, which was collected by Seibert near Pariacoto, has been exhibited at Longwood since 1967. Photo by Robert J. Armstrong.

early on developed a deep appreciation for these markets and used every opportunity he had to browse through the endless variety of local selections, looking for unusual plants. In an open-air market in Lima he found *Chenopodium quinoa* (65243), grown for its highly nutritious seeds, which are used in making soups; *Cucurbita moschata* (65275), known locally as *zapallo,* with tremendous fruits to 60 cm in diameter; and purple corn, *Zea mays* (65241–2), used for making *chicha morada* and *maza morada.* These unusual crops were exhibited for the first time in Longwood's vegetable garden in the summer of 1965.

On 17 February, Seibert departed for Philadelphia. Many of his collections were first sent to the USDA Inspection House in Miami, where they were started at the introduction garden. Among them were bulbs of *Paramongaia,* which were forwarded to Longwood in the spring of 1965. These came into bloom for the first time in January of 1967 and were exhibited in the conservatories the following month.

CHILEAN RECONNAISSANCE

Over the years a whole array of plants native to Mediterranean-climate regions of the world have been exhibited in Longwood's conservatories. Displays incorporating these plants have not only met with interest and acceptance from the public but have also proved that many Mediterranean plants are quite amenable to indoor conditions.

In South America the Mediterranean-climate region is situated in Chile. This country, stretching across thirty-six degrees in latitude, traverses several climatic zones. The Mediterranean climate prevails in central Chile, approximately covering the area between latitudes 32° south and 37° south. In 2001 a reconnaissance trip was organized, with the main purpose to observe and collect spring-flowering plants of central Chile. The team included Dr. Mark Bridgen, professor at the University of Connecticut, Rodney T. Eason, graduate student at the University of Delaware, and me. Upon landing in Santiago on 15 October, we were joined by Dr. Eduardo Olate, professor of Pontifica Universidad Católica de Chile, our host and guide for the entire trip.

Gentle giants of Nahuelbuta

The day after our arrival in Santiago we departed on a flight to the coastal city of Concepción, some 500 km to the south. This is the area where the Mediterranean climate of central Chile transitions to the cooler, wetter climate of southern Chile, which once supported extensive coniferous forests of *Araucaria araucana, Austrocedrus chilensis,* and *Fitzroya cupressoides.* In Concepción we rented a four-wheel-drive vehicle and drove south to the Cordillera de Nahuelbuta.

Along the road between Santa Juana and Nacimiento, a patch of fiery red-orange daylilylike flowers brought our car to an abrupt stop. The flowers, backlit by afternoon sun, suddenly roused us from a lethargy caused by long hours of driving through a countryside scourged with monotonous plantations of introduced eucalypts and pines. Before us, occupying a roadside bank, was a large colony of what turned out to be *Rhodophiala advena* (011815). After crawling up and sliding down the steep bank, we gave in to a frenzy of photographing and collecting. Our activities naturally brought out curious onlookers from a nearby homestead, who seemed amused by what must have appeared to be rather bizarre behavior. Still marveling at how a plant of such incredible beauty could grow so humbly along a roadside, we reluctantly returned to the vehicle and drove away.

Later in the afternoon we arrived at Parque Nacional Nahuelbuta, established primarily to protect the remaining tracts of forests of *Araucaria araucana,* monkey puzzle trees. *Araucaria* can be found in the Chilean and Argentinean Andes, usually growing on steep volcanic slopes. To the west of the Andes, the last remnant population is

A colony of *Rhodophiala advena* (011815) occupied a roadside bank between Santa Juana and Nacimiento. Photo by Tomasz Aniśko.

Chile occupies a narrow strip of land of nearly 760,000 km² between the Andes and the Pacific Ocean. It is 4200 km long but at no point wider than 350 km. The Cordillera de la Costa rises to 2200 m, while the highest peak in the Andes, Aconcagua, reaches 6960 m. Further south, both mountain chains gradually decrease in elevation. Chile is a land of climatic extremes. Much of northern Chile is a desert receiving negligible or no rainfall. The middle third of the country, between La Serena in the north and Concepción in the south, enjoys a Mediterranean climate and is the center of Chile's economic activities. In that region, annual rainfall ranges from about 80 mm in La Serena to 1270 mm in Concepción, and most of it comes in winter. Further south, annual precipitation increases while the summer dry season becomes shorter. The southernmost regions of Chile are bitterly cold and receive as much as 4000 mm of rain. Temperatures in Chile are moderate throughout most of the year thanks to the cold Humboldt Current. Like the climate, the vegetation of Chile varies greatly from north to south. The deserts of the north are replaced by steppe in central Chile. Mixed and evergreen forests predominate south of Río Bío-Bío but give way to cold steppes in Patagonia. Chile's isolation by desert to the north, mountains to the east, and ocean to the west resulted in a high rate of endemism of its flora, comparable to that of oceanic islands. Chile is home to about five thousand species, and of those more than half are endemic.

in the Cordillera de Nahuelbuta, which forms part of the coastal ranges.

Familiarity with individual *Araucaria* trees cultivated as ornamentals in the warmer parts of Europe and North America, even if sufficient to inspire one to visit the trees in their natural habitat, is not adequate preparation for the experience of entering a centuries-old *Araucaria* forest. Mountains and hills sparsely clad in these gentle, silent giants, and extending to the horizon, give one the sense of being in another world. Trees crowding the slopes like colossal parasols on a beach, the hypnotic movement of curtains of lichens hanging from the branches, massive trunks encased in thick bark reminiscent of the shell of a Goliath tortoise—all of these things together make such a strong impression as to induce a state of exhilaration and euphoria.

As the sun set over the *Araucaria* forest, we realized we had to rush down the mountain in order to return to the main highway before dark, and then reach Los Ángeles, a town southeast of Concepción, where we were to spend the night.

Black sand and seven waterfalls

Early the next morning the team departed Los Ángeles for Talca, about 250 km to the north. Past Chillán, we turned off the main highway and took a road toward the coast. In the afternoon we arrived in the small coastal town of Pelluhue, squeezed between black sand beaches and steep hills overlooking the Pacific Ocean. Along the beach, picturesque cliffs and rocks harbored a most interesting flora. Scarlet-red *Phycella bicolor* (011790, 011801), although more modest in size than its cousin *Rhodophiala*, was equally attractive. Impressive clumps of shrubby *Lobelia tupa,* up to 3 m across and 2 m high, were a revelation, as we were used to seeing only herbaceous members of that genus. This species' red flowers, arranged in 60 cm long spikes, are pollinated by hummingbirds. A couple of species of *Alstroemeria,* which were in bloom, seemed to favor crevices in the rocks, giving them some degree of protection from the wind.

We reached our destination, Talca, in late evening. The next morning we visited the Universidad de Talca, where we met with Flavia Schiappacasse Canepa, a professor of floriculture and former student of Bridgen. After showing us the research facilities at the university and sharing with us some of the plants being trialed there, Schiappacasse accompanied us to Altos de Lircay, a

Monkey puzzle trees, *Araucaria araucana,* growing in the Parque Nacional Nahuelbuta. Photo by Tomasz Aniśko.

nature reserve in the Andean foothills. Higher rainfall and a relatively short dry season allow for broad-leaved evergreen and mixed forests to flourish in the area. Southern beeches, including deciduous *Nothofagus obliqua* and evergreen *N. dombeyi,* predominate in these forests.

Approaching the park, we spotted an impressive yellow-flowering shrub. Upon closer inspection it turned out to be *Senecio yegua* (011809), making a show with its large panicles heavy with 5 cm wide flower heads backed by silvery gray leaves. Higher up the hills, inside the park, spring had not quite arrived, so plants in bloom were few and far between. A park ranger told us to come back in December, when the forests would become, in his words, "a virtual garden."

On 19 October, Schiappacasse, joined by Doris Lee, also Bridgen's former student, led us on yet another outing in the mountains, this time to the Reserva

Phycella bicolor (011790) occupies rocky cliffs along the black sand beaches of Pelluhue. Photo by Tomasz Aniśko.

The author is dwarfed by one of the centuries-old specimens of *Nothofagus dombeyi* that abound in Altos de Lircay, a nature reserve east of Talca. Photo by Tomasz Aniśko.

Shrubby *Senecio yegua* (011809) was spotted near Altos de Lircay. Photo by Tomasz Aniśko.

Resting along the trail in the Reserva Nacional Las Siete Tazas are, left to right, Lee, Schiappacasse Canepa, Eason, Olate, and Bridgen. Photo by Tomasz Aniśko.

The upper ridges of the coastal ranges are shrouded in clouds near Parque Nacional Fray Jorge. Photo by Tomasz Aniśko.

Nacional Las Siete Tazas, a nature reserve known for a series of seven majestic waterfalls. Like the day before, only the earliest bloomers were putting on a show. Noteworthy examples included *Lathyrus subandinus,* sporting eye-catching purple-blue flowers, seen in only one location, and *Rhodophiala splendens* (011783), another lovely example of this most garden-worthy genus. Upon returning to our vehicles several hours later, we bid farewell to Schiappacasse and Lee and headed off to Santiago.

El Norte Chico

On 20 October we continued north from Santiago toward the town of La Serena. The semiarid region between latitudes 28° south and 32° south is called El Norte Chico, The Little North. With every turn of the road the land appeared to be drier and the vegetation more xeric. Nevertheless, spring was in full swing, and we observed many plants in flower.

Further north, the coastal ranges rise to higher elevations, forcing the moisture carried by oceanic air to condense into clouds and create nearly permanent conditions of drizzle and fog along the top ridges, while a rain shadow affects the slopes and valleys to the east. This is also the area where Parque Nacional Fray Jorge has been established to protect the unique ecosystem of these ranges.

Once we reached the mountaintops in the park, we found ourselves surrounded by a virtual cloud forest, in stark contrast to the xeric flora at the base. Dense clouds limited visibility to 15 m, while ferocious winds rocked our vehicle left and right. Abundant moisture there supported a lush community of evergreen trees, shrubs, large herbs, and grasses. In a meadow, *Leucocoryne ixioides* flowered prolifically. Although a most charming plant in

Nolana paradoxa flowers in spring in great profusion despite the extreme conditions of the Atacama Desert. Photo by Tomasz Aniśko.

A lonely *Rhodophiala bagnoldii* grows on a beach in the Parque Nacional Llanos de Challe. Photo by Tomasz Aniśko.

every respect, this *Leucocoryne* had but one fault, as Eason described in his travelogue: "Later in the day, I regretted Mark and Eduardo's decision to collect bulbs of this plant as the flowers smell like rotting onions. Unfortunately, the plants were stored in the back of the 4-Runner near my head. Eventually, I became immune to the smell, but only after contemplating how to throw the bulbs out of the vehicle on several instances" (Eason 2002).

Driest place on earth
On 21 October we continued driving north toward the Atacama Desert, known as the driest place on earth. The desert stretches north from latitude 32° south to the border with Peru. The vegetation there is mostly restricted to a narrow strip along the coast where consistent fog provides moisture.

Although the desert landscape from afar appeared somber and lifeless, a closer examination revealed scores of brightly colored plants, including yellow-flowering shrubs, *Oxalis gigantea* and *Balbisia peduncularis;* ground-hugging *Nolana paradoxa,* displaying brilliant blue flowers; and an occasional slender *Nicotiana glauca* (011792).

North of Vallenar, we turned off the Pan-American Highway to reach Parque Nacional Llanos de Challe, situated in the coastal ranges. Our hope was to find *Leontochir ovallei,* the true gem of the desert. This plant, related to *Alstroemeria,* is endemic to Chile and grows only at Llanos de Challe. Unfortunately, the spring rains were late the year of our trip and the plants remained dormant underground. After much searching among crumbled rocks, I spotted an old seed head from the previous year, which still contained about twenty seeds (011798).

We then followed a dirt road deeper into the park until we reached the Pacific Ocean, at which point we turned south along the beach toward the town of Huasco. While driving along the beach we came upon a dry streambed filled with all sorts of flowers, various pink and purple *Calandrinia* species (011787–8), yellow *Cruckshanksia pumila* (011806), *Oxalis gigantea,* and *Rhodophiala bagnoldii.*

Honey palms

In Huasco we reversed our course and on 22 October began our travel south. The next day we headed off to the hills west of Santiago to study *matorral,* shrubby sclerophyll vegetation, typical of the coastal ranges and the Andean foothills of central Chile. On the way we spotted a truly magnificent old specimen of *Puya venusta,* a huge terrestrial bromeliad, forming a dense mound of silvery gray spiky leaves, topped with towering inflorescences carrying dark blue flowers subtended by red bracts. Further up into the hills, we came upon colonies of *Alstroemeria pelegrina* growing together with *Cestrum parqui* and *Sphacele salviae* (011789). By late afternoon we reached the coast in Zapallar, from where we drove south to Viña del Mar, Chile's main beach resort.

In Viña del Mar we were joined by Fernanda Larrain, Olate's student, who helped guide us around the area. Accompanied by Larrain, we headed off to the Parque Nacional La Campana, established mainly to save some of the last remaining groves of Chilean honey palms, *Jubaea chilensis.* Once abundant in the sclerophyll forests occupying valleys and lower slopes of the coastal ranges, these palms for centuries have been cut for their sugary sap. The sap, which flows for months from the severed end of the palm, is processed to make sugar, wine, and syrup, called *miel de palma* or palm honey. Among other noteworthy plants flowering in the park were *Aristolochia chilensis,* a small vine cascading over rocks, and *Drimys winteri,* a tall shrub with rhododendron-like foliage and large inflorescences of showy white flowers.

Back in Santiago we visited Pumahuida Vivero y Jardín, a nursery owned by Mónica Musalem, who specializes in Chilean native plants. Musalem is determined to bring native plants to Chilean gardens, which have traditionally relied entirely on exotic species and garden selections of mostly European origin. The wealth of

Puya venusta, found near Puente Quilimari, north of Los Molles, produces dark blue flowers subtended by red bracts. Photo by Tomasz Aniśko.

plants we saw in the Pumahuida reflected Musalem's extensive expertise and enthusiasm for the Chilean flora. We noticed many plants that we had unsuccessfully searched for during two weeks of scouting through Chile, including *Passiflora pinnatistipula* (011813), *Bomarea salsilla* (011811), and *Crinodendron hookerianum* (011812). This understandingly caused a lot of excitement in our group, and our desire to acquire these plants was very apparent. Musalem, concerned about the uncontrolled exploitation of Chilean flora by European and American collectors in the past, was at first somewhat uneasy about our taking these plants—most of which she had collected herself in the wild—but agreed to share them once we told her of our collaboration with the Pontifica Universidad Católica de Chile.

Remnants of once abundant groves of Chilean honey palms, *Jubaea chilensis,* are protected in the Parque Nacional La Campana east of Viña del Mar. Photo by Tomasz Aniśko.

Aristolochia chilensis cascades from a rock in the Parque Nacional La Campana. Photo by Tomasz Aniśko.

Drimys winteri, a large evergreen shrub, flowers prolifically in the Parque Nacional La Campana. Photo by Tomasz Aniśko.

Our trip ended on 28 October. Returning to the United States, we carried with us a modest bounty of thirty-six choice plants but also extensive notes and photographic documentation of many more species observed in bloom. The field observation formed the core of a thesis prepared after the trip by Eason (2002) and permitted compilation of a list of desired plants to be targeted during future expeditions.

BETWEEN THE FENCES

Based on the experience gained in Chile in 2001, a collecting expedition was planned two years later. To expand the range of plants we might encounter in Chile, the expedition started a few weeks later and included areas further south than the first trip. For this new round of collecting in Chile, I was joined by Tim Thibault, associate curator of Rancho Santa Ana Botanic Garden in Claremont, California. Our team was led again by Olate.

On the morning of 29 November, Thibault and I arrived in Santiago, where we were greeted by Olate. After picking up a rental car at the airport, we were on our way north. Spring was in full swing, and once we left the capital we were able to admire an explosion of wild flowers along the road. That was the idea, at any rate, until Olate told us that what we were seeing were invasive exotic plants, most notably North American *Lupinus arboreus* and European *Chrysanthemum coronarium*. In the course of this expedition we were to develop an appreciation for the scale of this problem, and the many ways in which introduced plants threaten the native flora in Chile.

Traveling on the Pan-American Highway, we stopped in several locations to look for bulbs, which we knew from the previous trip could often be found growing on sandy banks undercut during road construction. Indeed, a few stops later we had our first collections, including two forms of *Rhodophiala bagnoldii* (041–2), one with darker and the other with lighter pink flowers, and *Leucocoryne vittata* (044), which has white flowers with contrasting pink or purple markings.

An impressive specimen of *Puya venusta* spotted from the highway brought us to a stop near Puente Quilimari, just north of Los Molles. Since the area appeared fairly undisturbed, we decided to explore it, and after climbing a barbed-wire fence, we hiked from the road toward the ocean. In days to come we were to repeat this maneuver many times and in the process develop intimate familiarity with Chile's varied fences. As a result of a great portion of Chile's land being dedicated to pastures, it appeared as if a tightly knitted web of barbed wire was wrapped around the whole country. Our initial apprehension about climbing these fences was quickly dispelled by Olate, who clarified that the fences were meant to keep the cows in, not to keep the people out. Luckily for plant collectors, there are apparently no laws in Chile against trespassing, or at least none that are enforced. On the

Olate, left, and Thibault collect plants along the rocky shore of the Pacific near Puente Quilimari. Photo by Tomasz Aniśko.

other side of the fence, we entered into the coastal *matorral*. A number of plants were in bloom, including shrubs such as *Escallonia revoluta* and *Kageneckia oblonga* and perennials such as *Linum aquilinum* and *Alstroemeria diluta*. An even greater profusion of flowers was present on the rocky cliffs overlooking the ocean. Brightly colored *Alstroemeria pelegrina*, *Calandrinia grandiflora* (046), and *Schizanthus litoralis* were scattered among the boulders, while the mat-forming, prostrate *Nolana crassulifolia* (047) spilled over the rocks, enveloping them entirely or filling the crevices. From Los Molles we continued south for about 70 km along the coast, reaching Zapallar before nightfall.

The next morning we drove to the nearby mountains rising above Zapallar. Hiking through a sclerophyll forest in the valley of El Tigre turned out to be quite fruitful. On the south-facing slopes—which in the Southern Hemisphere are less exposed to sun—growing in the deep shade of evergreen trees, was *Senna stipulacea* (048), a shrub blooming with large, bright yellow flowers, and *Bomarea salsilla* (0410), a herbaceous climber related to *Alstroemeria*. In open sunny glades of the forest we found *Libertia sessiliflora* (0411), with pale lilac flowers, and *Alonsoa meridionalis* (0412) and *Lobelia excelsa* (049), both blooming bright red. On the north-facing, sun-baked slopes we collected *Conanthera campanulata* (0413), a cormous plant with gracefully pendant deep blue flowers, and *Flourensia thurifera* (0414), a shrub covered with large, yellow, daisylike inflorescences.

After lunch we drove first inland to El Melón and then back to the coast at Horcón, where Olate led us to a

Bomarea salsilla (0410), a herbaceous climber belonging to the Alstroemeriaceae, was collected in a shaded ravine of El Tigre. Photo by Tomasz Aniśko.

Scarlet-flowered *Lobelia excelsa* (049) was found growing in the sunny glades of El Tigre near Zapallar. Photo by Tomasz Aniśko.

large colony of yellow-flowering *Rhodophiala advena* (0416), which he knew of from his previous excursions in the area. Unfortunately, because of its proximity to Cau Cau, a popular beach, this population is threatened by development. Growing along with *Rhodophiala* were *Alstroemeria hookeri* ssp. *recumbens* (0417) and *Conanthera bifolia,* all together making a cheerful combination of yellow, pink, and blue flowers in this otherwise bleak habitat. For the night we returned to Zapallar.

On 1 December we headed to Farellones in the Andes, east of Santiago, to see if spring had yet arrived in the higher mountains, above 2000 m. First, in the lower hills of the Andes, we saw many new flowering plants, probably none more attractive than *Alstroemeria ligtu* ssp. *simsii* (0421), setting the entire hillside ablaze with orange flowers. This was our initiation to the major

undertaking involved in digging out *Alstroemeria* roots. This plant's fragile rhizomes are typically found at a depth of about 30 cm, while the easily breakable storage roots, essential for the plant's survival, reach to about 60 cm below the surface. Only by patiently and carefully removing soil and rocks from around the roots could we assure that the rhizome was not severed from the storage roots. Once several *Alstroemeria* plants were successfully excavated, we continued up the mountain on a steep, winding road. Approaching Farellones, we realized we had arrived too early to see most of the spring flora; therefore, we decided to turn back and return to this area at a later date.

Roadside refugia

After spending a night in Santiago, we were on the road again, this time heading to the Reserva Nacional Las Siete

Olate, left, and Thibault are surrounded by *Chusquea cumingii,* a native bamboo, and *Fabiana imbricata,* a solanaceous heatherlike shrub, growing above the timberline in the Reserva Nacional Las Siete Tazas. Photo by Tomasz Aniśko.

A yellow-flowered form of *Rhodophiala advena* (0416) collected near a popular beach, Cau Cau, at Horcón. Photo by Tomasz Aniśko.

Tazas situated in the lower ranges of the Andes near El Radal, some 250 km south of the capital. Upon our arrival we discovered that the cabins in which we were to stay were locked and the caretaker was nowhere to be found. Luckily, the scouts camping nearby told us about a hostel close to the park rangers' station. The hostel was open, saving us from driving back to El Radal late in the evening on a rather tortuous road.

In the morning, well rested from our long drive the day before, we started off on a trail along Río Claro, crossing the reserve. The river valley was densely forested, with *Nothofagus dombeyi* a dominant species. Among the more attractive understory shrubs was *Maytenus chubutensis* (0425), resembling boxwood in its habit but with reddish new growth, while *Fabiana imbricata* frequented the

open, exposed places. This latter shrub, despite its heatherlike appearance, is a member of Solanaceae. While typically it has very prolific, but rather dirty white flowers, occasionally we saw forms with flowers of a more defined lilac or purple color. One such attractive purple-flowered form (0426) enticed us enough to collect cuttings. This shrub not only mimicked a heather in its appearance, but above the timberline it became the dominant species, forming stands comparable to the heaths of the Northern Hemisphere. Later in the afternoon we departed Las Siete Tazas and drove to Lago Colbún, about 50 km east of Talca, to spend a night there.

Our destination for 4 December was Laguna del Maule in the high Andes near the Argentinean border. Driving on a road following Río Maule, we made several stops to browse through the roadside vegetation. During the course of this expedition we realized that the road-sides in Chile often offer refugia for plants that by and large have disappeared elsewhere. Inaccessible to grazing livestock and safe from herbicides applied in managed forest plantations, the roadsides, if not overrun by invasive exotic plants, provide many native plants their best chance for survival.

Although unsafe road conditions that day prevented us from reaching Laguna del Maule, we were able to make a number of interesting collections, including *Alstroemeria ligtu* ssp. *incarnata* (0427), with flowers in various shades of pink and salmon; *Calceolaria thyrsiflora* (0428), another shrubby member of the genus, this one with dark green foliage; and a bright red form of

Olate, left, and the author enjoy lunch in the valley of Río Maule. Photo by Tomasz Aniśko.

A colony of *Alstroemeria ligtu* ssp. *incarnata* (0427) with flowers in various shades of pink and salmon was found along the road leading to Laguna del Maule in the Andes, east of Talca. Photo by Tomasz Aniśko.

Shrubby *Calceolaria thyrsiflora* (0428) was spotted along Río Maule while traveling towards the Argentinean border, east of Talca. Photo by Tomasz Aniśko.

Salpiglossis sinuata (0430). In the afternoon we headed to Reserva Nacional Altos de Lircay near Vilches, northwest of Lago Colbún.

Black sand beaches

After spending another night at Lago Colbún, we departed for Constitución, a coastal town at the mouth of Río Maule. Then, driving along the coast, we stopped some 11 km south of La Trinchera to inspect vegetation on the fringes of the black sand dunes—a testimony of recent volcanic activity in the Andes—separating the road from the ocean. To our surprise in what appeared to be a very inhospitable habitat, we found a quite large population of *Rhodophiala splendens* (0436). Although the plants were clearly impoverished growing under these spartan conditions, their large scarlet flowers glistened in the setting sun like gems scattered in the otherwise austere landscape.

We started off on 6 December with an excursion to the rocky cliffs south of Constitución. Such cliffs, constantly subjected to the moderating influences of the ocean, are clad by an amazing variety of plants, and in places where the cliffs are accessible, they offer excellent plant-hunting possibilities. We collected a bumper crop of *Phycella* (0437) seeds and exceptionally dark purple *Calandrinia longiscapa* (0438) on one of the massive outcrops along the black sand beach.

Continuing south along the coast, we stopped in the small town of Pelluhue, where we explored rock formations similar to those in Constitución. From Pelluhue we

Mutisia subulata, a herbaceous vine found near Los Despachos, south of Cauquenes, boasted these showy gerbera-like inflorescences. Photo by Tomasz Aniśko.

The cliffs south of Constitución offered breathtaking views and a rich flora. Photo by Tomasz Aniśko.

turned inland toward Cauquenes. Near Los Despachos, some 20 km south of Cauquenes, we spotted along the road a beautiful *Mutisia subulata* vine covering a large shrub of *Acacia caven* and just opening its first inflorescences. Although we had seen several *Mutisia* species earlier on our trip, none enthused us like this one. It had large, dark pink, gerbera-like inflorescences, and from the number of buds waiting to open we could imagine what a prolific bloomer it must be. To our despair, though, there were no seeds to collect.

From Los Despachos we drove to Chillán, a town on the Pan-American Highway, and from there continued east to Termas de Chillán in the Andes.

Soaking up the rain

Termas de Chillán is a popular health spa in Chile, built near several thermal vents and sulfuric springs. The

morning after arriving there, we hiked to some of these thermal vents in the mountains. Hiking through the *Nothofagus* forest, we found *Maytenus disticha* (0483), a low-growing shrub with small, leathery, glossy leaves, which held much promise as a landscape plant for more warm-temperate parts of the United States. Above the timberline we saw large colonies of *Lathyrus subandinus,* a perennial species with prolific bicolor flowers, among which were interspersed *Olsynium philippi* and *Tristagma nivale* (0443).

On 8 December we left Termas de Chillán for Los Ángeles and the next morning drove to Parque Nacional Nahuelbuta in the Cordillera de Nahuelbuta, part of Chile's coastal ranges. We had awaited the opportunity to explore this park, known for its *Araucaria araucana* forest, with great anticipation. Arriving several weeks later than during the 2001 expedition, we hoped to see many more spring flowers in bloom. Unfortunately, this day also caught us in drenching rain. We pressed ahead, hoping for a break in the weather, but upon ascending to the top of the Cordillera de Nahuelbuta we were forced to admit defeat. A ferocious wind and a constant downpour made even walking barely possible. Fortunately, we were able to console ourselves with a few collections made along the road leading to the park. These included *Rhodophiala splendens* (0448), much larger than those collected near La Trinchera; *Teucrium bicolor* (0449), a subshrub of Lamiaceae, adorned with loose racemes of soft pink flowers; and *Ugni molinae* (0450), a myrtaceous shrub with delightfully fragrant flowers followed by equally aro-

The delightfully fragrant flowers of *Ugni molinae* (0450) are followed by red berries, which are used in preserves and liqueurs. Photo by Tomasz Aniśko.

Stunning flowers of *Rhodophiala splendens* (0448) collected on the way from Los Ángeles to Parque Nacional Nahuelbuta. Photo by Tomasz Aniśko.

matic red berries, used in Chile for making preserves and sweet liqueur.

On 10 December we changed direction and, hoping to run out from beneath the rain clouds, drove to the Termas de Tolguaca, a small spa in the Andes about 100 km south of Los Ángeles. Our attempts to stay dry turned out to be futile. The heavy rain followed us, and upon reaching the Termas de Tolguaca we were confined to the hotel for the rest of the day while the weather took a turn for the worse, the rain changing to snow and sleet. It became clear we would no longer be enjoying the balmy Mediterranean climate of central Chile, and needed to prepare ourselves for the capricious spring weather of the temperate southern regions.

The Andean backcountry

In the morning we took the road from Tolguaca to Parque Nacional Conguillio, about 80 km to the south. Along the way we collected several plants, including *Fuchsia magellanica* (0451) and *Alstroemeria aurea* (0452). Upon arriving in the park we rented a cabin and took a hike through the forest of *Araucaria* and *Nothofagus* along the shore of Laguna Conguillio. To our delight, the sky cleared in the evening, and we could see the majestic, snowcapped Volcán Llaima, 3125 m, dominating the horizon.

For 12 December we planned a 200 km loop, driving through the mountains toward the Argentinean border and returning to Conguillio for the night. First we headed south to Flor del Valle, a picturesque valley surrounded by tall, somber Andean peaks on all sides and lined with emerald pastures. We hiked up a steep slope in an attempt to explore the forest beyond the reach of grazing cows. After an exhausting climb, we gave up, however, as signs of overgrazing made it clear the cows were more fit than we thought and had plundered the forest quite far up the mountain. Our only collection at this site was *Sophora cassioides* (0453).

Upon reaching Melipeuco, we turned east to Icalma and from there north to Lonquimay. The day's collections included *Francoa appendiculata* (0456), *Gaultheria pumila* (0458), and *Mimulus luteus* (0457). Probably the most significant finding was *Drimys winteri* var. *andina* (0455), a shrubby variety of this beautiful Chilean tree. Plants we found near Reserva Nacional China Muerta

The bright yellow flowers of *Alstroemeria aurea* (0452) were spotted along the road from Tolguaca to Parque Nacional Conguillio. Photo by Tomasz Aniśko.

Rarely seen *Rhodophiala moelleri* (0461) was collected in the Andes between Curarrehue and Puerto Negro. Photo by Tomasz Aniśko.

were less than 1 m tall and had smaller leaves than the trees in the lowlands. Because of its compact growth and possibly greater cold hardiness, this variety may prove to be a better garden plant.

The following day we headed to Pucón, located on the east end of Lago Villarrica. Pucón welcomed us with drizzle, which intensified the next morning. Despite the weather, we started off on the road east to Curarrehue, taking a dirt track through the mountains to Puerto Negro. The road itself was in fairly bad shape, with fallen trees blocking it in several places and one of the bridges washed out. In addition, the constant rain and slippery surface made driving more difficult. To our relief, however, our four-wheel-drive vehicle, with Olate at the wheel, stood up to the test. What started off as a rather hopeless day for collecting turned out to be very rewarding when we came across *Rhodophiala moelleri* (0461), a rare member of the genus, which added a new purple-pink color to those we had collected previously. This was our last day collecting in the Andes, and we never saw that plant again.

Mission accomplished

On 15 December we headed to the coast again. By way of Loncoche, Lastarria, and Puentes, we reached Nueva Toltén in the afternoon. From there we turned south to Valdivia, making a stop near Queule, a small fishing village about 100 km north of Valdivia. A few kilometers south of Queule we explored windswept cliffs overlooking the Pacific. From our previous experience we knew that in

places such as this, free of grazing livestock, interesting plants could often be found. We were not disappointed this time, either. The most intriguing find in Queule was a prostrate form of *Escallonia rubra* var. *macrantha* (0466) with leathery, glossy leaves and large carmine-red flowers. Although at first we debated the identity of the plant, we all agreed it was a garden-worthy shrub.

Valdivia was an anxiously anticipated destination for us because of the unique Valdivian temperate rain forest, much of which still survives in the areas south of that city. This coastal region remains relatively undeveloped and has very few settlements. There are hardly any paved highways, and access can be gained only on logging roads. On the morning of 16 December we drove first from Valdivia to Niebla, a small village on the coast. A ferry in Niebla took us across Río Valdivia to Corral,

Crinodendron hookerianum (0470) is among the most desired shrubs indigenous to the Valdivian temperate rain forest. Photo by Tomasz Aniśko.

from where we continued south to Chaihuin. At that point our plan called for a drive inland to El Mirador, through the hills covered by the rain forest. In the meantime, however, the paved highway all but disappeared, and we had to rely on logging roads not marked on any of our maps. In other areas we had always been able to count on finding someone to ask for directions, but this was not the case in the rain forest; here we were on our own. After guessing a couple of times regarding which turns to take, we became increasingly skeptical about our chances of crossing this vast expanse of forest before night. Still, the hope of finding *Crinodendron hookeri-*

anum, one of the botanical gems inhabiting the Valdivian forest, motivated us to press forward.

Finally, at a rest stop, as Olate and I devoured our dry provisions, consisting of crackers and candy bars, Thibault, who had sought a moment of solitude behind the bushes, called on us to come see what he had found. There it was, *Crinodendron hookerianum* (0470), with its pendant, scarlet flowers, embedded in the most impenetrable growth of evergreen tress, shrubs, and vines imaginable.

With our mission thus accomplished, we soon decided to turn back and follow the road on which we had come.

On 17 December we boarded a flight from Valdivia to Santiago. We left behind the verdant hills of the southern coastal ranges and in less than two hours were back in the sun-scorched Central Valley. The last couple of days in Santiago were dedicated to cleaning seeds and cuttings, organizing herbarium specimens, and arranging for the phytosanitary certificates. One morning we paid a visit to Mónica Musalem's nursery, Pumahuida Vivero y Jardín, which, as we knew from the previous trip, grew a wide selection of Chilean native plants. Based on Musalem's suggestions, we picked a number of plants, among them *Alstroemeria revoluta* (0473), *Mitraria coccinea* (0474), and *Tecoma fulva* (0475), thus bringing the total number of collections for this expedition to 120.

Epilogue

The story of plant exploration for Longwood Gardens told in this book encompasses fifty expeditions that took place between 1956 and 2003. During that span of time, the world was transformed as the result of social, political, and technological changes. Plant exploration was not immune to the forces that shaped our societies and environment during the second half of the twentieth century; it too underwent a remarkable evolution. The expedition of Frank Kingdon Ward to Burma, the trip that began it all, was perhaps the last in the long tradition of what has been described as the Golden Age of plant collecting. A lonely professional plant explorer, who funds his endeavors through subscriptions from prominent public gardens and wealthy private collectors, embarks on a ten-month expedition to conduct a thorough exploration of a single mountain. His progress is slow, encumbered by lack of roads, primitive means of transportation, and dependence on a large entourage of porters. His main challenges are reaching a remote site, finding plants, and assuring they arrive alive at their destinations in Europe or America after a long sea journey.

Due to the relative ease of travel and transportation, expeditions now take weeks rather than months. The trips almost invariably involve teams of collaborators, none of whom are plant explorers by profession, but rather garden curators, university professors, or nurserymen. Team members share the costs of the expedition and combine their varied expertise. Help from local collaborators is essential, just as it was fifty years ago, but in place of porters, today's expeditions rely, often completely, on the participation of highly trained experts—botanists, horticulturists, or nurserymen—who are working in the area being explored. Finding plants in the field remains a matter of both skill and luck, but shipping them is easier than ever before. Thanks to the conveniences of polyethylene bags and air mail, packages containing unrooted cuttings can be delivered alive sometimes in less than a week from the time of collection.

On the other hand, the legal environment in which modern plant explorers have to operate could not be more different from that known to Frank Kingdon Ward. The framework of local, national, and international laws regulating access, transfer, and utilization of plants is more complex than ever. Some of these laws were enacted to facilitate conservation of species or habitats threatened with extinction. Others protect the proprietary rights to plants ascertained by commercial interests of individuals, organizations, or nations. Still others aim to prevent the introduction of exotic weeds, pests, and diseases, which might endanger economically significant crops or cause damage to the environment. Modern explorers, equipped with global positioning system receivers, cell phones, and off-road vehicles, can navigate through the most remote regions of the world with amazing efficiency, but they may find it increasingly difficult to map their way through the maze of regulations applied to plant collecting.

Fifty countries on six continents were visited in the course of the expeditions described in this book. In organizing these expeditions, Longwood Gardens did not act alone but collaborated with a wide range of institutions such as the USDA and the International Dendrological Research Institute; gardens and arboreta such as the Arnold Arboretum of Harvard University, Descanso Gardens, Holden Arboretum, Huntington Gardens, J. C. Raulston Arboretum, Morris Arboretum, Morton Arboretum, Rancho Santa Ana Botanic Garden, and U.S. National Arboretum; universities such as Harvard University, University of Connecticut, University of Virginia, and University of North Carolina; and nurseries such as Conard-Pyle Company, Rare Find Nursery, Saunders Brothers Nursery, and Woodland Nursery. And this is to name only a few. In fact, out of more than fifty explorers who participated in these expeditions, only sixteen were Longwood employees. To this list, dozens of cooperating institutions and individuals in foreign countries, equally important to the whole endeavor, would have to be added.

Their combined effort and more than six years of field work resulted in the introduction of more than thirteen thousand ornamental plants to the United States. The plants were widely distributed, freely shared, and evaluated to determine their suitability for cultivation. Many failed, and nobody knows how many of them exist today, but unquestionably their impact on gardening in America cannot be overestimated. Longwood Gardens' own collection was enlarged from about three thousand taxa in 1955 to more than thirteen thousand in the early 1970s and has remained at this level ever since. One-tenth of this increase can be credited to plant exploration.

Plant exploration for Longwood Gardens does not end with the fifty expeditions described in this book. Two teams went to Russia and Australia in 2004, another two traveled to China and Greece in 2005, and future expeditions are in the planning stages. As long as our fascination with plants of exquisite beauty continues, we will seek them out in the furthest regions of the world.

References

All unpublished materials are courtesy of Longwood Gardens Archives.

Anderson, E. 1965b. *Victoria* water lilies: plants which stir men's minds. *Missouri Botanical Garden Bulletin* 53 (5): 1–18.

Apps, D. A. 1986. Letter of 12 September to H. Marc Cathey of the U.S. National Arboretum.

Apps, D., and L. Batdorf. 1988. The search for and the evaluation of Korean daylily species. *The Daylily Journal* 43 (1): 11–19.

Barclay, A. S. 1956. Letter of 23 August to Walter H. Hodge.

Barclay, A. S. 1959. New considerations in an old genus: *Datura. Botanical Museum Leaflets, Harvard University* 18 (6): 245–272.

Brass, L. J. 1959. Letter of 14 January to Russell J. Seibert.

Brass, L. J. 1960. Letter of 13 July to Russell J. Seibert.

Campabadal, J. R. 1969. Letter of 6 June to Russell J. Seibert.

Cathey, H. M. 1986. Letter of 18 July to Frederick E. Roberts.

Creech, J. L. 1956a. Letter of 2 November to Walter H. Hodge.

Creech, J. L. 1956b. Letter of 10 November to Howard L. Hyland.

Creech, J. L. 1956c. Letter of 28 November to Howard L. Hyland.

Creech, J. L. 1957. Plant explorations: ornamentals in Southern Japan. Crops Research Division, ARS 34-1, Agricultural Research Service, USDA.

Creech, J. L. 1961a. *Camellia japonica* in Japan. *American Camellia Yearbook* 1961: 6–21.

Creech, J. L. 1961b. Letter of 3 May to Walter H. Hodge.

Creech, J. L. 1961c. Letter of 7 June to Walter H. Hodge.

Creech, J. L. 1961d. Letter of 23 July to Walter H. Hodge.

Creech, J. L. 1962a. Letter of 25 October to Carl O. Erlanson.

Creech, J. L. 1962b. Letter of 1 November to Carl O. Erlanson.

Creech, J. L. 1962c. Letter of 13 November to Carl O. Erlanson.

Creech, J. L. 1962d. Letter of 29 November to Russell J. Seibert.

Creech, J. L. 1963a. Letter of 30 August to Carl O. Erlanson.

Creech, J. L. 1963b. Letter of 13 September to Carl O. Erlanson.

Creech, J. L. 1963c. Letter of 31 October to Russell J. Seibert.

Creech, J. L. 1966a. Letter of 28 December to Russell J. Seibert.

Creech, J. L. 1966b. Ornamental plant explorations—Japan, 1961. Crops Research Division, ARS 34-75, Agricultural Research Service, USDA.

Creech, J. L. 1967a. Letter of 24 November to Quentin Jones of the USDA Agricultural Research Service.

Creech, J. L. 1967b. Letter of 24 November to Russell J. Seibert.

Creech, J. L. 1967c. Summary trip report: plant exploration to Taiwan, November 8 to December 18. USDA New Crops Research Branch, Beltsville, Maryland.

Creech, J. L. 1968. Letter of 10 January to Russell J. Seibert.

Creech, J. L. 1970a. Letter of 9 July to Howard L. Hyland.

Creech, J. L. 1970b. Plant exploration to the Soviet Union: July 15 to October 1. Proposal.

Creech, J. L. 1971a. A new look at Siberia: the ornamental plant possibilities. Lecture presented at Longwood Gardens, 15 December.

Creech, J. L. 1971b. Foreign travel report: USSR, June 23 to August 29. Crops Research Division, Agricultural Research Service, USDA.

Creech, J. L. 1971c. Letter of 16 July to Howard L. Hyland.

Creech, J. L. 1971d. Letter of 24 July to Howard L. Hyland.

Creech, J. L. 1971e. Letter of 6 August to Howard L. Hyland.

Creech, J. L. 1972. Plant collector in Siberia. *The University of Washington Arboretum Bulletin* 35 (3): 2–6.

Creech, J. L. 1974. Introduction of foreign plants to American gardens. Lecture presented at Longwood Gardens, 7 March.

Creech, J. L. 1987. A trip to Mt. Morrison mixes horticulture with adventure. *American Nurseryman* 165 (9): 130–132.

Creech, J. L. 1988. From Russia with plants. *American Nurseryman* 168 (1): 84–90.

Creech, J. L., and D. H. Scott. 1963. Memorandum of 18 October to M. W. Parker of the Crops Research Division, USDA Agricultural Research Service.

Crossan, D. F. 1969. Report on Longwood tropical study tour. Manuscript.

Darke, R. 1987a. New crops for Longwood Gardens. *Chimes* 151: 3.

Darke, R. 1987b. Plants and plantings. *Chimes* 154: 9.

Davis, W. 1996. *One River: Explorations and Discoveries in the Amazon Rain Forest*. New York: Simon and Schuster. 353.

de Freitas, C. L. 1969. Letter of 10 June to Russell J. Seibert.

de Vos, F. 1963. Plant exploring in Nepal. In *1963 National Capitol Flower and Garden Show Guide*. Washington, D.C.

de Vos, F. 1965a. Letter of 22 April to Henry T. Skinner of the U.S. National Arboretum.

de Vos, F. 1965b. Letter of 27 April to John L. Creech.

de Vos, F. 1965c. Letter of 8 May to John L. Creech.

de Vos, F. 1965d. Letter of 20 May to John L. Creech.

de Vos, F. 1965e. Letter of 22 June to Russell J. Seibert.

Dodson, C. H. 1964. Undated letter to Russell J. Seibert.

Eason, R. T. 2002. *Mediterranean Plants from Chile for Displays at Longwood Gardens*. M.S. Thesis, University of Delaware.

Fooks, C. T. 2002. Boxwood expedition to the Republic of Georgia. *The Boxwood Bulletin* 42 (1): 12–15.

Frierson, H. F. 2002. Boxwood in nature and gardens: travels to southern Russia and Ukraine. *The Boxwood Bulletin* 42 (2): 27–32.

Frierson, H. F. 2003. Boxwood in nature: travels to Azerbaijan and Georgia in 2002. *The Boxwood Bulletin* 42 (4): 69–76.

Gerlach, G. G. 1969. Letter of 14 July to Russell J. Seibert.

Higgins, J. J. 1970. Letter of 18 March to Russell J. Seibert.

Hodge, B. 1959a. Letter of 30 September to the Hodge family at Longwood.

Hodge, B. 1959b. Letter of 8 October to the Hodge family at Longwood.

Hodge, W. H. 1944. A botanist's Dominica diary. *Scientific Monthly* 58: 185–194, 281–291.

Hodge, W. H. 1956a. Letter of 16 August to Arthur S. Barclay.

Hodge, W. H. 1956b. Letter of 5 September to Arthur S. Barclay.

Hodge, W. H. 1956c. Letter of 5 September to Richard E. Schultes.

Hodge, W. H. 1956d. Letter of 5 December to Frederick G. Meyer.

Hodge, W. H. 1957a. Letter of 21 January to Frederick G. Meyer.

Hodge, W. H. 1957b. Letter of 10 June to Frank Kingdon Ward.

Hodge, W. H. 1957c. Letter of 11 November to Arthur S. Barclay.

Hodge, W. H. 1958a. Letter of 6 January to Arthur S. Barclay.

Hodge, W. H. 1958b. Letter of 2 September to Barbara T. Hodge.

Hodge, W. H. 1958c. Letter of 10 September to Barbara T. Hodge.

Hodge, W. H. 1958d. Letter of 10 September to Donald G. Huttleston.

Hodge, W. H. 1958e. Letter of 11 September to Barbara T. Hodge.

Hodge, W. H. 1958f. Letter of 12 September to Barbara T. Hodge.

Hodge, W. H. 1958g. Letter of 14 September to Barbara T. Hodge.

Hodge, W. H. 1958h. Letter of 20 September to Barbara T. Hodge.

Hodge, W. H. 1958i. Letter of 22 September to Barbara T. Hodge.

Hodge, W. H. 1958j. Letter of 27 September to Barbara T. Hodge.

Hodge, W. H. 1958k. Letter of 13 October to Barbara T. Hodge.

Hodge, W. H. 1959a. Letter of 19 January to Leonard J. Brass.

Hodge, W. H. 1959b. Letter of 20 October to Russell J. Seibert.

Hodge, W. H. 1959c. Letter of 22 October to Donald G. Huttleston, Gottlieb A. Hampfler, and Katherine Farquhar of Longwood Gardens.

Hodge, W. H. 1959d. The Longwood Gardens–USDA plant introduction program. *The National Horticultural Magazine* 38 (3): 164–167.

Hodge, W. H. 1960a. *Byblis gigantea. The American Horticultural Magazine* 39: 55–58.

Hodge, W. H. 1960b. New-Guinea trumpet-creeper. *The American Horticultural Magazine* 39: 184.

Hodge, W. H. 1960c. Two unusual hoyas. *The American Horticultural Magazine* 39: 231–232.

Hodge, W. H. 1961a. Longwood search: botanist collects plants and seed in Indonesia's Kebun Raya. *The New York Times* (22 January): X21.

Hodge, W. H. 1961b. Memorandum of 8 March to Russell J. Seibert.

Hodge, W. H. 1962. A rarely cultivated pitcher plant. *The American Horticultural Magazine* 41: 13–16.

Huttleston, D. G. 1960. Camellias at Longwood Gardens, Kennett Square, Pennsylvania. *Rhododendron and Camellia Year Book* (1960): 124–128.

Huttleston, D. G. 1969a. Letter of 16 July to Robert G. Wilson.

Huttleston, D. G. 1969b. Memorandum of 7 July to Russell J. Seibert.

Hyland, H. L. 1960. Summary report 1959–1960: new crops—Longwood ornamentals project.

Johnson, K. C. 1967. *Disa uniflora*: a method of cultivation and its hybridization with *D. racemosa. Journal of Botanical Society of South Africa* 53: 19–26.

Kim, K. 1997. Plant exploration to Shaanxi and Gansu provinces in China. *Holly Society Journal* 15 (2): 3–11.

Kingdon Ward, F. 1955. Letter of 30 September to Russell J. Seibert.

Kingdon Ward, F. 1956a. Letter of 10 August to Russell J. Seibert.

Kingdon Ward, F. 1956b. Plant hunting in Burma 1: the changing scene. *Gardener's Chronicle* 140: 8–9.

Kingdon Ward, F. 1956c. Plant hunting in Burma 2: against the odds. *Gardener's Chronicle* 140: 85.

Kingdon Ward, F. 1956d. Plant hunting in Burma 3: the real thing. *Gardener's Chronicle* 140: 185.

Kingdon Ward, F. 1956e. Plant hunting in Burma 4: the summit. *Gardener's Chronicle* 140: 287.

Kingdon Ward, F. 1956f. Plant hunting in Burma 5: the evergreen forest. *Gardener's Chronicle* 140: 486.

Kingdon Ward, F. 1956g. Plant hunting in Burma 6: Mindat ridge. *Gardener's Chronicle* 140: 656.

Kingdon Ward, F. 1957a. Plant hunting in Burma 7: orchids and all that. *Gardener's Chronicle* 141: 123.

Kingdon Ward, F. 1957b. Plant hunting in Burma 8: in the mist. *Gardener's Chronicle* 141: 576.

Kingdon Ward, F. 1958. A sketch of the flora and vegetation of Mount Victoria in Burma. *Acta Horti Gotoburgensis* 22: 53–74.

Kingdon Ward, F. 1960. *Pilgrimage for Plants*. London: George G. Harrap. 106–107.

Lighty, R. W. 1966a. Letter of 15 July to Russell J. Seibert.

Lighty, R. W. 1966b. Letter of 2 August to Russell J. Seibert.

Lighty, R. W. 1966c. Letter of 12 August to Katherine B. Farquhar and Donald G. Huttleston.

Lighty, R. W. 1966d. Letter of 17 August to Russell J. Seibert.

Lighty, R. W. 1966e. Letter of 25 August to Russell J. Seibert.

Lighty, R. W. 1966f. Letter of 4 September to Russell J. Seibert.

Lighty, R. W. 1966g. Letter of 30 September to Russell J. Seibert.

Lighty, R. W. 1966h. Letter of 7 October to Russell J. Seibert.

March, S. G. 1985. Collecting elite plants: Japan. Report.

Meyer, F. G. 1957a. Letter of 26 January to Walter H. Hodge.

Meyer, F. G. 1957b. Letter of 7 March to Walter H. Hodge.

Meyer, F. G. 1957c. Letter of 1 May to Russell J. Seibert.

Meyer, F. G. 1957d. Letter of 25 May to Russell J. Seibert.

Meyer, F. G. 1957e. Letter of 4 July to Howard L. Hyland.

Meyer, F. G. 1957f. Letter of 4 July to Walter H. Hodge.

Meyer, F. G. 1957g. Letter of 4 August to Walter H. Hodge.

Meyer, F. G. 1957h. Letter of 18 August to Walter H. Hodge.

Meyer, F. G. 1957i. Letter of 17 September to Walter H. Hodge.

Meyer, F. G. 1959a. Letter of 26 June to Walter H. Hodge.

Meyer, F. G. 1959b. Letter of 13 July to Walter H. Hodge.

Meyer, F. G. 1959c. Letter of 3 August to Walter H. Hodge.

Meyer, F. G. 1959d. Letter of 18 August to Walter H. Hodge.

Meyer, F. G. 1959e. Plant explorations: ornamentals in Italy, Southern France, Spain, Portugal, England, and Scotland. Crops Research Division, ARS 34-9, Agricultural Research Service, USDA.

Meyer, F. G. 1963. Plant exploration: ornamentals in the Netherlands, West Germany, and Belgium. Crops Research Division, ARS 34-32, Agricultural Research Service, USDA.

Paul, L. W. 1969. Rare orchid on display at Longwood Gardens. *American Horticultural Society Magazine* 48 (3): 138–139.

Rycroft, H. B. 1964. Letter of 27 February to Russell J. Seibert.

Schelpe, E. A. 1963. Letter of 21 November to Russell J. Seibert.

Schultes, R. E. 1956a. Letter of 8 August to Walter H. Hodge.

Schultes, R. E. 1956b. Letter of 21 August to Walter H. Hodge.

Schultes, R. E. 1956c. Letter of 18 September to Walter H. Hodge.

Schweinfurth U., and H. Schweinfurth-Marby. 1975. *Exploration in the Eastern Himalayas and the River Gorge Country of Southeastern Tibet.* Geoecological Research, vol. 3. Wiesbaden: Franz Steiner Verlag.

Seibert, D. 1962. Sailing across the Andes. *Travel* (September): 39–54.

Seibert, I. L. 1959a. Letter of 10 January to Seibert's children.

Seibert, I. L. 1959b. Letter of 20 January to Seibert's children.

Seibert, I. L. 1959c. South America. Trip diary.

Seibert, I. L. 1967. Houston to Yucatán, Mexico. Trip diary.

Seibert, I. L. 1968. Caribbean. Trip diary.

Seibert, I. L. 1971. El Salvador, Guatemala and Honduras. Trip diary.

Seibert, I. L. 1999. A treasure of memories. Manuscript.

Seibert, R. J. 1940. The Bignoniaceae of the Maya area. *Carnegie Institution of Washington Publication* 522: 375–434.

Seibert, R. J. 1948. The use of glands in a taxonomic consideration of the family Bignoniaceae. *Annals of the Missouri Botanical Garden* 35: 123–136.

Seibert, R. J. 1956a. Letter of 24 May to Carl O. Erlanson.

Seibert, R. J. 1956b. Letter of 12 September to Carl O. Erlanson.

Seibert, R. J. 1958a. Letter of 8 January to Howard L. Hyland.

Seibert, R. J. 1958b. Letter of 3 February to Samuel Ayres of the California Arboretum Foundation.

Seibert, R. J. 1959a. Letter of 19 March to Humberto Fabris.

Seibert, R. J. 1959b. Letter of 21 April to Carlos G. Cariola.

Seibert, R. J. 1960. Letter of 3 August to H. van Vloten of De Dorschkamp Forest Research Station in Wageningen, Netherlands.

Seibert, R. J. 1962. Letter of 2 April to Howard L. Hyland.

Seibert, R. J. 1963a. Letter of 18 July to Carl O. Erlanson.

Seibert, R. J. 1963b. Letter of 16 September to Everitt L. Miller.

Seibert, R. J. 1963c. Letter of 20 November to H. Brian Rycroft.

Seibert, R. J. 1963d. Letter of 6 December to F. W. Thorns of Durban Botanic Garden.

Seibert, R. J. 1963e. Memorandum of 18 December to the trustees of Longwood Foundation.

Seibert, R. J. 1964a. Letter of 17 March to H. Brian Rycroft.

Seibert, R. J. 1964b. Letter of 7 April to H. Brian Rycroft.

Seibert, R. J. 1964c. Letter of 5 May to L. Prosser of Saint George's Park.

Seibert, R. J. 1964d. Letter of 17 November to Michael H. Langford of the American Embassy in Lima.

Seibert, R. J. 1964e. Letter of 30 November to Ramón Ferreyra.

Seibert, R. J. 1964f. Plantsman's safari. *The Horticultural Society of New York Bulletin* 14 (9/10): 3–4.

Seibert, R. J. 1965a. Letter of 9 September to Edward A. Schelpe.

Seibert, R. J. 1965c. Report of 3 May to the trustees of Longwood Foundation.

Seibert, R. J. 1965d. South African ornamentals for American plant connoisseurs. *The Garden Journal* 15 (2): 67–68.

Seibert, R. J. 1966a. *Disa uniflora* at Longwood Gardens. *American Orchid Society Bulletin* 35: 367–369.

Seibert, R. J. 1966b. Letter of 24 January to Ger Verhaar.

Seibert, R. J. 1967a. "Cojomaria": *Paramongaia weberbaueri* Velarde, from Peru. *Plant Life* 23: 43–45.

Seibert, R. J. 1967b. Letter of 22 November to Iris M. Bannochie.

Seibert, R. J. 1967c. Letter of 28 December to Mary Plunkett of Longwood Gardens.

Seibert, R. J. 1967d. Memorandum of 30 June to the trustees of Longwood Foundation.

Seibert, R. J. 1968a. Letter of 5 February to Iris M. Bannochie.

Seibert, R. J. 1968b. Letter of 31 December to Robert G. Wilson.

Seibert, R. J. 1968c. Memorandum of 15 February to the trustees of Longwood Foundation.

Seibert, R. J. 1970a. Funds for exploring. *The New York Times* (4 January): D29.

Seibert, R. J. 1970b. Memorandum of 10 June to the trustees of Longwood Foundation.

Seibert, R. J. 1970c. Memorandum of 16 November to Longwood Program fellows.

Seibert, R. J. 1971. Letter of 21 June to Rex Thomas of the USDA Agricultural Research Service.

Spalding, G. H. 1962. Plant explorations: ornamentals in Australia. Crops Research Division, ARS 34-33, Agricultural Research Service, USDA.

Williams, L. 1958. Memorandum of 28 May to Howard L. Hyland of the USDA Agricultural Research Service.

Williams, L. 1959. Collecting ornamentals in southern Brazil. Manuscript.

Wilson, R. G. 1969. Letter of 5 August to Russell J. Seibert.

Winters, H. F. 1970a. Letter of 28 January to John L. Creech.

Winters, H. F. 1970b. Letter of 30 January to Russell J. Seibert.

Winters, H. F. 1970c. Letter of 18 February to Myra L. Haines of USDA Inspection House.

Winters, H. F. 1970d. Letter of 17 March to Howard L. Hyland of the USDA New Crops Research Branch.

Winters, H. F. . Letter of 27 March to John L. Creech.

Winters, H. F. 1970f. New germ plasm of ornamental plants from New Guinea. *Proceedings of the Tropical Region of the American Society for Horticultural Science* 14: 280–284.

Winters, H. F. 1970g. Plant collecting in New Guinea. Lecture presented at Longwood Gardens, 28 July.

Winters, H. F. 1972. Letter of 24 August to Russell J. Seibert.

Winters, H. F. 1976. *Microcitrus papuana,* a new species from Papua New Guinea (Rutaceae). *Baileya* 20 (1): 19–24.

Winters, H. F., and J. J. Higgins. 1970. Foreign travel report: Hawaii, New Caledonia, Australia, New Guinea, Philippines and Indonesia, January 4–April 14. Crops Research Division, Agricultural Research Service, USDA.

Woodson, R. E., and R. J. Seibert. 1937. Contributions toward a flora of Panama. I. Collections in the provinces of Chiriquí, Coclé, and Panama, by R. J. Seibert during the summer of 1935. *Annals of the Missouri Botanical Garden* 24: 175–210.

Woodson, R. E., and R. J. Seibert. 1939. Contributions toward a flora of Panama. III. Collections during the summer of 1938, chiefly by R. E. Woodson, Jr., P. H. Allen, and R. J. Seibert. *Annals of the Missouri Botanical Garden* 26: 265–324.

Yinger, B. R. 1989a. Plant trek: in pursuit of a hardy camellia. *Flower and Garden* 33 (2): 104–106.

Yinger, B. R. 1989b. Plant trek: on site with hardy camellias. *Flower and Garden* 33 (3): 6–66.

Index